THE APPLICATION OF TEACHINGS BY THE INTERNATIONAL COURT OF JUSTICE

How do the judges of the International Court of Justice, the most authoritative court in international law, use teachings when deciding cases? This work is the first book-length examination of how teachings are used in an important international institution. It uses three different methodologies: a traditional legal analysis, an empirical analysis where citations of teachings are counted and interviews with judges and staff. Three main patterns are identified: teachings have generally low weight, but this weight varies between different works and between different judges. The book suggests explanations for the patterns it identifies, in order to contribute to the understanding of not only when and how teachings are used, but also why they are used. It compares the Court's practice with that of other international courts and tribunals. This study fills a gap in the international legal literature and will be essential reading for scholars and practicing international lawyers.

Sondre Torp Helmersen is Associate Professor and Vice Dean for Research at the Faculty of Law, UiT The Arctic University of Norway. He has published widely on the sources of international law and other topics in leading journals. Before entering academia he worked at the Norwegian Ministry of Foreign Affairs.

STUDIES ON INTERNATIONAL COURTS AND TRIBUNALS

General Editors
Andreas Føllesdal, University of Oslo
Geir Ulfstein, University of Oslo

Studies on International Courts and Tribunals contain theoretical and interdisciplinary scholarship on legal aspects as well as the legitimacy and effectiveness of international courts and tribunals.

Other books in the series:

Mads Andenas and Eirik Bjorge (eds.) *A Farewell to Fragmentation: Reassertion and Convergence in International Law*

Cecilia M. Bailliet and Nobuo Hayashi (eds.) *The Legitimacy of International Criminal Tribunals*

Amrei Müller with Hege Elisabeth Kjos (eds.) *Judicial Dialogue and Human Rights*

Nienke Grossman, Harlan Grant Cohen, Andreas Follesdal, and Geir Ulfstein (eds.) *Legitimacy and International Courts*

Robert Howse, Hélène Ruiz-Fabri, Geir Ulfstein, and Michelle Q. Zang (eds.) *The Legitimacy of International Trade Courts and Tribunals*

Theresa Squatrito, Oran Young, Andreas Føllesdal, and Geir Ulfstein (eds.) *The Performance of International Courts and Tribunals*

Marlene Wind (ed.) *International Courts and Domestic Politics*

Christina Voigt (ed.) *International Judicial Practice on the Environment: Questions of Legitimacy*

Freya Baetens (ed.) *Legitimacy of Unseen Actors in International Adjudication*

Martin Scheinin (ed.) *Human Rights Norms in 'Other' International Courts*

Shai Dothan *International Judicial Review: When Should International Courts Intervene?*

Daniel Behn, Szilárd Gáspár-Szilágyi, and Malcolm Langford (eds.) *Adjudicating Trade and Investment Disputes: Convergence or Divergence?*

Silje Langvatn, Mattias Kumm, and Wojciech Sadurski (eds). *Public Reason and Courts*

Sondre Torp Helmersen *The Application of Teachings by the International Court of Justice*

THE APPLICATION OF TEACHINGS BY THE INTERNATIONAL COURT OF JUSTICE

SONDRE TORP HELMERSEN

UiT The Arctic University of Norway

CAMBRIDGE
UNIVERSITY PRESS

Shaftesbury Road, Cambridge CB2 8EA, United Kingdom

One Liberty Plaza, 20th Floor, New York, NY 10006, USA

477 Williamstown Road, Port Melbourne, VIC 3207, Australia

314–321, 3rd Floor, Plot 3, Splendor Forum, Jasola District Centre, New Delhi – 110025, India

103 Penang Road, #05–06/07, Visioncrest Commercial, Singapore 238467

Cambridge University Press is part of Cambridge University Press & Assessment, a department of the University of Cambridge.

We share the University's mission to contribute to society through the pursuit of education, learning and research at the highest international levels of excellence.

www.cambridge.org
Information on this title: www.cambridge.org/9781108928328

DOI: 10.1017/9781108933520

First published 2021
First paperback edition 2023

A catalogue record for this publication is available from the British Library

Library of Congress Cataloging-in-Publication data
Names: Helmersen, Sondre Torp, author.
Title: The application of teachings by the International Court of Justice / Sondre Torp Helmersen, University of Tromsø.
Description: Cambridge, United Kingdom ; New York, NY : Cambridge University Press, 2021. | Series: Studies on international courts and tribunals | Includes bibliographical references and index.
Identifiers: LCCN 2020046695 (print) | LCCN 2020046696 (ebook) | ISBN 9781108844147 (hardback) | ISBN 9781108928328 (paperback) | ISBN 9781108933520 (ebook)
Subjects: LCSH: International Court of Justice. | International courts.
Classification: LCC KZ6277 .H45 2021 (print) | LCC KZ6277 (ebook) | DDC 341.5/52–dc23
LC record available at https://lccn.loc.gov/2020046695
LC ebook record available at https://lccn.loc.gov/2020046696

ISBN   978-1-108-84414-7   Hardback
ISBN   978-1-108-92832-8   Paperback

CONTENTS

List of Figures   *page* xi
List of Tables   xii
Foreword   xiii
Preface   xxiii
Table of Cases   xxv
Table of Treaties   xxxviii
List of Abbreviations   xxxix

1 Introduction   1

  1.1 Argument and Outline   1

  1.2 Why Study the Application of Teachings by the
       ICJ   3

  1.3 Methodology   6
       1.3.1 Collecting Citations   6
       1.3.2 Analysing Citations   11
       1.3.3 Conducting Interviews   14
       1.3.4 The Concept of 'Weight'   16

2 The ICJ Statute Article 38(1)   18

  2.1 Introduction   18

  2.2 Guidance on the Application Teachings   20
       2.2.1 The Inclusion of Teachings   20
       2.2.2 'The Court, Whose Function Is to Decide in Accordance
              with International Law'   23
       2.2.3 '[S]hall Apply'   24
       2.2.4 '[J]udicial Decisions'   25
       2.2.5 '[T]eachings … of Publicists'   25
       2.2.6 '[T]he Most Highly Qualified   25
       2.2.7 '[O]f the Various Nations'   26

2.2.8 '[S]ubsidiary Means'   26

2.2.9 '[F]or the Determination of Rules of Law'   28

2.3 Defining 'Teachings'   29

2.3.1 Introduction   29

2.3.2 The Definition Does Not Determine Weight   30

2.3.3 The Term 'Teachings' (and Its Alternatives)   31

2.3.4 Teachings Are about Law   33

2.3.5 Teachings Are Not Produced by States   35

2.3.6 Teachings Are Not Produced by Official Institutions   36

3 The General Role of Teachings in the ICJ   43

3.1 Introduction   43

3.2 Majority Opinions Almost Never Cite Teachings   43

3.3 Individual Opinions Sometimes Cite Teachings   45

3.4 Teachings Are Used More Often Than They Are Cited   46

3.4.1 Introduction   46

3.4.2 Teachings Are Useful to Judges   46

3.4.3 Statements by Judges and Staff Members   48

3.4.4 Statements in Judicial Decisions   50

3.4.5 Judges Are Exposed to Teachings Through Pleadings   51

3.5 Reasons for the Absence of Citations   52

3.5.1 Introduction   52

3.5.2 The Quality of Teachings   53

3.5.3 Jealousy between Writers   53

3.5.4 The Court's Drafting Procedures and Style   54

3.5.5 Writers' Objectivity   55

3.5.6 The Lack of Diversity among Writers   57

3.5.7 The Court's Expertise   58

3.5.8 The Availability of Better Arguments   58

3.5.9 Teachings Lack Official Authority   59

3.5.10 Length and Complexity   60

3.5.11 Institutional Culture and Role   60

3.6   Other Patterns That Indicate Limited
      Weight   62
      3.6.1 Few Judges Cite Teachings in Every Opinion   62
      3.6.2 Judges Specify That They Agree with
             Teachings   62
      3.6.3 Teachings Are Used to 'Confirm'
             Conclusions   64
      3.6.4 A Lack of Engagement   65
      3.6.5 Justifications of Authority   66

3.7   Patterns That Indicate Some Weight   67
      3.7.1 Using Teachings as a Main Argument   67
      3.7.2 Citing Teachings That Criticise Judicial
             Decisions   69
      3.7.3 Criticising Insufficient Consideration of
             Teachings   69
      3.7.4 Efforts to Clarify Teachings   70
      3.7.5 References to Teachings That the Judge Disagrees
             With   74
      3.7.6 References to Disagreements in Teachings   76
      3.7.7 The Rate of Citation of Teachings Over Time   77

3.8   Teachings Have Lower Weight Than Other
      'Subsidiary Means'   80
      3.8.1 Introduction   80
      3.8.2 Judicial Decisions   80
      3.8.3 ILC Works   82

3.9   Explaining the Relatively Low Weight
      of Teachings   83
      3.9.1 Introduction   83
      3.9.2 Teachings Lack Official Authority   84
      3.9.3 Like Cases Should Be Treated Alike   85
      3.9.4 Expertise   86
      3.9.5 Quality   87
      3.9.6 Collectiveness and Diversity   88

3.10 Conclusion: The General Role of Teachings
      in the ICJ   90

4 Variations between Works   93

4.1 Introduction   93

4.2 Variations by Frequency   94
  4.2.1 The Most-Cited Writers in ICJ Opinions   94
  4.2.2 The Demographics of the Most-Cited Writers   98
  4.2.3 Explaining the Skewed Demographics of the Most-Cited Judges   99

4.3 Variations by Substance: Factors That Influence the Weight of Teachings   106
  4.3.1 Introduction   106
  4.3.2 Expertise   107
  4.3.3 Quality   110
  4.3.4 Official Positions   114
  4.3.5 Agreement between Multiple Writers   120

4.4 Reasons for Distinguishing between Teachings   123
  4.4.1 Introduction   123
  4.4.2 Increased Authority   123
  4.4.3 Saving Time   125
  4.4.4 Compliance with the ICJ Statute Article 38   126

4.5 The Collective Nature of Authority in International Law   127

4.6 Conclusion   128

5 Variations between Judges   131

5.1 Introduction   131

5.2 Variations by Frequency and Substance   131

5.3 Categorising Judges   134
  5.3.1 Introduction   134
  5.3.2 Category 1: Judges Who Never Cite Teachings   134
  5.3.3 Category 2: The Median   135
  5.3.4 Category 3: Judges Who Often Cite and Engage with Teachings   137

5.4 Factors That May Explain Variations Between Judges   138
  5.4.1 Introduction   138
  5.4.2 Strategic Citations   138

5.4.3 Philosophical Perspectives   139
5.4.4 Expertise   141
5.4.5 The Availability of Better Arguments   142
5.4.6 Practical Factors   142

5.5 Data That Correlate with Variations between Judges   146
5.5.1 Introduction   146
5.5.2 Permanent Judges and Judges Ad Hoc   146
5.5.3 Separate and Dissenting Opinions   147
5.5.4 Judges' Nationalities   148
5.5.5 Judges' Educations   150
5.5.6 Judges' Professional Backgrounds   152

5.6 Conclusion   155

6 Concluding Reflections   157

6.1 Teachings and the Development of International Law   157

6.2 Potentially Beneficial Adjustments of the Court's Practice   160
6.2.1 Introduction   160
6.2.2 Increased Diversity   162
6.2.3 Increased Transparency   164
6.2.4 Increased Regulation   166

6.3 The ICJ Compared to Other International Courts and Tribunals   168
6.3.1 Introduction   168
6.3.2 The General Role of Teachings   170
6.3.3 Variations between Teachings   175
6.3.4 Variations between Judges   177
6.3.5 Explaining Variations between Institutions   180

6.4 Avenues for Future Research   183

Appendices   185

Appendix 1 The Forty Most-Cited Writers   185

Appendix 2 Citations Per Judge   189

Appendix 3 Judges Engaging with Teachings   205

Appendix 4 Citations Per Judge (PCIJ)   207

Appendix 5 Judges' Citations Compared to
                Pleadings   208

Appendix 6 Most-Cited Writers in Pleadings   209

Bibliography   210
Index   227

FIGURES

3.1 Average number of citations of teachings per opinion
per year   *page* 78
3.2 Average number of citations of teachings per opinion per year, without the top
four judges   79
4.1 Writers' shares of all citations   95
4.2 Overrepresentation by groups of judges and writers   103
5.1 Groups of judges ranked by a total number of references to
teachings   132
5.2 The ten most-citing judges   133
5.3 Individual opinions per year   144
5.4 Number of opinions per year and number of citations of teachings
per year   145
5.5 Citations of teachings by judges' nationalities   151
5.6 Citations of teachings by judges' educations   153
5.7 Citations of teachings by judges' professional backgrounds   154

TABLES

4.1 The ten most-cited writers   *page* 94
4.2 Writers by number of judges citing them   97
4.3 Writers by number of 'justifications' of citations   97

xii

FOREWORD

How do judges justify their rulings? To what extent do judges refer to doctrine in order to explain their judicial decisions? To what extent may they actually be influenced by it, irrespective of whether they explicitly invoke it in their decisions? Moreover, should judges include citations more frequently, or are there counterarguments against doing so? This book is about the decision-making of the International Court of Justice, the principal judicial organ of the United Nations.[1] Specifically, it analyses the extent to which the Court explains its own judicial decisions by referring to writings of jurists in their independent capacities. The basic question addressed by the author is how and when the Court, or its individual members, makes explicit references to academic doctrine. This should command a keen interest among both academics and practitioners. Those who are interested in the inner workings of international law should pay close attention to this book's empirical findings and incisive questions.

Early formation of international law was largely linked to the development of customary rules. As the building block for the construction of such rules, state practice required scholarly research for it to be identified and interpreted. Compounded by traditions of confidentiality regarding diplomatic practice, there was also a dearth of open sources in this field. At early stages, natural laws were also invoked.[2] For such reasons, doctrine was long perceived to be a principal rather than a subsidiary source of international law.[3] In this situation, citing certain pre-eminent

---

[1] Article 92 of the Charter of the United Nations.

[2] Patrick Daillier, Mathias Forteau, and Alain Pellet, *Droit international public* (8th edn, L. G.D.J. 2009) 434–435.

[3] Max Sørensen, *Les sources du droit international: étude sur la jurisprudence de la cour permanente de justice internationale* (E. Munksgaard 1946) 180; André Oraison, 'L'Influence des Forces Doctrinales Académiques sur les Prononcés de la C.P.J.I. et de la C.I.J' (1999) 32 *Revue Belge de Droit International* 205, 211.

authors could moreover provide decisive legal authority in legal advice, pleadings and diplomatic negotiations.

In the eighteenth century, such citations were therefore also frequent in chanceries, cabinet meetings and royal courts. Emer de Vattel's 1758 treatise on the Law of Nations (*Droit des gens*) constitutes a classic case in point.[4] It became a privileged handbook for lawyers, diplomats and statesmen alike.[5] 'Vattel' epitomized pedigree. Not least for newly independent states, it served as a key introduction to state practice, but also to the conduct and language of foreign relations and to persuasive legal argument. Anecdotally, a copy of 'Law of Nations' that had been borrowed in 1789 was returned to the New York Society Library in 2010 – and all fees were waived, even though 221 years had passed. The book had been borrowed and used by the first president of the United States of America, George Washington, and it had been returned by his estate at Mount Vernon.[6] In the early history of the United States, Vattel was cited together with a handful of other authorities in key cabinet discussions, including by Alexander Hamilton and Thomas Jefferson in 1793, when interpreting a key treaty with France.[7] Even recent jurisprudence of United States courts continues to cite Vattel when interpreting statutory law referring to the law of nations at the time of the adoption of the US Federal Constitution.[8] Yet another significant example of his global influence, was the translation of 'Law of Nations' into Chinese by the 1840s, in the wake of the first Sino-British War, in keeping with the

---

[4] Emer de Vattel, *Le droit des gens, ou, principes de la loi naturelle, appliqués à la conduite et aux affaires des nations et des souverains* (1758), translated i.a. by Charles G. Fenwick, *The Law of Nations or the Principles of Natural Law Applied to the Conduct and to the Affairs of Nations and of Sovereigns* (Carnegie Institute of Washington 1916).

[5] Jean d'Aspremont, *Formalism and Sources of International Law: A Theory of the Ascertainment of Legal Rules* (Oxford University Press 2011) 64.

[6] The New York Society Library, 'Historic Mount Vernon Returns Copy of Rare Book Borrowed by George Washington in 1789 to The New York Society Library' (21 May 2010) nysoclib.org/about/historic-mount-vernon-returns-copy-rare-book-borrowed-george-washington-1789-new-york-society; Kevin J Hayes, *George Washington – A Life in Books* (Oxford University Press 2017) 264.

[7] Alexander Hamilton, 'Pacificus No. I, Gazette of the United States, 29 June 1793' in Alexander Hamilton, *Writings* (The American Library 2001) 801, 802–803; Thomas Jefferson, 'Opinion on the French Treaties, 28 April 1793' in Merrill D Petterson (ed.), *The Portable Thomas Jefferson* (Penguin Viking Press 1975) 268, 275–277.

[8] See American jurisprudence and a critical analysis in Brian Richardson, 'The Use of Vattel in the American Law of Nations' (2012) 106 *American Journal of International Law* 547–571.

interest shown by Chinese leaders in the Qing state in understanding international law.[9]

All of this was long before the twentieth century, with its vast codifications and progressive development of international law in a variety of conventions and other legal instruments, and the development of jurisprudence by standing international courts. Such instruments are now registered and publicly accessible, as is the jurisprudence of international courts. Access to potential building blocks for international legal argument has also been vastly improved by the development of collections and systematization of international legal materials. Access to evidence of State practice and jurisprudence, but also to sources of law stemming from international organisations is today further helped by digitalization and the Internet.[10] No wonder that the relative importance of citations of individual teachings has declined not only since the days of Vattel, but also after the establishment of universal standing courts of international law in the twentieth century.[11]

Sondre Torp Helmersen's analysis is centred on the citation practice in judicial decisions between 1923 and 2016, covering successively the Permanent Court of International Justice and its successor, the International Court of Justice. Hard evidence is provided on the basis of a thorough quantitative study. Simply put, the study confirms that majority opinions of the Court almost never cite teachings, while separate and dissenting opinions, particularly of a small and identifiable number of individual judges, sometimes do include such citations. Incidentally, this also confirms a degree of constancy in the PCIJ and the ICJ.[12]

[9]   Odd Arne Westad, *Restless Empire – China and the World since 1750* (Basic Books 2012) 81. On the reception of Henry Weaton's Elements of International Law (1836) translated into Chinese in 1864, see Rune Svarverud, *International Law as World Order in Late Imperial China: Translation, Reception and Discourse, 1847–1911* (Brill 2007) 90–91.

[10] See as varied references as, *inter alia*, Daillier, Forteau, and Pellet, *Droit*; Lassa Oppenheim, *International Law* (edited by Herch Lauterpacht), Volume 1 (Longmans, Green & Co. 1955) 33; G I Tunkin, *Theory of International Law* (George Allen and Unwin 1974) 186-187.

[11] Oraison, *Influence*, 210–214, speaks even of an indisputable hegemony ('*l'hégémonie incontestable*') of doctrine up to the middle of the nineteenth century and its manifestation in the work of the first international arbitral tribunals.

[12] Manley O Hudson, *The Permanent Court of International Justice 1920–1942: A Treatise* (Macmillan 1943) 615: 'The teachings of publicists are treated less favorably at the hands of the Court. No treatise or doctrinal writing has been cited by the Court. In connection with its conclusion in the *Lotus Case* that the existence of a restrictive rule of international law had not been conclusively proved, it referred to the 'teachings of publicists' without attempting to assess their value, but it failed to find in them any useful indication. Individual judges have not been so restrained in their references to the teachings of

This empirical basis constitutes, in turn, an Archimedes' lever for asking a number of incisive questions as to the actual role of teachings. The author supplements the collection and analysis of citations with interviews, which also contribute to fleshing out possible hypotheses. On this basis, the author puts forward personal reflections that will undoubtedly pave the way for future debate. The further analysis of these trends deserves careful reading, together with the questions asked by the author to map out their possible explanations. The author provides several leads, also referring to anonymized interviews with two judges and a number of drafters. Interestingly, the answers differ somewhat, while general tendencies are clear.

The book is structured and written in an accessible style and with an intelligible presentation that eases swift comprehension of quantitative methods, and key distinguishing features and trends among the various findings. This is combined with humility as to possible interpretations, with an invitation to further research in the future. The book also describes the close relationship that exists between practitioners and theoreticians of international law (we should incidentally not forget that neither Grotius nor Vattel, among others, were academic writers, they were practitioners).

Judicial behaviouralists, American realists and certain Scandinavian realists, first among whom Alf Ross (1899–1979), have exercised influence not least in the Nordic countries and provided strong arguments to pay particular attention to what judges say is law. Studying the latter as a particular social phenomenon, and considering law from the perspective of what judges will do and decide, has paved the way for debatable 'predictive' or 'prognosis' theories.[13] However, a careful study of judicial activity should, in any case, inform legal analysis. In doing so, Sondre Torp Helmersen has entered the 'engine room' of international law, by considering whether and to what extent judges refer to particular teachings.

This reader would be inclined to caution against equating frequency of 'citations' with actual influence. The judges of the International Court of Justice draft and negotiate judicial decisions, whose function it is to transcend academic debates and contribute to effective peaceful

---

publicists; they have not hesitated to cite living authors, and even the published works of members of the Court itself.'

[13] Karl L Llewellyn, *Jurisprudence; Realism in Theory and Practice* (University of Chicago Press 1962); Alf Ross, *A Textbook of International Law – General Part* (Longmans, Green and Co. 1947) 80. For a critical approach, see Martti Koskenniemi, 'Introduction: Alf Ross and Life Beyond Realism' (2003) 14 *European Journal of International Law* 653–659.

settlement of international disputes, in accordance with the stated aims and means of the Charter of the United Nations (Articles 2 and 33). The Court is constituted of judges who are experts in their own right and have themselves a lengthy experience in drafting legal opinions or advice in practice and/or academia. While united by the common legal system of international law, international judges stem from different domestic traditions and legal cultures.[14] Dissenting Opinions have traditionally been identified in continental Europe as largely stemming from a Common Law tradition.[15] French authors refer to various kinds of doctrine, and may also distinguish subtly between the English notion of 'teachings' (in the plural) and the French 'doctrine' (in the singular), with a possible emphasis on identification of concurrent doctrinal opinions. A distinction is also suggested between purely 'academic doctrine' and more 'targeted doctrine', since independent opinions may take different forms depending on whether they have been engaged in specific procedures, be they normative, diplomatic, arbitral or judicial.[16] May the negotiation and formulation of broad-based majority opinions, in fact, ultimately require applying 'Ockham's razor', or a *'lex parcimoniae'*, i.e. a law of briefness, with regard to references to individual authors? Could such parsimony actually facilitate consensus building? Aren't there reasons for judges to concentrate instead on the fine-tuning of a common understanding of the relevant facts of the case, and on the other means at their disposal to contribute to the peaceful resolution of the dispute before them? And, to use yet another metaphor: may doctrine sometimes rather be part of legal 'scaffolding' in early argumentation, awaiting eventually removal in the final stages of construction?

This reader would also venture questions as to whether there may be a discrete continuous 'dialogue' between the Court and doctrine, if one considers the actual patterns and channels of indirect communication that are part of the broader discourse of international law. International courts do not receive 'feedback' from any central legislative body, as

---

[14] Antoine Garapon and Ioannis Papadopoulos, *Juger en Amérique et en France* (Odile Jacob 2003) 198–203. On the difficulties in bridging obstacles to understanding alien legal cultures, as concepts emerge within a culture at a particular juncture, see Joseph Raz, *Between Authority and Interpretation* (Oxford University Press 2009) 31–36 and 41–46.

[15] See, among many examples, Oraison, *Influence*, 207; A. P. Sereni, *Les opinions indivi-duelles et dissidents des juges des tribunaux internationaux* (A. Pedone 1964) 819–857, and Ijaz Hussain, *Dissenting and Separate Opinions at the World Court* (Martinus Nijhoff Publishers 1984), both referred to by Oraison, *Influence*, footnote 6.

[16] Oraison, *Influence*, 207.

opposed to what may happen in domestic legal systems. It may, never-theless, not be entirely far-fetched to consider various 'feedback' possibilities through academic and other arenas, which contribute to a continuous conversation that may, in turn, influence the future jurisprudence of the court.

A possible illustration may be provided by adjudication in the field of maritime delimitation of the continental shelf and exclusive economic zones. The International Court of Justice has over the years undoubtedly contributed decisively to developing substantive law in this regard. According to Kaye in 2008, it has indeed been 'difficult to think of another area of international law since World War II where international adjudication has had such a clear field in which to operate'.[17] It may be easy today to forget major academic discussions and controversies over a number of years in this field. They were related to debates concerning the methods that might best lead to an 'equitable result' in delimitation of continental shelf or exclusive economic zones pursuant to Articles 74 and 83 of the United Nations Convention on the Law of the Sea. Without entering into the history and content of these divergences, a lively debate had arisen, which included warnings against any future methodological lack of coherence by the Court. In 2001, the Court's President, Gilbert Guillaume, noted, however, that a breakthrough had been achieved. The law of maritime delimitation had 'reached a new level of unity and certainty, whilst conserving the necessary flexibility'.[18] What had indeed happened? In 1993, the Court reached an almost unanimous decision (14–1) in the case of Maritime Delimitation in the area between Greenland and Jan Mayen (Denmark v. Norway), that contributed to legal certainty as to key issues of method in cases of coastal states with opposite coasts.[19] The same basic approach was subsequently adopted for states with adjacent coasts in the judgment in 2001 in the case of

---

[17] Stuart Kaye, 'Lessons Learned from the Gulf of Maine Case: The Development of Maritime Boundary Delimitation Jurisprudence Since UNCLOS III' (2008) 14 *Ocean and Coastal Law Journal* 73, 74.

[18] Statement of the President of the International Court of Justice, Judge Gilbert Guillaume, on 31 October 2001 to the Sixth Committee of the United Nations General Assembly, *Official Records of the General Assembly*, Fifty-sixth session, Sixth Committee, 12th meeting [summary record]. These observations were included in Gilbert Guillaume, *La cour internationale de Justice à l'aube du XXIème siècle: Le regard d'un juge* (A. Pedone 2003) 287–301.

[19] *Maritime Delimitation in the Area between Greenland and Jan Mayen, Judgment, I.C.J. Reports 1993*, 38.

Maritime Delimitation between Qatar and Bahrain.[20] This unified methodology has largely characterized the jurisprudence since, in keeping with President Guillaume's observations. That the Court played such a decisive role does not mean that academic doctrine did not contribute to these advances. This reader would not fail to acknowledge the teachings, among others, of Prosper Weil (1926–2018), including his landmark contribution to doctrine in a seminal analysis of jurisprudence of maritime delimitation, at a crucial juncture, in 1988.[21] His 'feedback' as to the Court's previous case-law and his analysis with a view to promoting cogent methodological ways forward have been noted.[22] It is only fair to assume that his contributions also had an influence, in spite of lack of explicit references to them in judgments. This may, incidentally, also have to do with the fact that Prosper Weil was himself *inter alia* co-arbitrator in the Arbitral Tribunal between Canada and France in the Saint Pierre and Miquelon case, and, counsel of Norway in the Greenland/Jan Mayen case. In Oraison's parlance, he could therefore easily also have been categorized as a contributor to 'targeted doctrine'.[23]

Moreover, international law does not live in a vacuum. Societal developments, technological paradigm shifts and leaps in scientific knowledge speak in favour of understanding the role of doctrine as a privileged semiconductor or avenue for interdisciplinary cross-fertilization influencing international law. Thus, a pioneering international lawyer who cogently expounded the importance of cooperation as regards transboundary hydrocarbon deposits on the continental shelf and indicated a future methodology, was Professor Juraj Andrassy (1896–1977) of the university of Zagreb, in his 1951 course at the Hague Academy of International Law.[24] This prescient 'teaching' was held shortly after the 1945 Truman

---

[20] *Maritime Delimitation and Territorial Questions between Qatar and Bahrain, Merits, Judgment, I.C.J. Reports 2001*, 40. See Guillaume, *La cour*, 294.

[21] Prosper Weil, *Perspectives du droit de la délimitation maritime* (A. Pedone 1988), translated into English: *The Law of Maritime Delimitation: Reflections* (Cambridge University Press, 1989), reviewed by Natalino Ronzitti in (1990) 84 *American Journal of International Law* 321.

[22] Ronzitti, 'Review'; Kaye, 'Lessons', 78 and 90; Vaughan Lowe, 'The Role of Equity in International Law' (1992) 12 *Australian Year Book of International Law* 54, 74.

[23] *Case concerning the delimitation of maritime areas between Canada and France*, Decision of 10 June 1992, R.I.A.A. vol. XXI (UN 2006) 265.

[24] Juraj Andrassy, 'Les Relations internationales de voisinage' (1951) 79 Recueil des Cours 215.

Proclamation on the Continental Shelf.[25] The issue he highlighted was subsequently referred to in 1969 by the Court in the North Sea Continental Shelf judgment, without citations.[26] The contributions of Professor Andrassy may also reflect the interdisciplinary strengths of the academic community in Zagreb, which was also famous for its geophysicists, including in particular Andrija Mohorovičić (1857–1936).[27]

There should thus not be any doubt about the real influence of teachings, ranging from the role of transmitters, go-betweens or inter-connectors between a wealth of legal raw material and the ultimate determination of rules of law.

Going back to the negotiation of article 38 of the PCIJ and then the ICJ Statute, it may also be worthwhile to carefully study its negotiating history in the Advisory Committee that in the summer of 1920 considered key elements of the future Statute.[28]

There was basic agreement among the ten Committee members that the Court must not act as a legislator.[29] Moreover, the Norwegian member, Hagerup, stated, that an overarching requirement was to 'avoid the possibility of the Court declaring itself incompetent (*non-liquet*) through lack of applicable rules'.[30] Furthermore, 'if there is a rule of international law, the Court must apply it'.[31]

Lord Phillimore, referred to serious differences of opinion that 'arose from the continental idea of justice; at the outset strict limitations are imposed on the judges, then through fear of restricting them too much they are given complete freedom within these limits. The English system

---

[25] US Presidential Proclamation No. 2667, Policy of the United States with Respect to the Natural Resources of the Subsoil and Sea Bed of the Continental Shelf, 28 September 1945. See, inter alia, *North Sea Continental Shelf, Judgment, I.C.J. Reports 1969*, p. 3, 33.

[26] *North Sea Continental Shelf*, 51. See also Maurice K Kamga, 'L'affermissement des principes juridiques applicables à l'exploitation des gisements pétroliers ou gaziers transfrontaliers en mer' (2017) 22 *African Yearbook of International Law* 271, 272.

[27] On Andrija Mohorovičić and the phenomenon of discontinuity coined the 'Moho' after him, together with other synergies between Earth sciences and the formation of international law, see Rolf Einar Fife, 'The Limits in the Seas: The Need to Establish Secure Maritime Boundaries; Some Thoughts on the Contributions of Earth Scientists to Legal Determinacy with Regard to the Extent of the Continental Shelf Beyond 200 Miles' in *Proceedings of the Twentieth Anniversary Commemoration of the opening for Signature of the United Nations Convention on the Law of the Sea* (UN 2002) 81, 92.

[28] ACJ, *Procès-Verbaux of the Proceedings of the Committee June 16th–July 24th 1920 with Annexes* (Van Langenhyusen Brothers 1920).

[29] ACJ, *Procès-Verbaux*, 295 (Lapradelle).

[30] ACJ, *Procès-Verbaux*, 295–296, 307 ff, 314, 317, 332, 338 (Hagerup).

[31] ACJ, *Procès-Verbaux*, 295.

is different: the judge takes an oath 'to do justice according to law'.[32] This led the Committee's chair, Baron Descamps of Belgium, to agree that one should avoid pronouncing a non-liquet, but the judge 'must be saved from applying [general principles of law] as he pleased'. For this reason he urged that 'the judge render decisions in keeping with the dictates of the legal conscience of civilised peoples and for this same purpose make use of the doctrines of publicists carrying authority'.[33] Descamps here introduced the reference to doctrine, in order to counter arbitrariness. The reference to doctrine was, however, far from uncontroversial, as the Italian member, Foreign Office legal adviser Arturo Ricci-Busatti 'denied most emphatically that the opinion of the authors could be considered as a source of law, to be applied by the court'.[34] This is where Descamps explained the 'auxiliary character' of these elements of interpretation.[35] He stressed that doctrine as an element of interpretation 'could only be of a subsidiary nature; the judge could only use it in a supplementary way to clarify the rules of international law'. Moreover, '[d]octrine and jurisprudence no doubt do not create law; but they assist in determining rules that exist'.[36] The American member of the Committee, Root, put on record that he was opposed to 'granting the judges – in addition to their ordinary task of applying international law – the power to some extent to create it'.[37] In this context, he referred to the risk otherwise of major challenges in having great powers, or other states, not agreeing to the proposed system and thus refusing to sign on.

In terms of parsimony of citations, this reader has the opinion that a sound of silence may, in fact, conceal the depth of prior research and use of doctrine. It may also mask solid legal scaffolding, sometimes better revealed in individual opinions. At the same time, the debate among the key drafters of the provisions of the Statute of the PCIJ, may also provide

---

[32] ACJ, *Procès-Verbaux*, 315 (Phillimore).

[33] ACJ, *Procès-Verbaux*, 318–9 (Descamps).

[34] ACJ, *Procès-Verbaux*, 332 (Ricci-Busatti).

[35] ACJ, *Procès-Verbaux*, 334 (Descamps). The reference to doctrine being an 'auxiliary' and therefore helpful support, but not a primary source is clearly reflected in the French authentic version of the provision in Article 38 of the Statute (auxiliaire). This concurs today with the Spanish version in the Statute of the ICJ (auxiliar). Although German is not an authentic language version of the Statute, its translation expresses the same nuance 'als Hilfsmittel zur Festellung von Rechtsnormen', see inter alia Matthias Herdegen, *Völkerrecht*)16th ed., C. H. Beck 2017) 171–172.

[36] ACJ, *Procès-Verbaux*, 336 (Descamps).

[37] ACJ, *Procès-Verbaux*, 339 (Root).

some indication as to reasons for the exercise of caution in the use of citations in majority opinions.

This book will undoubtedly trigger many further and possibly entirely different reflections. The author's underlying precise analysis, supplemented with his useful comparisons with the practice of certain other jurisdictions, provides solid food-for-thought in this regard.

Rolf Einar Fife
September 2020

PREFACE

This book is based on the PhD thesis with the same title that I submitted at the University of Oslo in January 2018. I owe great thanks to my supervisors, Geir Ulfstein and Michael Waibel. Their contributions to the thesis have been invaluable, both on the abstract level of big ideas and on the concrete level of small (but important) details. The assessment committee, with Ole Kristian Fauchald, Sir Michael Wood, and Christine Chinkin, gave much important advice on how the thesis could be improved and made more suitable for publication as a book. I am also grateful to the three anonymous reviewers solicited by Cambridge University Press, whose comments contributed to many significant improvements to the text. Joost Pauwelyn was the external commentator at my midway assessment in Oslo in January 2016. He also gave a number of useful comments. Lorand Bartels supervised my LLM thesis at the University of Cambridge, on the application of teachings by the WTO Appellate Body, which served as a prototype for the thesis project. His comments were important in the early stages of the thesis.

Many others have provided valuable thoughts and discussions. They include Alice Ruzza, Andreas L Paulus, Anna Andersson, Avidan Kent, Bård Sverre Tuseth, Carola Lingaas, Christoffer Conrad Eriksen, Dag Michalsen, Damien Charlotin, Eyal Benvenisti, Gentian Zyberi, Hilde K Ellingsen, Inger Johanne Sand, Jamie Trinidad, Johann Ruben Leiss, Jon Christian F Nordrum, Karen Alter, Lee Epstein, Letizia Lo Giacco, Love Rönnelid, Luíza Leão Soares Pereira, Mads Andenæs, Martti Koskenniemi, Malcolm Langford, Martin Ratcovich, Massimo Fabio Lando, Matthew William Saul, Michael A Becker, Niccolò Ridi, Odile Ammann, Ola Mestad, Omri Sender, Pål Wrange, Rabia Akbulut, Ran Guo, Sergio Puig, Sofie AE Høgestøl, Stian Øby Johansen, Wolfgang Alschner, and Zuzanna Godzimirska. I am particularly grateful to the five anonymous judges and employees at the International Court of Justice (ICJ) who agreed to give the interviews that are cited throughout the thesis. At Cambridge University Press, Tom Randall deftly steered the project through the editorial process and Gemma Smith provided excellent editorial assistance. Above all, Gaiane Nuridzhanian has supported, inspired, and motivated me from start to finish.

Three texts partly based on the thesis have been published elsewhere: 'Finding "the Most Highly Qualified Publicists": Lessons from the International Court of Justice' (2019) 30 *European Journal of International Law* 509 is based on Sections 4.3 to 4.5 of this book. 'Scholarly-Judicial Dialogue in International Law' (2017) 16 *The Law & Practice of International Courts and Tribunals* 464 is partly based on some of the findings presented in Chapter 3 of this book. 'How the application of teachings can affect the legitimacy of the International Court of Justice' in Avidan Kent, Nikos Skoutaris, and Jamie Trinidad (eds.), *The Future of International Courts: Regional, Institutional and Procedural Challenges* (Routledge 2019) 181 is similar to Section 6.2 of this book.

The thesis includes six appendices, most of which contain data from an examination of the ICJ's decisions and opinions. The full background document that contains these data was too big to be included in the printed book. I am happy to provide it on request.

The cover painting is by my grandfather Odd Helmersen (1922-2012). It depicts the archipelago of Lofoten, where he spent most of his life.

Sondre Torp Helmersen
Tromsø
September 2020

TABLE OF CASES

International Court of Justice

Question of the Delimitation of the Continental Shelf between Nicaragua and Colombia beyond 200 Nautical Miles from the Nicaraguan Coast (Nicaragua v. Colombia), Preliminary Objections, Judgment, I.C.J Reports 2017, p. 100
Declaration of Judge Robinson
Obligations Concerning Negotiations Relating to Cessation of the Nuclear Arms Race and to Nuclear Disarmament (Marshall Islands v. United Kingdom), Jurisdiction and Admissibility, Judgment, I.C.J. Reports 2016, p. 833
Dissenting Opinion of Judge Cançado Trindade
Dissenting Opinion of Judge Crawford
Separate Opinion of Judge Tomka
Armed Activities on the Territory of the Congo (Democratic Republic of the Congo v. Uganda), Order of 11 April 2016, I.C.J. Reports 2016, p. 222
Declaration of Judge Cançado Trindade
Alleged Violations of Sovereign Rights and Maritime Spaces in the Caribbean Sea (Nicaragua v. Colombia), Preliminary Objections, Judgment, I.C.J. Reports 2016, p. 3
Dissenting Opinion of Judge Ad Hoc Caron
Obligation to Negotiate Access to the Pacific Ocean (Bolivia v. Chile), Preliminary Objection, Judgment, I.C.J. Reports 2015, p. 592
Declaration of Judge Bennouna
Separate Opinion of Judge Cançado Trindade
Declaration of Judge Gaja
Questions Relating to the Seizure and Detention of Certain Documents and Data (Timor-Leste v. Australia), Request for the Modification of the Order Indicating Provisional Measures of 3 March 2014, Order of 22 April 2015, I.C.J. Reports 2015, p. 556
Separate Opinion of Judge Cançado Trindade
Application of the Convention on the Prevention and Punishment of the Crime of Genocide (Croatia v. Serbia), Judgment, I.C.J. Reports 2015, p. 3
Dissenting Opinion of Judge Cançado Trindade
Separate Opinion of Judge Ad Hoc Kreća
Separate Opinion of Judge Owada

Dissenting Opinion of Judge Ad Hoc Vukas

Questions Relating to the Seizure and Detention of Certain Documents and Data (Timor-Leste v. Australia), Provisional Measures, Order of 3 March 2014, I.C.J. Reports 2014, p. 147

Separate Opinion of Judge Cançado Trindade

Certain Activities Carried Out by Nicaragua in the Border Area (Costa Rica v. Nicaragua); Construction of a Road in Costa Rica along the San Juan River (Nicaragua v. Costa Rica), Provisional Measures, Order of 22 November 2013, I.C.J. Reports 2013, p. 354

Separate Opinion of Judge Cançado Trindade

Request for Interpretation of the Judgment of 15 June 1962 in the Case concerning the Temple of Preah Vihear (Cambodia v. Thailand) (Cambodia v. Thailand), Judgment, I.C.J. Reports 2013, p. 281

Separate Opinion of Judge Cançado Trindade

Certain Activities Carried Out by Nicaragua in the Border Area (Costa Rica v. Nicaragua); Construction of a Road in Costa Rica along the San Juan River (Nicaragua v. Costa Rica), Order of 16 July 2013, Provisional Measures, I.C.J. Reports 2013, p. 230

Dissenting Opinion of Judge Cançado Trindade

Frontier Dispute (Burkina Faso/Niger), Judgment, I.C.J. Reports 2013, p. 44

Separate Opinion of Judge Cançado Trindade

Separate Opinion of Judge Yusuf

Whaling in the Antarctic (Australia v. Japan), Declaration of Intervention of New Zealand, Order of 6 February 2013, I.C.J. Reports 2013, p. 3

Separate Opinion of Judge Cançado Trindade

Territorial and Maritime Dispute (Nicaragua v. Colombia), Judgment, I.C.J. Reports 2012, p. 624

Declaration of Judge Keith

Questions Relating to the Obligation to Prosecute or Extradite (Belgium v. Senegal), Judgment, I.C.J. Reports 2012, p. 422

Separate Opinion of Judge Cançado Trindade

Dissenting Opinion of Judge Ad Hoc Sur

Ahmadou Sadio Diallo (Republic of Guinea v. Democratic Republic of the Congo), Compensation, Judgment, I.C.J. Reports 2012, p. 324

Separate Opinion of Judge Cançado Trindade

Declaration of Judge Greenwood

Jurisdictional Immunities of the State (Germany v. Italy: Greece Intervening), Judgment, I.C.J. Reports 2012, p. 99

Dissenting Opinion of Judge Cançado Trindade

Separate Opinion of Judge Keith

Judgment No. 2867 of the Administrative Tribunal of the International Labour Organization upon a Complaint Filed against the International Fund for Agricultural Development, Advisory Opinion, I.C.J. Reports 2012, p. 10

Separate Opinion of Judge Cançado Trindade

Application of the Interim Accord of 13 September 1995 (the Former Yugoslav Republic of Macedonia v. *Greece), Judgment of 5 December 2011, I.C.J. Reports 2011,* p. 644
    Dissenting Opinion of Judge Ad Hoc Roucounas
    Separate Opinion of Judge Shahabuddeen
    Separate Opinion of Judge Simma
Request for Interpretation of the Judgment of 15 June 1962 in the Case Concerning the Temple of Preah Vihear (Cambodia v. *Thailand) (Cambodia* v. *Thailand), Provisional Measures, Order of 18 July 2011, I.C.J. Reports 2011,* p. 537
    Separate Opinion of Judge Cançado Trindade
Jurisdictional Immunities of the State (Germany v. *Italy), Application for Permission to Intervene, Order of 4 July 2011, I.C.J. Reports 2011,* p. 494
    Separate Opinion of Judge Cançado Trindade
Application of the International Convention on the Elimination of All Forms of Racial Discrimination (Georgia v. *Russian Federation), Preliminary Objections, Judgment, I.C.J. Reports 2011,* p. 70
    Dissenting Opinion of Judge Cançado Trindade
Ahmadou Sadio Diallo (Republic of Guinea v. *Democratic Republic of the Congo), Merits, Judgment, I.C.J. Reports 2010,* p. 639
    Separate Opinion of Judge Cançado Trindade
    Joint Declaration of Judges Keith and Greenwood
    Dissenting Opinion of Judge Ad Hoc Mahiou
Accordance with International Law of the Unilateral Declaration of Independence in Respect of Kosovo, Advisory Opinion, I.C.J. Reports 2010, p. 403
Separate Opinion of Judge Cançado Trindade
    Declaration of Judge Tomka, Vice President
Jurisdictional Immunities of the State (Germany v. *Italy), Counter-Claim, Order of 6 July 2010, I.C.J. Reports 2010,* p. 310
    Dissenting Opinion of Judge Cançado Trindade
Pulp Mills on the River Uruguay (Argentina v. *Uruguay), Judgment, I.C.J. Reports 2010,* p. 14
Joint Dissenting Opinion Judges Al-Khasawneh and Simma
    Separate Opinion of Judge Cançado Trindade
Dispute Regarding Navigational and Related Rights (Costa Rica v. *Nicaragua), Judgment, I.C.J. Reports 2009,* p. 213
    Declaration of Judge Ad Hoc Guillaume
Application of the Convention on the Prevention and Punishment of the Crime of Genocide (Croatia v. *Serbia), Preliminary Objections, Judgment, I.C.J. Reports 2008,* p. 412
    Separate Opinion of Judge Abraham
Sovereignty over Pedra Branca/Pulau Batu Puteh, Middle Rocks and South Ledge (Malaysia/Singapore), Judgment, I.C.J. Reports 2008, p. 12
    Declaration of Judge Bennouna
    Separate Opinion of Judge Ad Hoc Sreenivasa Rao

Territorial and Maritime Dispute between Nicaragua and Honduras in the Caribbean Sea (Nicaragua v. Honduras), Judgment, I.C.J. Reports 2007, p. 659
Dissenting Opinion of Judge Ad Hoc Torres Bernárdez
Ahmadou Sadio Diallo (Republic of Guinea v. Democratic Republic of the Congo), Preliminary Objections, Judgment, I.C.J. Reports 2007, p. 582
Declaration of Judge Ad Hoc Mahiou
Separate Opinion of Judge Ad Hoc Mampuya
Application of the Convention on the Prevention and Punishment of the Crime of Genocide (Bosnia and Herzegovina v. Serbia and Montenegro), Judgment, I.C.J. Reports 2007, p. 43
Separate Opinion of Judge Ad Hoc Kreća
Dissenting Opinion of Judge Ad Hoc Mahiou
Separate Opinion of Judge Tomka
Armed Activities on the Territory of the Congo (Democratic Republic of the Congo v. Uganda), Judgment, I.C.J. Reports 2005, p. 168
Dissenting Opinion of Judge Ad Hoc Kateka
Legal Consequences of the Construction of a Wall in the Occupied Palestinian Territory, Advisory Opinion, I.C.J. Reports 2004, p. 136
Separate Opinion of Judge Elaraby
Avena and Other Mexican Nationals (Mexico v. United States of America), Judgment, I.C.J. Reports 2004, p. 12
Declaration of Vice-President Ranjeva
Legal Consequences of the Construction of a Wall in the Occupied Palestinian Territory, Order of 30 January 2004, I.C.J. Reports 2004, p. 3
Dissenting Opinion of Judge Buergenthal
Application for Revision of the Judgment of 11 September 1992 in the Case Concerning the Land, Island and Maritime Frontier Dispute (El Salvador/Honduras: Nicaragua Intervening) *(El Salvador v. Honduras), Judgment, I.C.J. Reports 2003, p. 392*
Dissenting Opinion of Judge Ad Hoc Paolillo
Oil Platforms (Islamic Republic of Iran v. United States of America), Judgment, I.C.J. Reports 2003, p. 161
Separate Opinion of Judge Ad Hoc Rigaux
Dissenting Opinion of Judge Elaraby
Application for Revision of the Judgment of 11 July 1996 in the Case Concerning Application of the Convention on the Prevention and Punishment of the Crime of Genocide (*Bosnia and Herzegovina v. Yugoslavia*), Preliminary Objections (*Yugoslavia v. Bosnia and Herzegovina*), *Judgment, I.C.J. Reports 2003, p. 7*
Separate Opinion of Judge Ad Hoc Mahiou
Frontier Dispute (Benin/Niger), Formation of Chamber, Order of 27 November 2002. I.C.J. Reports 2002, p. 613
Declaration of Judge Oda
Land and Maritime Boundary between Cameroon and Nigeria (Cameroon v. Nigeria: Equatorial Guinea Intervening), Judgment, I.C.J. Reports 2002, p. 303

Dissenting Opinion of Judge Ad Hoc Ajibola
Dissenting Opinion of Judge Koroma
Separate Opinion of Judge Ad Hoc Mbaye
Armed Activities on the Territory of the Congo (New Application: 2002) (Democratic Republic of the Congo v. Rwanda), Provisional Measures, Order of 10 July 2002, I.C.J. Reports 2002, p. 219
Declaration by Judge Elaraby
Arrest Warrant of 11 April 2000 (Democratic Republic of the Congo v. Belgium), Judgment, I.C.J. Reports 2002, p. 3
Dissenting Opinion of Judge Al-Khasawneh
Dissenting Opinion by Judge Ad Hoc Bula-Bula
Separate Opinion of President Guillaume
Joint Separate Opinion of Judges Higgins, Kooijmans, and Buergenthal
Dissenting Opinion of Judge Ad Hoc Van den Wyngaert
Sovereignty over Pulau Ligitan und Pulau Sipadan (Indonesia/Malaysia), Application for Permission to Intervene, Judgment, I.C.J. Reports 2001, p. 575
Separate Opinion of Judge Ad Hoc Weeramantry
LaGrand (Germany v. United States of America), Judgment, I.C.J. Reports 2001, p. 466
Maritime Delimitation and Territorial Questions between Qatar and Bahrain, Merits, Judgment, I.C.J. Reports 2001, p. 40
Joint Dissenting Opinion of Judges Bedjaoui, Ranjeva, and Koroma
Separate Opinion of Judge Fortier
Arrest Warrant of 11 April 2000 (Democratic Republic of the Congo v. Belgium), Provisional Measures, Order of 8 December 2000, I.C.J. Reports 2000, p. 182
Declaration by Judge Ad Hoc Van den Wyngaert
Dissenting Opinion by Judge Ad Hoc Bula-Bula
Aerial Incident of 10 August 1999 (Pakistan v. India), Jurisdiction of the Court, Judgment, I.C.J. Reports 2000, p. 12
Dissenting Opinion of Judge Ad Hoc Pirzada
Kasikili/Sedudu Island (Botswana/Namibia), Judgment, I.C.J. Report 1999, p. 1045
Dissenting Opinion of Vice-President Weeramantry
Legality of Use of Force (Yugoslavia v. Belgium), Provisional Measures, Order of 2 June 1999, I.C.J. Reports 1999, p. 124
Dissenting Opinion of Vice-President Weeramantry
LaGrand (Germany v. United States of America), Provisional Measures, Order of 3 March 1999, I.C.J. Reports 1999, p. 9
Separate Opinion of President Schwebel
Fisheries Jurisdiction (Spain v. Canada), Jurisdiction of the Court, Judgment, I.C.J. Reports 1998, p. 432
Dissenting Opinion of Judge Torres-Bernárdez, Judge Ad Hoc
Dissenting Opinion of Vice-President Weeramantry
Land and Maritime Boundary between Cameroon and Nigeria, Preliminary Objections, Judgment, I.C.J. Reports 1998, p. 275
Dissenting Opinion of Vice-President Weeramantry

Oil Platforms (Islamic Republic of Iran v. United States of America), Counter-Claim, Order of 10 March 1998, I.C.J. Reports 1998, p. 190
  Dissenting Opinion by Judge Ad Hoc Rigaux
Application of the Convention on the Prevention and Punishment of the Crime of Genocide, Counter-claims, Order of 17 December 1997, I.C.J. Reports 1997, p. 243
  Separate Opinion of Judge Ad Hoc Lauterpacht
  Dissenting Opinion of Vice-President Weeramantry
Gabčikovo-Nagymaros Project (Hungary/Slovakia), Judgment, I.C.J. Reports 1997, p. 7
  Dissenting Opinion of Judge Fleischhauer
  Separate Opinion of Vice-President Weeramantry
Oil Platforms (Islamic Republic of Iran v. United States of America), Preliminary Objection, Judgment, I.C.J. Reports 1996, p. 803
  Separate Opinion of Judge Shahabuddeen
Application of the Convention on the Prevention and Punishment of the Crime of Genocide, Preliminary Objections, Judgment, I.C.J. Reports 1996, p. 595
  Dissenting Opinion of Judge Ad Hoc Kreća
  Joint Declaration of Judge Shi and Judge Vereshchetin
Legality of the Threat or Use of Nuclear Weapons, Advisory Opinion, I.C.J. Reports 1996, p. 226
  Dissenting Opinion of Judge Higgins
  Dissenting Opinion of Judge Koroma
  Dissenting Opinion of Vice-President Schwebel
  Dissenting Opinion of Judge Shahabuddeen
  Declaration of Judge Vereshchetin
  Dissenting Opinion of Judge Weeramantry
Legality of the Use by a State of Nuclear Weapons in Armed Conflict, Advisory Opinion, I.C.J. Reports 1996, p. 66
  Dissenting Opinion of Judge Weeramantry
  Land and Maritime Boundary between Cameroon and Nigeria, Provisional Measures, Order of 15 March 1996, I.C.J. Reports 1996, p. 13
  Separate Opinion by Judge Ajibola
Request for an Examination of the Situation in Accordance with Paragraph 63 of the Court's Judgment of 20 December 1974 in the Nuclear Tests (New Zealand v. France) Case, I.C.J. Reports 1995, p. 288
  Dissenting opinion by Judge Ad Hoc Sir Geoffrey Palmer
  Dissenting opinion by Judge Weeramantry
East Timor (Portugal v. Australia), Judgment, I.C.J. Reports 1995, p. 90
  Dissenting Opinion of Judge Weeramantry
  Separate Opinion of Judge Shahabuddeen
  Dissenting Opinion of Judge Skubiszewski
Maritime Delimitation and Territorial Questions between Qatar and Bahrain, Jurisdiction and Admissibility, Judgment, I.C.J. Reports 1995, p. 6
  Dissenting Opinion of Vice-President Schwebel

Application of the Convention on the Prevention and Punishment of the Crime of Genocide, Provisional Measures, Order of 13 September 1993, I.C.J. Reports 1993, p. 325
  Separate Opinion of Judge Ajibola
  Separate Opinion of Judge Ad Hoc Lauterpacht
  Separate Opinion of Judge Shahabuddeen
  Separate Opinion of Vice-President Weeramantry
Maritime Delimitation in the Area between Greenland and Jan Mayen, Judgment, I.C.J. Reports 1993, p. 38
  Separate Opinion of Judge Ajibola
  Separate Opinion of Judge Shahabuddeen
  Separate Opinion of Judge Weeramantry
Land, Island and Maritime Frontier Dispute (El Salvador/Honduras: Nicaragua Intervening), Judgment of 11 September 1992, I.C.J. Reports 1992, p. 351
  Dissenting Opinion of Judge Oda
  Separate Opinion of Judge Torres-Bernárdez
Certain Phosphate Lands in Nauru (Nauru v. Australia), Preliminary Objections, Judgment, I.C.J. Reports 1992, p. 240
  Separate Opinion of Judge Shahabuddeen
Questions of Interpretation and Application of the 1971 Montreal Convention Arising from the Aerial Incident at Lockerbie (Libyan Arab Jamahiriya v. United States of America), Provisional Measures, Order of 14 April 1992, I.C.J. Reports 1992, p. 114
  Dissenting Opinion by Judge Weeramantry
Questions of Interpretation and Application of the 1971 Montreal Convention Arising from the Aerial Incident at Lockerbie (Libyan Arab Jamahiriya v. United Kingdom), Provisional Measures, Order of 14 April 1992, I.C.J. Reports 1992, p. 3
  Dissenting Opinion by Judge Weeramantry
Arbitral Award of 31 July 1989, Judgment, I.C.J. Reports 1991, p. 53
  Declaration of Judge Mbaye
  Separate Opinion of Judge Ni
  Separate Opinion of Judge Shahabuddeen
  Dissenting Opinion of Judge Weeramantry
Passage through the Great Belt (Finland v. Denmark), Provisional Measures, Order of 29 July 1991, I.C.J. Reports 1991, p. 12
  Separate Opinion of Judge Shahabuddeen
Land, Island and Maritime Frontier Dispute (El Salvador/Honduras), Application to Intervene, Judgment, I.C.J. Reports 1990, p. 92
Land, Island and Maritime Frontier Dispute (El Salvador/Honduras), Application to Intervene, Order of 28 February 1990, I.C.J. Reports 1990, p. 3
  Dissenting Opinion of Judge Shahabuddeen
Applicability of Article VI, Section 22, of the Convention on the Privileges and Immunities of the United Nations, Advisory Opinion, I.C.J. Reports 1989, p. 177
  Separate Opinion of Judge Shahabuddeen

Land, Island and Maritime Frontier Dispute (El Salvador/Honduras), Composition of Chamber, Order of 13 December 1989, I.C.J. Reports 1989, p. 162
Separate Opinion Judge Shahabuddeen
Aerial Incident of 3 July 1988 (Islamic Republic of Iran v. United States of America), Order of 13 December 1989, I.C.J. Reports 1989, p. 132
Separate Opinion by Judge Schwebel
Separate Opinion by Judge Shahabuddeen
Elettronica Sicula S.P.A. (ELSI), Judgment, I.C.J. Reports 1989, p. 15
Dissenting Opinion of Judge Schwebel
Border and Transborder Armed Actions (Nicaragua v. Honduras), Jurisdiction and Admissibility, Judgment, I.C.J. Reports 1988, p. 69
Separate Opinion of Judge Shahabuddeen
Military and Paramilitary Activities in and against Nicaragua (Nicaragua v. United States of America). Merits, Judgment. I.C.J. Reports 1986, p. 14
Dissenting Opinion of Judge Sir Robert Jennings
Separate Opinion of Judge Lachs
Dissenting Opinion of Judge Oda
Dissenting Opinion of Judge Schwebel
Continental Shelf (Libyan Arab Jamahiriya/Malta), Judgment, I.C.J. Reports 1985, p. 13
Dissenting Opinion of Judge Oda
Separate Opinion of Judges Ruda, Bedjaoui, and Jiménez de Aréchaga
Dissenting Opinion of Judge Schwebel
Military and Paramilitary Activities in and against Nicaragua (Nicaragua v. United States of America), Jurisdiction and Admissibility, Judgment, I.C.J. Reports 1984, p. 392
Separate Opinion of Judge Sir Robert Jennings
Dissenting Opinion of Judge Schwebel
Delimitation of the Maritime Boundary in the Gulf of Maine Area, Judgment, I.C.J. Reports 1984, p. 246
Military and Paramilitary Activities in and against Nicaragua (Nicaragua v. United States of America), Declaration of Intervention, Order of 4 October 1984, I.C.J. Reports 1984, p. 215
Dissenting Opinion of Judge Schwebel
Military and Paramilitary Activities in and against Nicaragua (Nicaragua v. United States of America), Provisional Measures, Order of 10 May 1984, I.C.J. Reports 1984, p. 169
Dissenting Opinion of Judge Schwebel
Continental Shelf (Libyan Arab Jamahiriya/Malta), Application to Intervene, Judgment, I.C.J. Reports 1984, p. 3
Dissenting Opinion of Judge Ago
Separate Opinion of Judge Jiménez de Aréchaga
Dissenting Opinion of Judge Schwebel
Dissenting Opinion of Vice-President Sette-Camara

Continental Shelf (Tunisia/Libyan Arab Jamahiriya), Judgment, I.C.J. Reports 1982, p. 18
  Separate Opinion of Judge Ago
  Dissenting Opinion of Judge Oda
Aegean Sea Continental Shelf, Judgment, I.C.J. Reports 1978, p. 3
  Dissenting Opinion of Judge de Castro
  Separate Opinion of Judge Tarazi
Western Sahara, Advisory Opinion, I.C.J. Reports 1975, p. 12
  Separate Opinion of Judge Dillard
Nuclear Tests (Australia v. France), Judgment, I.C.J. Reports 1974, p. 253
  Dissenting Opinion of Judge de Castro
Fisheries Jurisdiction (United Kingdom v. Iceland), Merits, Judgment, I.C.J. Reports 1974, p. 3
  Separate Opinion of Judge de Castro
  Separate Opinion of Judge Dillard
  Declaration by Judge Ignacio-Pinto
  Separate Opinion of Judge Sir Humphrey Waldock
Application for Review of Judgement No. 158 of the United Nations Administrative Tribunal, Advisory Opinion, I.C.J. Reports 1973, p. 166
  Dissenting Opinion of Judge de Castro
  Separate Opinion of Judge Dillard
Appeal Relating to the Jurisdiction of the ICAO Council, Judgment, I.C.J. Reports 1972, p. 46
  Separate Opinion of Judge Dillard
Legal Consequences for States of the Continued Presence of South Africa in Namibia (South West Africa) Notwithstanding Security Council Resolution 276 (1970), Advisory Opinion, I.C.J. Reports 1971, p. 16
  Separate Opinion of Judge De Castro
  Separate Opinion of Judge Dillard
  Dissenting Opinion of Judge Gerald Fitzmaurice
Barcelona Traction, Light and Power Company, Limited, Judgment, I.C.J. Reports 1970, p. 3
  Separate Opinion of Judge Ammoun
  Separate Opinion of Judge Sir Gerald Fitzmaurice
  Separate Opinion of Judge Jessup
  Separate Opinion of Judge Padilla Nervo
  Dissenting Opinion of Judge Riphagen
  Separate Opinion of Judge Tanaka
North Sea Continental Shelf, Judgment, I.C.J. Reports 1969, p. 3
  Separate Opinion of Judge Fouad Ammoun
  Dissenting Opinion of Vice-President Koretsky
  Dissenting Opinion of Judge Sorensen
South West Africa, Second Phase, Judgment, I.C.J. Reports 1966, p. 6
  Dissenting Opinion of Judge Jessup

Dissenting Opinion of Judge Koretsky
Declaration of President Spender
Separate Opinion of Judge van Wyk
*Barcelona Traction, Light and Power Company, Limited, Preliminary Objections,
    Judgment, I.C.J. Reports 1964, p. 6*
Dissenting Opinion of Judge Armand-Ugon
Declaration by Judge Koretsky
Dissenting Opinion of Judge Morelli
*South West Africa Cases (Ethiopia v. South Africa; Liberia v. South Africa), Preliminary
    Objections, Judgment of 21 December 1962: I.C.J. Reports 1962, p. 319*
Separate Opinion of Judge Jessup
Dissenting Opinion of Judge van Wyk
Dissenting Opinion of President Winiarski
*Certain Expenses of the United Nations (Article 17, paragraph 2, of the Charter),
    Advisory Opinion of 20 July 1962: I.C.J. Reports 1962, p. 151*
Dissenting Opinion of President Winiarski
*Case concerning the Temple of Preah Vihear (Cambodia v. Thailand), Merits, Judgment
    of 15 June 1962: I.C.J. Reports 1962, p. 6*
Separate Opinion of Vice-President Alfaro
Separate Opinion of Sir Gerald Fitzmaurice
*Case concerning the Arbitral Award made by the King of Spain on 23 December 1906,
    Judgment of 18 November 1960: I.C.J. Reports 1960, p. 192*
Dissenting Opinion of Judge Urrutia Holguin
*Case concerning Right of Passage over Indian Territory (Merits), Judgment of
    12 April 1960: I.C.J. Reports 1960, p. 6*
Dissenting Opinion of Judge Fernandes
*Case Concerning the Aerial Incident of July 27th, 1955 (Israel v. Bulgaria), Preliminary
    Objections, Judgment of May 26th, 1959: I.C.J. Reports 1959, p. 127*
Joint Dissenting Opinion by Judges Sir Hersch Lauterpacht, Wellington Koo and Sir
    Percy Spender
*Case Concerning the Application of the Convention of 1902 Governing the Guardianship
    of Infants (Netherlands v. Sweden), Judgment of November 28th, 1958: I.C.J.
    Reports 1958, p. 55*
Separate Opinion of Judge Sir Hersch Lauterpacht
Separate Opinion of Sir Percy Spender
Case of Certain Norwegian Loans, Judgment of July 6th, 1957: I.C.J. Reports 1957, p. 9
Separate Opinion of Judge Sir Hersch Lauterpacht
*South West Africa–Voting Procedure, Advisory Opinion of June 7th, 1955: I.C.J. Reports
    1955, p. 67*
Separate Opinion of Judge Lauterpacht
Nottebohm Case (Second Phase), Judgment of April 6th, 1955: I.C.J. Reports 1955, p. 4
*Effect of Awards of Compensation Made by the U.N. Administrative Tribunal, Advisory
    Opinion of July 13th, 1954: I.C.J. Reports 1954, p. 47*
Dissenting Opinion by Judge Levi Carneiro

The Minquiers and Ecrehos Case, Judgment of November 17th, 1953: I.C.J. Reports 1953, p. 47
  Individual Opinion of Judge Levi Carneiro
Anglo-Iranian Oil Co. Case (jurisdiction), Judgment of July 22nd, 1952: I.C.J. Reports 1952, p. 93
  Dissenting Opinion of Judge Levi Carneiro
Ambatielos case (jurisdiction), Judgment of July 1st, 1952: I.C.J. Reports 1952, p. 28
  Dissenting Opinion of President McNair
Fisheries case, Judgment of December 18th, 1951: I.C.J. Reports 1951, p. 116
  Dissenting Opinion of Sir Arnold McNair
Anglo-Iranian Oil Co. Case, Order of July 5th, 1951: I.C.J. Reports 1951, p. 89
  Dissenting Opinion of Judge Levi Carneiro
Colombian-Peruvian Asylum Case, Judgment of November 20th 1950: I.C.J. Reports 1950, p. 266
  Dissenting Opinion by Judge Azevedo
  Dissenting Opinion by M Caicedo Castilla
Interpretation of Peace Treaties, Advisory Opinion: I.C.J. Reports 1950, p. 65
  Dissenting Opinion by Judge Zoričič
Corfu Channel case, Judgment of April 9th, 1949: I.C.J. Reports 1949, p. 4
  Dissenting Opinion by Judge Azevedo
  Dissenting Opinion by Judge Winiarski
Admission of a State to the United Nations (Charter, Art. 4), Advisory Opinion: I.C.J. Reports 1948, p. 57
  Individual Opinion by M Azevedo
  Dissenting Opinion by M Krylov
  Dissenting Opinion by M Zoričič

Permanent Court of International Justice

Electricity Company of Sofia and Bulgaria, Order, 26 February 1940, P.C.I.J. Series A/B No. 80, p. 4
The Panevezys-Saldutiskis Railway Case, Judgment 28 February 1939, P.C.I.J. Reports Series A/B No. 76, p. 4
  Dissenting Opinion by Jonkheer van Eysinga
The Diversion of Water from the Meuse, Judgment 28 June 1937, P.C.I.J. Reports Series A/B No. 70, p. 4
Individual Opinion by Mr Hudson
Lighthouses Case between France and Greece, Judgment 17 March 1934, P.C.I.J. Series A/B No. 62, p. 4
Separate Opinion by M Séfériadès
Legal Status of Eastern Greenland, Judgment 5 April 1933, P.C.I.J. Series A/B No. 53, p. 22
Dissenting Opinion by M Vogt
Free Zones of Upper Savoy and the District of Gex (second phase), Order made on 6 December 1930, P.C.I.J. Series A No. 24, p. 4

Observations by M Kellogg

Opinion by M Dreyfus

Case Concerning the Payment in Gold of Brazilian Federal Loans Contracted in France (France v. United States of America), Judgment No. 15, 12 July 1929, P.C.I.J. Reports Series A No. 21, p. 93

Dissenting Opinion by M Pessôa

Dissenting Opinion by M de Bustamante

Case Concerning the Payment of Various Serbian Loans in France (France v. Kingdom of the Serbs, Croats and Slovenes), Judgment No. 14, 12 July 1929, P.C.I.J. Reports Series A No. 20, p. 5

Dissenting Opinion by M Pessôa

The Case of the S.S. 'Lotus' (France v. Turkey), Judgment No. 9, 7 September 1927, P.C.I.J. Reports Series A No. 10, p. 4

Dissenting Opinion by Lord Finlay

Dissenting Opinion by M Moore

Case Concerning Certain German Interests in Polish Upper Silesia (The Merits) (Germany v. Poland), Judgment No. 7, 25 May 1926, P.C.I.J. Reports Series A No. 7, p. 4

Case Concerning Certain German Interests in Polish Upper Silesia, Judgment No. 6, 25 August 1925, P.C.I.J. Reports Series A No. 6, p. 3

The Mavrommatis Palestine Concessions, Judgment No. 2, 30 August 1924, P.C.I.J. Reports Series A No. 2, p. 6

Dissenting Opinion by M Moore

Advisory Opinion Given by the Court on September 10th 1923 on Certain Questions Relating to Settlers of German Origin in the Territory Ceded by Germany to Poland, Advisory Opinion No. 6, 10 September 1923, P.C.I.J. Reports Series B No. 6, p. 5

Questions of Jaworzina (Polish–Czechoslovakian Frontier), Advisory Opinion No. 8, 6 December 1923, P.C.I.J Reports Series B No. 8, p. 5

Case of the S.S. 'Wimbledon', Judgment, 17 August 1923, P.C.I.J. Reports Series A No. 1, p. 15

Dissenting Opinion by M Schücking 47

Case of the S.S. 'Wimbledon', Judgment, 28 June 1923, P.C.I.J. Reports Series A No. 1, p. 11

WTO Appellate Body

United States – Final Anti-Dumping Measures on Stainless Steel from Mexico, WT/DS344/AB/R, 30 April 2008

Japan – Taxes on Alcoholic Beverages, WT/DS8/AB/R, WT/DS10/AB/R, WT/DS11/AB/R, 4 October 1996

Special Court for Sierra Leone

Prosecutor v. Charles Ghankay Taylor, Judgment, SCSL-03–01-T, 18 May 2012

International Centre for Settlement of Investment Disputes

Guardian Fiduciary Trust Ltd f/k/a Capital Conservator Savings & Loan Ltd v. *Former Yugoslav Republic of Macedonia*, ICSID Case No. ARB/12/31, Award, 22 September 2015

OPIC Karimum Corporation v. *The Bolivarian Republic of Venezuela*, ICSID Case No. ARB/10/14, Award, 28 May 2013

Tidewater Inc. and Others v. *The Bolivarian Republic of Venezuela*, ICSID Case No ARB/10/5, Decision on Jurisdiction, 8 February 2013

Hussein Nuaman Soufraki v. *The United Arab Emirates*, ICSID Case No. ARB/02/7, Decision of the Ad Hoc Committee on the Application for Annulment of Mr Soufraki, 5 June 2007

Other Arbitral Awards

PCA, *The South China Sea Arbitration (The Republic of Philippines* v. *The People's Republic of China)*, Case 2013–19, Award, 12 July 2016

UNCITRAL, *AWG Group Ltd* v. *The Argentine Republic*, Decision on Liability (30 July 2010) 73

Affaire des Biens Britanniques au Maroc Espagnol (Espagne contre Royaume-Uni), (1924) 2 RIAA 615

United Kingdom National Courts

Supreme Court, *R* v. *Secretary of State for Exiting the European Union* [2017] UKSC 5

Court of Appeals, *Serdar Mohammed and Others* v. *Secretary of State for Defence* [2015] EWCA Civ 843

House of Lords, *White* v. *Jones*, Lord Mustill [1995] 2 AC 207

High Court of Justice, *Bastin* v. *Davies* [1950] 1 All ER 1095

Privy Council, *re: Piracy jure gentium* [1934] AC 586

High Court of Justice, *R* v. *Sussex Justices, Ex parte McCarthy* [1923] 1 KB 256

Privy Council, *Kronprinsessan Margreta* [1921] AC 486

English High Court of Justice, *West Rand Central Gold Mining Co.* v. *R* [1905] 2 KB 391

Court for Crown Cases Reserved, *R* v. *Keyn* [1876] 2 Ex D 63

Court of Admiralty, *The 'Renard'* [1778] 165 All ER 51

United States National Courts

Court of Appeals for the Second Circuit, *Flores* v. *Southern Peru Copper Corp.* 343 F 3d 140 (2nd Cir. 2003)

Supreme Court, *The Paquete Habana* 175 US 677 (1900)

TABLE OF TREATIES

Covenant of the League of Nations, Paris, 28 June 1919, in Force 10 January 1920, 225
    CTS 195
Statute of the Permanent Court of International Justice, Geneva, 13 December 1920, in
    Force 8 October 1921, 6 LNTS 390
Statute of the International Court of Justice, San Francisco, 26 June 1945, in Force
    24 October 1945, 33 UNTS 933
Convention for the Protection of Human Rights and Fundamental Freedoms, Rome,
    4 November 1950, in Force 3 September 1953, 213 UNTS 221
Convention on the Settlement of Investment Disputes between States and Nationals of
    Other States, Washington, 18 March 1965, in Force 14 October 1966, 575
    UNTS 159
Vienna Convention on the Law of Treaties, Vienna, 23 May 1969, in Force
    27 January 1980, 1155 UNTS 331
United Nations Convention on the Law of the Sea, Montego Bay, 10 October 1982, in
    Force 16 November 1994, 1833 UNTS 3
Annex VI: Statute of the International Tribunal for the Law of the Sea
Marrakesh Agreement Establishing the World Trade Organization, Marrakesh,
    15 April 1994, in Force 1 January 1995, 1869 UNTS 401
Annex 2: Understanding on Rules and Procedures Governing the Settlement of
    Disputes
Rome Statute of the International Criminal Court, Rome, 17 July 1998, in Force
    1 July 2002, 2187 UNTS 3

ABBREVIATIONS

ACJ	Advisory Committee of Jurists
ALI	American Law Institute
CTS	Consolidated Treaty Series
ECtHR	European Court of Human Rights
HRC	UN Human Rights Committee
IACtHR	Inter-American Court of Human Rights
ICC	International Criminal Court
ICJ	International Court of Justice
ICRC	International Committee of the Red Cross
ICSID	International Centre for Settlement of Investment Disputes
ICTY	International Criminal Tribunal for the Former Yugoslavia
IDI	Institute of International Law
ILA	International Law Association
ILC	International Law Commission
ITLOS	International Tribunal for the Law of the Sea
LNTS	League of Nations Treaty Series
NGO	Nongovernmental Organisation
OAS	Organization of American States
OECD	Organization for Economic Cooperation and Development
PCA	Permanent Court of Arbitration
PCIJ	Permanent Court of International Justice
RIAA	Reports of International Arbitral Awards
UN	United Nations
UNCITRAL	UN Commission on International Trade Law
UNESCO	United Nations Educational, Scientific, and Cultural Organization
UNGA	United Nations General Assembly
UNTS	United Nations Treaty Series
WTO	World Trade Organization

1

Introduction

1.1   Argument and Outline

This book examines how the ICJ applies 'the teachings of the most highly qualified publicists', as per the ICJ Statute Article 38(1). Teachings are listed in Article 38(1) and are something that the judges 'shall apply'.[1] The question that this book tries to answer is what role they currently play in the most authoritative international judicial institution.

This book is divided into six chapters. After this introduction, the book continues with an examination of the guidance that the ICJ Statute Article 38(1) gives on the application of teachings. Chapter 3 examines the general role that teachings apparently have in the ICJ. The examination shows that teachings seem to have limited weight. There are nonetheless variations between teachings and between judges. Those variations are explored in Chapters 4 and 5, respectively. The various chapters also present explanations for the patterns that they identify and suggest factors that can predict variations. Chapter 6 gives concluding reflections.

The book's findings pertain to the ICJ and the ICJ Statute Article 38(1). The ICJ is an authoritative court that is respected by other courts and tribunals and other international lawyers,[2] and the ICJ Statute Article 38(1) reflects customary international law.[3] Therefore, the book's findings have implications for international law generally. This means that much of the book can be read as not only an examination of the ICJ's application of teachings but also a discussion of the role and status of teachings in international law generally. Section 6.3 provides a comparison between the ICJ's practice and those of other courts and tribunals.

The results of the book should be interesting to a number of audiences. Academics can use the results and methodology in further research, and

---

they get an opportunity to see how the judges view their writings. Judges themselves may be interested in seeing an academic analysis of their practice, and they may use this in order to reflect on their approach. Practitioners who wish to convince judges, which include not only counsel but also judges themselves, should be interested in knowing how much resonance different arguments may have with judges.[4] Chapters 3 and 4 give some guidance on which teachings to employ, how much of them to employ, and how to employ them, in order to maximise the chance of convincing judges. Chapter 5 shows which judges are most receptive to arguments based on teachings.

As part of its argument, the book is able to test some assumptions about teachings that are commonly held but rarely tested empirically. As explained in Section 2.3.6, writers are split on whether works produced by the ILC should be considered as teachings. This book finds no clear support for either proposition in the ICJ's practice. ILC works are not classified as teachings in this book. Section 3.4.2 shows that several writers assume that teachings are more important when judges are dealing with unwritten law, as opposed to when interpreting written instruments such as treaties. The book finds support for this assumption in the ICJ's practice. Section 3.5 presents various theories from other writers about why the ICJ's majority opinions rarely cite teachings. This book finds that many of them have little explanatory power. Writers assume that teachings have less weight than judicial decisions and ILC works, which is what this book also finds (Section 3.8). According to Section 3.10, some writers assume that teachings have some weight, but this book finds that the ICJ as a whole assign teachings low weight. Chapter 4 notes that writers also assume that the weight of teachings varies between works, which is what this book finds. Many writers support at least some of the factors identified by the book as determining the weight given to a work of teachings. Section 5.4 shows that writers have identified some factors that can explain the different attitudes of different judges towards teachings, and these factors are mostly confirmed by the book (the book also adds some factors of its own). Finally, Section 5.5.4 presents several writers who assume that civil law systems are more positive towards citing teachings than are common law

---

[4] Similarly Nora Stappert, 'A New Influence of Legal Scholars? The Use of Academic Writings at International Criminal Courts and Tribunals' (2018) 31 *Leiden Journal of International Law* 963, 965; (in the context of US national law) John Henry Merryman, 'The Authority of Authority: What the California Supreme Court Cited in 1950' (1954) 6 *Stanford Law Review* 613, 613.

systems, although some writers doubt this. The results in this book support the doubters.

1.2 Why Study the Application of Teachings by the ICJ

Existing sources tell little about the role of teachings in international law generally or the ICJ specifically. The ICJ Statute[5] Article 38(1) provides some simple directions, but nothing more, as explained in Chapter 2. Another question is whether the directions in Article 38(1) are observed in the ICJ's practice. This cannot be answered by the Statute itself, and it is examined in this book. Some existing books and articles discuss the role of teachings in international law,[6] but usually without the examples, data, or examinations of the kind that are found in this book. Existing teachings therefore give limited guidance on the topic[7] and are often limited to repeating the same common assumptions about teachings.[8] Some authors examine the application of teachings by other institutions using empirical methods reminiscent of those that are used in this book. Their results are compared with those from this book in Section 6.3.

While the role of teachings in the ICJ is not well explained by relevant sources or other teachings, the topic is important in practice. Teachings are explicitly recognised in the ICJ Statute Article 38(1) and are frequently cited by many of the Court's judges in individual opinions. It would be valuable to get a more detailed picture of the role teachings actually play in the ICJ's decision-making process. This book aims to provide such a picture.

---

[5] Statute of the International Court of Justice, San Francisco, 26 June 1945, in force 24 October 1945, 33 UNTS 933.

[6] For example, Alain Pellet, 'Article 38' in Andreas Zimmermann and others (eds.), *The Statute of the International Court of Justice: A Commentary* (2nd edn, Oxford University Press 2012) 731, 868–870; Hugh Thirlway, *The Sources of International Law* (Oxford University Press 2014) 126–128. Most international law textbooks cover teachings, but notable absences are V D Degan, *Sources of International Law* (Martinus Nijhoff 1997); Antonio Cassese, *International Law* (2nd edn, Oxford University Press 2005); Vaughan Lowe, *International Law* (Oxford University Press 2007).

[7] Sir Michael Wood, 'Teachings of the Most Highly Qualified Publicists (Art. 38 (1) ICJ Statute)', *Max Planck Encyclopedia of Public International Law* (article last updated October 2010) http://opil.ouplaw.com/view/10.1093/law:epil/9780199231690/law-9780199231690-e1480, para 16.

[8] Jörg Kammerhofer, 'Lawmaking by scholars' in Catherine Brölmann and Yannick Radi (eds.), *Research Handbook on the Theory and Practice of International Lawmaking* (Edward Elgar 2016) 305, 307.

This book examines how often and in what ways ICJ opinions cite teachings. Judicial decisions are a publicly available material where teachings are cited, and they are relatively authoritative.[9] Teachings are also cited in pleadings,[10] various legal advice,[11] and official communications,[12] but they lack either the publicity or authority of judicial decisions. Organisations such as the IDI, ILA, and ILC cite teachings in their texts,[13] and at least the ILC is comparable to judicial decisions in terms of authority.[14] This book nonetheless focuses on the ICJ.

The ICJ is chosen over other courts and tribunals because it is the only permanent judicial institution with general jurisdiction in international law.[15] This gives it a unique authority,[16] even though there is no formal

---

[9] Gleider Hernández, 'Interpretative Authority and the International Judiciary', in Andrea Bianchi, Daniel Peat, and Matthew Windsor (eds.), *Interpretation in International Law* (Oxford University Press 2015) 166, 166; Jean d'Aspremont, 'Non-State Actors and the Social Practice of International Law', in Math Noortmann, August Reinisch, and Cedric Ryngaert (eds.), *Non-State Actors in International Law* (Hart 2015) 11, 20–21.

[10] For example, Hersch Lauterpacht, *The Development of International Law by the International Court* (Stevens and Sons 1958) 25; James Crawford, *Brownlie's Principles of Public International Law* (8th edn, Oxford University Press 2012) 43; Thirlway, *Sources*, 127.

[11] For example, Bruno Simma, 'Remarks by Bruno Simma' (2000) 94 *American Society of International Law Proceedings* 319, 319 ('[f]oreign offices'); Alina Kaczorowska, *Public International Law* (4th edn, Routledge 2010) 59 ('legal advisers to states'); Malcolm N Shaw, *International Law* (7th edn, Cambridge University Press 2014) 80 ('States' and 'officials').

[12] Manfred Lachs, *The Teacher in International Law* (2nd edn, Martinus Nijhoff 1987) 195–199; Peter Malanczuk, *Akehurst's Modern International Law* (7th edn, Routledge 1997) 52; (more reservedly) Shabtai Rosenne, *Practice and Methods of International Law* (Oceana Publications 1984) 119.

[13] Karol Wolfke, *Custom in Present International Law* (2nd edn, Martinus Nijhoff 1993) 156; Wood, 'Teachings', para 15.

[14] Section 3.8.

[15] James Crawford, *Chance, Order, Change: The Course of International Law* (Brill 2014) 216; Mads Andenas and Eirik Bjorge, 'Introduction: From Fragmentation to Convergence' in International Law', in Mads Andenas and Eirik Bjorge (eds.), *A Farewell to Fragmentation: Reassertion and Convergence in International Law* (Cambridge University Press 2015) 1, 6.

[16] For example, Maurice Mendelson, 'The International Court of Justice and the Sources of International Law' in Vaughan Lowe and Malgosia Fitzmaurice (eds.), *Fifty Years of the International Court of Justice: Essays in Honour of Sir Robert Jennings* (Cambridge University Press 1996) 63, 83; Pierre-Marie Dupuy, 'The Danger of Fragmentation or Unification of the International Legal System and the International Court of Justice' (1998) 31 *NYU Journal of International Law and Politics* 791, 791; ILC, *First report on formation and evidence of customary international law by Michael Wood, Special Rapporteur (A/CN.4/663)* (UN 2013) 28.

hierarchy among international courts.[17] The ICJ's predecessor, the PCIJ, is also covered. Statistics and findings from the PCIJ are presented alongside those from the ICJ in several places in this book. Numbers, figures, and graphs refer only to the ICJ, unless anything else is explicitly stated. National courts also cite teachings when applying international law,[18] possibly at a greater rate than many international courts and tribunals.[19] However, national courts have 'less weight' than international courts and tribunals in international law[20] and are not systematically examined in this book.

The book covers separate and dissenting ICJ opinions as well as declarations,[21] using the term 'individual' opinions.[22] Since only five of the ICJ's majority opinions have cited teachings,[23] examining individual opinions is necessary in order to get a fuller picture of the role that teachings play in the ICJ. One ICJ judge explains that 'references [...] may even be in the draft judgment but get taken out before the final judgment is issued'.[24] Therefore, as sources of what actually happens in practice in international courts and tribunals, individual opinions are probably more accurate than majority opinions.[25] This is true regardless of the fact that individual opinions are generally seen as less authoritative

[17] For example, Crawford, *Chance*, 216; D J Harris, *Cases and Materials on International Law* (8th edn, Sweet & Maxwell 2015) 42; Kenneth Keith, 'Challenges to the Independence of the International Judiciary: Reflections on the International Court of Justice' (2017) 30 *Leiden Journal of International Law* 137, 153.

[18] Wood, 'Teachings', para 14; Shaw, *International Law*, 80; Sandesh Sivakumaran, 'The Influence of Teachings of Publicists on the Development of International Law' (2017) 66 *International and Comparative Law Quarterly* 1, 27.

[19] For example, Lauterpacht, *Development*, 25; Crawford, *Brownlie's*, 43; L C Green, *International Law: A Canadian Perspective* (2nd edn, The Carswell Company 1988) 70.

[20] Georg Schwarzenberger, *International Law, Volume 1: International Law as Applied by International Courts and Tribunals: I* (3rd edn, Stevens and Sons 1957) 32; John H Currie, *Public International Law* (2nd edn, Irwin Law 2008) 109.

[21] As in, for example, Stewart Manley, 'Citation Practices of the International Criminal Court: The Situation in Darfur, Sudan' (2017) 30 *Leiden Journal of International Law* 1003, 1004.

[22] For example, *South West Africa, Second Phase, Judgment, I.C.J. Reports 1966*, p. 6, Declaration of President Spender 54–57; Gleider I Hernández, *The International Court of Justice and the Judicial Function* (Oxford University Press 2014) 98.

[23] As discussed in Section 3.2.

[24] ICJ Judge 1.

[25] For example, Crawford, *Brownlie's*, 43; Mendelson, 'Sources', 84; Robert Kolb, *The International Court of Justice* (Hart 2013) 1014; D W Greig, *International Law* (2nd edn, Butterworths 1976) 48. Similarly Shabtai Rosenne, *The Perplexities of Modern International Law* (Martinus Nijhoff 2004) 44.

than majority opinions.[26] Judge Ammoun in *Barcelona Traction* holds that the 'authority' of the Court's decisions 'derives, *inter alia*, from the very fact that their judgments include the dissenting or separate opinions'.[27] Therefore, majority and individual opinions should be read together – a point other ICJ judges have also made in their extra-judicial writings.[28]

A caveat when examining individual opinions is that some may reflect the Court's practices more accurately than others, depending on how close they are to the Court's median approach.[29] Two international judges mention that certain colleagues are 'far reaching' or 'dissenters'.[30] This book alleviates this problem by examining every individual opinion. The more opinions that underlie the conclusions that are drawn, the better the chance that these conclusions are not based on the opinions of outlier judges. The book also identifies a 'median' approach among the judges in Section 5.3.3 and identifies four outliers (Cançado Trindade, Weeramantry, Shahabuddeen, and Kreća). When relevant, statistics are presented with and without the outliers.

1.3   Methodology

1.3.1   Collecting Citations

This book covers all decisions made by the Court from its beginning to 5 October 2016, the final decisions being the judgments on preliminary objections in the three *Marshall Islands* cases.[31] The ICJ gave its first

---

[26] For example, Michel Virally, 'The Sources of International Law', in Max Sørensen (ed.), *Manual of Public International Law* (St. Martin's Press 1968) 116, 153–154; Daniel Terris, Cesare P R Romano, and Leigh Swigart, *The International Judge: An Introduction to the Men and Women Who Decide the World's Cases* (Oxford University Press 2007) 126.

[27] *Barcelona Traction, Light and Power Company, Limited, Judgment, I.C.J. Reports 1970*, p. 3, Separate Opinion of Judge Ammoun 316.

[28] Sir Robert Jennings, 'The Collegiate Responsibility and Authority of the International Court of Justice', in Yoram Dinstein (ed.), *International Law at a Time of Perplexity: Essays in Honour of Shabtai Rosenne* (Martinus Nijhoff 1989) 343, 346; Mohamed Shahabuddeen, *Precedent in the World Court* (Cambridge University Press 1996) 178 and 196.

[29] Rosenne, *Methods*, 99, argues that this affects the weight of each opinion.

[30] Quoted in Terris, Romano, and Swigart, *International Judge*, 66–67.

[31] Of the three, the one published last in the ICJ reports is *Obligations Concerning Negotiations Relating to Cessation of the Nuclear Arms Race and to Nuclear Disarmament (Marshall Islands v. United Kingdom), Jurisdiction and Admissibility, Judgment, I.C.J. Reports 2016*, p. 833.

opinion, in *Admission of a State to the UN*, in 1948.[32] The book also covers all PCIJ's decisions, from *Wimbledon* (1923) to *Electricity Company of Sofia and Bulgaria* (1940).[33]

The Court distinguishes between three types of decisions and opinions: orders, judgments, and advisory opinions.[34] No distinction is made between them here in terms of weight, in line with the Court's own practice.[35]

The Court is normally composed of fifteen permanent judges, plus up to two judges ad hoc. Six of the ICJ's cases were decided by 'chambers', composed of fewer than the normal fifteen to seventeen judges, under the ICJ Statute Article 26.[36] Chamber decisions should perhaps have less weight than regular decisions, due the lower number of judges involved and the resultant reduction of geographical diversity.[37] In practice, however, chambers decisions seem to be given the same weight as regular decisions, at least by the ICJ itself.[38] Chambers decisions are therefore treated the same as regular decisions in this book.

This book is based on a reading of decisions and opinions. The decisions and opinions were downloaded as PDF files from the Court's official website in English-language versions, but in French if no English version was available.[39] All citations of teachings were collected, copied into a separate document, and then manually counted and analysed.[40]

---

[32] *Admission of a State to the United Nations (Charter, Art. 4), Advisory Opinion: I.C.J. Reports 1948*, p. 57.

[33] *Case of the S.S. "Wimbledon", Judgment, 28 June 1923, P.C.I.J. Reports Series A No. 1*, p. 11; *Electricity Company of Sofia and Bulgaria, Order, 26 February 1940, P.C.I.J. Series A/B No. 80*, p. 4.

[34] ICJ, 'Judgments, Advisory Opinions and Orders' (2017) www.icj-cij.org/en/decisions.

[35] *Interpretation of Peace Treaties, Advisory Opinion: I.C.J. Reports 1950*, p. 65, Dissenting Opinion by Judge Zoričič 101. Similarly, for example, *Legal Consequences for States of the Continued Presence of South Africa in Namibia (South West Africa) notwithstanding Security Council Resolution 276 (1970), Advisory Opinion, I.C.J. Reports 1971*, p. 16, Separate Opinion of Judge De Castro 173–174; Shahabuddeen, *Precedent*, 165–171.

[36] ICJ, 'Chambers and Committees' (2017) www.icj-cij.org/en/chambers-and-committees.

[37] Section 4.6.

[38] Shahabuddeen, *Precedent*, 176; Paolo Palchetti, 'Article 27', in Andreas Zimmermann and others (eds.), *The Statute of the International Court of Justice: A Commentary* (2nd edn, Oxford University Press 2012) 502, 504–505.

[39] ICJ, 'List of All Cases' (2017) www.icj-cij.org/en/list-of-all-cases.

[40] The methodology is thus similar to, for example, Ole Kristian Fauchald, 'The Legal Reasoning of ICSID Tribunals – An Empirical Analysis' (2008) 19 *European Journal of International Law* 301, 302; Michael Peil, 'Scholarly Writings as a Source of Law: A Survey of the Use of Doctrine by the International Court of Justice' (2012) 1 *Cambridge Journal of International and Comparative Law* 136, 147–148; Manley, 'Citation', 1004.

Citations of teachings have also been collected from pleadings in some ICJ cases. The ICJ cases in question are the three with the most citations of teachings in individual opinions: *Jan Mayen*,[41] *Pulp Mills*,[42] and the merits phase of *Bosnia Genocide*.[43] All oral and written pleadings are included.

Citations of teachings that concern national law rather than international law are counted when those teachings are used to find the content of international law. National law can also be used as a fact,[44] and teachings can be applied as part of that process, but that is not counted in this book.

An international court or tribunal may also refer to another tribunal's or a counsel's reference to teachings. Such 'indirect' references are counted in this book.[45] Courts and tribunals do not repeat every reference to teachings made by other tribunals or counsel. This may be taken to mean that 'indirect' references do have some significance. At the same time, an 'indirect' reference may be seen as less significant than one that a court or tribunal makes purely on its own initiative.

International courts and tribunals sometimes preface references to teachings with the phrase 'see generally' (or something similar). Such references are presumably intended mainly to give background to the topic under discussion rather than provide support for specific legal conclusions. However, the teachings may still have affected the judge's writings and decisions. These 'general' references are therefore counted in this book.[46]

The traditional way of applying teachings is to use their substance as support for a conclusion on the content of international law. However,

---

[41] *Maritime Delimitation in the Area between Greenland and Jan Mayen, Judgment, I.C.J. Reports 1993*, p. 38.

[42] *Pulp Mills on the River Uruguay (Argentina v. Uruguay), Judgment, I.C.J. Reports 2010*, p. 14.

[43] *Application of the Convention on the Prevention and Punishment of the Crime of Genocide (Bosnia and Herzegovina v. Serbia and Montenegro), Judgment, I.C.J. Reports 2007*, p. 43.

[44] *Case Concerning certain German interests in Polish Upper Silesia (The Merits) (Germany v. Poland), Judgment No. 7, 25 May 1926, P.C.I.J. Reports Series A No. 7*, p. 4, 19; James Crawford, *International Law as an Open System: Selected Essays* (Cameron May 2002) 22.

[45] As in Stappert, 'Influence', 969. By contrast, some studies of national law exclude such citations, for example, Blake Rohrbacher, 'Decline: Twenty-Five Years of Student Scholarship in Judicial Opinions' (2006) 80 *American Bankruptcy Law Journal* 553, 555; Brent E Newton, 'Law Review Scholarship in the Eyes of the Twenty-First-Century Supreme Court Justices: An Empirical Analysis' (2012) 4 *Drexel Law Review* 399, 402.

[46] They are excluded by Fauchald, 'Legal Reasoning', 351.

a tribunal can also make an inference about the content of international law from the fact that something is *not* stated in relevant teachings. Such applications of teachings are counted in this book. An example can be found in an opinion by Judge Krylov in *Corfu Channel*, where he noted that the island of Corfu had 'not been found worthy of special attention' by a Greek international law textbook.[47] Judge Lauterpacht in the *Voting Procedure* case noted the lack of 'disposition among authors who commented in detail upon' the various rules he was discussing to 'question their propriety in any way'.[48] In *Land, Island and Maritime Frontier Dispute*, when discussing the legal status of the Gulf of Fonseca, Judge Oda found it significant that '[t]here was no mention of the Gulf' in two specific works on international law.[49]

Some citations of teachings are imprecise. They are references in which a judge gives the name of one or more authors without naming any specific work.[50] An imprecise reference may even be more significant than a precise one, if the implication is that the judge considers it so seminal and obvious that every reader should know the details without the judge having to state them. However, counting such references is difficult. It can be difficult to know whether the judge is referring to an individual as writer or in another capacity. An illustration is Vice-President Alfaro in the *Temple* case, who referred to the views of 'Spanish jurists'.[51] It is, moreover, not possible to know how many works of teachings the judge may have had in mind for each writer. In some cases, it is not even clear how many individuals the judge has in mind. Because of these difficulties, 'imprecise' references are not counted in this book.

For the purpose of counting references, where a single work of teachings is cited more than once in the same paragraph (in the text or the footnotes), it is considered a single citation for statistical purposes.[52]

---

[47] *Corfu Channel case, Judgment of April 9th, 1949: I.C.J. Reports 1949*, p. 4, Dissenting Opinion by Judge Krylov 74.

[48] *South-West Africa–Voting Procedure, Advisory Opinion of June 7th, 1955: I.C.J. Reports 1955*, p. 67, Separate Opinion of Judge Lauterpacht 111.

[49] *Land, Island and Maritime Frontier Dispute (El Salvador/Honduras: Nicaragua intervening), Judgment of 11 September 1992, I.C.J. Reports 1992*, p. 351, Dissenting Opinion of Judge Oda 747.

[50] For example, *Admission of a State to the UN,* Individual Opinion by M. Azevedo 73.

[51] *Case concerning the Temple of Preah Vihear (Cambodia* v. *Thailand), Merits, Judgment of 15 June 1962: I.C.J. Reports 1962*, p. 6, Separate Opinion of Vice-President Alfaro 39.

[52] As in Wes Daniels, '"Far Beyond the Law Reports": Secondary Source Citations in the United States Supreme Court Opinions October Terms 1900, 1940, and 1978 (1983) 76 *Law Library Journal* 1, 3; Russell Smyth, 'Citing Outside the Law Reports: Citations of

Multiple citations to the same work in different paragraphs in the same opinion are counted as multiple citations.[53] References of multiple editions or volumes of the same work in the same paragraph are counted as distinct citations.[54] Examples include Judge ad hoc Van den Wyngaert in *Arrest Warrant*, who cited different versions of *Oppenheim's International Law*.[55] The judge's choice of whether to split something into multiple paragraphs or not is a matter of style. The approach taken in this book may therefore seem arbitrary, but there is no alternative that seems less arbitrary.

Different judicial decisions and opinions have different lengths. For statistical purposes in this book, they are still counted as a single decision or opinion, without any adjustment for length. Regardless of length, every opinion may involve a contested legal question and may cite teachings. This is illustrated by the fact that even the shortest individual opinions can cite teachings[56] and that one judge (Cançado Trindade) in one opinion managed to include forty-three references to teachings on a single page.[57] It would have been possible to count references to teachings per page of judicial decision,[58] but this would have been problematic since some decisions include more factual discussions or summaries of the parties' submissions.

Secondary Authorities on the Australian State Supreme Courts Over the Twentieth Century' (2009) 18 *Griffith Law Review* 692, 704.

[53] These are counted as a single citation by Vaughan Black and Nicholas Richter, 'Did She Mention My Name?: Citation of Academic Authority by the Supreme Court of Canada, 1985–1990' (1993) 16 *Dalhousie Law Journal* 377, 381; Tony Cole, 'Non-Binding Documents and Literature', in Tarcisio Gazzini and Eric De Brabandere (eds.), *International Investment Law: The Sources of Rights and Obligations* (Martinus Nijhoff 2012) 289, 304.

[54] These are counted as a single citation by Black and Richter, 'My Name', 380.

[55] *Arrest Warrant of 11 April 2000 (Democratic Republic of the Congo v. Belgium), Judgment, I.C.J. Reports 2002*, p. 3, Dissenting Opinion of Judge ad hoc Van den Wyngaert 149, where the different versions have different editors.

[56] For example, *Arbitral Award of 31 July 1989, Judgment, I.C.J. Reports 1991*, p. 53, Declaration of Judge Mbaye 80 and *Frontier Dispute (Benin/Niger), Formation of Chamber, Order of 27 November 2002. I.C.J. Reports 2002*, p. 613, Declaration of Judge Oda 616 are only one page long.

[57] *Obligation to Negotiate Access to the Pacific Ocean (Bolivia v. Chile), Preliminary Objection, Judgment, I.C.J. Reports 2015*, p. 592, Separate Opinion of Judge Cançado Trindade 8.

[58] P Lee Petherbridge and David L Schwartz, 'An Empirical Assessment of the Supreme Court's Use of Legal Scholarship' (2012) 106 *Northwestern University Law Review* 995, 1005.

Judges' number of citations per opinion does not include their participation in majority opinions. The counting is limited to individual opinions. One reason for this is that the ICJ's majority opinions are prepared by a drafting committee that usually has three members, and it is not possible to know which judges were members of the drafting committee in any specific case.[59] The president or vice-president is usually a member unless they disagree with the majority decision, but beyond that the selection is secret.[60] According to Hugh Thirlway, the Court's former Registrar, some judges 'never participate in a Drafting Committee'.[61] Where multiple judges have co-authored an individual opinion, the citations in the opinion are included in the citation counts of each of the individual judges.[62]

1.3.2 Analysing Citations

ICJ judges have said nothing explicitly about the role teachings play in their decision-making.[63] The closest examples are the PCIJ's *Lotus* decision, where the majority deliberately left open 'the question as to what [teachings'] value may be from the point of view of establishing the existence of a rule of customary law',[64] and Judge Shahabuddeen's opinion in *Border and Transborder Armed Actions*, where he wrote that the teachings he cited do not 'prevail over [...] the ordinary and natural meaning of' a treaty'.[65] The latter statement is in line with the term 'subsidiary' in the ICJ Statute Article 38(1) and is therefore discussed

---

[59] Thore Neumann and Bruno Simma, 'Transparency in International Adjudication' in Anne Peters and Andrea Bianchi (eds.), *Transparency in International Law* (Cambridge University Press 2013) 436, 458.

[60] ICJ, 'Resolution Concerning the International Judicial Practice of the Court (Rules of Court, Article 19)' (12 April 1976) www.icj-cij.org/en/other-texts/resolution-concerning-judicial-practice, Article 6.

[61] Hugh Thirlway, 'The Drafting of ICJ Decisions: Some Personal Recollections and Observations' (2006) 5 *Chinese Journal of International Law* 15, 23.

[62] Smyth, 'Outside', 704.

[63] More generally Stefan Talmon, 'Determining Customary International Law: The ICJ's Methodology between Induction, Deduction and Assertion' (2015) 26 *European Journal of International Law* 417, 441 ('[t]he Court rarely explicitly states its methodology for determining the rules of international law'); Sivakumaran, 'Influence', 26 ('[a]ctors often do not explain their thought processes').

[64] *The Case of the S.S. 'Lotus' (France* v. *Turkey), Judgment No. 9, 7 September 1927, P.C.I.J. Reports Series A No. 10*, p. 4, 26.

[65] *Border and Transborder Armed Actions (Nicaragua* v. *Honduras), Jurisdiction and Admissibility, Judgment, I.C.J. Reports 1988*, p. 69, Separate Opinion of Judge Shahabuddeen 148–149.

further in Section 2.2.8. Because there are no more examples of judges explicitly discussing or explaining their application of teachings, a conventional legal analysis of the ICJ's opinions is unhelpful.

Instead, this book uses quantitative and qualitative approaches to examine the ICJ's application of teachings.[66] The quantitative approach involves counting the number of references to teachings in each decision and by each judge. The qualitative approach involves an analysis of the terms and phrases used by judges when citing teachings, as well as the specific context of the citation. In many sections not all the relevant examples have been included, in order to maintain the flow of the text. The guiding idea has been that examples are included to the extent that they add analytical value to the text, instead of aiming to give an exhaustive listing of all relevant examples. An example of quantitative analysis is Section 3.2, which notes that the ICJ's majority opinions rarely cite teachings, and infers from this that teachings are treated as having low weight. An example of qualitative analysis is Section 4.3.3, where it is noted that some judges use terms such as 'expert' and 'valuable' about works that they cite, and this is used to infer that judges treat expertise and quality as factors that affect the weight of teachings.

The two methodological approaches should together give quite an accurate picture of how ICJ judges apply teachings in their opinions. A quantitative approach alone provides more limited information.[67] There is also a risk that '[w]hen what matters is what is countable, what is countable determines what matters'.[68] This book does not count citations for the sake of counting citations, but does so as one part of a purposely designed research methodology.

The book counts the number of citations of teachings and breaks them down by judge and case. Another possibility would be to examine the

---

[66] For example, Manley, 'Citation', 1006; (in the context of national law) Bart Sloan, 'What Are We Writing For? Student Works As Authority and Their Citation by the Federal Bench, 1986–1990' (1992) 62 *George Washington Law Review* 221, 229; Keith Stanton, 'Use of Scholarship by the House of Lords in Tort Cases' in James Lee (ed.), *From House of Lords to Supreme Court: Judges, Jurists and the Process of Judging* (Hart 2011) 201, 203–204.

[67] For example, Jean d'Aspremont in 'EJIL Editors' Choice of Books' (2015) 26 *European Journal of International Law* 1027, 1041; Cole, 'Non-Binding', 305; (in the context of national law) Fred R Shapiro and Michelle Pearse, 'The Most-Cited Law Review Articles of All Time' (2012) 110 *Michigan Law Review* 1483, 1518.

[68] Sarah M H Nouwen, '"*As You Set out for Ithaka*": Practical, Epistemological, Ethical, and Existential Questions about Socio-Legal Empirical Research in Conflict' (2014) 27 *Leiden Journal of International Law* 227, 230.

percentage of citations of all materials that were citations of teachings,[69] but that is not attempted here. In some parts of the book, the empirical results are linked with data on judge-related demographics. For example, Section 5.5.4 finds that judges from OECD member states cite less often than other judges do, while judges who are former academics cite more teachings than judges who are former diplomats. It would also have been interesting to examine, for example, whether judges cite more teachings by writers from states that are involved in the specific case. A rejected proposal during the drafting of the ICJ Statute Article 38(1) was to limit the Court to citing *only* writers from the states involved in the case,[70] which implies that writers' nationalities have some significance. However, it has not been practically possible to examine this in detail, because it is difficult to find reliable demographic data on all but the most famous of the 1280 writers the ICJ and its judges have cited.

Judges can cite something without having read or been influenced by it[71] and be influenced by something without citing it.[72] The latter point is also made by former ICJ President Jennings.[73] There are several indications that ICJ judges read more teachings than they cite, which are discussed in Section 3.4. This means that citations are not exhaustive, and teachings probably have a 'hidden' influence on ICJ judges. The examination of judicial decisions that is undertaken in this book will show how judges argue about teachings in their written opinions. It does

[69] As done by Michael Bohlander, 'The Influence of Academic Research on the Jurisprudence of the International Criminal Tribunal for the Former Yugoslavia – A First Overview' (2003) 3 *The Global Community Yearbook of International Law & Jurisprudence* 195, 197; Fauchald, 'Legal Reasoning', 302.

[70] ACJ, *Procès-Verbaux of the Proceedings of the Committee June 16th–July 24th 1920 with Annexes* (Van Langenhuysen Brothers 1920) 336; Peil, 'Writings', 140.

[71] For example, Kammerhofer, 'Lawmaking', 322–323; Jack Goldsmith, 'Remarks by Jack Goldsmith' (2000) 94 *ASIL Proceedings* 318, 318; Lord Rodger of Earlsferry, 'Judges and Academics in the United Kingdom' (2010) 29 *University of Queensland Law Journal* 29, 30–31.

[72] For example, G I Tunkin, *Theory of International Law* (George Allen and Unwin 1974) 187; (in the context of national law) Jack Beatson, 'Legal Academics: Forgotten Players or Interlopers?' in Andrew Burrows, David Johnston, and Reinhard Zimmermann (eds.), *Judge and Jurist: Essays in Memory of Lord Rodger* (Oxford University Press 2013) 523, 526; Petherbridge and Schwartz, 'Empirical', 1000.

[73] Robert Y Jennings, 'What is International Law and How Do We Know It When We See It' in Martti Koskenniemi (ed.), *Sources of International Law* (Ashgate 2000) 27, 46–47; Robert Y Jennings, 'Reflections on the Subsidiary Means for the Determination of Rules of Law', in *Studi di diritto internazionale in onore di Gaetano Arangio-Ruiz*, vol. I (Editoriale Scientifica 2004) 319, 328.

not necessarily reflect fully what judges think about teachings. It is a legal rather than a psychological examination.[74]

Because of this 'hidden influence', writers are divided on the usefulness of analysing citations in judicial decisions. Some believe such analyses are useful,[75] while others are sceptical.[76] Yet others take an intermediate view.[77] The best assessment is made by Sivakumaran, who calls 'citation by courts and tribunals [...] a useful measure of influence', but adds that it 'is not the same as influence', and 'only one measure of influence'.[78] Citations are only a reasonably accurate and necessarily imperfect proxy of weight, in a study where a proxy must necessarily be used.[79] The study undertaken in this book reveals one thing (how judges argue), but not something else (what judges think). This is inevitable no matter what methodology is used in a scholarly work. The results that the book does give are important enough in themselves.[80]

1.3.3   Conducting Interviews

The study of judicial decisions is supplemented by interviews with judges and staff at the ICJ.[81] The interviews are cited throughout book. Two (current or former) ICJ judges and three (current or former) ICJ staff members were interviewed. The staff members had been involved in the

---

[74] Max Sørensen, *Les sources du droit international: étude sur la jurisprudence de la cour permanente de justice internationale* (E. Munksgaard 1946) 188.

[75] For example, Greig, *International Law*, 48; Lachs, *Teacher*, 192; (in the context of national law) Theodore Eisenberg and Martin T Wells, 'Ranking and Explaining the Scholarly Impact of Law Schools' (1998) 27 *Journal of Legal Studies* 373, 377.

[76] For example, Kammerhofer, 'Lawmaking', 323; Jean d'Aspremont, *Formalism and the Sources of International Law* (Oxford University Press 2011) 210; (in the context of national law) Richard A Mann, 'The Use of Legal Periodicals by Courts and Journals' (1986) 26 *Jurimetrics Journal* 400, 400.

[77] For example, (in the context of national law) Neil Duxbury, *Judges and Jurists: An Essay on Influence* (Hart 2001) 1, 6, 8–9, and 13; Fábio P Shecaira, *Legal Scholarship as a Source of Law* (Springer 2013) 15 and 18; Edward Rubin, 'Seduction, Integration and Conceptual Frameworks: The Influence of Legal Scholarship on Judges' (2010) 29 *University of Queensland Law Journal* 101, 13.

[78] Sivakumaran, 'Influence', 3.

[79] Sivakumaran, 'Influence', 26.

[80] Lawrence Friedman and others, 'State Supreme Courts: A Century of Style and Citation' (1981) 33 *Stanford Law Review* 773, 794.

[81] Other examples of the use of interviews when studying international judges include Terris, Romano, and Swigart, *International Judge*, xvi-xvii; Lyndel V Prott, *The Latent Power of Culture and the International Judge* (Professional Books 1979) xxi; Ruth Mackenzie and others, *Selecting International Judges: Principle, Process, and Politics* (Oxford University Press 2010) 180.

process of deciding cases and writing opinions for the Court. The judges and staff members are anonymised throughout the book[82] and are only identified as 'ICJ Judge 1', 'ICJ Judge 2', 'ICJ Employee 1', 'ICJ Employee 2', and 'ICJ Employee 3'.

One aim of the interviews was to discover the views and experiences of the interviewees. An important point was also to reveal interesting information about the ICJ's application of teachings that were not captured by qualitative and quantitative analysis of judicial decisions. The judges' opinions and experiences are used to support or rebut hypotheses that are suggested, but not proven, by the qualitative and quantitative analyses. The interviews constitute no more or less than the expressed views of a selection of individuals about the ICJ's application of teachings. This provides interesting background for and elaboration of many of the discussions in the book, and that is all they are meant to do.

The interviewees were selected through personal connections with people employed at the Court, who agreed to be interviewed themselves or referred to others who did. There was no opportunity to choose interviewees freely, and thus the sample of interviewees could not be deliberately designed.[83] When interviewees are not deliberately chosen, there is a risk of selection bias. For example, the judges and staff members who are willing to and interested in being interviewed by a researcher could generally be inclined to give different answers from other judges or staff members. It is not possible for this book to fully control for such risks.

The interviews were semi-structured insofar as they used a predetermined set of questions, but they gave the interviewees significant freedom to choose which questions to focus on and to elaborate on related matters.[84] Some of the questions were quite direct and in some sense 'leading'. Leading questions can affect the answers given by an interviewee,[85] but they may also make interviews more reliable.[86] The interviews therefore started with more open-ended questions, with more specific and pointed questions as the discussions progressed, before moving on a new topic with a new open-ended question.

---

[82] Svend Brinkmann and Steinar Kvale, *InterViews: Learning the Art of Qualitative Research Interviewing* (3rd edn, Sage 2015) 94–95.

[83] This is similar to the challenge faced by Terris, Romano, and Swigart, *International Judge*, xvii.

[84] Similarly Ibid., xvi.

[85] Brinkmann and Kvale, *InterViews,* 199.

[86] Ibid., 200.

1.3.4   The Concept of 'Weight'

The rest of book discusses the 'weight' of teachings.[87] This is a measure of how much teachings affect how a judge views and decides a legal question. The ICJ used the term 'weight' when describing its attitude to reports by the HRC in *Diallo*.[88] Other writers use other terms for similar concepts, such as 'influence', 'authority', and 'persuasiveness'.[89] Different terms are sometimes used interchangeably[90] and often without being explicitly defined, but 'weight' is used in this book.

An ICJ employee describes how teachings can, for example, 'frame how [judges] approach an issue', in addition to making someone 'change their mind'.[91] The ICJ's former Registrar Thirlway claims that teachings may 'tip the scale' in difficult cases.[92] However, the weight discussed in this does not presuppose that a judge changes their mind. A judge could hold a particular view before consulting teachings and have this view confirmed by the teachings. In that case the judge would be affected by the teachings, by becoming more certain, but teachings would not have changed the judge's mind. A simplified illustration is to think of 'legal certainty' as a range between 0 and 100 for a legal question with two possible outcomes. Zero means completely sure of one view, 100 means completely sure of opposite. Fifty means the judge is unable to decide between the two. Teachings can, for example, have a weight of 'two'. A judge may then be at forty-nine before consulting teachings, and then be pushed to fifty-one. In this case, the judge's mind has been changed. However, the judge may have been at sixty before consulting teachings, and if the teachings have a weight of thirty, the judge will be at ninety afterwards. The judge's view has been affected, but the teachings have not changed

---

[87]   As in, for example, Thirlway, *Sources*, 126–127; Crawford, *Brownlie's*, 43; Martin Dixon, *Textbook on International Law* (7th edn, Oxford University Press 2013) 49.

[88]   *Ahmadou Sadio Diallo (Republic of Guinea* v. *Democratic Republic of the Congo), Merits, Judgment, I.C.J. Reports 2010*, p. 639, 664.

[89]   Bohlander, 'Influence', 195; Fernando Lusa Bordin, 'Reflections of Customary International Law: The Authority of Codification Conventions and ILC Draft Articles In International Law (2014) 63 *International and Comparative Law Quarterly* 535, 538; Cole, 'Non-Binding', 300 and 304.

[90]   For example, by Gregory Scott Crespi, 'The Influence of a Decade of Statutory Interpretation Scholarship on Judicial Rulings: An Empirical Analysis' (2000) 53 *SMU Law Review* 9, 9; Dixon, *Textbook*, 49.

[91]   ICJ Employee 1.

[92]   Thirlway, *Sources*, 127.

the judge's mind. Thus, the concept of weight is not a matter of either–
or, but rather a continuum from low to high.[93]

When multiple teachings are referred to for the same point in
a decision, it can be difficult to disentangle the weight of any individual
work. Often in such cases all that can be done is to analyse the weight of
the teachings as a whole.

The ICJ Statute Article 38(1)(d) designates teachings as 'subsidiary
means', as discussed in Section 2.2.8. This means that teachings can have
weight, since their role is limited to affecting those who interpret rules, as
opposed to creating those rules. The designation of teachings as subsidiary means does not tell us *how much* weight teachings have in the ICJ.[94]
The rest of the book attempts to do so.

Having a law degree usually means that one has done at least part of
one's studies on the basis of teachings. In this sense, most, if not all,
practising lawyers, including judges, base at least some of their knowledge
and skills on teachings.[95] Teachings thus exert an influence on students'
thinking that is likely to persist after graduation and as they become
practising lawyers.[96] This could be considered a form of 'weight', even
though it would be of an indirect and peripheral nature compared to most
of the 'weight' that is studied in this book. Because of its nature, it is also
more difficult to measure and will not be analysed further in this book.

---

[93] This is also how Fuad Zarbiyev, 'Saying Credibly What the Law Is: On Marks of Authority
in International Law' (2018) 9 *Journal of International Dispute Settlement* 291, 309, sees
the concept of 'authority'.

[94] Aldo Zammit Borda, 'A Formal Approach to Article 38(1)(d) of the ICJ Statute from the
Perspective of the International Criminal Courts and Tribunals' (2013) 24 *European
Journal of International Law* 649, 655.

[95] Lord Goff, 'The Search for Principle' (1983) 67 *Proceedings of the British Academy*
169, 185.

[96] William Twining and others, 'The Role of Academics in the Legal System' in
Mark Tushnet and Peter Cane (eds.), *The Oxford Handbook of Legal Studies* (Oxford
University Press 2005) 920, 927.

2

The ICJ Statute Article 38(1)

2.1 Introduction

The ICJ's operation is regulated by the ICJ Statute, which was adopted as an annex to the UN Charter in 1945. The ICJ Statute Article 38(1) (d) is a rare example of a treaty (or other official instrument) that explicitly mentions teachings. The aim of this chapter is to show what guidance the provision gives on the ICJ's application of teachings, in order to provide a framework for the subsequent analysis of the Court's and the judges' practice. This is done by interpreting the terms of the provision (Section 2.2). The term 'teachings' requires a precise definition, which requires some space, and it is therefore singled out in Section 2.3.

This section discusses what that provision says about the Court's application of teachings, in order to provide a framework for the subsequent analysis, explanation, and assessment of the Court's and the judges' practice.

The relevant wording of the ICJ Statute Article 38(1) is as follows:

> The Court, whose function is to decide in accordance with international law such disputes as are submitted to it, shall apply: . . . the teachings of the most highly qualified publicists of the various nations, as subsidiary means for the determination of rules of law.

It is also possible to consider teachings to be a 'means' of treaty interpretation under the VCLT[1] Article 32 and equivalent customary international law.[2] However, since the ICJ Statute Article 38(1)(d) also applies to treaties, there is a strong presumption that the VCLT Article 32 does not say anything else than the ICJ Statute Article 38(1)(d) as regards the application of teachings in treaty

---

[1] Vienna Convention on the Law of Treaties, Vienna, 23 May 1969, in force 27 January 1980, 1155 UNTS 331.
[2] Fauchald, 'Legal Reasoning', 351.

interpretation. The VCLT Article 32 is, therefore, not discussed separately here.

The ICJ Statute Article 38 is accused of being poorly drafted,[3] 'outdated',[4] and unclear.[5] Even so, the provision does indicate various aspects of how teachings are to be applied by ICJ judges. These aspects are discussed in the rest of this chapter. Chapters 3 to 5 analyse the Court's and the judges' application of teachings, which offers the opportunity to test whether these practices adhere to the wording of Article 38(1).[6] The examination shows that the Court and the judges mostly adhere to Article 38(1) but not always. Section 6.2 highlights possible benefits from adjusting the Court's and the judges' practices. It uses compliance with Article 38(1) as part of its arguments, including on diversity (Section 6.2.2) and transparency (Section 6.2.3).

The following discussions draw on the preparatory works of the PCIJ and ICJ statutes. The wording of the PCIJ Statute[7] Article 38(4) has almost the same wording as the ICJ Statute Article 38(1)(d), which is why the PCIJ Statute's preparatory works are still relevant. The creation of the PCIJ Statute was mandated by Article 14 of the Covenant of the League of Nations.[8] The Council of the League of Nations created the ACJ, whose *Procès-Verbaux* contain the only substantive discussions on the role of teachings in the preparatory works.[9] The preparatory works also include the Committee's report,[10] records of the eighth and tenth sessions of the Council,[11]

---

[3] Philip Allott, 'Interpretation—An Exact Art' in Andrea Bianchi, Daniel Peat, and Matthew Windsor (eds.), *Interpretation in International Law* (Oxford University Press 2015) 373, 378. Similarly, for example, RP Dhokalia, *The Codification of Public International Law* (Manchester University Press 1970) 167; Wood, 'Teachings', para. 6.

[4] Rosenne, *Perplexities*, 27. Similarly, Wood, 'Teachings', para. 6; Kaczorowska, *International Law*, 32.

[5] Peil, 'Writings', 138.

[6] This is a partial response to the concern voiced by Jennings, 'What is International Law', 29 that 'it is an open question whether [Article 38] is now in itself a sufficient guide to the content of modern international law'.

[7] Statute of the Permanent Court of International Justice, Geneva, 13 December 1920, in force 8 October 1921, 6 LNTS 390.

[8] Covenant of the League of Nations, Paris, 28 June 1919, in force 10 January 1920, 225 CTS 195.

[9] Antônio Augusto Cançado Trindade, 'Statute of the International Court of Justice', *Audiovisual Library of International Law* (2017) http://legal.un.org/avl/ha/sicj/sicj.html.

[10] ACJ, *Procès-Verbaux*, 693.

[11] Procès-Verbal of the Eight Session of the Council of the League of Nations (September 1920) *League of Nations Official Journal* 304, 318–321; Procès-Verbal of the Tenth Session of the Council of the League of Nations (November–December 1920) *League of Nations Official Journal* 4, 12–22.

the Council's report to the Assembly of the League of Nations, the records of the meetings and final report of the subcommittee that was then established by the Assembly's Third Committee, the Third Committee's draft PCIJ Statute, and the records of the Assembly's twentieth and twenty-first sessions.[12] As will be shown later, the final text of the PCIJ Statute was a compromise that masked disagreements over the role of teachings.[13] Disagreements concerned in particular what 'subsidiary' was supposed to mean, and how active a role teachings could be allowed to play.

The preparatory works to the ICJ Statute include the recommendations of 10 February 1944 of the Inter-Allied Committee on the Future of the Permanent Court of International Justice and the Proposals for the Establishment of a General International Organization (1944). A UN Committee of Jurists produced a draft ICJ Statute in 1945, which was discussed further at the UN Conference on International Organization, where the Statute was adopted along with the UN Charter. The discussions related to the ICJ Statute are mainly found in volumes XIII and XIV of the Documents of the United Nations Conference on International Organization,[14] but these contain no substantive discussion on the application of teachings.

2.2   Guidance on the Application Teachings

2.2.1   The Inclusion of Teachings

It is notable that Article 38(1) mentions teachings at all. The ICJ Statute Article 38 is the ICJ's applicable law clause. Such clauses also exist for other courts and tribunals but without mentioning teachings. Examples include the UNCLOS Article 293, the Rome Statute[15] Article 21, and the

---

[12]   League of Nations, *Permanent Court of International Justice Documents concerning The Action Taken by the Council of the League of Nations under Article 14 of the Covenant and the Adoption by the Assembly of the Statute of the Permanent Court* (League of Nations1921) 20–27; 82–96; 172; 225–256.

[13]   Peil, 'Writings', 140.

[14]   UN Committee of Jurists, *Documents of the United Nations Conference on International Organization San Francisco, 1945* (UN Information Organizations 1945). The discussions relevant to Article 38(1) are found in vol. XIII page 392 and vol. XIV page 670.

[15]   Rome Statute of the International Criminal Court, Rome, 17 July 1998, in force 1 July 2002, 2187 UNTS 3.

ICSID Convention[16] Article 42.[17] There are also examples of official instruments regulating what judicial decisions are to contain. These provisions include the ICJ Rules of Court[18] Article 95(1), the ITLOS Rules of the Tribunal[19] Article 125, the Rome Statute Article 74(5), the ECtHR Rules [20] Article 74(h), and the ICSID Convention Article 48(3). None of these mentions teachings.

The original draft of the PCIJ Statute, presented by Baron Descamps (the President of the Committee) on 1 July 1920, did not include teachings in the listing that was to become Article 38(1).[21] Teachings were included in two other drafts, which said 'the opinions of writers' and 'the opinions of the best qualified writers', respectively.[22] A final compromise included 'the doctrines of the best qualified writers of the various nations as a means for the application and development of law',[23] which the drafting committee changed to what became Article 38(4).[24]

Teachings were more significant in international law in the past.[25] They were originally included in the PCIJ Statute, which was adopted in 1920. At that time the number and extent of treaties were even lower than they are at present.[26] Back then there were also fewer collections of treaties,[27] and less publicly available or collected State practice.[28] The international judiciary was much weaker in 1920 than it is today, and

---

[16] Convention on the Settlement of Investment Disputes Between States and Nationals of Other States, Washington, 18 March 1965, in force 14 October 1966, 575 UNTS 159.

[17] Isabelle Van Damme, *Treaty Interpretation by the WTO Appellate Body* (Oxford University Press 2009). Thirteen points out that WTO tribunals do not have applicable law clauses.

[18] ICJ, 'Rules of Court (1978)' (1978) www.icj-cij.org/en/rules.

[19] ITLOS, 'Rules of the Tribunal' (17 March 2009) www.itlos.org/fileadmin/itlos/documents/basic_texts/Itlos_8_E_17_03_09.pdf.

[20] ECtHR, 'Rules of Court' (14 November 2016) www.echr.coe.int/Documents/Rules_Court_eng.pdf.

[21] ACJ, *Procès-Verbaux*, 306; Peil, 'Writings', 138.

[22] ACJ, *Procès-Verbaux*, 344 and 351.

[23] Ibid., 337.

[24] Ibid., 567 and 584; Peil, 'Writings', 140.

[25] For example, ILC, Third report on identification of customary international law by Michael Wood, Special Rapporteur (A/CN.4/682) (UN 2015) 44. For example, Tunkin, Theory, 186; John F Murphy, *The Evolving Dimensions of International Law: Hard Choices for the World Community* (Cambridge University Press 2010) 26 suggest different past eras as the heyday of teachings.

[26] Gideon Boas, *Public International Law: Contemporary Principles and Perspectives* (Edward Elgar 2012) 114; Tim Hillier, *Sourcebook on Public International Law* (Cavendish 1998) 94.

[27] Lauterpacht, *Development*, 24.

[28] For example, Edwin D Dickinson, 'Changing Concepts and the Doctrine of Incorporation' (1932) 26 *American Journal of International Law* 239, 259; Lauterpacht, *Development*, 24;

there were fewer judicial decisions available.[29] These factors may explain why the PCIJ Statute included teachings.[30] The inclusion of teachings in the ICJ Statute may also be a result of the significantly unwritten nature of international law.[31]

The other applicable law clauses that were mentioned earlier and that do not mention teachings were concluded later than the PCIJ Statute. The ICSID Convention was concluded in 1965, the UNCLOS in 1982, and the Rome Statute in 1998. This too indicates that the time of the PCIJ Statute's conclusion was a factor in its inclusion of teachings.

Another sign of the decline of teachings is that the ICJ's *Handbook*, which was last updated in 2013, includes a chapter titled 'The Court applies international law', which discusses each of the elements in the ICJ Statute Article 38 *except* teachings and 'general principles of law'.[32] Teachings were significant enough to be included in the Statute in 1920, but not significant enough to be discussed separately in the *Handbook* in 2013.

The inclusion of teachings in the ICJ Statute is in any case unnecessary. While it may be said to authorise the Court to apply teachings,[33] that is superfluous. There is no sign that the Court or its judges would otherwise be prohibited from citing teachings. While other courts and tribunals do not have teachings mentioned in their statutes, many nonetheless cite them, even in majority opinions.[34] Unless the citation of teachings is explicitly prohibited, which it is and has been in certain national legal

---

Patrick Daillier, Mathias Forteau, and Alain Pellet, *Droit International Public* (8th edn, L. G.D.J. 2009) 434–435.

[29] For example, DP O'Connell, *International Law*, vol. I (2nd edn, Stevens and Sons 1970) 35; Wolfke, *Custom*, 156; Cole, 'Non-Binding', 311.

[30] GJH Van Hoof, *Rethinking the Sources of International Law* (Kluwer 1993) 177; Anthony Carty, *The Decay of International Law? A Reappraisal of the Limits of Legal Imagination In International Affairs* (Manchester University Press 1986) 13; Daillier, Forteau, and Pellet, *Droit International*, 434.

[31] For example, Robert Jennings, 'International Lawyers and the Progressive Development of International Law' in Jerzy Makarczyk (ed.), *Theory of International Law at the Threshold of the 21st Century: Essays in Honour of Krzysztof Skubiszewski* (Kluwer 1996) 413, 413; Hillier, *Sourcebook,* 94; Andraz Zidar, 'Interpretation and the International Legal Profession: Between Duty and Aspiration' in Andrea Bianchi, Daniel Peat, and Matthew Windsor (eds.), *Interpretation in International Law* (Oxford University Press 2015) 133, 142.

[32] ICJ, 'Handbook' (last updated 31 December 2013) www.icj-cij.org/files/publications/hand book-of-the-court-en.pdf, 95–99.

[33] Twining and others, 'Academics', 945.

[34] Chapter 6.3.2.

systems,[35] judges can cite them regardless of whether doing so is expressly mentioned in an applicable law clause.

2.2.2 'The Court, Whose Function Is to Decide in Accordance with International Law'

The ICJ Statute, including Article 38(1), formally applies only to the ICJ ('the Court').[36] However, there is widespread agreement that the provision reflects customary international law.[37] The ICJ may also have made the same assumption when writing that 'the sources of international law which Article 38 of the Statute requires the Court to apply' and 'sources of law enumerated in Article 38 of the Statute'.[38] This means that the provision is relevant to other courts and tribunals too, as well as to anyone else seeking to interpret and apply international law. Other international courts and tribunals seem to adhere to it in practice.[39] According to the ICJ Statute Article 38(1), the Court 'is to decide in accordance with international law'. This was not included in Article 38 of the PCIJ Statute. Committee 1 at the UN Conference on International Organization noted that the addition 'will accentuate' the 'character of the' Court 'as an organ of international law'.[40]

---

[35] Ibid.

[36] Gerald G Fitzmaurice, 'Some Problems Regarding the Formal Sources of International Law' in Martti Koskenniemi (ed.), *Sources of International Law* (Ashgate 2000) 57, 77. Similarly, for example, Murphy, *Dimensions*, 15; William W Bishop, 'General Course on Public International Law' (1965) 115 *Recueil des Cours* 147, 214.

[37] For example, ALI, *Restatement of the Law of Foreign Relations of the United States*, vol. I (ALI Publishers 1987) 29; ILC, *Survey of International Law in Relation to the Work of Codification of the International Law Commission: Preparatory work within the purview of article 18, paragraph 1, of the of the International Law Commission – Memorandum submitted by the Secretary-General* (A/CN.4/1/Rev.1) (UN 1949) 22, Martti Koskenniemi, 'Introduction' in Martti Koskenniemi (ed.), *Sources of International Law* (Ashgate 2000) xi xi. Although, for example, Richard A Falk, 'On the Quasi-Legislative Competence of the General Assembly' (1966) 60 *American Journal of International Law* 782, 782 is sceptical.

[38] *Military and Paramilitary Activities in and against Nicaragua (Nicaragua v. United States of America), Merits, Judgment. I.C.J. Reports 1986*, pp. 14, 38, 92; GM Danilenko, *Law-Making in the International Community* (Martinus Nijhoff 1993) 36.

[39] RP Anand, 'The International Court of Justice and the Development of International Law' (1965) 7 *International Studies* 228, 229. For international criminal courts and tribunals: Borda, 'Formal Approach', 651; Stappert, 'Influence', 965.

[40] UN Committee of Jurists, *Documents of the United Nations Conference on International Organization San Francisco, 1945*, vol. XIII (UN Information Organizations 1945) 392; elaborated on by Danilenko, *Law-Making*, 33–34.

The UNCLOS[41] Articles 74(1) and 83(1) mention 'international law, as referred to in Article 38 of the [ICJ Statute]', which seems to build on an assumption that the provision reflects customary international law.

That the ICJ Statute Article 38(1) reflects customary international law means that many of the arguments and conclusions of this book are significant not only with regard to the ICJ itself but also with regard to international law generally. Other courts and tribunals nonetheless apply teachings differently from the ICJ, as explored in Section 6.3.

Another aspect of the phrase 'the Court' is that Article 38(1) is thus addressed to the Court as a collective. It is the Court as such that is to 'apply . . . teachings'. Individual judges vary greatly in their approach to teachings, as shown in Chapter 5.

2.2.3   '[S]hall Apply'

Article 38(1) further says that the Court 'shall apply' teachings. This does not mean that the Court or its judges are obliged to *cite* teachings.[42] An ICJ judge does not 'think that Article 38 itself tells you when to refer to something and when not to do it. It allows you to do it, but that is all'.[43] Jennings, who was an ICJ judge, writes that the ICJ 'is required . . . to consult the writings of the most eminent publicists',[44] but does not say anything about citing. An ICJ employee reports that they are 'not aware of anyone who feels under an obligation to refer to scholarship. In some ways it is the opposite, a tradition or responsibility not to cite scholarship.'[45] The practice of the Court as a whole and of many judges of not citing teachings is not contrary to the ICJ Statute Article 38(1).

Hersch Lauterpacht, who was also an ICJ judge, nonetheless seems to argue that more citation of teachings would be more in line with the intentions behind Article 38(1).[46] Section 6.2.3 argues that more citations of teachings in ICJ opinions could have potential benefits for the Court.

---

[41] United Nations Convention on the Law of the Sea, Montego Bay, 10 October 1982, in force 16 November 1994, 1833 UNTS 3.

[42] According to *Hussein Nuaman Soufraki* v. *The United Arab Emirates*, ICSID Case No. ARB/02/7, Decision of the ad hoc Committee on the Application for Annulment of Mr Soufraki, 5 June 2007, 58, the same is true for ICSID awards.

[43] ICJ Judge 1.

[44] R Y Jennings, 'The Progressive Development of International Law and Its Codification' (1947) 24 *British Yearbook of International Law* 301, 308.

[45] ICJ Employee 2.

[46] Lauterpacht, *Development*, 24–25.

2.2.4   '[J]udicial Decisions'

Article 38(1)(d) includes teachings alongside 'judicial decisions'. From this, it may seem that the two are supposed to have the same status in international law. However, the ICJ seems to display a strong preference for judicial decisions, as discussed in Section 3.8.2.

2.2.5   '[T]eachings . . . of Publicists'

Article 38(1)(d) mentions 'teachings' and 'publicists' in the plural. This may mean that what is to be applied are not the views of individual writers singularly but rather the collective views of multiple writers. Descamps in the ACJ was open to letting judges consider 'the concurrent teaching of the authors whose opinions have authority'.[47] Elsewhere he used the term 'coinciding doctrine'.[48] This seems to express the same point. This book does find that the ICJ assigns greater weight to teachings when multiple writers agree (Section 4.3.5).

2.2.6   '[T]he Most Highly Qualified

Article 38(1)(d) limits itself to 'the *most highly qualified* publicists' (emphasis added). This seems to mean that the judges are to make a selection of the best writers, and only consult these.[49] Statements in the preparatory works express the same meaning, when mentioning 'authors whose opinions have authority',[50] 'widely recognised authors',[51] 'the best qualified writers',[52] and 'qualified authors'.[53] However, making such a selection is difficult.[54] In practice, judges are free to consult whom they like.

Another problem with an interpretation that excludes certain writers is that Article 38(1) is not necessarily exhaustive, as discussed in Section 2.3.2. If it is not, the Court and the judges may also cite writers who are

---

[47] ACJ, *Procès-Verbaux*, 323; Peil, 'Writings', 138.

[48] ACJ, *Procès-Verbaux*, 332.

[49] Anthony D'Amato, 'What Does It Mean to be an Internationalist?' (1989) 10 *Michigan Journal of International Law* 102, 102.

[50] ACJ, *Procès-Verbaux*, 323; Peil, 'Writings', 138.

[51] Ibid., 333.

[52] Ibid., 351.

[53] Ibid., 336.

[54] Clive Parry, *The Sources and Evidence of International Law* (Manchester University Press 1965) 108; Rebecca M M Wallace and Olga Martin-Ortega, *International Law* (7th edn, Sweet & Maxwell 2013) 30. Similarly Georg Schwarzenberger, 'The Inductive Approach to International Law' (1947) 60 *Harvard Law Review* 539, 559–560.

not among the 'most highly qualified', even though those writers are not covered by the wording of Article 38(1)(d).

Another meaning of the term is also possible: It may mean that the Court is to treat different writings as having different levels of weight, depending on how 'qualified' the writer is. This also seems to be happening in practice. In Section 4.3, it is inferred that ICJ judges seem to view teachings as having more weight if the judge considers the writer to be an expert, or if the writer has held some important official position (which may be seen as a proxy for being 'highly qualified').

2.2.7   '[O]f the Various Nations'

The writers mentioned in Article 38(1)(d) are supposed to be 'of the various nations'. International law is universal in that it is binding on all states. It should therefore be of interest to legal writers from any country, who can write texts that may inform the Court in its deliberations. As shown in Section 4.2.2, however, the writers who are cited the most by the ICJ come from a small selection of Western countries. This raises the question of what the Court and the judges are to do if the 'most highly qualified publicists' are found not in 'the various nations' but only in a few of them.

Article 38(1)(d) cannot instruct the judges to consult the most highly qualified publicists of *each* of the various nations. It would not be practically possible to mention hundreds of writers for every legal point, even if one relevant piece of writing from each 'nation' could be found. On the other hand, the Article cannot be read as referring to the most highly qualified publicists regardless of whether they all come from the same nation. It is a general principle of treaty interpretation that each term of a provision is to be given effect.[55] The correct interpretation must lie somewhere in between the two extremes. For example, it may be that the judges must at least consider texts from different parts of the world and try not to display apparent bias towards any specific nations or regions. The benefits of this are explored in Section 6.2.

2.2.8   '[S]ubsidiary Means'

Article 38(1)(d) says that teachings are a 'subsidiary means for the determination of rules of law'. The Statute does not have a term for the

---

[55] For example, Richard Gardiner, *Treaty Interpretation* (2nd edn, Oxford University Press 2017) 179–181.

opposite of 'subsidiary'. This book uses 'principal'.[56] An alternative term is 'primary',[57] but that is usually used in a different context, as the opposite of 'secondary rules'.[58]

That teachings are 'subsidiary' means they cannot create international law.[59] This was also a view of the ACJ.[60]

The French version of the Statute uses 'auxiliaire' for 'subsidiary'.[61] That term emphasises the supplementary role that judicial decisions are supposed to have, while 'subsidiary' emphasises their 'subordinate' role.[62] These are two different aspects of the function of teachings in international law, but there is no contradiction between them.

'Subsidiary means' can only help determine the content of the 'principal means', through which international law is created.[63] Judge Shahabuddeen adhered to this when stating that teachings do not 'prevail over' the ordinary meaning of a treaty.[64] Teachings can be used to interpret a treaty, as well as to ascertain the content of customary international law or a general principle of law. Teachings can also be used when determining the content of other subsidiary means, such as judicial decisions, which can in turn be used to interpret a treaty or ascertain the content of customary international law or a general principle of law.

It is possible to question the reality of the distinction between 'principal' and 'subsidiary means'.[65] The distinction may break down for

---

[56] Schwarzenberger, *International Law*, 26–28; Peil, 'Writings', 137.

[57] Donald W Greig, 'Sources of International Law' in Sam Blay, Ryszard Piotrowicz, and Martin Tsamenyi (eds.), *Public International Law: An Australian Perspective* (2nd edn, Oxford University Press 2005) 52, 79.

[58] Jean d'Aspremont, 'The Idea of "Rules" in the Sources of International Law' (2014) 84 *British Yearbook of International Law* 103, 107.

[59] For example, Schwarzenberger, 'Inductive', 551; Gerald Fitzmaurice, 'The General Principles of International Law Considered from the Standpoint of the Rule of Law' (1957) 92 *Recueil des cours* 1, 97; Thirlway, *Sources*, 8 and 117.

[60] ACJ, *Procès-Verbaux*, 306, 322, 333–334, 336, 338, 344, 620, and 680.

[61] Kaczorowska, *International Law*, 32 claims that the 'words do not have the same meaning', but she provides no further explanation.

[62] Manley O Hudson, *The Permanent Court of International Justice 1920–1942: A Treatise* (Macmillan 1943) 612–613.

[63] Ibid., 612; Lachs, *Teacher*, 194; Pellet, 'Article 38', 853–854.

[64] *Border and Transborder Armed Actions*, Separate Opinion of Judge Shahabuddeen 148–149.

[65] For example, J R Y Jennings, 'The Judiciary, International and National, and the Development of International Law' (1996) 45 *International and Comparative Law Quarterly* 1, 3–4; Fitzmaurice, 'Problems', 78; Louis Henkin quoted in Antonio Cassese, *Five Masters of International Law* (Hart, 2011) 191.

subsidiary means that are particularly authoritative. The ICJ's decisions are an example. The ICJ has stated that it 'does not legislate',[66] but in practice it contributes to the creation of international law.[67]

ICJ judges apply teachings only as a subsidiary means and not as the sole basis of a right or obligation. When teachings are used in that way, they will have a certain 'weight', depending on how much they affect the user.[68] Saying that teachings are 'subsidiary means' does not in itself say anything about their weight. This book proposes that the weight of teachings depends on certain factors that are described in Section 4.3.

It is also possible to talk about 'sources' of international law, which teachings are probably not.[69] The ACJ did not agree on this point.[70] Most international law textbooks discuss teachings in a chapter on 'the sources of international law' (or something similar). The term 'source' is not used in ICJ Statute or in other relevant binding instruments. It does not have any legal significance, and it is too contested and ambiguous to be of much help.[71] This book instead uses the terminology of the ICJ Statute Article 38(1), where teachings are a 'subsidiary means'.[72] Whether teachings are also a 'source of international law' is a terminological question, without substantive consequences for arguments made in this book. If a choice has to be made, teachings should not be considered a 'source'.

2.2.9   '[F]or the Determination of Rules of Law'

Teachings are to be applied 'for the determination of rules of law'. Teachings can thus be applied in order to find rules that are based on

---

[66] *Legality of the Threat or Use of Nuclear Weapons, Advisory Opinion, I.C.J. Reports 1996,* p. 226, 237. Similar statements are found in *Fisheries Jurisdiction (United Kingdom v. Iceland), Merits, Judgment, I.C.J. Reports 1974,* pp. 3, 23–24; *South West Africa, Second Phase,* 48.

[67] Section 6.1.

[68] As defined in Section 1.3

[69] For example, ALI, *Restatement,* 29–30; Van Hoof, *Rethinking,* 169 and 176; Terris, Romano, and Swigart, *International Judge,* 115, although certain writers do consider teachings a 'source', such as Parry, *Sources,* 107; D'Amato, 'Internationalist', 102; Peil, 'Writings', 137–138. As does the Privy Council, *re: Piracy jure gentium* [1934] AC 586, 588.

[70] ACJ, *Procès-Verbaux,* 332–333; Van Hoof, *Rethinking,* 176; Peil, 'Writings', 139.

[71] For example, Robert Jennings and Arthur Watts (eds.), *Oppenheim's International Law,* vol. I (9th edn, Longman 1992) 23; P E Corbett, 'The Consent of States and the Sources of the Law of Nations' (1925) 6 *British Yearbook of International Law* 20, 30; Crawford, *Open System,* 22.

[72] Georg Schwarzenberger, 'The Province of the Doctrine of International Law' (1956) 9 *Current Legal Problems* 235, 236.

treaties or customary international law or on general principles of law. In the ACJ Descamps envisaged teachings to be used only to find 'general principles of law', in cases where neither treaty nor custom was available, in order to avoid a *'non liquet'* (a situation where the Court cannot say whether something is legal or illegal).[73] Teachings are not subject to any such limitations, and that is in line with the wording of the ICJ Statute.

Moreover, the role of teachings in the international legal system goes beyond 'the determination of rules of law'. Teachings are, for example, an important source of information and ideas and contribute to the development of the law. This is discussed further in Sections 3.4.2 and 6.1.

2.3   Defining 'Teachings'

2.3.1   Introduction

This book examines the application of 'teachings' by the ICJ. The purpose of this section is to define the term, as it is used in the ICJ Statute. The definition is clear in its core: academic books and articles in journals that are not produced by states, intergovernmental organisations, or courts and tribunals and that may be used to answer legal questions. However, there are some debatable aspects of the definition of teachings, which will be discussed later. The ICJ has not defined 'teachings', neither in majority nor in individual opinions. A precise definition of the concept is necessary in order to make a precise assessment of its application.

Teachings include a variety of media. This includes speeches and lectures,[74] as well as letters. All of these media have been cited in individual ICJ opinions.[75] The opinions have not cited blog posts,[76] so it is not necessary to classify them for the purposes of this book. The line between a long and thorough blog post and a short journal article, case note, or editorial may be fleeting and overlapping. Some texts are published both on blogs and in journals, including editorials for the

---

[73] ACJ, *Procès-Verbaux*, 318–319; Peil, 'Writings', 139; Carty, *Decay*, 13.

[74] For example, ILC, *Report of the International Law Commission Sixty-eighth session (2 May-10 June and 4 July-12 August 2016) (A/71/10)* (UN 2016) 111; Sivakumaran, 'Influence', 23.

[75] Letters in, for example, *Application of the Convention on the Prevention and Punishment of the Crime of Genocide (Croatia v. Serbia), Judgment, I.C.J. Reports 2015*, p. 3, Separate Opinion of Judge ad hoc Kreća 502; speeches in, for example, *Corfu Channel*, Dissenting Opinion by Judge Azevedo 109; *Nicaragua, 1986*, Separate Opinion of Judge Lachs 159–160.

[76] For example, Lord Carnwath of the UK Supreme Court cited 'the UK Constitutional Law Blog site' in *R v. Secretary of State for Exiting the European Union* [2017] UKSC 5 para 274.

European Journal of International Law (which are usually also published on the blog *EJIL: Talk!*). Some journals publish short articles that can be shorter than long blog posts, and some journals are only published online. The classification of blog posts should ultimately depend on whether they contain independent and substantive analysis of legal questions. If they do, they should be considered teachings.

2.3.2   *The Definition Does Not Determine Weight*

It may be necessary to classify a text as one or another 'principal' or 'subsidiary means' in order to know when and how it can or must be applied. For example, whether a text is a valid treaty or merely a draft will affect how lawyers use it. Distinctions can also be made within a single category. One judicial decision may have more weight than another judicial decision. One type of teachings may be more important than another, as argued in Chapter 4. Moreover, a text can have weight and play a role in ICJ judges' legal decisions without being mentioned in the ICJ Statute Article 38(1) at all. This is because the ICJ Statute Article 38(1) does not have to be exhaustive.[77] Therefore, how a text is classified under the ICJ Statute Article 38(1), or whether it belongs there at all, does not determine what weight the text will have. It is unnecessary to discuss whether ILC texts belong in the ICJ Statute Article 38, for example.[78] While it does matter whether something is a 'subsidiary means' (as opposed to a binding 'principal means'), it is less important *which* 'subsidiary means' it is classified as.

The purpose of this section is therefore only to determine what is examined in the rest of the book. The definition of teachings that is presented here does not change the overall conclusions that are reached in later chapters of the book. For example, if ILC texts were counted as teachings, the conclusion that teachings have low weight (Section 3.10) would still stand, although it would be necessary to clarify that it is 'non-ILC teachings' that have low weight. The definition of 'teachings' is more of a terminological than a substantive question.

---

[77] For example, Maarten Bos, 'The Recognised Manifestations of International Law: A New Theory of "Sources"' (1977) 20 *German Yearbook International Law* 9, 18; Hillier, *Sourcebook,* 95; Joost Pauwelyn, 'Is It International Law or Not, and Does It Even Matter?' in Joost Pauwelyn, Ramses Wessel, and Jan Wouters (eds.), *Informal International Lawmaking* (Oxford University Press 2012) 125, 133.

[78] Sir Arthur Watts, *The International Law Commission 1949–1998,* vol. I (Oxford University Press 1999) 15.

2.3.3   The Term 'Teachings' (and Its Alternatives)

Various terms similar to 'teachings' are used in various sources. The French version of the ICJ Statute uses 'doctrine'. The ICJ's majority opinions have used 'the writings of publicists' and 'writers',[79] 'the literature',[80] and 'legal thinking'.[81]

Individual ICJ opinions have used an even wider variety of terms. It is possible to distinguish between terms that denote the writer (the 'publicists' in the ICJ Statute Article 38(1)) and terms that denote their works ('teachings' in the ICJ Statute). Terms for 'publicists' include, in addition to 'publicists' itself,[82] 'author' or 'authors',[83] 'writer' or 'writers',[84] and many more. Terms for teachings include, in addition to 'teachings'[85] itself, (the) 'doctrine',[86] 'writing' or 'writings',[87] (the) 'literature',[88] 'scholarship',[89] and many more. Judges have also used

---

[79] *Nottebohm Case (second phase), Judgment of April 6th, 1955: I.C.J. Reports 1955*, p. 4, 22–23; *Nuclear Weapons*, 259.

[80] *LaGrand (Germany* v. *United States of America), Judgment, I.C.J. Reports 2001*, p. 466, 501 and 508.

[81] *North Sea Continental Shelf, Judgment, I.C.J. Reports 1969*, p. 3, 35.

[82] For example, *South West Africa, Second Phase*, Separate Opinion of Judge van Wyk 132; *North Sea*, Separate Opinion of Judge Fouad Ammoun 142; *Jan Mayen*, Separate Opinion of Judge Weeramantry 239.

[83] For example, *Colombian-Peruvian asylum case, Judgment of November 20th 1950: I.C.J. Reports 1950*, p. 266, Dissenting Opinion by Judge Azevedo 341; *Voting Procedure*, Separate Opinion of Judge Lauterpacht 111, *South West Africa, Second Phase*, Dissenting Opinion of Judge Koretsky 242.

[84] For example, *Anglo-Iranian Oil Co. Case, Order of July 5th, 1951: I.C.J. Reports 1951*, p. 89, Dissenting Opinion of Judge Levi Carneiro 164; *Case concerning the Application of the Convention of 1902 governing the Guardianship of Infants (Netherlands* v. *Sweden), Judgment of November 28th, 1958: I.C.J. Reports 1958*, p. 55, Separate Opinion of Judge Sir Hersch Lauterpacht 96; *Barcelona Traction, 1970*, Separate Opinion of Judge Ammoun 292 and 312.

[85] *Oil Platforms (Islamic Republic of Iran* v. *United States of America), Judgment, I.C.J. Reports 2003*, p. 161, Separate Opinion of Judge ad hoc Rigaux 387–388.

[86] For example, *Asylum*, Dissenting Opinion by Judge Azevedo 338; *Barcelona Traction, 1970*, Separate Opinion of Judge Tanaka 119 and Separate Opinion of Judge Jessup 193.

[87] For example, *Temple*, Separate Opinion of Vice-President Alfaro 41; *Barcelona Traction, 1970*, Separate Opinion of Judge Ammoun 304 ('legal writing'); *Oil Platforms, 2003*, Separate Opinion of Judge ad hoc Rigaux 232 ('doctrinal writing').

[88] For example, *Appeal Relating to the Jurisdiction of the ICAO Council, Judgment, I.C.J. Reports 1972*, p. 46, Separate Opinion of Judge Dillard 112; *Border and Transborder Armed Actions*, Separate Opinion of Judge Shahabuddeen 134; *East Timor (Portugal* v. *Australia), Judgment, I.C.J. Reports 1995*, p. 90, Dissenting Opinion of Judge Weeramantry 210.

[89] *Land, Island and Maritime Frontier Dispute, 1992*, Dissenting Opinion of Judge Oda 747.

terms that merely denote a specific type of text, such as 'treatises',[90] or 'works' in general,[91] or simply the term 'text'.[92] The terminology is thus not uniform. Some judges use multiple terms, even on the same page of an opinion.[93] They make no apparent distinction between the various terms.

The PCIJ Statute preparatory works also use a variety terms,[94] including 'doctrine' or 'doctrines,[95] 'teaching' or 'teachings',[96] 'authors',[97] 'writers',[98] and 'publicists'.[99] They do not, however, define the concept. They give only one example of what it covers, which is texts from the IDI.[100] The preparatory works to the ICJ Statute use the term 'doctrine',[101] but do not discuss the concept in much detail. The ILC's works on customary international law have used 'teachings' and 'writings' (in the Special Rapporteur's *Third Report*, in the draft conclusions and commentaries adopted on the first reading and in the conclusions adopted on the second reading and the accompanying statement of the chair of the drafting committee).[102] Teachings themselves use a variety of terms to denote teachings, including terms mentioned earlier.

---

[90] Ibid.; *Legality of Use of Force (Yugoslavia* v. *Belgium), Provisional Measures, Order of 2 June 1999, I.C.J. Reports 1999*, p. 124, Dissenting Opinion of Vice-President Weeramantry 191–192.

[91] *Arbitral Award of 31 July 1989*, Dissenting Opinion of Judge Weeramantry 167; *Oil Platforms, 2003*, Separate Opinion of Judge ad hoc Rigaux 387–388; *Pulp Mills*, Separate Opinion of Judge Cançado Trindade 171.

[92] *Jan Mayen*, Separate Opinion of Judge Weeramantry 261.

[93] For example, *Nuclear Tests (Australia* v. *France), Judgment, I.C.J. Reports 1974*, p. 253, Dissenting Opinion of Judge de Castro 381; *Arbitral Award of 31 July 1989*, Separate Opinion of Judge Shahabuddeen 108; *Land and Maritime Boundary between Cameroon and Nigeria (Cameroon* v. *Nigeria: Equatorial Guinea intervening), Judgment, I.C.J. Reports 2002*, p. 303, Dissenting Opinion of Judge ad hoc Ajibola 582.

[94] Sivakumaran, 'Influence', 4. Van Hoof, *Rethinking*, 176 also interprets a reference to 'the legal conscience of civilized nations' in ACJ, *Procès-Verbaux*, 323 as meaning teachings.

[95] ACJ, *Procès-Verbaux*, 319, 331–334, and 336.

[96] Ibid., 323 and 324.

[97] Ibid., 332 and 334.

[98] Ibid., 333–335.

[99] Ibid., 335.

[100] Ibid., 336; Sivakumaran, 'Influence', 12.

[101] UN Committee of Jurists, *Documents of the United Nations Conference on International Organization San Francisco, 1945 Volume XIV* (UN Information Organizations 1945) 377 and 670.

[102] ILC, *Third report*, 41 and 44; ILC, *Report of the Sixty-eighth session*, 78 and 111; ILC, *Identification of customary international law, Statement of the Chair of the Drafting Committee* (25 May 2018) 15; ILC, *Identification of Customary International Law, Text of the draft conclusions as adopted by the Drafting Committee on second reading (17 May 2018)* (A/CN.4/L.908) 4.

In short, various terms are used in different texts. 'Teachings' is used in this book, since that is what the ICJ Statute uses. Even though 'teachings of … publicists' has academic connotations, the term is considered equivalent with the other terms mentioned here, thus encompassing writings by authors who are not full-time academics.[103]

2.3.4   Teachings Are about Law

One aspect of the definition of 'teachings' as used in this book is that it concerns law. Only texts that say something about law can be considered teachings. This means that texts that are concerned with facts are not teachings.[104] An example of the latter is generalist encyclopaedias.[105] Moreover, State practice and official documents may be reported in academic legal journals, as when the 'Truman Declaration' was reported in the 1946 volume of the *American Journal of International Law*.[106] This does not count as teachings. A treaty collection reproduces the text of a treaty, which is a matter of fact.[107] Similarly, books that merely collect and reproduce judicial decisions are not teachings.[108] A history text may document historical facts, which may amount to State practice, which may in turn be part of the basis for determining customary international law.[109] The history text will nonetheless not be teachings. Individual ICJ opinions have cited dictionaries.[110] Dictionaries can inform the reader of how a word is used in practice. That is a factual matter. Dictionaries can aid the interpretation

---

[103] ILC, *Report of the Sixty-eighth session*, 111. The opposite approach is nonetheless taken by Michelle Harner and Jason A Cantone, 'Is Legal Scholarship Out of Touch? An Empirical Analysis of the Use of Scholarship in Business Law Cases' (2011) 19 *University of Miami Business Law Review* 1, 14.

[104] Peil, 'Writings', 149–150; Fauchald, 'Legal Reasoning', 351.

[105] As cited in *Fisheries case, Judgment of December 18th, 1951: I.C.J. Reports 1951*, p. 116, Dissenting Opinion of Sir Arnold McNair 170.

[106] Cited in ibid., 159.

[107] J G Merrills, *International Dispute Settlement* (5th edn, Cambridge University Press 2011) 142. Treaty collections were cited, for example, by *Ambatielos case (jurisdiction), Judgment of July 1st, 1952: I.C.J. Reports 1952*, p. 28, Dissenting Opinion of President McNair 59–61. *Anglo-Iranian Oil Co.*, Dissenting Opinion of Judge Levi Carneiro 156.

[108] Stanton, 'Scholarship', 211. Such collections are cited in, for example, *Temple*, Separate Opinion of Vice-President Alfaro 44 and 47–48.

[109] Anthea Elizabeth Roberts, 'Traditional and Modern Approaches to Customary International Law: A Reconciliation' (2001) 95 *American Journal of International Law* 757, 775.

[110] For example, *Effect of awards of compensation made by the U.N. Administrative Tribunal, Advisory Opinion of July 13th, 1954: I.C.J. Reports 1954*, p. 47, Dissenting Opinion by Judge Levi Carneiro 92; *Barcelona Traction, Light and Power Company, Limited,*

of a word found in a legal text. A dictionary does not, however, try to say what the law is. The same is the case of 'legal' dictionaries, that is, dictionaries that define terms as used in a legal context.[111] Thus, no dictionary will be considered as teachings in this book.[112]

The exact line between law and fact can be unclear. An illustration is found in Judge Levi Carneiro's opinion in the ICJ's *Minquiers and Ecrehos* case. He cited an international law book according to which England had title to certain maritime areas in the past.[113] Ascertaining such a title is a question of law, and that is how Carneiro used the statement. However, he also referred to a geography book that made a similar claim but used it merely as a basis for saying that England took 'interest' in the maritime areas.[114] Such interest is a matter of fact, not law, so the reference was not used to establish international law. So, the first reference counts as teachings, the second does not.

A distinct category of non-legal texts is academic works in other disciplines than law. Non-fiction writers who have been cited by individual judges include Plato,[115] Churchill,[116] and Gandhi.[117] Playwrights and novelists have also been cited, such as Shakespeare,[118] Tolstoy,[119] and Proust.[120] There are also citations of religious texts, including the

---

Preliminary Objections, Judgment, I.C.J. Reports 1964, p. 6, Dissenting Opinion of Judge Morelli 108.

[111] As cited in, for example, *Application of the Convention on the Prevention and Punishment of the Crime of Genocide, Preliminary Objections, Judgment, I.C.J. Reports 1996*, p. 595, Dissenting Opinion of Judge ad hoc Kreća 748.

[112] As in Black and Richter, 'My Name', 380, but contrary to Peil, 'Writings', 150–151; Stappert, 'Influence', 971.

[113] *The Minquiers and Ecrehos case, Judgment of November 17th, 1953: I.C.J. Reports 1953*, p. 47, Individual Opinion of Judge Levi Carneiro 87.

[114] Ibid., 88.

[115] For example, *North Sea*, Separate Opinion of Judge Fouad Ammoun 137; *Pulp Mills*, Separate Opinion of Judge Cançado Trindade 158; *Jurisdictional Immunities of the State (Germany v. Italy), Counter-Claim, Order of 6 July 2010, I.C.J. Reports 2010*, p. 310, Dissenting Opinion of Judge Cançado Trindade 344.

[116] *Nuclear Weapons*, Dissenting Opinion of Judge Weeramantry 472–473.

[117] For example, *Marshall Islands* v. *United Kingdom*, Dissenting Opinion of Judge Cançado Trindade 26–32.

[118] For example, *Croatia Genocide, 2015*, Dissenting Opinion of Judge Cançado Trindade 295.

[119] For example, *Marshall Islands* v. *United Kingdom*, Dissenting Opinion of Judge Cançado Trindade 26–32.

[120] *Request for Interpretation of the Judgment of 15 June 1962 in the Case concerning the Temple of Preah Vihear (Cambodia v. Thailand) (Cambodia v. Thailand), Provisional Measures, Order of 18 July 2011, I.C.J. Reports 2011*, p. 537, Separate Opinion of Judge Cançado Trindade 570.

Quran,[121] the *Tao Te Ching*,[122] and the *Bible*.[123] None of these are 'teachings' under the ICJ Statute Article 38(1).

2.3.5 *Teachings Are Not Produced by States*

Another requirement for a text to be defined as 'teachings' is that it is not produced by a state.[124] Teachings are thus distinct from official documents. State officials and counsel may write teachings in their individual capacity, but when they act on behalf of a state, they do not produce teachings.[125] Pleadings are not teachings, even when the pleadings are reproduced in teachings.[126]

An interesting question in this connection is how to classify the statements of 'experts' who comment on legal matters.[127] The use of such experts is somewhat common in investment arbitration,[128] but not in the ICJ.[129] Such experts give their views on law that is relevant to the case at hand, which is similar to the role teachings can play. There are few specific examples of ICJ opinions that cite statements by such experts. Judge ad hoc van Wyk in *South West Africa* referred to 'the evidence of Professor Possony, Professor van den Haag and Professor Manning' to 'prove' that a rule was 'not universally observed'.[130] Judge Sir Arnold McNair in *Fisheries* cited an 'opinion supplied' by 'Dr. Ræstad [...] at the

---

[121] *Nuclear Weapons*, Dissenting Opinion of Judge Weeramantry 481.

[122] *Gabčikovo-Nagymaros Project (Hungary/Slovakia), Judgment, I.C.J. Reports 1997*, p. 7, Separate Opinion of Vice-President Weeramantry 106.

[123] For example, *Croatia Genocide, 2015*, Dissenting Opinion of Judge Cançado Trindade 361–362.

[124] Cole, 'Non-Binding', 312–314.

[125] Wood, 'Teachings', para 13; Peil, 'Writings', 149. However Rosenne, *Perplexities*, 50–52 mentions opinions of state and intergovernmental organisation lawyers under heading of 'The teachings of publicists'.

[126] As cited in, for example, *Temple*, Separate Opinion of Vice-President Alfaro 45.

[127] ICJ, 'Rules of Court (1978)' (1978) www.icj-cij.org/en/rules, Articles 57, 58, 65, 68, and 71 mention 'witnesses and experts'.

[128] For example, *Tidewater Inc. and others* v. *The Bolivarian Republic of Venezuela*, ICSID Case No ARB/10/5, Decision on Jurisdiction, 8 February 2013, para 104 and 183; *OPIC Karimum Corporation* v. *The Bolivarian Republic of Venezuela*, ICSID Case No. ARB/10/14, Award, 28 May 2013, para 71; *Guardian Fiduciary Trust Ltd f/k/a Capital Conservator Savings & Loan Ltd* v. *Former Yugoslav Republic of Macedonia*, ICSID Case No. ARB/12/31, Award, 22 September 2015, para 133.

[129] ICJ, 'Handbook' (last updated 31 December 2013) www.icj-cij.org/files/publications/handbook-of-the-court-en.pdf, 57 (regarding experts generally, which includes experts on factual matters) .

[130] *South West Africa, Second Phase*, Separate Opinion of Judge van Wyk 170.

request of the Public Prosecutor' in a national law case that McNair discussed.[131] A difference between teachings and experts is that the latter is called upon for the purpose of a specific dispute.[132] An additional difference is that whereas teachings are usually pre-existing written materials the judges read, in the ICJ at least, experts give oral evidence directly to the judges.[133] Because they are different, the views of legal experts are not counted as teachings for the purpose of this book.[134]

Preparatory works to treaties are largely produced by states. They are therefore not teachings.[135] Some preparatory works are produced by the ILC. Since ILC texts are not considered teachings, as explained in Section 2.3.6, preparatory works produced by the ILC are also not teachings.

2.3.6   Teachings Are Not Produced by Official Institutions

Teachings are often produced by individuals, but they can also be produced collectively by groups or institutions.[136] Such organisations include intergovernmental organisations and their various organs, which are composed of states and thus cannot produce teachings. UNCITRAL is an example.[137] There are also *private* organisations, whose works fall within the definition of teachings. Texts produced by international courts or tribunals are not teachings. They include, of course, judicial decisions, as well as individual opinions,[138] advisory opinions, and general comments. Courts also produce other texts, such

---

[131] *Fisheries case*, Dissenting Opinion of Sir Arnold McNair 182.

[132] J Romesh Weeramantry, *Treaty Interpretation in Investment Arbitration* (Oxford University Press 2012) 139.

[133] ICJ, 'Handbook' (last updated 31 December 2013) www.icj-cij.org/files/publications/handbook-of-the-court-en.pdf, 57.

[134] Fauchald, 'Legal Reasoning', 351 counted '[s]ome instances where legal experts were interviewed as witnesses and where their statements were taken into account as interpretive arguments [...] as "legal doctrine"'.

[135] Peil, 'Writings', 150.

[136] Cole, 'Non-Binding', 304.

[137] According to UNCITRAL, 'FAQ – Origin, Mandate and Composition of UNCITRAL' (2017) www.uncitral.org/uncitral/en/about/origin_faq.html#drafting, its membership comprises 'elected member States representing different geographic regions'.

[138] Individual opinions are nonetheless classified as teachings in, for example, *Barcelona Traction, 1970*, Separate Opinion of Judge Ammoun 317; Pellet, 'Article 38', 869. S A Riga Sureda, *Investment Treaty Arbitration: Judging under Uncertainty* (Cambridge University Press 2012) 135–137 classifies individual opinions as 'halfway' between teachings and decisions.

as reports produced by judges in their official capacity, but these are also not teachings.[139]

Texts submitted by private individuals or organisations as 'amicus curiae' briefs could also be considered teachings. Like the opinions of 'legal experts', amicus curiae briefs are prepared for the purpose of a specific case. They are, therefore, somewhat different from regular teachings.[140] While amicus curiae briefs have been accepted by certain other international courts and tribunals,[141] no ICJ opinion has cited amicus curiae briefs that discuss a point of law, and therefore their classification does not matter to this book. If a classification has to be made, they should probably be seen as a form of teachings.

The IDI and ILA are private organisations whose works count as teachings.[142] The IDI was mentioned as a producer of teachings in preparatory works to the PCIJ Statute, which also assumed that their works would have greater weight than other teachings.[143] This classification of IDI and ILA works also finds support in individual ICJ opinions.[144] ILC works seem more divided about how to classify the IDI and ILA's works. The Special Rapporteur's *First report on formation and evidence of customary international law* classifies the IDI under 'other bodies' separately from 'writings',[145] but the Special Rapporteur's *Third report on identification of customary international law* includes the IDI in 'writings'.[146] The IDI and

---

[139] As cited by, for example, *Admission of a State to the UN*, Dissenting Opinion by M. Zoričič 94; *Barcelona Traction, 1964*, Dissenting Opinion of Judge Armand-Ugon 117–118 and Declaration by Judge Koretsky 48–49.

[140] Carsten Stahn and Eric De Brabandere, 'The Future of International Legal Scholarship: Some Thoughts on "Practice", "Growth" and "Dissemination"' (2014) 27 *Leiden Journal of International Law* 1, 2; Jochen von Bernstorf, 'The Relationship Between Theory and Practice in International Law' in Jean d'Aspremont and others (ed.), *International Law as a Profession* (Cambridge University Press 2017) 222, 225.

[141] Eric De Brabandere, 'Rationale of amicus curiae interventions in international economic and investment disputes' (2011) 12 *Chicago Journal of International Law* 85, 94.

[142] For example, Jennings, 'Subsidiary Means', 329; Moustapha Sourang, 'Jurisprudence and Teachings' in Mohammed Bedjaoui (ed.), *International Law: Achievements and Prospects* (Martinus Nijhoff/UNESCO 1991) 283, 285; Daillier, Forteau, and Pellet, *Droit international*, 436.

[143] ACJ, *Procès-Verbaux*, 336.

[144] *Jurisdictional Immunities of the State (Germany v. Italy: Greece intervening), Judgment, I. C.J. Reports 2012*, p. 99, Dissenting Opinion of Judge Cançado Trindade 198; *Arrest Warrant, 2002*, Dissenting Opinion of Judge ad hoc Van den Wyngaert 154 and 167; *Dispute regarding Navigational and Related Rights (Costa Rica v. Nicaragua), Judgment, I. C.J. Reports 2009*, p. 213, Declaration of Judge ad hoc Guillaume 294.

[145] ILC, *First report*, 41 and 44.

[146] ILC, *Third report*, 55.

the ILA are NGOs. Texts that are prepared or published by other NGOs also count as teachings. So too do texts that are published by universities, such as *Harvard Research in International Law*.[147]

The IDI and the ILA are private entities. They are not constituted or formally authorised by states. A contrast can be drawn with what may be called 'state-empowered bodies', which are 'international bodies created by two or more states and granted authority to make decisions or take actions, such as developing, interpreting, applying, and enforcing international law'.[148] One example is the ILC.[149] It is a subsidiary organ of the UNGA , which consists of states.[150] The ILC's members are elected by states, but serve in a personal capacity.[151] The ILC's tasks are 'the promotion of the progressive development of international law and its codification', according to the *ILC Statute*[152] Article 1). This distinction is difficult to maintain in practice, as the ILC has recognised.[153]

The work of the ILC may result in the conclusion of a treaty. Such treaties will not, of course, be teachings. The question is how to classify the works that the ILC produces prior to or independent of the conclusion of a treaty.[154] The UNGA, may 'take note' of a text from the ILC, as it did, for example, with the final text on the *Responsibility of States for Internationally Wrongful Acts* (2001).[155] Such texts are nonetheless

---

[147] Documented in, for example, James T Kenny, 'Manley O. Hudson and the Harvard Research in International Law 1927–1940' (1977) 11 *The International Lawyer* 319, and cited in, for example, *Corfu Channel*, Dissenting Opinion by Judge Azevedo 101.

[148] Anthea Roberts and Sandesh Sivakumaran, 'Lawmaking by Nonstate Actors: Engaging Armed Groups in the Creation of International Humanitarian Law' (2012) 37 *Yale Journal of International Law* 107, 116; repeated by Sivakumaran, 'Influence', 5; Sandesh Sivakumaran, 'Beyond States and Non-State Actors: The Role of State-Empowered Entities in the Making and Shaping of International Law' (2017) 55 *Columbia Journal of Transnational Law* 343, 346.

[149] Roberts and Sivakumaran, 'Nonstate Actors', 116–117; Sivakumaran, 'Influence', 5; Sivakumaran, 'Beyond', 346 and 352–353.

[150] UNGA Resolution 174 (II) (21 November 1948) created the ILC.

[151] ILC, 'About the Commission' (last updated 31 July 2017) http://legal.un.org/ilc/ilcintro .shtml; Mark E Villiger, *Customary International Law and Treaties* (Martinus Nijhoff 1985) 79; Shabtai Rosenne with the Assistance of Yaël Ronen, *The Law and Practice of the International Court 1920–2005*, vol. III (4th edn, Martinus Nijhoff 2006) 1559–1560.

[152] 'Statute of the International Law Commission' (1947), adopted by the UNGA in resolution 174 (II) of 21 November 1947, as amended by resolutions 485 (V) of 12 December 1950, 984 (X) of 3 December 1955, 985 (X) of 3 December 1955 and 36/39 of 18 November 1981.

[153] ILC, *Yearbook of the International Law Commission 1956, Vol 2 (A/CN.4/SER.A/1956/Add1)* (UN 1957) 255–256.

[154] Similarly Shaw, *International Law*, 85–86.

[155] UNGA Resolution 56/83 (12 December 2001) para 3.

produced by the ILC.[156] The UNGA's involvement should increase the weight of the relevant text. This involvement also shows that the contours of the term 'teachings' are fluid, in that the difference between teachings and official institutional texts is a matter of degree rather than an unequivocal separation of two isolated concepts. A line nonetheless has to be drawn somewhere. In this book, ILC texts that have been 'taken note of' by the UNGA will be classified together with other ILC texts, and neither counts as teachings. ILC texts are often commented on by states. Such comments express the views of the State and are not teachings. They can express *opinio juris*.[157] It is possible to distinguish between texts that are adopted by the ILC as such and texts that are prepared by individual Special Rapporteurs.[158] The latter are closer to teachings, although neither is counted in this book.

During the drafting of the PCIJ Statute, there was a suggestion to include codification work by the League of Nations Assembly within the definition of teachings. This was rejected.[159] The League of Nations Assembly was the predecessor of the UNGA. The Hague Codification Conference may be seen as a precursor of the ILC. It was distinct from the Assembly, like the ILC is distinct from the UNGA today. Therefore, the rejection of the proposal regarding the Assembly says little about the legal status of texts produced by the Conference (or by the ILC).

The ICJ's opinions have never said anything direct about whether ILC texts are teachings, but there are examples of judges who seem to assume either one or the other in their individual opinions. Judges have discussed the ILC and its works as something other than 'the literature',[160] (the) 'doctrine',[161] and 'legal writers'.[162] However, this does not necessarily

---

[156] ILC, *Survey*, 16.

[157] As used in Eduardo Jiménez de Aréchaga, 'International Law in the Past Third of a Century' (1978) 159 *Recueil des cours* 1, 24. *Fisheries case*, Dissenting Opinion of Sir Arnold McNair 163.

[158] Alan Boyle and Christine Chinkin, *The Making of International Law* (Oxford University Press 2007) 200 classify 'the reports of individual special rapporteurs' as teachings.

[159] League of Nations, *Permanent Court of International Justice Documents concerning The Action Taken by the Council of the League of Nations under Article 14 of the Covenant and the Adoption by the Assembly of the Statute of the Permanent Court* (League of Nations 1921) 68.

[160] *Application of the Interim Accord of 13 September 1995 (the former Yugoslav Republic of Macedonia v. Greece), Judgment of 5 December 2011, I.C.J. Reports 2011*, p. 644, Separate Opinion of Judge Simma 704.

[161] *Diallo, 2010*, Dissenting Opinion of Judge ad hoc Mahiou 828; *Croatia Genocide, 2015*, Separate Opinion of Judge ad hoc Kreća 475.

[162] *North Sea*, Separate Opinion of Judge Fouad Ammoun 116.

mean that ILC texts are not 'teachings' in the ICJ Statute, since that category may be broader than the terms used by these judges. The ILC and its works have also, by contrast, been discussed by judges as part of 'the literature'[163] and 'legal doctrine'.[164] Judges have also called ILC works '*travaux préparatoires*' or 'preparatory works'.[165] This may mean that the judges in question did not consider ILC texts to be teachings. It may, however, simply reflect the fact that the ILC's work resulted in the conclusion of a treaty, which necessarily makes the relevant ILC texts preparatory works to the treaty, but without being a general comment on whether any or all ILC works count as teachings. One ICJ judge who was interviewed does not consider ILC works as teachings, saying that the ILC 'does not fit into Article 38 in any obvious way'.[166]

The ILC's *Survey of International Law in Relation to the Work of Codification of the International Law Commission* of 1949, probably prepared by Hersch Lauterpacht,[167] seems ambivalent on the question of its own classification. The *Survey* states that certain ILC texts 'would be at least in the category of writings of the most highly qualified publicists, referred to in Article 38', but it adds that 'their authority would be considerably higher', including due to 'the resources of the United Nations'.[168] The Special Rapporteur's *Third report on identification of customary international law* includes ILC texts under 'writings'.[169] However, this is not done in the later draft *Customary International Law Conclusions* (adopted on the first reading),[170] apparently due to scepticism from states.[171] The ILC Statute Article 15 says that 'the

---

[163] *Dispute regarding Navigational and Related Rights*, Declaration of Judge ad hoc Guillaume 294.

[164] *Arrest Warrant of 11 April 2000 (Democratic Republic of the Congo v. Belgium)*, *Provisional Measures, Order of 8 December 2000, I.C.J. Reports 2000*, p. 182, Declaration by Judge ad hoc Van den Wyngaert 232.

[165] For example, *North Sea*, Dissenting Opinion of Judge Sorensen 254; *Jan Mayen*, Separate Opinion of Judge Shahabuddeen 142 and 148; *Maritime Delimitation and Territorial Questions between Qatar and Bahrain, Merits, Judgment, I.C.J. Reports 2001*, p. 40, Joint Dissenting Opinion of Judges Bedjaoui, Ranjeva and Koroma 203.

[166] ICJ Judge 1.

[167] Lawrence Preuss, 'Survey of International Law in Relation to the Work of Codification of The International Law Commission. Memorandum submitted by the Secretary General. (Doc. A/CN.4/1/Rev.l.)' (1949) 43 *American Journal of International Law* 829 (the text is formally attributed to the UN Secretary General).

[168] ILC, *Survey*, 16. Harris, *Cases*, 57 agrees.

[169] ILC, *Third report*, 55.

[170] ILC, *Report of the Sixty-eighth session*, 111–112.

[171] According to the accompanying ILC, *Fourth report on identification of customary international law by Michael Wood, Special Rapporteur (A/CN.4/695)* (UN 2016) 10.

expression "codification of international law" is used for convenience as meaning the more precise formulation and systematization of rules of international law in fields where there already has been extensive State practice, precedent and doctrine'. This mention of 'doctrine' may be taken to mean that the ILC's own works do not count as 'doctrine', a term that may be synonymous with 'teachings'. The ILC itself has, in a decision on 'Documentation and publications', called ILC works '*travaux préparatoires*',[172] but this is just as inconclusive as when it is done by judges, as discussed earlier.

Writers are divided on whether ILC works should count as teachings. Some discuss them in the same textbook chapters,[173] others separately.[174] This separation is not decisive, however; for example, Bos discusses ILC works and 'doctrine' separately, but considers ILC works to be teachings.[175] Some writers hold that ILC works are teachings,[176] while others disagree.[177] Some writers are more ambivalent.[178]

In this book, ILC works are not classified as teachings. They will instead be used as a contrast to teachings, in the same way as judicial decisions. Texts from the ILC's predecessor, the Hague Codification Conference,[179] are treated in the same way.[180]

The ICRC is another entity whose texts have been cited in the ICJ's opinions. It claims to have a 'hybrid nature', being 'a private association

---

[172] ILC, *Report of the International Law Commission, Sixty-fifth session (6 May–7 June and 8 July–9 August 2013) (A/68/10)* (UN 2013) 118.

[173] For example, Parry, *Sources*, 114; Wolfke, *Custom*, 156; Daillier, Forteau, and Pellet, *Droit international*, 434–436, 870.

[174] For example, O'Connell, *International Law*, 29–31 and 35–57; Taslim O Elias, 'Modern Sources of International Law' in Wolfgang Friedmann, Louis Henkin, and Oliver Lissitzyn (eds.), *Transnational Law in a Changing Society: Essays In Honor of Philip C. Jessup* (Columbia University Press 1972) 34, 37–41 and 63–67; Shaw, *International Law*, 80–81 and 84–86.

[175] Bos, 'Manifestations', 61–63 and 64–65, and 64.

[176] For example, Wood, 'Teachings', para 11; ALI, *Restatement*, 38; Bordin, 'Reflections', 537.

[177] Gerald Fitzmaurice, 'The Contribution of the Institute of International Law to the Development of International Law' (1973) 138 *Recueil des cours* 203, 220; Watts, *International Law Commission*, 14–15.

[178] For example, André Oraison, 'L'Influence des Forces Doctrinales Académiques sur les Prononcés de la C.P.J.I. et de la C.I.J' (1999) 32 *Revue Belge de Droit International* 205, 208; John Dugard, *International Law: A South African Perspective* (4th edn, Juta and Co 2011) 37–38; Borda, 'Formal Approach', 656–657; Rosenne, *Perplexities*, 52.

[179] The relationship between the conference and the ILC is explained further at ILC, 'About the Commission' (last updated 31 July 2017) http://legal.un.org/ilc/ilcintro.shtml, and in UN, *The Work of the International Law Commission*, vol. I (8th edn, UN 2012) 1–6.

[180] Crawford, *Brownlie's*, 43.

formed under the Swiss Civil Code',[181] but that its 'functions and activities [...] are mandated by the international community of States'.[182] Compared to the ILC, states are far less involved, if at all, in the creation of ICRC texts.[183] Works produced by the ICRC are, therefore, considered teachings for the purposes of this book.[184] The ICRC's 'Report on the Work of the Conference of Government Experts', which was cited in the ICJ's *Wall* opinion,[185] is a special case. That work is not considered as teachings, because it was prepared by 'government experts'.

[181] Gabor Rona, 'The ICRC's status: in a class of its own', *ICRC* (17 February 2004) www .icrc.org/eng/resources/documents/misc/5w9fjy.htm.

[182] Ibid. Similarly Boyle and Chinkin, *Making,* 204–205.

[183] Boyle and Chinkin, *Making,* 205.

[184] English Court of Appeals, *Serdar Mohammed and others* v. *Secretary of State for Defence* [2015] EWCA Civ 843, para 171; Boas, *Contemporary,* 115.

[185] *Legal Consequences of the Construction of a Wall in the Occupied Palestinian Territory, Advisory Opinion, I.C.J. Reports 2004,* p. 136, 175.

3

The General Role of Teachings in the ICJ

3.1 Introduction

This chapter examines the general role of teachings in the ICJ. One striking fact is that the Court's majority opinions almost never cite teachings, described in Section 3.2. This is taken as an indication that teachings have limited weight in the ICJ. Individual opinions sometimes cite teachings, as described in Section 3.3. This nuances the overall picture somewhat, as it suggests that individual judges use teachings even though the Court does not cite them. This hypothesis is examined more closely in Section 3.4. Section 3.5 presents possible explanations for the absence of citations in majority opinions and shows that many of the explanations that have been proposed by other authors are unconvincing. Section 3.6 presents other patterns in the Court's and judges' practice, in addition to the absence of citations, which suggest that teachings have limited weight. Section 3.7 presents some patterns that support the opposite conclusion. Section 3.8 then compares the Court's use of teachings with its use of judicial decisions and works produced by state-empowered bodies. These are also 'subsidiary means' under the ICJ Statute Article 38(1), but they are assigned significantly more weight than teachings. Explanations for this different treatment are presented in Section 3.9. Section 3.10 draws an overall conclusion, which is that teachings generally have low weight in the ICJ.

3.2 Majority Opinions Almost Never Cite Teachings

Citations of teachings are almost completely absent from the ICJ's majority opinions.[1] This is despite the ICJ Statute Article 38(1)(d) saying that the ICJ 'shall apply [. . .] teachings', which is thus not interpreted by the Court to mean that the Court must *cite* teachings.[2]

---

[1] Jennings and Watts (eds.), *Oppenheim's*, 42–43.

[2] Section 2.2.3.

43

A decision by the Court in *Land, Island and Maritime Frontier Dispute* made reference to 'the successive editors of Oppenheim's *International Law*' and to 'G. Gidel, *Le droit international de la mer* (1934), Vol. 3' as well as to a work by Sir Cecil Hurst.[3] The *Namibia* opinion cited a work by Jan Smuts.[4] In *Kasikili/Sedudu Island*, there is a reference to a document produced by the IDI.[5] Works produced by the ICRC have been cited in the *Wall* opinion[6] and the *Nicaragua* judgment.[7] The merits judgment of *Bosnia Genocide* referred to Raphael Lemkin's book *Axis Rule in Occupied Europe* (1944).[8] However, this reference concerned the 'etymology of the word [...] genocide', that is, apparently more of a dictionary function than the function of teachings that is discussed in this book.[9] That reference is therefore not counted as a reference to teachings. Some of the ICJ's majority opinions contain general references without naming specific works.[10] In its judgment in the *Nottebohm Case (second phase)*, the Court referred to 'the writings of publicists' and 'the opinions of writers'.[11] The *Nuclear Weapons* advisory opinion contains a reference to 'writers'.[12] In *North Sea* the Court mentioned 'legal thinking',[13] while in *LaGrand* it mentioned 'the literature'.[14] The PCIJ's majority opinions have also made non-specific references to teachings.[15] These include references, in majority opinions, to 'general opinion',[16] 'an almost universal opinion',[17] '*une doctrine constante*',[18] 'teachings of legal

---

[3] *Land, Island and Maritime Frontier Dispute, 1992*, 592 and 594.

[4] *Namibia*, 48.

[5] *Kasikili/Sedudu Island (Botswana/Namibia), Judgment, I.C.J. Report 1999*, p. 1045, 1062.

[6] *Wall, Advisory Opinion*, 176.

[7] *Nicaragua, 1986*, 124–125.

[8] *Bosnia Genocide, 2007*, 125.

[9] Section 2.3.4.

[10] Rosenne and Ronen, *Law and Practice*, 1558; Crawford, *Brownlie's*, 43; Pellet, 'Article 38', 869.

[11] *Nottebohm*, 22–23.

[12] *Nuclear Weapons*, 259.

[13] *North Sea*, 35.

[14] *LaGrand, 2001*, 501 and 508.

[15] For example, Sørensen, *Sources*, 181–182; Crawford, *Brownlie's*, 43.

[16] *Case of the S.S. 'Wimbledon,' Judgment, 17 August 1923, P.C.I.J. Reports Series A No. 1*, p. 15, 28.

[17] *Advisory opinion given by the Court on September 10th 1923 on certain questions relating to settlers of German origin in the territory ceded by Germany to Poland, Advisory Opinion No. 6, 10 September 1923, P.C.I.J. Reports Series B No. 6*, p. 5, 36.

[18] *Questions of Jaworzina (Polish-Czechoslovakian Frontier), Advisory Opinion No. 8, 6 December 1923, P.C.I.J Reports Series B No. 8*, p. 5, 37 (italics added).

authorities',[19] and 'teachings of publicists' and 'all or nearly all writers'.[20] In short, the ICJ has cited specific works of teachings on a point of law only seven times, in five cases. The ICJ's docket held a total of 155 cases as of 5 October 2016.[21]

Thus, teachings were cited in majority opinions on average 0.04 times per case and in only 3 per cent of the Court's cases. Section 1.3.2 argued that citations of teachings in judicial decisions can be taken as an indication that the judges assigned some weight to teachings (albeit without being decisive proof of this). Thus, the lack of citation of teachings in ICJ decisions should at least suggest that teachings have limited weight.[22]

3.3 Individual Opinions Sometimes Cite Teachings

In individual opinions the picture is quite different. Teachings are cited 4370 times across 1256 individual opinions, giving an average citation rate of 3.5. Teachings are cited in 407 of the opinions, that is, approximately 32 per cent.

A small number of judges are responsible for a large share of all citations, as explained in Section 5.2. The top four most-citing judges (Cançado Trindade, Weeramantry, Shahabuddeen, and Kreća) are alone responsible for 2613 of the 4370 citations.

References to teachings are also found in individual PCIJ opinions.[23] The PCIJ's 130 individual opinions have cited teachings 61 times, which gives an average of just under 0.5. Of the 130 opinions 22 cited teachings, which is 17 per cent.

In the ICJ, among the judges who have written at least one individual opinion, 68 per cent have cited teachings (112 out of 165 judges). In the PCIJ, a smaller share of judges has cited teachings in their individual opinions. Only 14 of the total 40 judges who have written at least one individual PCIJ opinion have cited teachings, 35 per cent of the total.

The more frequent citation of teachings in individual opinions indicates that teachings play a significantly bigger role in the ICJ than the lack

---

[19] *Case Concerning Certain German Interests in Polish Upper Silesia, Judgment No. 6, 25 August 1925, P.C.I.J. Reports Series A No. 6*, p. 3, 20.

[20] *Lotus*, 26.

[21] The count in Peil, 'Writings', 151 is higher than in this book, because it includes ILC works.

[22] Sørensen, *sources*, 183.

[23] Ibid., 183–185.

of citation in majority opinions would suggest. This hypothesis is explored further in the following section 3.4.

3.4 Teachings Are Used More Often Than They Are Cited

3.4.1 Introduction

There are multiple indications that ICJ judges use teachings more often than they cite them. Teachings are useful to judges, as argued in Section 3.4.2, so it would be strange if judges did not use teachings at all. The following section presents direct statements by the Court's judges and staff confirming that teachings are frequently used (Section 3.4.3). Judges have also made statements in judicial decisions that imply the same (Section 3.4.4). Finally, judges are exposed to teachings through pleadings (Section 3.4.5).

3.4.2 Teachings Are Useful to Judges

Judges' use of teachings flows from their usefulness. Teachings are 'the everyday first reference of the practising international lawyer'.[24] It is natural that they should also be used by ICJ judges, which is what this section aims to show.

Teachings can improve the quality of judicial reasoning.[25] They can also save judges' time, insofar as they can spend less time on searching for sources.[26] That is especially useful for judges who work under time pressure, as discussed in Section 5.4.6. Teachings can provide information about judicial decisions, as can be seen when judges mention where they found a decision.[27] Teachings can also provide information about other teachings.[28]

---

[24] Dixon, *Textbook*, 49. Similarly, for example, Nicholas Greenwood Onuf, 'Global Law-Making and Legal Thought' in Nicholas Greenwood Onuf (ed.), *Law-Making in the Global Community* (Carolina Academic Press 1982) 1, 20; Anthony Aust, *Handbook of International Law* (2nd edn, Cambridge University Press 2010) 5.

[25] Cole, 'Non-Binding', 308–309.

[26] Ibid. Similarly Frank K Richardson, 'Law Reviews and the Courts' (1983) 5 *Whittier Law Review* 385, 389; Wolfke, *Custom*, 156.

[27] *Temple*, Separate Opinion of Vice-President Alfaro, for example, 44, 47–48, 50–51; *Barcelona Traction, 1970*, Separate Opinion of Judge Jessup 168; *Elettronica Sicula S.P. A. (ELSI), Judgment, I.C.J. Reports 1989*, p. 15, Dissenting Opinion of Judge Schwebel 118.

[28] Examples include *Western Sahara, Advisory Opinion, I.C.J. Reports 1975*, p. 12, Separate Opinion of Judge Dillard 121; *Sovereignty over Pedra Branca/Pulau Batu Puteh, Middle*

A particularly useful function of teachings is the provision of information about and syntheses of State practice and *opinio juris* in order to establish customary international law. Teachings can therefore be more useful in attempts to ascertain the content of unwritten law (such as customary international law), as opposed to the content of written law (such as treaties).[29] A plausible reason for this is that treaties and other written law in themselves generally give a good indication of the content of the law, while unwritten law often requires a significant effort, in terms of information gathering and analysis, just to establish the basic outline of a rule. Teachings can assist in this, as described earlier. An indication that teachings are more useful for unwritten than written law is that ICJ judges have cited teachings far more when discussing unwritten law. Of a total of 4370 references to teachings in individual ICJ opinions, 2582 (59 per cent) concerned unwritten law, while 1267 (29 per cent) concerned written law. The final 521 (12 per cent) were given when interpreting judicial decisions.

However, these numbers are not conclusive evidence that teachings are *more useful* for dealing with unwritten law. The numbers do not take into account the times judges tried to find unwritten and written law. If judges discussed unwritten law more often, this could explain some of the discrepancy. It is unlikely to explain the entire discrepancy, however. Sir Percy Spender's opinion in *Guardianship of Infants* can serve as an illustration. The opinion sought to interpret a treaty and to ascertain a rule of customary international law, but cited teachings only on the latter point.[30] The numbers presented here are thus an indication that supports, but does not prove, the assumption that teachings are more useful for finding unwritten law. Other writers share this view,[31] as does the ILC's Special Rapporteur in the *Third Report on Identification of Customary International Law.*[32]

ICJ judges also cite teachings more often in individual opinions attached to judgments than in those that are attached to orders.

Rocks and South Ledge (Malaysia/Singapore), Judgment, I.C.J. Reports 2008, p. 12, Separate Opinion of Judge ad hoc Sreenivasa Rao 168.

[29] Peil, 'Writings', 153–157. The US Supreme Court, *The Paquete Habana* 175 US 677 (1900), 700 considered teachings useful as 'evidence' of 'customs and usages of civilized nations'. Stephen Hall, *International Law* (2nd edn, LexisNexis Butterworths 2006) 59, rightly points out that this statement is 'too narrow', since teachings are also useful when dealing with written instruments such as treaties.

[30] *Guardianship of Infants*, Separate Opinion of Sir Percy Spender 116, 123–124, and 127.

[31] Tunkin, *Theory*, 186; Wolfke, *Custom*, 156; Danilenko, *Law-Making*, 257.

[32] ILC, *Third report*, 41.

Individual opinions attached to orders cite teachings on average 3 times, whereas individual opinions attached to judgments cite teachings on average 4.1 times.[33] Orders may involve less contested legal questions, and teachings may for that reason be more useful in judgments. Moreover, orders generally concern ICJ-specific procedural law, whereas judgments generally involve substantive questions of international law that are not specific to the ICJ. Teachings may be more useful in judgments, where ICJ judges deal with questions that they may be less familiar with.

Teachings also play a role in the development of the law, a theme that is taken up again in Section 6.1.

There are also dangers of using teachings, such as a potential for inaccuracies,[34] and their use as a substitute for consulting primary sources.[35] Even so, teachings are useful to judges, and it is plausible that judges should consult them when deciding cases.

3.4.3   Statements by Judges and Staff Members

One ICJ judge explains that judges always have teachings in mind when writing and discussing and cite them in notes and deliberations, and that many judges have read the same works when preparing a case.[36] However, another judge warns that while '[t]he court does refer to published work in its deliberations', 'it does so less than you might think [. . .] it is more a background consideration for judges'.[37]

---

[33] The category of 'orders' includes preliminary objections, provisional measures, interventions, and other orders, while the 'judgment' category includes decisions on merits and compensation. This classification is not based on how a decision is formally classified on the Court's website. Using the Court's website's classification would be arbitrary, since the same types of decisions seem to be classified differently in different cases. For example, *Land, Island and Maritime Frontier Dispute Order 1990, I.C.J. Reports 1990*, p. 3 is an order, while *Land, Island and Maritime Frontier Dispute (El Salvador/Honduras), Application to Intervene, Judgment, I.C.J. Reports 1990*, p. 92 is a judgment, even though both concern intervention.

[34] For example, Lachs, *Teacher*, 191; (in the context of national law) Neil N Bernstein, 'The Supreme Court and Secondary Source Material: 1965 Term' (1968) 57 *Georgetown Law Journal* 55, 62; Bart Sloan, 'Student Works', 225.

[35] Anthea Elizabeth Roberts, 'Traditional', 775. Similarly, for example, J S Watson, 'Legal Theory, Efficacy and Validity in the Development of Human Rights Norms in International Law' (1979) 3 *University of Illinois Law Forum* 609, 636; Van Hoof, *Rethinking*, 178.

[36] ICJ Judge 2.

[37] ICJ Judge 1.

An ICJ judge says that there is an unwritten rule saying that the Court's majority opinions shall not cite teachings.[38] This is supported by Judge Tomka, the Court's former President.[39] Tomka is part of the Court's median according to Section 5.3.3, which means that he is not averse to citing teachings in individual opinions.

The ICJ has an 'amazing library',[40] and 'in the judges' offices [...] they do have books [...] on the shelves'.[41] Moreover, '[t]he ICJ Registry, for each case, prepares a bibliography of scholarship relating to the case'.[42] As an ICJ employee points out, the practice of producing bibliographies 'seems to indicate an institutional [...] assumption that scholarship is important and useful and should be consulted'.[43] The same ICJ employee reports that 'most judges keep abreast of international legal scholarship', '[a]t least on things they are interested in'.[44] Clerks include citations in background documents that they prepare for the judges.[45] ICJ employees also report that judges 'pay attention to' subsequent scholarly commentary on their decisions.[46]

Hugh Thirlway, formerly the Court's Registrar, writes that although teachings may 'tip the scale', it is 'unlikely' that judges would write that in the decision.[47] The two ICJ judges who were interviewed confirm that the judges use teachings more than the lack of citations in majority opinions might suggest.[48] Former ICJ Judge and President, Humphrey Waldock says the same in extrajudicial writings.[49] Kammerhofer reports 'anecdotal evidence about the Court's internal procedures' which 'supports the intuition that the judges and the Registry utilise scholarship to a significant degree'.[50]

---

[38] Ibid. Similarly Jennings, 'Judiciary', 9.

[39] Judge Tomka quoted in Amelia Keene (ed.), 'Outcome Paper for the Seminar on the International Court of Justice at 70' (2016) 7 *Journal of International Dispute Settlement* 238, 260.

[40] ICJ Employee 2.

[41] ICJ Employee 3.

[42] ICJ Employee 2. Similarly Rosenne, *Methods*, 119.

[43] ICJ Employee 2.

[44] Ibid.

[45] ICJ Employee 1; ICJ Employee 2; ICJ Employee 3.

[46] ICJ Employee 1. Similarly ICJ Employee 2; (in the context of national law) Judith S Kaye, 'One Judge's View of Academic Law Review Writing' (1989) 39 *Journal of Legal Education* 313, 314.

[47] Thirlway, *Sources*, 127. Similarly, for example, Wolfke, *Custom*, 156; Greig, 'Sources', 83.

[48] ICJ Judge 1; ICJ Judge 2.

[49] Humphrey Waldock, 'General Course on Public International Law' (1962) 106 *Recueil des cours* 1 96. Similarly, for example, Pellet, 'Article 38', 869.

[50] Kammerhofer, 'Lawmaking', 307.

3.4.4 *Statements in Judicial Decisions*

An additional indication that teachings are used without being cited is that judges who cite teachings seem to have read more of them than they cite. This is a possible inference from the use of terms such as 'for example',[51] 'e.g.',[52] 'in particular',[53] '*inter alia*',[54] and 'among others',[55] before references to teachings. Judges have also referred to teachings in plural (e.g., 'writers',[56] authors',[57] 'the doctrine',[58] and the like) while only citing one or two works.

Judge Dillard in the *ICAO* case mentioned that the 'literature' on one question was 'sparse', which should mean that he had a good general idea of what it contained.[59] In the *Fisheries jurisdiction (UK)* case, Judge Dillard mentioned where '[a]dditional references' could be found, which may mean that he was familiar with these.[60] Something similar was done by Judge Weeramantry in the *Nuclear Weapons* case, where he mentioned a 'list of German authors cited by Oppenheim' without elaborating further.[61] Judge De Castro in the *Nuclear Tests (Australia)*

---

[51] For example, *ICAO*, Separate Opinion of Judge Dillard 97; *Land, Island and Maritime Frontier Dispute, 1992*, Separate Opinion of Judge Torres-Bernárdez 635, 636; *Jan Mayen*, Separate Opinion of Judge Weeramantry 245.

[52] For example, *Jurisdictional Immunities, 2012*, Separate Opinion of Judge Keith 169; *Request for Interpretation of the Judgment of 15 June 1962 in the Case concerning the Temple of Preah Vihear (Cambodia v. Thailand) (Cambodia v. Thailand), Judgment, I.C.J. Reports 2013*, p. 281, Separate Opinion of Judge Cançado Trindade 339–340 and 345; *Marshall Islands v. United Kingdom*, Dissenting Opinion of Judge Crawford 3.

[53] For example, *Diallo, 2010*, Dissenting Opinion of Judge ad hoc Mahiou 825–826; *Questions relating to the Seizure and Detention of Certain Documents and Data (Timor-Leste v. Australia), Provisional Measures, Order of 3 March 2014, I.C.J. Reports 2014*, p. 147, Separate Opinion of Judge Cançado Trindade 6.

[54] For example, *Arbitral Award of 31 July 1989*, Separate Opinion of Judge Shahabuddeen 108; *Bosnia Genocide, 2007*, Dissenting Opinion of Judge ad hoc Mahiou 406; *Obligation to Negotiate Access to the Pacific Ocean*, Separate Opinion of Judge Cançado Trindade 3.

[55] *Certain Activities Carried Out by Nicaragua in the Border Area (Costa Rica v. Nicaragua); Construction of a Road in Costa Rica along the San Juan River (Nicaragua v. Costa Rica), Order of 16 July 2013, Provisional Measures, I.C.J. Reports 2013*, p. 230, Dissenting Opinion of Judge Cançado Trindade 268.

[56] *Barcelona Traction, 1970*, Dissenting Opinion of Judge Riphagen 344–345; *Namibia*, Separate Opinion of Judge De Castro 207; *Land and Maritime Boundary, 2002*, Separate Opinion of Judge ad hoc Mbaye 530.

[57] *Interpretation of Peace Treaties*, Dissenting Opinion by Judge Zoričić 106.

[58] *South West Africa, Second Phase*, Dissenting Opinion of Judge Jessup 421–422; *Arrest Warrant, 2000*, Dissenting Opinion by Judge ad hoc Bula-Bula 227; *Bosnia Genocide, 2007*, Dissenting Opinion of Judge ad hoc Mahiou 410.

[59] *ICAO*, Separate Opinion of Judge Dillard 112.

[60] *Fisheries Jurisdiction (United Kingdom v. Iceland)*, Separate Opinion of Judge Dillard 71.

[61] *Nuclear Weapons*, Dissenting Opinion of Judge Weeramantry 545.

case referred to only two works of teachings 'for brevity's sake', which means that he knew of more teachings that he could have referred to.[62] A similar approach is found in an opinion by Judge ad hoc Sir Geoffrey Palmer, which said that teachings were 'so vast on the subject that [they] cannot be cited'.[63] In the *Gabčikovo* case Vice-President Weeramantry mentioned a topic that had 'long been the subject of' teachings, but mentioned only one example of those teachings.[64] Judge Cançado Trindade in the *Kosovo* case described the view of 'most' teachings, but only referred to one 'notable exception'.[65] In the same vein an opinion by Judge ad hoc Paolillo referred to one text representing a 'minority view' among teachings, which implies that he was also familiar with the majority view.[66] Judge Jessup in the *South West Africa* case wrote that '[o]ne can cite many views on each side of the question' that he was discussing, yet 'call[ed] attention merely to' three works.[67]

However, none of this necessarily means that the judges excluded references to teachings that affected their decisions. It could simply be that they were aware of the existence of more teachings than they were able to consult. It could also be that the judge has communicated with someone who informed them of the existence of more teachings, such as a clerk or counsel. In that case, the teachings may have influenced the clerk or counsel, who may in turn have influenced the judge. However, the teachings would at best have had an indirect effect on the judge's decision.

3.4.5   *Judges Are Exposed to Teachings Through Pleadings*

ICJ judges are exposed to large amount of teachings through the parties' pleadings. This is, for example, noted by Jennings, the Court's former

---

[62] *Nuclear Tests (Australia)*, Dissenting Opinion of Judge de Castro 378.

[63] *Request for an Examination of the Situation in Accordance with Paragraph 63 of the Court's Judgment of 20 December 1974 in the Nuclear Tests (New Zealand v. France) Case, I.C.J. Reports 1995*, p. 288, Dissenting Opinion by Judge ad hoc Sir Geoffrey Palmer 409.

[64] *Gabčikovo*, Separate Opinion of Vice-President Weeramantry 118.

[65] *Accordance with International Law of the Unilateral Declaration of Independence in Respect of Kosovo, Advisory Opinion, I.C.J. Reports 2010*, p. 403, Separate Opinion of Judge Cançado Trindade 550–551.

[66] *Application for Revision of the Judgment of 11 September 1992 in the Case concerning the* Land, Island and Maritime Frontier Dispute (El Salvador/ Honduras: Nicaragua intervening) *(El Salvador v. Honduras), Judgment, I.C.J. Reports 2003*, p. 392, Dissenting Opinion of Judge ad hoc Paolillo 421.

[67] *South West Africa, Second Phase*, Dissenting Opinion of Judge Jessup 370–371.

President.[68] Not all of these are cited in the judges' opinions. This alone means that judges have been exposed to a larger number of teachings than they cite.

The examination of pleadings in three ICJ cases that is done in this book shows that among the 261 citations of teachings in pleadings, 96 of the authors cited were also cited in the judges' individual opinions. Thus, judges cited 37 per cent, slightly more than one third, of the authors cited in pleadings.

This may mean that the judges did not find the remaining authors useful. A different explanation is that the judges were influenced by some of the remaining writers, even though they were not cited. In any case, some overlap between pleadings and judges' opinions should be expected, since both should be inclined to cite the leading works in the field.

3.5   Reasons for the Absence of Citations

3.5.1   Introduction

As noted in Section 3.2, the ICJ's majority opinions have cited teachings only seven times, across five cases. Even so, Section 3.4 argues that the Court and its judges use teachings more often than the citation rates suggest. This section seeks to identify the reasons behind this discrepancy.

The absence of citations discussed here is not unique to teachings. The ICJ generally does not cite judicial decisions from other institutions[69] and often cites little or no state practice when applying customary international law.[70]

Similarly, in the ILC's *1966 Yearbook*, individual ILC members explained why there were no references to teachings in the final report on the law of treaties.[71] The reasons they gave were that it did not want to 'give the impression that the Commission had taken no account of the works of' writers who were not cited, that 'the Commission was an organ

---

[68]   Robert Jennings, 'General Course on Principles of International Law' (1967) 121 *Recueil des cours* 323, 343. Similarly Dickinson, 'Concepts', 259; Hall, *International Law*, 59.

[69]   Boyle and Chinkin, *Making*, 297. Similarly Harris, *Cases*, 41–42.

[70]   Bordin, 'Reflections', 548. Similarly, for example, Antonio Cassese, 'The International Court of Justice: It Is High Time to Restyle the Respected Old Lady' in Antonio Cassese (ed.), *Realizing Utopia: The Future of International Law* (Oxford University Press 2012) 239, 248; Talmon, 'Determining', 434–440.

[71]   ILC, *Yearbook of the International Law Commission 1966 Volume I Part II, A/CN.4/Ser.A/ 1966* (UN 1967) 295–296.

of the United Nations and of the General Assembly', that '[t]here was no necessity', 'not to confuse the Commission's justification for its commentaries with any bibliography which might be prepared by the Secretariat for the diplomatic conference', and that the ILC 'might be accused of discrimination'.[72] Those justifications overlap with some of those discussed later. The statements seem to imply that teachings at least played a role in the drafting of the report, and that the drafters chose not to acknowledge this role by including citations. This is supported by one member's statement that the text had its 'roots not only in the works consulted by the Special Rapporteur but also in the literature in many different languages on which the individual members had relied'.[73]

3.5.2   The Quality of Teachings

One proposed explanation is the varying quality of teachings.[74] It may therefore be 'difficult' or 'embarrassing' to pick the best works.[75] One ICJ judge explains that 'it is really difficult to reach an objective selection, if you single out particular writers that come from particular legal traditions, that have particular views', and 'if you have to do it on a comprehensive basis it is going to be impossible because there is so much being written'.[76] Teachings do vary in quality, as explored in Section 4.3.3, but that does not explain why the ICJ's majority opinions rarely cite them. The varying quality of teachings applies equally to judges writing individual opinions and to other international and national courts and tribunals, even though these often cite teachings.[77] This is therefore unsatisfactory as an explanation.

3.5.3   Jealousy between Writers

A further proposed explanation for the Court's lack of citation is the potential for jealousy between authors.[78] Judge Tomka, a former

---

[72] Ibid.

[73] Ibid., 295.

[74] Pellet, 'Article 38', 869. Similarly Mendelson, 'Sources', 84.

[75] For example, Schwarzenberger, 'Inductive', 559–560; Rosenne, *Methods*, 119; Parry, *Sources*, 108.

[76] ICJ Judge 1.

[77] Section 6.3.

[78] For example, Pellet, 'Article 38', 869; Crawford, *Brownlie's*, 42–43. Lord Mustill acknowledges this as a reason not to cite teachings in British House of Lords, *White* v. *Jones*, Lord Mustill, [1995] 2 AC 207, 292.

President of the Court, has endorsed this view, stating that 'the Court would never refer to the writings of qualified publicists as it would not elevate a particular author to the status of "the most highly qualified publicists" as referred to in Article 38'.[79] This is confirmed by an ICJ employee, who suggests that the Court's judges 'do not like giving [writers] a hierarchy'.[80] While this issue will likely also arise for individual judges and other courts and tribunals, it may be felt particularly keenly by the ICJ, due to its nature, role, and culture. This is elaborated on in Section 3.5.11.

3.5.4   The Court's Drafting Procedures and Style

The Court's collegiate drafting procedure has also been proposed as a reason for the lack of citations of teachings.[81] One ICJ judge explains that 'the size of a body makes a difference, because there is a tendency to resist putting in more material than is necessary when having to persuade fifteen [...] judges'.[82] The WTO Appellate Body also has a collective drafting procedure,[83] yet it has cited teachings in 19 per cent of its reports until 2013.[84] Whereas each WTO Appellate Body report is the responsibility of three WTO Appellate Body members, the ICJ's decisions are issued by the whole fifteen- to seventeen-member bench.[85] Even so, the ICJ's decisions are usually drafted mainly by three judges, who convene in a drafting committee.[86] The drafting procedure of the ICJ can be one explanation for why the Court's majority opinions do not cite teachings, but it seems unlikely to be the only explanation.

The Court's '"broad-brush" approach to reasoning' may be another explanation for the lack of teachings references.[87] This is certainly possible. Refuting the claim would require a comparative study of the

---

[79] Judge Tomka quoted in Keene (ed.), 'Outcome Paper', 260.

[80] ICJ Employee 1.

[81] For example, Hall, *International Law*, 59; Wood, 'Teachings', para 10; Crawford, *Brownlie's*, 42–43.

[82] ICJ Judge 1.

[83] Terris, Romano, and Swigart, *International Judge*, 61.

[84] Sondre Torp Helmersen, 'The Use of Scholarship by the WTO Appellate Body' (2016) 7 *Goettingen Journal of International Law* 309, 317. The article reports a figure of 26 per cent but includes ILC works. Without ILC works, teachings are cited in 21 out of 110 reports, that is, 19 per cent.

[85] Unless the 'chambers' procedure is used (as described in Section 1.3.1).

[86] Section 1.3.1.

[87] Maurice Mendelson, 'Sources', 84.

approaches of different individual judges and other international courts and tribunals, which is not done in this book.

3.5.5 Writers' Objectivity

The possibility that authors are biased or influenced by self-interest rather than objectivity could keep the Court from citing teachings.[88] The existence of such biases has been noted by Max Huber in the *Spanish Zone of Morocco* arbitration,[89] by Judge Bustamante in the PCIJ,[90] and by an ICJ employee.[91] Several writers have themselves nonetheless held that writers are generally objective.[92]

Writers may, moreover, have been involved in specific cases or disputes about which they write, for example, as a judge, arbitrator, or counsel.[93] Many writers work as counsel or judges at some point in their career.[94] Writers can also have some connections with a party to a case or dispute on which they comment, for example, as an employee, external counsel, or recipient of research funding.[95] Writers can also be

---

[88] Hilary Charlesworth, 'Law-Making and Sources' in James Crawford and Martti Koskenniemi (eds.), *The Cambridge Companion to International Law* (Cambridge University Press 2012) 187, 197; Sørensen, *sources*, 187–188.

[89] *Affaire des Biens Britanniques au Maroc Espagnol (Espagne contre Royaume-Uni)*, (1924) 2 RIAA 615, 640.

[90] *Case Concerning the Payment in Gold of Brazilian Federal Loans Contracted in France (France v. United States of America), Judgment No. 15, 12 July 1929, P.C.I.J Reports Series A No. 21*, p. 93, Dissenting Opinion by M. de Bustamante 133.

[91] ICJ Employee 2 ('is the commentary written by somebody who has spent their life as an advocate for the issue that is the subject of the treaty being commented on? Because if that is the case, you have to look at their comments through that lens, and assume that they [...] have a particular way of looking at it and interest in it being interpreted in a certain way').

[92] For example, O'Connell, *International Law*, 37; Lachs, *Teacher*, 204; Ruben E Agpalo, *Public International Law* (Rex 2006) 11. However, ILC, *Report of the Sixty-eighth session*, 111; D'Amato, 'Internationalist', 104; Lauterpacht, *Development*, 24; L Oppenheim, 'The Science of International Law: Its Task and Method' (1908) 2 *American Journal of International Law* 313, 334, 345 and 353; Oscar Schachter, *International Law in Theory and Practice* (Martinus Nijhoff 1991) 38 disagree.

[93] Pellet, 'Article 38', 869–870; Anthea Roberts, *Is International Law International?* (Oxford University Press 2017) 4.

[94] Manfred Lachs, 'Teaching and Teachings of International Law' (1976) 151 *Recueil des cours* 161, 220; Lachs, *Teacher*, 199–209.

[95] Andrea Bianchi, 'The Game of Interpretation in International Law: The Players, the Cards, and Why the Game is Worth the Candle', in Andrea Bianchi, Daniel Peat, and Matthew Windsor (eds.), *Interpretation in International Law* (Oxford University Press 2015) 34, 43.

influenced by future job prospects.[96] The ICJ Statute Article 17(2) prevents judges from participating in cases 'in which [the judge] has previously taken part as agent, counsel, or advocate for one of the parties, or as a member of a national or international court, or of a commission of enquiry, or in any other capacity'.[97] Similar rules are found, for example, in the ITLOS Statute[98] Article 7(2) and 8(1), the Rome Statute Article 41(2)(a) , and the ECtHR Rules Article 4(2). There are also general rules about maintaining 'impartiality' and avoiding 'conflicts of interest', for example, in the Rome Statute Article 40(2) and the ECHR[99] Article 21(3). The Burgh House Principles on the Independence of the International Judiciary have similar language.[100] There are no such rules for writers. Trying to prevent writers from writing about cases they have been involved in altogether is not a good solution, since the writings of an 'insider' can be uniquely useful. Writers should, however, inform the reader about any affiliation with cases and parties on which they are commenting.[101] There is nonetheless a risk that writers withhold such information.[102]

It is up to judges to avoid biased writers,[103] but an easier response may simply be to refrain from citing teachings altogether. However, this should apply equally to all courts and tribunals as well as individual ICJ judges, who do cite teachings. It may be that the ICJ's unique institutional role, where disputes gain a relatively high degree of political visibility by a prestigious court that is part of the UN system, means that its disputes are inherently more political than those of many other international courts and tribunals. In some sense, even launching a case before the

---

[96] A. H. Qureshi, 'Editorial Control and the Development of International Law' (1990) 61 *Political Quarterly* 328, 332; Muthucumaraswamy Sornarajah, *Resistance and Change in the International Law on Foreign Investment* (Cambridge University Press, 2015) 100 (describing more generally 'a long tradition [. . .] of working to further the interests of multinational corporations in the expectation of monetary rewards').

[97] Elaborated on in ICJ, 'Practice Directions' (amended on 20 January 2009 and 21 March 2013) www.icj-cij.org/en/practice-directions, VII and VIII.

[98] UNCLOS Annex VI: Statute of the International Tribunal for the Law of the Sea.

[99] Convention for the Protection of Human Rights and Fundamental Freedoms, Rome, 4 November 1950, in force 3 September 1953, 213 UNTS 221.

[100] Sands, McLachlan, and Mackenzie, 'The Burgh House Principles on the Independence of the International Judiciary' (2005) 4 *Law and Practice of International Courts and Tribunals* 247, para 7.1, 8.1, 9.1, and 9.2.

[101] Kenneth Ripple, 'The Judge and the Academic Community' (1989) 50 *Ohio State Law Journal* 1237, 1239; J E Côté, 'Far-Cited' (2001) 39 *Alberta Law Review* 640, 655).

[102] Beatson, 'Academics', 535.

[103] Goldsmith, 'Remarks', 318.

ICJ is a political act. If so, the proposed explanation of political disputes and potentially biased writers is, like lack of diversity among writers, incomplete without reference to the Court's institutional role, which is discussed further in Section 3.5.11.

3.5.6   The Lack of Diversity among Writers

Another reason given for the lack of citations of teachings in the ICJ's majority opinions is that writers tend to stem only from a few countries.[104] Former ICJ Judge Buergenthal has pointed to the need to 'avoid criticism that' the Court is 'influenced by the views of one or the other region of the world'.[105] One ICJ judge notes that '[t]he Court sees itself as universal [. . .] and references to literature are almost always going to be to literature from North America or Europe. So that is another question, or another concern, that you appear to be favouring one sector rather than another'.[106] In the same vein, an opinion by Judge Shahabuddeen cited a letter from Philip C. Jessup, who argued that '[t]he Court, *qua* Court, naturally hesitates to cite individuals or national courts lest it appear to have some bias or predilection'.[107] This is also true of other international courts and tribunals – a circumstance that should also keep them from citing teachings. However, uniquely for the ICJ, the ICJ Statute Article 38(1)(d) says that the 'most highly qualified publicists', whose 'teachings' the Court 'shall apply', are to be drawn 'from the various nations'. This can plausibly be interpreted to mean that it is better for the Court not to cite any writers at all if it cannot cite writers from different parts of the world. However, the ICJ Statute Article 38(1)(d) applies equally to individual judges and is widely assumed to reflect customary international law,[108] which makes its directions applicable to other courts and tribunals as well. It may nonetheless be a particular concern for the ICJ's majority opinions, due to their unique role in international law, as discussed in Section 3.5.11. The ICJ is the only permanent, global, generalist international court. It has a special responsibility for

---

[104]   Mendelson, 'Sources', 83; Pellet, 'Article 38', 869.

[105]   Judge Buergenthal quoted in Terris, Romano, and Swigart, *International Judge*, 98.

[106]   ICJ Judge 1.

[107]   *Applicability of Article VI, Section 22, of the Convention on the Privileges and Immunities of the United Nations, Advisory Opinion, I.C.J. Reports 1989*, p. 177, Separate Opinion of Judge Shahabuddeen 220.

[108]   Section 2.2.2.

the integrity and acceptance of international law. It is therefore plausible that the lack of diversity of relevant teachings may be why the ICJ's majority opinions rarely cite them.

3.5.7 The Court's Expertise

Some writers argue that the ICJ's majority opinions do not cite teachings because the judges are themselves legal experts.[109] While the judges are experts when composing a majority opinion, they are equally expert when composing individual opinions, many of which do cite teachings. The ICJ as an institution of fifteen to seventeen judges may nonetheless be seen as more expert than any individual judge. However, other courts and tribunals are also composed of experts and still cite teachings in their decisions. A potential counterargument is that no other court or tribunal matches the ICJ's expertise. This is difficult to assess, and the most important factor will be each institution's view of its own expertise. The ICJ's expertise probably has some explanatory power for its near lack of references to teachings in majority opinions, but it is difficult to say more precisely how much.

3.5.8 The Availability of Better Arguments

Individual opinions in the ICJ espouse views that by definition differ from the views of the majority of the Court's judges. Because they are supported by a minority of the judges, the views expounded in individual opinions may have less support in the available sources than do majority opinions. There may be nothing better than teachings available to cite, which will mean that individual judges generally have a greater incentive to cite teachings in their opinions than judges in the majority.[110] The very act of disagreeing with one's colleagues may also prompt judges to rely more on teachings.[111] This can be seen as a form of 'strategic' citation of teachings, which is also discussed in Section 5.4.2. The availability of better arguments may thus at least explain some of the discrepancy between citations in majority and individual opinions.

---

[109] Mendelson, 'Sources', 84.

[110] Manley, 'Citation', 1006; (in the context of national law) Daniels, 'Beyond', 12.

[111] Manley, 'Citation', 1006; (in the context of Canadian national law) Black and Richter, 'My Name', 388.

3.5.9 *Teachings Lack Official Authority*

Teachings lack official authority, since they are not created by states.[112]

Judges can be seen as political actors who respond to incentives in their judicial practice. Like other lawyers, they aspire to have their legal work accepted by others. Judges Bedjaoui, Ranjeva, and Koroma in the *Qatar/ Bahrain* case cited teachings to express the idea that judges 'are subject to criticism' and are 'influenced by popular reaction'.[113] Courts therefore need 'techniques which will make their judgments more persuasive and enhance their legitimacy'.[114]

An absence of references to teachings may make a judicial decision look more authoritative.[115] As one ICJ judge explains, the Court 'tries to be definitive, and being definitive involves abstracting itself from particular positions'.[116] Furthermore, frequent citation of teachings 'gives these sorts of references a bad name, because you do it too often. People think it is a form of decoration'.[117] The same judge also says, '[o]ne thing about references to literature is that they date, whereas references to cases or to the ILC do not to the same extent'.[118] Something similar is pointed out by an ICJ employee, who argues that a judicial decision 'should [be] inherently authoritative', and that 'loading it with up references to scholarship' could be counterproductive.[119] Judicial decisions are generally assigned more weight than teachings.[120] If a judge relies on teachings in a decision, the significance of the decision may be pulled down towards the level of teachings.

The negative effect of citations of teachings on the authority of judicial opinions may be especially relevant to the ICJ, which has a special status in international law, as discussed in Section 3.5.11. However, there may also be strategic arguments in favour of citing teachings, which are explored in Section 5.4.2, to explain variations in citation rates between ICJ judges.

---

[112] Van Hoof, *Rethinking,* 177; (in the context of national law) Bernstein, 'Secondary', 63; Nigel Simmonds, *Law as a Moral Idea* (Oxford University Press 2008) 164.

[113] *Qatar and Bahrain, 2001,* Joint Dissenting Opinion of Judges Bedjaoui, Ranjeva and Koroma 151.

[114] Ibid.

[115] (In the context of English law) Earlsferry, 'Judges', 32; Alexandra Braun, 'Burying the Living? The Citation of Legal Writings in English Courts' (2010) 58 *American Journal of Comparative Law* 27, 42.

[116] ICJ Judge 1.

[117] ICJ Judge 1.

[118] Ibid.

[119] ICJ Employee 2.

[120] Section 3.8.2.

A related argument is that the weight of teachings in international law is largely bound up in the identities of specific writers, as explored in Section 4.2. Citing more teachings would expose this. This dependence on personalities could be considered unsuitable for international courts, which seek to maintain an impersonal and institutional identity.

3.5.10   Length and Complexity

Citing teachings in a judicial decision makes the decision longer,[121] which means that it takes longer to write and to read. It can also make the decision more complex by obscuring the judge's reasoning.[122] This is an argument against citing teachings.[123] It is not certain that this is something the ICJ is concerned about, but it is a possible explanation for why majority opinions do not cite teachings.

3.5.11   Institutional Culture and Role

An 'institutional culture' may affect how the ICJ approaches teachings.[124] An ICJ judge agrees that not citing teachings 'is part of the [Court's] institutional culture'.[125] Judge Buergenthal, who served at the ICJ as well as the IACtHR, compares the two institutions and finds the ICJ to be 'more formal and to some extent formalistic in its judicial approach'.[126]

The ICJ is the only permanent generalist international law court, the oldest surviving international court, and the one with the most authority.[127] The Court's role goes beyond settling disputes; it is also supposed to uphold 'common values of the international community'.[128] It must thus appear neutral, including in its choices of individual writers and writers of different countries. It will also wish to give the appearance that its decisions are on a higher plane than mere teachings. Because of this, the ICJ may better maintain the authority and acceptability of its decisions by refraining from citing teachings in majority opinions.

---

[121] John Henry Merryman, 'Toward a Theory of Citations: An Empirical Study of the Citation Practice of the California Supreme Court in 1950, 1960, and 1970' (1977) 50 *Southern California Law Review* 381, 423; Smyth, 'Outside', 701.

[122] Earlsferry, 'Judges', 32.

[123] Beatson, 'Academics', 537–538.

[124] Sivakumaran, 'Influence', 28; Kammerhofer, 'Lawmaking', 323.

[125] ICJ Judge 1.

[126] Judge Buergenthal quoted in Terris, Romano, and Swigart, *International Judge*, 97–98.

[127] Section 1.2.

[128] Hernández, *Judicial Function*, 204.

A notable aspect of the ICJ's general jurisdiction is that it can be called on to ascertain or interpret any treaty as well as customary international law (and even general principles of law). Other courts and tribunals are, by contrast, often limited to interpreting a specific treaty or set of treaties. It is argued in Section 3.4.2 that teachings are more useful when ascertaining customary international law than when interpreting treaties. This could mean that teachings should be cited more often by the ICJ than by others. Even so, the ICJ's majority opinions almost never cite teachings,[129] while several other courts and tribunals do so more often.[130]

It was mentioned in Section 3.5.3 that the desire to avoid jealousy between authors has been proposed as a reason why the ICJ does not cite teachings, but that other courts and tribunals apparently do not see it the same way. The argument should be seen in light of the ICJ's unique status and role. It is because of the ICJ's unique features that it wishes to avoid jealousy between authors. An ICJ judge thus explains that it would be below the prestige, nature, function, and status of the Court to allow writers to jockey for being cited.[131]

An indication of the existence of different cultures in different institutions would be if a judge changed their approach to teachings when moving from one institution to another, in line with observable differences between the two institutions. This book provides enough data for one case study, that of Judge Shahabuddeen. He was a member of both the ICJ and the ICTY. In the ICTY Judge Shahabuddeen was an outlier who cited teachings far more than other judges,[132] just as he has done in the ICJ. This may look like an argument against the existence of institutional cultures. However, the ICJ's institutional culture seems mainly to concern the majority rather than individual opinions. Moreover, it is not possible to know which, if any, ICJ cases where Judge Shahabuddeen was a member of the drafting committee.[133] His practices therefore do not disprove the hypothesis that the ICJ's practice in majority opinions is (at least to some extent) driven by the Court's institutional culture.

---

[129] Section 3.2.

[130] Section 6.3.2.

[131] ICJ Judge 2.

[132] Bohlander, 'Influence', 198–208.

[133] Section 1.3.1.

3.6   Other Patterns That Indicate Limited Weight

3.6.1   *Few Judges Cite Teachings in Every Opinion*

Of the 165 ICJ judges who have written at least one individual opinion and the 112 of them again who have cited teachings, only 25 (15 per cent of the 165) have cited teachings in all of their individual opinions. Of these 25, only Ajibola and El-Erian were permanent judges, the rest were ad hoc (Ajibola was both permanent and ad hoc). Of the 23 judges who were ad hoc, 20 wrote only one or two opinions in total. Even Judge Cançado Trindade, who alone is responsible for 34 per cent of the ICJ's references to teachings, has not cited teachings in every opinion; of his 37 opinions, 6 do not cite teachings. A potential reason for Judge Cançado Trindade's numerous references to teachings is his philosophical approach to adjudication, as discussed in Section 5.4.3.

Most, if not all, of the cases that come before the ICJ involve some disputed issue of law. In these cases, teachings will generally be, at least tangentially, relevant to the legal issues in question.[134] Thus, the judges could cite teachings if they wished. Judges writing individual opinions may choose to focus entirely on questions of fact rather than law, in which case there is not much opportunity to cite teachings. However, in practice, most individual opinions involve questions of law as well as questions of fact. Thus, it seems that even judges writing individual opinions often choose not to cite teachings even when they are available and relevant. This is another indication of the low weight of teachings.

3.6.2   *Judges Specify That They Agree with Teachings*

Even among those judges who do cite teachings, some specify that they 'agree' with the teachings to which they refer.[135] Judges have also used other phrases with the meaning, such as that they 'share' the views of teachings,[136]

---

[134]   Black and Richter, 'My Name', 382 argue that this is the case for the Canadian Supreme Court.

[135]   For example, *Nuclear Tests (Australia)*, Dissenting Opinion of Judge de Castro 382; *Qatar and Bahrain, 2001*, Separate Opinion of Judge Fortier 458; *Arrest Warrant, 2002*, Joint Separate Opinion of Judges Higgins, Kooijmans and Buergenthal 79.

[136]   *Application of the Convention on the Prevention and Punishment of the Crime of Genocide, Provisional Measures, Order of 13 September 1993, I.C.J. Reports 1993*, p. 325, Separate Opinion of Judge Ajibola 403; *Arrest Warrant, 2002*, Separate opinion of Judge ad hoc Bula-Bula 108.

'incline towards'[137] them, 'have reached the same conclusion as' them.[138] Some judges characterise teachings with terms that mean that the judge happens to agree them. This includes 'correct' or 'correctly',[139] 'right', 'rightly', or 'rightfully',[140] and 'quite properly'.[141] Other characterisations with similar meaning include 'appropriate',[142] 'apt',[143] and 'apposite'.[144] Examples of more complicated phrases are 'for this judge the range of judicial choice for this Court is well summed up by' teachings,[145] '[t]he Court would have been well advised to follow' teachings,[146] and that the judge 'cannot do better than' teachings.[147] Judges have also simply used the phrases '[i]n my opinion',[148] 'in my view',[149] and 'I think'[150] when citing teachings.

---

[137] *Land, Island and Maritime Frontier Dispute (El Salvador/Honduras), Composition of Chamber, Order of 13 December 1989, I.C.J. Reports 1989*, p. 162, Separate opinion Judge Shahabuddeen 169.

[138] *Wall, Advisory Opinion*, Separate Opinion of Judge Elaraby 258.

[139] For example, *Continental Shelf (Libyan Arab Jamahiriya/Malta), Judgment, I.C.J. Reports 1985*, p. 13, Separate Opinion of Judges Ruda, Bedjaoui and Jiménez de Aréchaga 84; *Arrest Warrant, 2002*, Dissenting Opinion of Judge Al-Khasawneh 96; *Bosnia Genocide, 2007*, Separate Opinion of Judge Tomka 315.

[140] For example, *Aegean Sea Continental Shelf, Judgment, I.C.J. Reports 1978*, p. 3, Separate Opinion of Judge Tarazi 60; *Pedra Branca/Pulau Batu Puteh*, Declaration of Judge Bennouna 129; *Croatia Genocide, 2015*, Separate Opinion of Judge ad hoc Kreća 452.

[141] *South West Africa, Second Phase*, Dissenting Opinion of Judge Jessup 370–371.

[142] *North Sea*, Dissenting Opinion of Vice-President Koretsky 168; *Jan Mayen*, Separate Opinion of Judge Ajibola 289; *Land and Maritime Boundary, 2002*, Separate Opinion of Judge ad hoc Mbaye 536.

[143] *Armed Activities on the Territory of the Congo (Democratic Republic of the Congo v. Uganda), Judgment, I.C.J. Reports 2005*, p. 168, Dissenting Opinion of Judge ad hoc Kateka 372.

[144] *Questions of Interpretation and Application of the 1971 Montreal Convention arising from the Aerial Incident at Lockerbie (Libyan Arab Jamahiriya v. United Kingdom), Provisional Measures, Order of 14 April 1992, I.C.J. Reports 1992*, p. 3, Dissenting Opinion by Judge Weeramantry 57; *Questions of Interpretation and Application of the 1971 Montreal Convention arising from the Aerial Incident at Lockerbie (Libyan Arab Jamahiriya v. United States of America), Provisional Measures, Order of 14 April 1992, I.C.J. Reports 1992*, p. 114, Dissenting Opinion by Judge Weeramantry 167.

[145] *Nuclear Tests (New Zealand) Examination*, Dissenting opinion by Judge ad hoc Sir Geoffrey Palmer 418.

[146] *Oil Platforms, 2003*, Dissenting Opinion of Judge Elaraby 304–305.

[147] Ibid., Separate Opinion of Judge ad hoc Rigaux 372–373.

[148] *South West Africa, Second Phase*, Separate Opinion of Judge van Wyk 132.

[149] *Land and Maritime Boundary, 2002*, Dissenting Opinion of Judge Koroma 481–482; *Bosnia Genocide, 2007*, Separate Opinion of Judge Tomka 330.

[150] *Land, Island and Maritime Frontier Dispute, Order 1990*, Dissenting Opinion of Judge Shahabuddeen 53.

A particularly interesting example is Judge Schwebel's comments in the ICJ's *Libya-Malta* case, when referring to an author who 'in [his] view, rightly' stated the law.[151] However, he also called the author 'distinguished'.[152] The use of terms such as 'distinguished' is discussed in Section 4.3.2 and seems to mean that the judge views the writer as particularly authoritative. Thus, even when citing an authoritative writer, Schwebel felt the need to specify his agreement with the teachings.

An example from the PCIJ is found in Lord Finlay's dissenting opinion in the *Lotus* case. He cited teachings by 'Mr. Oppenheim', and added that the cited 'passage, in my opinion, is an accurate statement of the international law applicable'.[153]

These examples suggest that, at least among those judges and in those cases, teachings were cited because the judges agreed with the views they found there, after an independent assessment of whether the teachings were correct. If the weight of teachings depends entirely on whether the judge happens to agree with them, they do not actually have any intrinsic weight. Thus, the examples cited here support the view that teachings have low weight.[154] A counterargument to this, however, is that judges sometimes cite teachings they disagree with, as discussed in Section 3.7.5.

3.6.3   Teachings Are Used to 'Confirm' Conclusions

Some judges cite teachings to 'confirm' their own view of a legal question or a conclusion previously arrived at by means of other sources.[155] This suggests that teachings have been accorded little, if any, independent weight. Something similar is the application of teachings as 'support', as done by Judge Weeramantry in the *Nuclear Weapons* advisory opinion.[156] Judges Keith and Greenwood in *Diallo* first mentioned what they saw as the ordinary meaning of a treaty term and how 'monitoring bodies' agreed with it, and added that 'so too' did teachings.[157] Judge Cançado Trindade in the *Kosovo* advisory opinion

---

[151] *Libyan Arab Jamahiriya/Malta, 1985*, Dissenting Opinion of Judge Schwebel 185.
[152] Ibid.
[153] *Lotus*, Dissenting Opinion by Lord Finlay 56–57.
[154] Braun, 'Burying', 47.
[155] For example, *Nicaragua, 1986*, Dissenting Opinion of Judge Schwebel 384; *Arrest Warrant, 2002*, Separate opinion of Judge ad hoc Bula-Bula 116; *Bosnia Genocide, 2007*, Dissenting Opinion of Judge ad hoc Mahiou 414.
[156] *Nuclear Weapons*, Dissenting Opinion of Judge Weeramantry 532–533.
[157] *Diallo, 2010*, Joint Declaration of Judges Keith and Greenwood 718.

discussed a distinction that was 'endorsed in' teachings.[158] Judge Shahabuddeen in *Border and Transborder Armed Actions* first stated his own view of the law and then, in a separate sentence, cited teachings to explain it.[159] Vice-President Weeramantry in *Land and Maritime Boundary between Cameroon and Nigeria* found that teachings 'reinforce[d]' a point.[160] All of these examples seem essentially to be about citing teachings in order to 'confirm' a view.

An example is also found in the PCIJ. The dissenting opinion by Schücking in *Wimbledon* discussed various sources and finally added that '[s]uch is also the doctrine of the writers on international law'.[161]

That judicial decisions cite teachings merely in order to 'confirm' conclusions implies that teachings have low weight. While teachings are 'subsidiary',[162] the role they play may still go beyond merely 'confirming' conclusions that are reached by other means. They can be particularly useful in answering difficult legal questions, where other sources are silent or contradictory.[163]

3.6.4   A Lack of Engagement

Section 3.7 gives examples of judges seeming to assign some weight to teachings, and such applications of teachings may be classified as 'engagement' with teachings.[164] The point in this section is that those examples constitute only a small minority of the references to teachings in ICJ opinions. Thus, even the ICJ judges who do cite teachings in their opinions often engage little with the contents of those

---

[158] *Kosovo*, Separate Opinion of Judge Cançado Trindade 596–597.

[159] *Border and Transborder Armed Actions*, Separate Opinion of Judge Shahabuddeen 140–141.

[160] *Land and Maritime Boundary between Cameroon and Nigeria*, *Preliminary Objections, Judgment, I.C.J. Reports 1998*, p. 275, Dissenting Opinion of Vice-President Weeramantry 373–374.

[161] *Wimbledon, 17 August 1923*, Dissenting Opinion by M. Schücking 47.

[162] Section 2.2.8.

[163] Shecaira, *Scholarship,* 77. Similarly Thomas L Ambro, 'Citing Legal Articles in Judicial Opinions: A Sympathetic Antipathy' (2006) 80 *American Bankruptcy Law Journal* 547, 549; Harner and Cantone, 'Out of Touch', 49–50.

[164] Antonios Tzanakopoulos, 'Judicial Dialogue as a Means of Interpretation' in Helmut Philipp Aust and Georg Nolte (eds.), *The Interpretation of International Law by Domestic Courts* (Oxford University Press 2016) 72, 89: 'engagement' is in this context taken to mean to neither 'adopt [an] argument wholesale' nor 'merely ignore it'.

teachings.[165] A lack of engagement with teachings suggests that they have low weight.[166]

Some judges cite teachings mostly in footnotes, and others in the main text of their opinions. This, however, is not necessarily an indicator of engagement (or lack thereof). It can be merely a matter of style.[167] As an illustration one may compare, for example, the opinions of Judge Riphagen and Judge Ammoun in the merits phase of the *Barcelona Traction* case.[168] Riphagen supplied each of his references in the main text of his opinion, while Ammoun included his mostly in footnotes. Ammoun nonetheless cited more teachings than did Riphagen and also engaged more with them.

3.6.5   *Justifications of Authority*

Judges sometimes seem to attempt to justify the authority of the teachings they cite by referring to the quality of the text, the expertise or official position of the writer, or the fact that multiple writers agree. Examples are collected in Section 4.3. The most obvious are where judges use terms such as 'authority' or 'authoritative' about the cited teachings, but all of the examples count as judges justifying the authority of teachings. Judges have also referred to the 'weight',[169] 'significan[ce]',[170] 'direct

---

[165] (In the context of national law) Crespi, 'Influence', 21; Shecaira, *Scholarship*, 49.

[166] Stephen M Schwebel, 'The Inter-active Influence of the International Law Court of Justice and the International Law Commission' in Calixto A Armas Barea and others (eds.), *Liber Amicorum in Memoriam of Judge José María Ruda* (Kluwer 2000) 479, 486; Stanton, 'Scholarship', 204.

[167] The opposite view is apparently taken by James Cameron and Kevin R Gray, 'Principles of International Law in The WTO Dispute Settlement Body' (2001) 50 *International and Comparative Law Quarterly* 248, 259.

[168] *Barcelona Traction, 1970*, Dissenting Opinion of Judge Riphagen 287, 289, 291–293, 295, 297–298, 300, 302–304, 308–309, 312–314, 316, 322, 324, 328–330, 332–333 and Separate Opinion of Judge Ammoun 337, 345, 348.

[169] For example, *Bosnia Genocide, 1993*, Separate Opinion of Vice-President Weeramantry 386; *Application of the Convention on the Prevention and Punishment of the Crime of Genocide, Counter-claims, Order of 17 December 1997, I.C.J. Reports 1997*, p. 243, Dissenting Opinion of Vice-President Weeramantry 290. *Aerial Incident of 10 August 1999 (Pakistan v. India), Jurisdiction of the Court, Judgment, I.C.J. Reports 2000*, p. 12, Dissenting Opinion of Judge ad hoc Pirzada 78 used both 'authority' and 'weight'.

[170] *South West Africa Cases (Ethiopia v. South Africa; Liberia v. South Africa), Preliminary Objections, Judgment of 21 December 1962: I.C.J. Report: 1962*, p. 319, Dissenting Opinion of President Winiarski 451; *Nuclear Weapons*, Declaration of Judge Vereshchetin 281.

interest',[171] and 'importance'[172] of specific authors or teachings. Judges have also written that they 'have benefited greatly and gratefully' from teachings,[173] and that teachings 'strengthen me in my opinion'.[174] These tendencies, on the one hand, suggest that certain works are seen (by some judges and in some cases) as having some weight. On the other, the need to do this in respect of certain specific works suggests that the category of teachings as a whole generally has low weight.[175]

This tendency to justify the authority of teachings can be contrasted with judges' use of judicial decisions. The judges who justify the authority of teachings generally do not see any need to justify the authority of judicial decisions. This suggests that judicial decisions are seen as having greater significance in themselves, independently of the position and expertise of the judge and the quality of the text. This contrast indicates that teachings generally have low weight, at least when compared to judicial decisions, which are compared further in Section 3.8.2.

3.7 Patterns That Indicate Some Weight

3.7.1 Using Teachings as a Main Argument

In some opinions, judges have cited only teachings when drawing certain legal conclusions. In these cases, judges do *not* use teachings as a basis of rights and obligations, which they cannot be.[176] The legal conclusions are (either implicitly or explicitly) based on treaties, customary international law, or general principles of law. However, that teachings are cited prominently or even exclusively makes it seem like they have played a significant role in the judges' legal reasoning. Examples can be found in the opinions of Judge Cançado Trindade in *Whaling*[177] and *Kosovo*,[178]

---

[171] *Case concerning the Aerial Incident of July 27th, 1955 (Israel v. Bulgaria), Preliminary Objections, Judgment of May 26th, 1959: I.C.J. Reports 1959,* p. 127, Joint Dissenting Opinion by Judges Sir Hersch Lauterpacht, Wellington Koo and Sir Percy Spender 174.

[172] *Guardianship of Infants,* Separate Opinion of Judge Sir Hersch Lauterpacht 96.

[173] *Land, Island and Maritime Frontier Dispute, Order 1990,* Dissenting Opinion of Judge Shahabuddeen 21.

[174] *Case concerning Right of Passage over Indian Territory (Merits), Judgment of 12 April 1960: I.C.J. Reports 1960,* p. 6, Dissenting Opinion of Judge Fernandes 140.

[175] Braun, 'Burying', 47.

[176] Section 2.2.8.

[177] *Whaling in the Antarctic (Australia v. Japan), Declaration of Intervention of New Zealand, Order of 6 February 2013, I.C.J. Reports 2013,* p. 3, Separate Opinion of Judge Cançado Trindade 22.

[178] *Kosovo,* Separate Opinion of Judge Cançado Trindade 576.

Judge Jessup in *South West Africa*,[179] Judge Krylov in *Corfu*,[180] Judge Tanaka in *Barcelona Traction*,[181] and Judge Ammoun in *North Sea*.[182]

In *Barcelona Traction*, Judge Sir Gerald Fitzmaurice cited only teachings when asserting that '[t]here has, doctrinally, been much discussion and controversy as to what is the correct test to apply in order to determine the national status of corporate entities', and that an 'element of fluidity is still present in this field'.[183] Fitzmaurice thus applied teachings not to assert the existence of a rule, but rather to show that the law was uncertain. That is also significant. Fitzmaurice did the same later in the same opinion, discussing 'the law of the State Succession' and referring to teachings when asserting 'it is somewhat doubtful whether [a rule existed] yet'.[184] Judge Riphagen, also in *Barcelona Traction*, seemed to rely solely on how scholars interpreted a treaty. He mentioned 'treaties' where 'the nationality of the natural persons who manage a company is a factor in determining the link between a State and that company' and by way of an example mentioned that '[a]ccording to information given by Foighel in *Nationalization and Compensation*, 1963, p. 235, this is the case in a treaty, with an attached aide-mémoire, of 27 September 1948 between Switzerland and Yugoslavia'.[185] Judge Riphagen thus appears not to have interpreted the treaty himself, but instead relied entirely on the interpretation found in teachings. The teachings may also have been the source of Judge Riphagen's knowledge of the treaty in the first place. In *Guardianship of Infants*, Judge Sir Percy Spender referred to 'authorities' cited by the parties and found that they 'at least should satisfy one' of the legal conclusion he reached.[186]

There is also an example in the PCIJ, in Moore's dissenting opinion in *Mavrommatis*. He wrote that 'it will suffice' to cite teachings to find that '[t]he requirement of jurisdiction' is 'fundamental and peremptory' in international law.[187]

---

[179]   *South West Africa, Second Phase*, Dissenting Opinion of Judge Jessup 418.

[180]   *Corfu Channel*, Dissenting Opinion by Judge Krylov 74.

[181]   *Barcelona Traction, 1970*, Separate Opinion of Judge Tanaka 119.

[182]   *North Sea*, Separate Opinion of Judge Fouad Ammoun 120 and 140.

[183]   *Barcelona Traction, 1970*, Separate Opinion of Judge Sir Gerald Fitzmaurice 83.

[184]   Ibid., 101.

[185]   *Barcelona Traction, 1970*, Dissenting Opinion of Judge Riphagen 348.

[186]   *Guardianship of Infants*, Separate Opinion of Sir Percy Spender 124.

[187]   *The Mavrommatis Palestine Concessions*, Judgment No. 2, 30 August 1924, P.C.I.J. Reports Series A No. 2, p. 6, Dissenting Opinion by M. Moore 59–60.

3.7.2 Citing Teachings That Criticise Judicial Decisions

There are examples of judges citing teachings that criticise judicial decisions, and apparently using this as a basis for discounting the value of the decisions in question. Since judicial decisions normally have more weight than teachings, it is significant that those judges apparently see teachings as authoritative enough to discredit judicial decisions.

For example, Judge Dillard in *Fisheries Jurisdiction (UK)* apparently used teachings to show that the PCIJ's discussion of 'the much discussed question of State autonomy and freedom of State action and presumptions flowing from such concepts' in the *Lotus* decision was 'controversial'.[188] This 'controversy' was apparently Judge Dillard's reason for not giving much weight to pronouncements in the *Lotus* decision. Teachings criticising an earlier decision were thus used to distinguish the case at hand.[189]

In *Barcelona Traction*, Judge Padilla Nervo referred 'to arbitral decisions and claims commissions', cited by 'the Applicant'. He then dismissed the decisions by citing a statement by Schwarzenberger, who wrote that '[t]hese decisions do not necessarily give expression to rules of customary international law'.[190] Also in *Barcelona Traction*, Judge Sir Gerald Fitzmaurice cited teachings when writing that '[i]t could be asked for instance whether the *Nottebohm* case itself was rightly decided'.[191]

Judge van Wyk in *South West Africa* provides another example. Judge van Wyk claimed that the ICJ's 'majority opinion' in *Namibia* 'has elicited strong criticism from highly qualified publicists'.[192] This was an argument for not relying on it when determining whether the League of Nations Mandate for South West Africa survived the dissolution of the League of Nations.

3.7.3 Criticising Insufficient Consideration of Teachings

Some judges have criticised judicial decisions and other sources for not taking teachings sufficiently into account. Judge De Castro in the *Namibia* case discussed whether 'the unanimity rule was applicable to [League of Nations] mandates' and opined that two ICJ cases had 'rather

---

[188] *Fisheries Jurisdiction (United Kingdom v. Iceland),* Separate Opinion of Judge Dillard 59.

[189] The concept of 'distinguishing a case' is discussed in the context of international law by, for example, Shahabuddeen, *Precedent*, 110–127 and Hernández, *Judicial Function*, 174–177.

[190] *Barcelona Traction, 1970,* Separate Opinion of Judge Padilla Nervo 247.

[191] Ibid., Separate Opinion of Judge Sir Gerald Fitzmaurice 81.

[192] *South West Africa, Second Phase*, Separate Opinion of Judge van Wyk, 132.

weak [authority]'.[194] This was in part because they were contradictory, and the relevant parts were obiter dicta, but it was also because they did 'not [take] into consideration the arguments and facts based on practice indicated in' pleadings before the Court and 'legal writings' (i.e., teachings).[195] This must mean that (at least according to this judge) the authority of judicial decisions can be reduced if they fail to take into account the views of teachings.

In a similar vein, Judge Oda, in a dissenting opinion in *Libya/Malta*, criticised the majority opinion and gave as a reason for his dissent that '[r]eference should have been made' by the majority to two specified works of teachings.[196] In another decision he criticised the majority for not being 'aware' of and not 'probing' relevant teachings.[197] This also implies that some level of authority is granted teachings. Judge ad hoc Kreća in *Croatia Genocide* mentioned that the ILC cited teachings to support a finding, but criticised the ILC for mentioning only one academic article on the point in question.[198] A similar example is found in Judge ad hoc Torres Bernárdez's opinion in *Territorial and Maritime Dispute between Nicaragua and Honduras*. Torres Bernárdez argued, in the context of maritime delimitation, that '[t]he Court should have assessed the virtues of the bisector method in relation to the actual "coastal configuration"'. This was something, he noted, that 'scholarly opinion has not failed to emphasize'.[199]

One function of a legal argument can be to 'redistribute argumentative burdens'.[200] That is a fitting description of what judges apparently see teachings as having done in the cases mentioned here.

3.7.4 *Efforts to Clarify Teachings*

One way of ascribing significance to teachings is to attempt to clarify their meaning (which is similar to how one would try to interpret a treaty

---

[194] *Namibia*, Separate Opinion of Judge De Castro, 201.

[195] Ibid.

[196] *Libyan Arab Jamahiriya/Malta, 1985*, Dissenting Opinion of Judge Oda 140.

[197] *Nicaragua, 1986*, Dissenting Opinion of Judge Oda 257–258.

[198] *Croatia Genocide, 2015*, Separate Opinion of Judge ad hoc Kreća 495.

[199] *Territorial and Maritime Dispute between Nicaragua and Honduras in the Caribbean Sea (Nicaragua v. Honduras), Judgment, I.C.J. Reports 2007*, p. 659, Dissenting Opinion of Judge ad hoc Torres Bernárdez, 820.

[200] For example, Armin von Bogdandy and Ingo Venzke, *In Whose Name? An Investigation of International Courts' Public Authority and Its Democratic Justification* (Oxford University Press 2014) 19.

or a judicial decision). While teachings 'are not [. . .] to be construed as if they were [. . .] a statute',[201] their meaning can be unclear. An attempt to interpret them implies that the views of teachings should not be discarded or overlooked just because they are not immediately discernible, and that it is desirable to ascertain the content of teachings before arriving at a final conclusion about the law.

One example is Judge Sir Robert Jennings in the *Nicaragua* case, who, when discussing the views of Hans Kelsen, said that 'Kelsen would hardly have used the word "revolutionary" if he had thought of [the UN Charter being binding on non-parties] as depending upon a development of customary international law'.[202] In *Application for Review of Judgment No. 158 of the United Nations Administrative Tribunal*, Judge De Castro pointed out that an expression used in teachings was 'ambiguous'.[203] Thus, he cited teachings even though they were not immediately helpful and even tried to clarify them. Judge Shahabuddeen in *Land, Island and Maritime Frontier Dispute* said that 'both writers would have had good reason for not going so far', in an attempt to ascertain the intentions of the teachings he was citing.[204] Similar examples are found in opinions of Judge Cançado Trindade in *Diallo*;[205] Judges Lauterpacht, Koo, and Spender in *Aerial Incident 1955 Israel-Bulgaria*;[206] and Judge Shahabuddeen in *Bosnia Genocide*.[207]

Some judges have corrected the parties' views of teachings. Judge Levi Carneiro's opinion in *Anglo-Iranian Oil Co.* included a lengthy discussion to show how one of the parties' understanding of a specific work was incorrect[208] and discussed opposing views from other teachings.[209] Similarly, Judge Shahabuddeen in the *Nauru* case mentioned a dispute

---

[201] *Border and Transborder Armed Actions*, Separate Opinion of Judge Shahabuddeen 148–149.

[202] *Nicaragua, 1986*, Dissenting Opinion of Judge Sir Robert Jennings 531–532.

[203] *Application for Review of Judgement No. 158 of the United Nations Administrative Tribunal, Advisory Opinion, I.C.J. Reports 1973*, p. 166, Dissenting Opinion of Judge de Castro 277.

[204] *Land, Island and Maritime Frontier Dispute, Order 1990*, Dissenting Opinion of Judge Shahabuddeen 38.

[205] *Ahmadou Sadio Diallo (Republic of Guinea v. Democratic Republic of the Congo), Compensation, Judgment, I.C.J. Reports 2012*, p. 324, Separate Opinion of Judge Cançado Trindade 355–356.

[206] *Aerial Incident of July 27th, 1955*, Joint Dissenting Opinion by Judges Sir Hersch Lauterpacht, Wellington Koo and Sir Percy Spender 174 and 178–179.

[207] *Application of the Interim Accord*, Separate Opinion of Judge Shahabuddeen 355.

[208] *Anglo-Iranian Oil Co.*, Dissenting Opinion of Judge Levi Carneiro 163–164.

[209] Ibid., 167.

between the parties over the interpretation of a specific work.[210] In the PCIJ, the dissenting opinion by Jonkheer van Eysinga in the *Panevezys-Saldutiskis Railway Case* mentions teachings cited by the 'Lithuanian Agent' in the case, but adds that 'if one continues to read' the cited page, 'one realizes that Borchard really only has in mind the line of conduct of the United States Department of State in the sphere of the Claims Commissions'.[211] The conclusion is that the work in question does not support the claim made by the agent.

In other opinions judges have used other sources or documents in order to interpret teachings. In an opinion in *Aerial Incident of 3 July 1988*, Judge Shahabuddeen used a judicial opinion to interpret teachings.[212] He discussed the filing of memorials and referred to 'a practice under which, if such an objection was filed before the Memorial, the Court could in its discretion decline to recognize or treat it as such and direct that it be filed after the Memorial'.[213] Judge Shahabuddeen then read an article by Judge Jiménez de Aréchaga in light of that 'practice' and in light of a judicial opinion by Jiménez de Aréchaga, and found them compatible. In another example, in *Libya/ Malta* Judge Jiménez de Aréchaga stated that '[a] textual argument serves to confirm the correctness of Judge Morelli's opinion'.[214] The 'textual argument' concerned a treaty provision, and Judge Morelli was cited as an author of teachings, not as a judge. Thus, Judge Jiménez de Aréchaga used the wording of a treaty to confirm the view of a writer. This is the opposite of what was described in Section 3.6.3 (writers being used to confirm a conclusion arrived at by other means), and it suggests that Jiménez de Aréchaga assigned significant weight to teachings in that case. In the *Gabčikovo* case, Vice-President Weeramantry used other teachings to clarify a work of teachings (a work by Hugo Grotius).[215] The other works were thus used as commentary on Grotius, even though, formally speaking, Grotius's works too are merely teachings. Vice-President

---

[210]   *Certain Phosphate Lands in Nauru (Nauru v. Australia), Preliminary Objections, Judgment, I.C.J. Reports 1992*, p. 240, Separate Opinion of Judge Shahabuddeen 284.

[211]   *The Panevezys-Saldutiskis Railway Case, Judgment 28 February 1939, P.C.I.J. Reports Series A/B No. 76*, p. 4, Dissenting Opinion by Jonkheer van Eysinga 33–34.

[212]   *Aerial Incident of 3 July 1988 (Islamic Republic of Iran v. United States of America), Order of 13 December 1989, I.C.J. Reports 1989*, p. 132, Separate Opinion by Judge Shahabuddeen 157.

[213]   *Aerial Incident of 3 July 1988*, Separate Opinion by Judge Shahabuddeen 157.

[214]   *Continental Shelf (Libyan Arab Jamahiriya/Malta), Application to Intervene, Judgment, I.C.J. Reports 1984*, p. 3, Separate Opinion of Judge Jiménez de Aréchaga 57.

[215]   *Gabčikovo*, Separate Opinion of Vice-President Weeramantry 96.

Weeramantry's approach therefore suggests not only that teachings can be authoritative enough to require clarification but also that some teachings (such as those of Grotius) have more weight than others. The latter point is pursued further in Chapter 4.

Some judges have compared the views of a single writer across multiple works. Judge Sir Hersch Lauterpacht in *Guardianship of Infants* cited a work of teachings, and his impression was that the writer 'expressed a different view' in another work.[216] In *Border and Transborder Armed Actions (Nicaragua v. Honduras)*, Judge Shahabuddeen found it 'possible [...] to discern some movement in this important area on the part of a thoughtful mind', when discussing the possibility that 'Mr. Garcia-Amador' had changed his views on the legal question that Shahabuddeen was discussing.[217] In the PCIJ, the Dissenting opinion by M. Bustamante in the *Brazilian Loans* case considered teachings concerning the effect of fluctuating currency exchange rates on payment obligations. Bustamante pointed out that '[i]n the first place, a distinction must be drawn between those who wrote before the world war and those who studied the question after 1914'.[218] He then argued that 'the requirements of the national situation [...] have a great influence on [...] teachings' and remarked that '[i]n order to avoid this stumbling block, we have quoted pre-war authors in preference to others'. Bustamante seems to be under the impression that writers were more acutely affected by national interests in the years after World War I than in the years before, and he takes this into account when consulting teachings.

Other judges show that they made a close reading of teachings. An opinion by Judge ad hoc Caron in *Alleged Violations of Sovereign Rights and Maritime Spaces* cited teachings, with 'emphasis added'.[219] Judge ad hoc Caron thus wished to emphasise a specific part of the citation, suggesting an active engagement with the text. Judge Shahabuddeen in *Border and Transborder Armed Actions* explicitly mentioned having done a 'close reading' of certain teachings.[220] Judge Abraham in *Croatia Genocide* argued that a writer 'appears very hesitant on the

---

[216] *Guardianship of Infants*, Separate Opinion of Judge Sir Hersch Lauterpacht 96.

[217] *Border and Transborder Armed Actions*, Separate Opinion of Judge Shahabuddeen 148–149.

[218] *Brazilian Loans*, Dissenting Opinion by M. de Bustamante 133.

[219] *Alleged Violations of Sovereign Rights and Maritime Spaces in the Caribbean Sea (Nicaragua v. Colombia), Preliminary Objections, Judgment, I.C.J. Reports 2016*, p. 3, Dissenting Opinion of Judge ad hoc Caron 77.

[220] *Border and Transborder Armed Actions*, Separate Opinion of Judge Shahabuddeen 149–150.

point' he was discussing.[221] Similarly, some judges have cited writers who 'clearly',[222] 'emphatically',[223] 'strongly',[224] or 'forcefully'[225] stated their views. Judges have also found that teachings were 'clear',[226] 'strong',[227] or 'categorical'.[228] Other judges have mentioned how a writer 'did not intend' a certain meaning,[229] that a writer 'stated' something 'with very considerable hesitation',[230] and that a writer who 'strongly' expressed a view 'also expressed some reservations'.[231]

3.7.5   References to Teachings That the Judge Disagrees With

Judges sometimes discuss teachings with which they disagree,[232] implying that teachings have some independent weight.[233] These cases must be distinguished from those in which a judge cites teachings with which they have come to agree only after reading them. In such cases teachings may have had significant weight. However, when examining citations of teachings in judicial decisions, as in this book, such cases are indistinguishable from those in which judges cite teachings that happen to agree with their preconceived opinion.

---

[221] *Application of the Convention on the Prevention and Punishment of the Crime of Genocide (Croatia v. Serbia), Preliminary Objections, Judgment, I.C.J. Reports 2008*, p. 412, Separate Opinion of Judge Abraham 533.

[222] *Aerial Incident of July 27th, 1955,* Joint Dissenting Opinion by Judges Sir Hersch Lauterpacht, Wellington Koo and Sir Percy Spender 178–179; *Kasikili/Sedudu Island,* Dissenting Opinion of Vice-President Weeramantry 1174.

[223] *Military and Paramilitary Activities in and against Nicaragua (Nicaragua v. United States of America), Jurisdiction and Admissibility, Judgment, I.C.J. Reports 1984*, p. 392, Dissenting Opinion of Judge Schwebel 626–627.

[224] *Bosnia Genocide, 1993,* Separate Opinion of Vice-President Weeramantry 386.

[225] For example, *Marshall Islands v. United Kingdom,* Dissenting Opinion of Judge Cançado Trindade 33.

[226] *South West Africa,* Dissenting Opinion of Judge van Wyk 603–604.

[227] *Nuclear Weapons,* 279; *Oil Platforms (Islamic Republic of Iran v. United States of America), Preliminary Objection, Judgment, I.C.J. Reports 1996*, p. 803, Separate Opinion of Judge Shahabuddeen 826.

[228] *Asylum,* Dissenting Opinion by M. Caicedo Castilla 365.

[229] *South West Africa,* Dissenting Opinion of Judge van Wyk 604.

[230] *Guardianship of Infants,* Separate Opinion of Judge Sir Hersch Lauterpacht 96.

[231] *Bosnia Genocide, 1993,* Separate Opinion of Vice-President Weeramantry 386.

[232] Kammerhofer, 'Lawmaking', 322; (in the context of national law) Richard A Posner, 'The Theory and Practice of Citations Analysis, with Special Reference to Law and Economics', *John M. Olin Program in Law and Economics Working Paper* Number 83 (1999) http://chicagounbound.uchicago.edu/cgi/viewcontent.cgi?article=1577&context=law_and_economics, 6.

[233] Posner, 'Citations Analysis', 9; Duxbury, *Judges,* 15.

Section 3.6.2 noted how many judges specify their agreement with teachings. This, it was argued, is a sign that teachings have low weight. The argument in this section is that even though (some) judges feel free to disagree with teachings, (some) judges nonetheless do cite (some) teachings with which they disagree. This makes teachings seem more significant than if judges cited only teachings that they agreed with.

Phrases that indicate disagreement include 'but see',[234] 'contra',[235] that a work 'does not persuade me',[236] and that its assertions are 'doubtful'.[237] Other judges have criticised teachings for 'bias',[238] for having 'extra legal intentions'[239] and for having 'already played its role',[240] and questioned whether 'it is fully reflective of the range of potential characteristics of a rule of customary international law'.[241]

Judge Oda in *Land, Island and Maritime Frontier Dispute* noted that while scholars were unanimous, this had 'little [. . .] value' because their conclusions were based on a single award from the PCA, which they, according to Judge Oda, had read too much into.[242] Judge Oda moreover disagreed twice with teachings he cited in *Tunisia/Libya*, once even after calling them 'very worthwhile'.[243]

Judge ad hoc Mahiou in the *Bosnia Genocide case* agreed with one aspect of the majority opinion which, he noted, 'contradicted the [rash] opinion of one author'.[244] Vice-President Weeramantry introduced in the same case his reference to teachings with which he disagreed by stating that 'account must, however, be taken of' them.[245] The use of the word 'must' may suggest that he felt a sense of obligation to do so.

---

[234] *South West Africa, Second Phase*, Dissenting Opinion of Judge Jessup 422.

[235] *Arrest Warrant, 2002*, Separate opinion of Judge ad hoc Bula-Bula 225.

[236] *Nuclear Weapons*, Dissenting Opinion of Judge Shahabuddeen, 387.

[237] *Arrest Warrant, 2002*, Joint Separate Opinion of Judges Higgins, Kooijmans and Buergenthal 70–71.

[238] *Whaling*, Separate Opinion of Judge Cançado Trindade 38.

[239] *Bosnia Genocide, 2007*, Separate Opinion of Judge ad hoc Kreća 535.

[240] *Diallo, 2010*, Separate Opinion of Judge Cançado Trindade 804–805.

[241] *Question of the Delimitation of the Continental Shelf between Nicaragua and Colombia beyond 200 Nautical Miles from the Nicaraguan Coast (Nicaragua v. Colombia), Preliminary Objections, Judgment, I.C.J. Reports 2016*, p. 100, Declaration of Judge Robinson 212.

[242] *Land, Island and Maritime Frontier Dispute, 1992*, Declaration of Judge Oda, 748.

[243] *Continental Shelf (Tunisia/Libyan Arab Jamahiriya), Judgment, I.C.J. Reports 1982*, p. 18, Dissenting Opinion of Judge Oda 200.

[244] *Bosnia Genocide, 2007*, Dissenting Opinion of Judge ad hoc Mahiou 383.

[245] *Bosnia Genocide, 1993*, Separate Opinion of Vice-President Weeramantry 378.

Other examples of judges citing teachings they disagree with include, among others, Judge Azevedo in *Corfu Channel*,[246] Judge Shahabuddeen in *Border and Transborder Armed Actions*,[247] and Judge Ammoun in *Barcelona Traction*.[248]

3.7.6   References to Disagreements in Teachings

There are also examples of judges citing works of teachings that disagree with each other. In most cases this is significant for the same reason as the references to teachings with which the judge disagrees, since a judge who cites opposing teachings will often have to disagree with at least one of the opposing sides. Judges could thus have limited themselves to citing the side they agreed with or they could have ignored the teachings altogether. References to opposing teachings are also significant for another reason: Section 4.3.5 argues that teachings will, all else being equal, have more weight when multiple works agree. When judges nonetheless cite works that disagree with each other, it may be taken to mean that teachings can have some weight even when some writers disagree.

For example, judges have cited teachings when arguing that they were 'divided',[249] that '[o]ne can cite many views on each side',[250] that there exist 'opposing views'[251] or 'schools',[252] that there was scholarly 'controversy',[253] and that a legal matter 'has been much debated'.[254] Further examples of judges citing disagreements in teachings include, among many others, Judge De Castro in *Namibia*,[255] President Winiarski in *South West Africa*,[256] and President Guillaume in *Arrest Warrant*.[257]

Another example seems to be Judge Ammoun in *Barcelona Traction*, who referred to 'J. L. Brierly', who did not 'ventur[e] so far as G. Scelle, or

---

[246] *Corfu Channel*, Dissenting Opinion by Judge Azevedo 98.

[247] *Border and Transborder Armed Actions*, Separate Opinion of Judge Shahabuddeen 134.

[248] *Barcelona Traction, 1970*, Separate Opinion of Judge Ammoun 291 and 312.

[249] *South West Africa, Second Phase*, Dissenting Opinion of Judge Jessup 370–371; *Border and Transborder Armed Actions*, Separate Opinion of Judge Shahabuddeen 148–149; *Passage through the Great Belt (Finland v. Denmark), Provisional Measures, Order of 29 July 1991, I.C.J. Reports 1991*, p. 12, Separate Opinion of Judge Shahabuddeen 28.

[250] *South West Africa, Second Phase*, Dissenting Opinion of Judge Jessup 370–371.

[251] *Western Sahara*, Separate Opinion of Judge Dillard 121.

[252] *Nuclear Weapons*, Dissenting Opinion of Judge Weeramantry 545.

[253] *Jan Mayen*, Separate Opinion of Judge Weeramantry 261.

[254] *Jan Mayen*, Separate Opinion of Judge Shahabuddeen 134.

[255] *Namibia*, Separate Opinion of Judge De Castro 206–207 and 215.

[256] *South West Africa*, Dissenting Opinion of President Winiarski 451.

[257] *Arrest Warrant, 2002*, Separate Opinion of President Guillaume 36–37.

as the Latin American jurists'.[258] This seems to be an example of nuancing, rather than contrasting, teachings. Judge ad hoc Mampuya in *Diallo* cited teachings that opposed the position adopted in an ILC instrument.[259] ILC works are not classified as teachings in this book,[260] but the example is even more significant since ILC works are usually credited with even more weight than teachings (as argued in Section 3.8.3).

3.7.7   *The Rate of Citation of Teachings Over Time*

Section 3.8.2 argues that teachings have less weight than judicial decisions. This should mean that where both judicial decisions and teachings are available, judicial decisions will be cited more often.[261] A court's catalogue of judicial decisions will necessarily grow over time. There is no formal '*stare decisis*' or system of 'binding' precedent in international law,[262] but there are de facto systems of precedent.[263] Thus, with more available judicial decisions, whose weight is greater than that of teachings, it should follow that the need to cite teachings decreases. Greater availability of judicial decisions does not in itself reduce the *weight* of teachings.[264] Rather, *the rate of citations* of teachings is reduced, as a consequence of the increased availability of judicial decisions combined with their greater weight compared to teachings.

However, as Figure 3.1 shows, the rate of citations of teachings in ICJ opinions has actually *increased* over time. The years are on the (horizontal) x-axis, while the number of references and share of opinions with references are on the (vertical) y-axis. The figure includes a trend line.

This could be taken to mean that the ICJ assigns relatively high weight to teachings (compared to other courts and tribunals), or at least that the weight has increased over time. However, the increase in the citations of teachings is largely driven by a few 'outlier' judges. Section 1.3.2 noted the

---

[258] *Barcelona Traction, 1970,* Separate Opinion of Judge Ammoun 331–332.

[259] *Ahmadou Sadio Diallo (Republic of Guinea v. Democratic Republic of the Congo), Preliminary Objections, Judgment, I.C.J. Reports 2007,* p. 582, Separate Opinion of Judge ad hoc Mampuya 635.

[260] Section 2.3.6.

[261] Waldock, 'General Course', 976.

[262] ICJ Statute Article 59, and, for example, Onuf, 'Global', 19; Rosenne and Ronen, *Law and Practice,* 763 and 765, and many others.

[263] For example, Schwarzenberger, *International Law,* 31; Terris, Romano, and Swigart, *International Judge,* 118; Boas, *Contemporary,* 113.

[264] Kammerhofer, 'Lawmaking', 307.

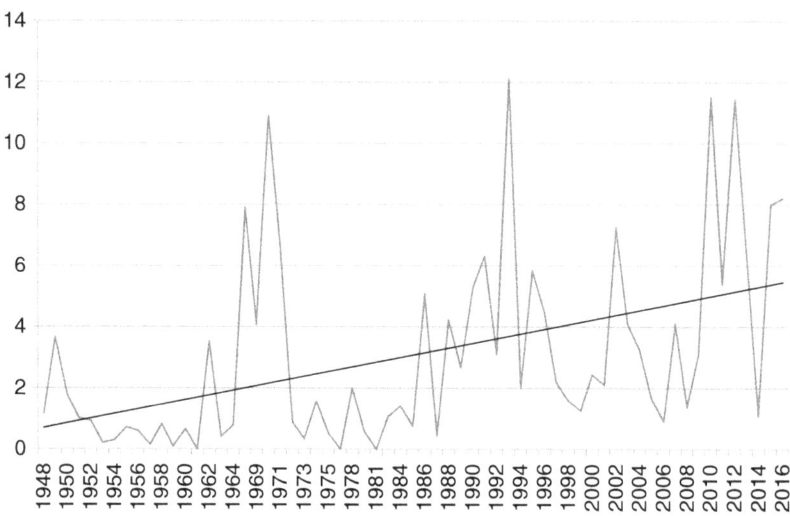

Figure 3.1   Average number of citations of teachings per opinion per year

importance of not drawing general conclusions from a limited number of such outliers. Judge Cançado Trindade alone has provided 1513 of the total 4370 references, that is, more than a third (35 per cent). Weeramantry has 462 references, Kreća 396, and Shahabuddeen 242, as shown in Appendix 2. As noted in Section 3.3, these four judges (out of 165) have cited teachings 2613 times, that is, 60 per cent of the total. While the Court has been in operation from 1946, these four judges served from 1988 to 1997 (Shahabuddeen), 1991 to 2000 (Weeramantry), 1993 to 2015 (Kreća, as judge ad hoc), and 2009 to the present (Cançado Trindade). If these four judges are removed from the statistics, the trend in citations of teachings in individual ICJ opinions over time is flatter, with a slight decline, as shown in Figure 3.2.

The outsize importance of these four judges could be taken as a coincidence. They happened to be elected and appointed relatively recently, thus skewing the statistics of citations of teachings over time. It may also have something to do with the fact that it has only recently been possible, or perhaps easier, to elect or appoint such judges. The ICJ today is more experienced, established, and confident than it was in its early history. The election and appointment of the four outlier judges (three as permanent judges and one as a recurring judge ad hoc) could therefore be more than a mere coincidence and actually be a reflection of the changing nature and context of the Court.

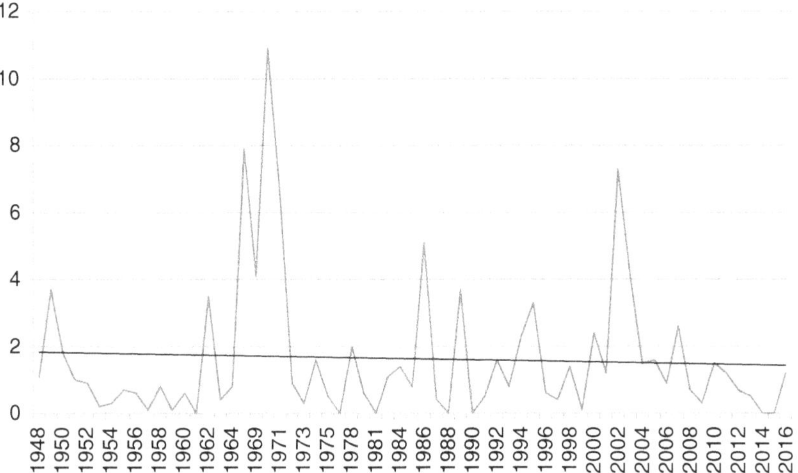

Figure 3.2 Average number of citations of teachings per opinion per year, without the top four judges

In the PCIJ, the average number of citations of teachings per opinion has increased over time. So has the share of the individual PCIJ's opinions per year that cite teachings.

More generally, variations in the citation of teachings over time could be caused by a multitude of reasons. As the catalogue of case law grows, teachings may be needed to navigate it. Moreover, since new teachings are published every year,[265] the amount of potentially relevant teachings should also increase, which may in turn increase the rate of citations of teachings.[266] At the same time, the existing teachings will grow increasingly outdated and need to be supplemented with newer, more relevant teachings. If international law teachings generally take a turn towards topics and approaches that are of little use to judges, the rate of citation is likely to decline. This book does not attempt to say whether it has happened in international law.[267] Various coincidences may also play a role; for example, that certain cases decided in more recent times may have been dissimilar to earlier cases,

---

[265] Jean d'Aspremont, 'Wording in International Law' (2012) 25 *Leiden Journal of International Law* 575, 587 adds that the amount published each year seems to grow too.

[266] Merryman, 'Theory', 407.

[267] For example, Michael D McClintock, 'The Declining Use of Legal Scholarship by Courts: An Empirical Study' (1998) 51 *Oklahoma Law Review* 659, 667–682 note this possibility in the United States.

resulting in fewer relevant judicial decisions, and in turn resulting in a greater need to rely on teachings. Moreover, a court may cite teachings strategically early in its existence in order to assert its place in and gain acceptance by the international community. Alternatively, a court or judge may respond to a similar need for acceptance by *not* citing teachings. They may do so on the assumption that it will make an opinion look more authoritative (as discussed in Section 5.4.2), for example, because states may be more accepting of opinions that do not lean on the writings of scholars who are neither appointed or elected by nor accountable to states (as discussed in Section 3.9.2).

The conclusion is that it is difficult to infer much about the weight of teachings from the rate of citations of teachings over time. That the rate has not declined can be taken as a sign that teachings have some weight, but there are numerous alternative explanations.

3.8 Teachings Have Lower Weight Than Other 'Subsidiary Means'

3.8.1 Introduction

The weight of teachings can be most accurately described by comparing it with something else. The following sections compare it with the weight of two other 'subsidiary means' (as per the ICJ Statute Article 38): judicial decisions and texts by state-empowered bodies (mainly the ILC).[268] ICJ judges generally assign both more weight than teachings, as will be shown later.

3.8.2 Judicial Decisions

Certain ICJ opinions seem to agree that judicial decisions have more weight than teachings.[269]

Vice-President Ranjeva in *Avena* cited teachings which in turn cited judicial decisions and wrote that '[t]he [...] precedent provides support' for his interpretation.[270] This may mean that even though teachings also

---

[268] The latter term is defined in Section 2.3.6.

[269] This is supported by, for example, Jennings, 'General Course', 341; Borda, 'Formal Approach', 660, but, for example, M Akehurst, 'The Hierarchy of the Sources of International Law' (1975) 47 *British Yearbook of International Law* 273, 280 seems to disagree.

[270] *Avena and other Mexican Nationals (Mexico v. United States of America), Judgment, I.C.J. Reports 2004*, p. 12, Declaration of Vice-President Ranjeva 76.

agreed with Vice-President Ranjeva's opinion, they could not '[provide] support' in the way that judicial decisions could.

In *Prosecute or Extradite*, after discussing a series of judicial decisions, Judge Cançado Trindade summarised them as a 'development', which had also been 'acknowledged [...] in' teachings.[271] Thus, the role of teachings was seen as merely to 'acknowledge' the development of the law which otherwise was driven by judicial decisions.

In *Guardianship of Infants*, Judge Sir Hersch Lauterpacht cited teachings while explaining that there was 'little judicial practice directly applicable to' the 'matter' at issue.[272] A possible inference is that had there been more judicial practice, Lauterpacht may not have seen the need to cite teachings.

Former ICJ judge Fitzmaurice writes that when counsel cite judicial decisions it is because one 'cannot ignore' them, as opposed to teachings, which are cited because they support one's argument, they have 'illustrative value', or they put something well.[273]

Moreover, even the most enthusiastic users of teachings seem to prefer judicial decisions when they are available. For example, even though Judge Shahabuddeen is among the judges who cite teachings most often, his opinion in *East Timor* frequently cited only judicial decisions.[274] That judicial decisions have more weight than teachings was also assumed in the PCIJ Statute's preparatory works, as 'M. de Lapradelle thought that jurisprudence was more important than doctrine'.[275]

As shown in Section 3.2, the ICJ's majority opinions rarely cite teachings, and many ICJ judges never do so. Majority opinions do cite ICJ decisions, but rarely the judicial decisions from other institutions, as noted in Section 3.5.1. In any case, teachings will more or less always cite relevant ICJ practice when answering specific questions of international law. This contrast indicates an unequal relationship between judicial decisions and teachings, where judicial decisions have far more weight. Similarly, ICJ judges frequently apply teachings in order to interpret judicial decisions,[276] whereas the opposite is rarely seen (a

---

[271] *Questions relating to the Obligation to Prosecute or Extradite (Belgium v. Senegal), Judgment, I.C.J. Reports 2012*, p. 422, Separate Opinion of Judge Cançado Trindade 536.

[272] *Guardianship of Infants*, Separate Opinion of Judge Sir Hersch Lauterpacht 96.

[273] Fitzmaurice, 'Problems', 76.

[274] *East Timor*, Separate Opinion of Judge Shahabuddeen, for example, 120–123, 125–126.

[275] ACJ, *Procès-Verbaux*, 336.

[276] Section 3.4.2.

rare example is cited in Section 3.7.4, from Judge Shahabuddeen in *Aerial Incident of 3 July 1988*).

Judicial decisions are generally not subject to the types of 'justifications' that are discussed in Section 4.3, that is, with judges justifying references by emphasising quality, expertise, official status, or agreement between writers. This indicates that judicial decisions have more inherent weight than teachings, since judges do not find it necessary to explain or justify why they are cited.

3.8.3   ILC Works

While the ICJ's majority opinions have cited teachings only seven times,[277] they cite judicial decisions and ILC works liberally.[278] This is one indication that works produced by state-empowered bodies are granted more weight than teachings.[279]

That the ICJ follows the ILC was assumed in statements made before the ILC in 1974, by among others Sir Humphrey Waldock, who represented the ICJ.[280] In 1997, the then-President of the Court, Judge Schwebel, gave a speech to the UNGA, where he highlighted 'the breadth and depth of the importance given' the ILC works on State responsibility in *Gabčikovo*.[281] Thirlway, the Court's former Registrar, mentions that in *Bosnia Genocide*, the ICJ treated the ILC's *Responsibility of States for Internationally Wrongful Acts*[282] Article 16 as customary international law, even though the ILC itself was unsure about the status of the rule.[283] According to Judge ad hoc Mahiou in *Diallo*, states 'have had to consider the draft ILC Articles on Diplomatic Protection'.[284] These examples show the weight accorded by the ICJ to ILC works, which seems to be greater than what it grants teachings.

---

[277] Section 3.2.

[278] Pellet, 'Article 38', 824 and 870; Peil, 'Writings', 152; Sivakumaran, 'Influence', 27.

[279] This assumption is supported by, for example, Virally, 'Sources', 154; Jennings, 'International Lawyers', 413; Schwebel, 'Influence', 480.

[280] ILC, *Yearbook of the International Law Commission 1974, Volume II Part One* (UN 1975) 162.

[281] UNGA, *Fifty-second Session, 36th plenary meeting* (27 October 1997) www.icj-cij.org /files/press-releases/9/3009.pdf, 2.

[282] ILC, *Yearbook of the International Law Commission, 2001, vol. II (Part Two) (A/CN.4/ SER.A/2001/Add.1)* (UN 2007).

[283] Thirlway, *Sources*, 19. This is also discussed by Dixon, *Textbook*, 47.

[284] *Diallo, 2007*, Declaration of Judge ad hoc Mahiou 621.

Even so, the ICJ's majority opinion in *North Sea* held that Article 6 of the 1958 Geneva Convention on the Continental Shelf, 'the relevant parts of which were adopted almost unchanged from the draft of the International Law Commission', was 'not at all de lege lata or [...] an emerging rule of customary international law'.[285] This was, however, in line with what the ILC had intended. The provision was meant as an attempt at progressive development rather than codification. Some individual judges have questioned whether certain ILC works reflect customary international law.[286] This is not controversial, however. To assume that all ILC works necessarily reflect customary international law would be contrary to the ILC Statute Article 1,[287] according to which the ILC's tasks include not only the 'codification' of international law but also 'the promotion of' its 'progressive development'.

The ILC has occasionally been subject to such 'justifications'.[288] References to ILC works have even been justified by the very fact that they are ILC works.[289] However, references to ILC works tend to be justified much less often than references to teachings, which should mean that ILC works generally have more weight than teachings.

3.9 Explaining the Relatively Low Weight of Teachings

3.9.1 Introduction

The following sections try to explain why teachings have low weight (as demonstrated previously) and less weight than judicial decisions and ILC texts (as shown in Section 3.8). Various possible explanations are discussed, but not all of them are found to have much explanatory power.

---

[285] *North Sea*, 38.

[286] *Gabčikovo,* Dissenting Opinion of Judge Fleischhauer 206; *Diallo, 2007,* Separate Opinion of Judge ad hoc Mampuya 635–636; *Prosecute or Extradite,* Dissenting Opinion of Judge ad hoc Sur 614.

[287] Similarly, David D Caron, 'The ILC Articles on State Responsibility: The Paradoxical Relationship between Form and Authority' (2002) 96 *American Journal of International Law* 857, 866.

[288] For example, *North Sea*, Dissenting Opinion of Vice-President Koretsky 160; *Nicaragua, Jurisdiction and Admissibility 1984*, Separate Opinion of Judge Sir Robert Jennings 552; *Maritime Delimitation and Territorial Questions between Qatar and Bahrain, Jurisdiction and Admissibility, Judgment, I.C.J. Reports 1995*, p. 6, Dissenting Opinion of Vice-President Schwebel 28–30.

[289] *Nicaragua, Jurisdiction and Admissibility 1984*, p. 392, Dissenting Opinion of Judge Schwebel 570 and 621–622.

3.9.2   Teachings Lack Official Authority

Section 3.5.9 notes that teachings have no official authority, since they are not created by states.[290] This is the essential difference between international courts and tribunals and state-empowered bodies, on the one hand, and scholars, on the other, since the former are created and empowered by and interact with states.[291] For the ILC this point is made by an ICJ employee[292] and a former ILC Chairman.[293] One ICJ judge explains that 'the ILC itself is part of a process of consideration by states, so it is an articulation of practice which states comment on [. . .]. So the reasons that impel the Court to refer to the ILC are the reasons that impel it not to refer to individual authors'.[294] An ICJ majority opinion took into account 'the rejection by the ILC of the concept of international crimes when it prepared the final draft of its Articles on State Responsibility, a decision reflecting the strongly negative reactions of a number of States to any such concept'.[295]

Some authors work at universities, which may be government owned, but this does not imply State endorsement of the resulting writings. Writers who work for states (e.g., in ministries, agencies, or courts) or official institutions tend to specify that they are writing in their personal capacity when publishing teachings.

The role of states in the ILC can be contrasted with their role in the ICRC. In this book ICRC works are mostly classified as teachings, because the ICRC does not have the same official status or state involvement as the ILC.[296] Nonetheless, according to Judge ad hoc Bula-Bula it gives 'the authorized interpretation' of the First Geneva Convention.[297] ICRC works have some weight, but the difference in state authorisation

---

[290] Van Hoof, *Rethinking*, 177; (in the context of national law) Bernstein, 'Secondary', 63; Simmonds, *Idea*, 164.

[291] For judicial decisions, for example, Rosenne, *Methods*, 119. Similarly Van Hoof, *Rethinking*, 171 and 177; David Lefkowitz, 'The Sources of International Law: Some Philosophical Reflections' in Samantha Besson and John Tasioulas (eds.), *The Philosophy of International Law* (Oxford University Press 2010) 187, 192–194. State involvement in the prime example of a State-empowered body, the ILC, is discussed in Section 2.3.6.

[292] ICJ Employee 1 ('the states are so heavily involved in the ILC').

[293] Robert Rosenstock, 'The ILC and State Responsibility' (2002) 96 *American Journal of International Law* 792, 794.

[294] ICJ Judge 1.

[295] *Bosnia Genocide, 2007,* 170.

[296] Section 2.3.6.

[297] *Arrest Warrant, 2002,* Separate opinion of Judge ad hoc Bula-Bula 122–123.

and involvement means that ICRC works carry less weight than ILC works. This shows that the degree of state empowerment and involvement in an institution should be seen as a continuum, with more state empowerment leading to gradually more weight.[298]

3.9.3 Like Cases Should Be Treated Alike

Judicial decisions are presumably given weight by international courts and tribunals for reasons of consistency.[299] Like cases should be treated alike,[300] which is an important reason why legal systems generally have (formal or informal) systems of precedent.[301] This consideration does not apply to the application of teachings (nor to works produced by state-empowered bodies). However, the views expressed in teachings can be relied on in good faith, and it can therefore be argued that deviating from them is undesirable.[302] Even so, the desirability of treating like cases alike explains some of the difference in weight between judicial decisions and teachings.

A related argument is that the authors of teachings are free to change their minds, even after a judge has cited their works, which could sow doubt about the correctness of the judge's reasoning.[303] However, judges too can to some extent change their mind. International law does not have formal *stare decisis*, but it does have de facto systems of precedent.[304] This means that writers can more readily change their minds than judges, which in turn means that applying teachings provides less stability than applying judicial decisions. This is plausible as a partial reason why teachings are assigned less weight than judicial decisions.

---

[298] Rosenne, *Perplexities*, 52; Hall, *International Law*, 59; Crawford, *Brownlie's*, 43, place the ILC on the same level as texts produced by collective, but not state-empowered, bodies such as the IDI. Bordin, 'Reflections', 558–559, is correct in disagreeing with this.

[299] Rosenne and Ronen, *Law and Practice*, 1554.

[300] Shahabuddeen, *Precedent*, 40; Hernández, *Judicial Function*, 171.

[301] WTO Appellate Body, *United States – Final Anti-Dumping Measures on Stainless Steel from Mexico*, WT/DS344/AB/R, 30 April 2008, 66–67; WTO Appellate Body, *Japan – Taxes on Alcoholic Beverages*, WT/DS8/AB/R, WT/DS10/AB/R, WT/DS11/AB/R, 4 October 1996, 14; UNCITRAL, *AWG Group Ltd v. The Argentine Republic*, Decision on Liability (30 July 2010) 73.

[302] Lord Goddard CJ in English High Court of Justice, *Bastin v. Davies* [1950] 1 All ER 1095, 1096.

[303] Braun, 'Burying', 73, explains that this has been used to justify the English convention against citing living authors in judicial decisions.

[304] Section 3.7.7.

3.9.4   *Expertise*

Another factor giving judicial decisions and works produced by state-empowered bodies weight is that courts and state-empowered bodies are usually staffed by experts.[305] The ILC includes academics, who may be seen as 'highly qualified publicists' in their own right and who often dominate debates.[306] International courts and tribunals often have a clause in their statute requiring the members to be international law experts.[307]

However, many writers are also experts. The 'most highly qualified publicists' are by definition experts. The two groups can be compared, but the result depends on how they are defined and delineated. If one compares all international judges and members of state-empowered bodies with anyone who has written texts that fall under the definition of 'teachings' given in Section 2.3, the latter category will be much larger. Since Courts and state-empowered bodies are highly selective and contain a much smaller number of people, it is logical to assume their average expertise is higher. International judges and members of state-empowered bodies are generally elected or appointed late in their career and are therefore older than the average writer and have more legal experience. In short, all international judges and members of state-empowered bodies have on average more expertise than everyone who has written 'teachings'. If the category of writers is narrowed down to only 'the most highly qualified publicists', the result may be different. However, that term is unclear and subjective, as discussed in Section 2.2.6. It is not possible to assess exactly how many writers qualify as 'most highly qualified' and therefore not possible to compare the average expertise of such writers with that of judges.

While it can therefore be concluded that judges and members of state-empowered bodies have on average more expertise than writers, this is primarily because one category is bigger than the other. If a judge picks out a random judicial decision and a random work of teachings, the author of the judicial decision will (on average) be more expert than the author of the teachings. However, that is not how judges work in practice. Rather than citing randomly, they seek out the most authoritative works.

---

[305]   Schwarzenberger, *International Law*, 31; Shaw, *International Law*, 86.

[306]   Boyle and Chinkin, *Making*, 173.

[307]   For example, ICJ Statute Article 2; Marrakesh Agreement Establishing the World Trade Organization, Marrakesh, 15 April 1994, in force 1 January 1995, 1869 UNTS 401, Annex 2: Understanding on Rules and Procedures Governing the Settlement of Disputes Article 17.3; Rome Statute Article 36(3)(b).

This is at least what ICJ judges seem to do, and it is what their incentives are telling them to do: Each judge wants to make their opinion as authoritative and persuasive as possible and will therefore wish to cite the most respected teachings.[308] The writer of the most authoritative work on a given issue cannot be presumed to have any less expertise than the judge who writes the most authoritative judicial decision. Sometimes the two will be the same person. In light of this, expertise loses its explanatory power for why teachings have low weight.

A further complicating factor is that judges and members of state-empowered bodies may have to have a more generalist, as opposed to specialist, form of legal expertise. While ILC special rapporteurs and members of specialised international courts are often appointed or elected precisely for their specialised expertise, regular ILC members and members of the ICJ are more often generalists. Doctoral students who have just finished their theses are supposed to be experts on the particular issue they have studied, and they may know more about it than the average international judge knows about an issue that happens to come before them.

In conclusion, expertise does not explain why judicial decisions and works by state-empowered bodies have more weight than teachings.[309]

3.9.5   Quality

Yet another factor giving judicial decisions and works produced by state-empowered bodies weight is their quality.[310] While teachings may also be of high quality,[311] it is possible that the procedures used in international courts and tribunals and state-empowered bodies give their works a particular quality that cannot be replicated by teachings.

Judicial decisions are created through an adversarial process[312] and are based on actual disputes.[313] However, teachings too may be part of and subject to adversarial (academic) debates.[314] As for the argument that judicial decisions apply the law to real disputes, a counterargument is that

---

[308]   Sections 4.4.2 and 5.4.2.

[309]   Fitzmaurice, 'Problems', 75–76.

[310]   Crawford, *Brownlie's*, 44.

[311]   Sienho Yee, 'Article 38 of the ICJ Statute and Applicable Law: Selected Issues in Recent Cases' (2016) 7 *Journal of International Dispute Settlement* 472, 491–492.

[312]   Jennings, 'General Course', 341. Similarly, for example, Schwarzenberger, *International Law*, 31.

[313]   Jennings, 'General Course', 341. Similarly Fitzmaurice, 'Problems', 76; Weeramantry, *Treaty Interpretation*, 137.

[314]   Beatson, 'Academics', 532.

the academic detachment of teachings may result in a more reflective and comprehensive legal reasoning.[315]

State-empowered bodies produce their work through a process of dialogue and negotiation, which generally yields a solid result.[316] However, certain procedures may instead *reduce* the quality of the resulting works. The need for consensus may lead to watered-down or unclear conclusions.[317]

Another point is that judges and members of state-empowered bodies may face greater time constraints than scholars, which may reduce their opportunity to refine their arguments. This need not necessarily be the case though. It can depend, for example, on the scholar's teaching load, the caseload of a judge, and how much assistance is available to them. An ICJ judge, for example, may well have more time to reflect on the resolution of a case that stretches over several years than an academic has to reflect on each of the several research articles that they may be expected to produce in a given year.

A further argument is that courts and state-empowered bodies have good research facilities.[318] However, many scholars also have access to excellent libraries and are often helped by academic colleagues and assistants. Therefore, 'facilities' is not a good reason to assume that the quality of judicial decisions and works by state-empowered bodies is higher than that of teachings.

In conclusion, quality does not explain the relatively low weight of teachings.[319]

3.9.6 Collectiveness and Diversity

International courts and state-empowered bodies are collective entities, which add to the weight of their decisions and works.[320] A possible

---

[315] Ian McLeod, *Legal Method* (9th edn, Palgrave Macmillan 2013) 109. Similarly Goff, 'Search', 184; Gerard V La Forest, 'Who is Listening to Whom? The Discourse Between the Canadian Judiciary and Academics' in Basil S Markesinis (ed.), *Law Making, Law Finding and Law Shaping: The Diverse Influences* (Oxford University Press, Oxford 1997) 69, 69.

[316] Rosenne, *Methods*, 121. Similarly Pellet, 'Article 38', 870; John Dugard, 'How Effective is the International Law Commission in the Development of International Law? A Critique of the ILC on the Occasion of Its Fiftieth Anniversary' (1998) 23 *South African Yearbook of International Law* 34, 38.

[317] Oscar Schachter, 'Law-Making in the United Nations' in Nandasiri Jasentuliyana (ed.), *Perspectives on International Law* (Kluwer 1995) 119, 132.

[318] Schwarzenberger, *International Law*, 32 regarding the ICJ.

[319] Hernández, 'Interpretative Authority', 168.

[320] ILC, *Third report*, 45; Watts, *International Law Commission*, 15.

argument for this is that the chance of a claim being correct increases with the number of people who agree that it is correct (all else being equal). This intuitive notion does not always hold true, however. For example, before Copernicus, Keppler, and Galilei, many scientists agreed that the sun revolved around the earth, but that did not make it true. In international law, by contrast, one may argue that if enough lawyers agree that something is true, it is by definition true.[321] The increased weight that comes from being produced by a collective body also applies to collective works of teachings, including books and articles with multiple authors, as well as works by bodies such as the ILA and IDI.

International courts and state-empowered bodies usually have regionally diverse memberships. International courts are generally made up of judges representing the major regions of the states parties. Many court instruments say that two judges should be nationals of the same state.[322] They also require that the judges should represent different geographical regions.[323] Thus, while many judges may have some or all of their education from the same Western States, as in the ICJ,[324] they are diverse in terms of geographical and cultural background.[325] The ILC Statute contains provisions identical to those of the ICJ Statute mentioned earlier, in Article 2(2) and Article 8, respectively. This diversity increases the weight of judicial decisions[326] and works by state-empowered bodies,[327] compared to the weight of teachings. Judges interviewed for the book *The International Judges* agree that this diversity matters.[328] This includes Judge Ammoun, who in *Barcelona Traction* argues that judicial

---

[321] For example, Lefkowitz, 'Philosophical Reflections', 189–190; Pauwelyn, 'Is It International Law', 140; Andrea Bianchi, 'Reflexive Butterfly Catching: Insights from a Situated Catcher' in Joost Pauwelyn, Ramses Wessel, and Jan Wouters (eds.), *Informal International Lawmaking* (Oxford University Press 2012) 200, 210.

[322] ICJ Statute Article 3(1), Rome Statute Article 36(7), Statute of the Inter-American Commission on Human Rights, 1 October 1979, OAS Resolution 447 (IACHR Statute) Article 4(2).

[323] ICJ Statute Article 9; DSU Article 17.3; ITLOS Statute 3(2); ECHR Article 20; Rome Statute 36(8)(a) (which also mandates '[a] fair representation of female and male judges').

[324] Section 5.5.5.

[325] Rosenne and Ronen, *Law and Practice*, 388.

[326] Schwarzenberger, *International Law*, 31; Schachter, *Theory*, 38–39; Bos, 'Manifestations', 64.

[327] For example, Parry, *Sources*, 114; Dhokalia, *Codification*, 172; Crawford, *Brownlie's*, 44.

[328] Terris, Romano, and Swigart, *International Judge*, 64 report that '[t]here [. . .] seems to be general agreement between judges and observes that [. . .] a bench made of a blend of people with different backgrounds is a crucial asset'.

decisions gain 'increased authority' from their diversity.[329] This point has a link to the argument the Court could benefit from citing a more diverse set of authors, which is presented in Section 6.2.2.

3.10   Conclusion: The General Role of Teachings in the ICJ

This chapter has shown that teachings are almost never cited in majority opinions, and even when cited in individual opinions they are in many instances assigned low weight by ICJ judges. There are also some examples of judges apparently assigning some weight to teachings, but those are the exception rather than the rule. They mainly come from a small subset of the ICJ's judges. Such variations between judges are discussed further in Chapter 5. The overall conclusion is that teachings have generally low weight.[330]

Another finding is that teachings are used more often than they are cited (Section 3.4). In line with that, Thirlway, the Court's former Registrar, claims that teachings 'probably would' be able to 'tip the scale' in a case 'where a court would not consider itself authorized to find the existence of a customary rule'.[331] Thirlway does not give specific examples, presumably for reasons of confidentiality. One ICJ judge calls Thirlway's statement 'a bit exaggerated', but acknowledges that teachings do 'have weight'.[332] Another judge says that 'I cannot off-hand think of one [example]', but also that '[i]t is not impossible, [. . .] certainly not'.[333] One ICJ employee can 'think of some cases' where the judges were 'spending more time with scholarship than others, but not necessarily in a way that translated into any clear outcomes'.[334]

As for why ICJ majority opinion rarely cite teachings, most of the explanations proposed by others either collapse when they are held up to the practices of other courts or of individual judges, or only make full sense when viewed in light of the ICJ's institutional role. The most plausible theory for why the ICJ's majority opinions do not cite teachings

---

[329]   *Barcelona Traction, 1970*, Separate Opinion of Judge Ammoun 317.

[330]   Scholars are somewhat divided on this. For example, Joost Pauwelyn, *Conflict of Norms in Public International Law: How WTO Law Relates to Other Rules of International Law* (Cambridge University Press 2003) 51 emphasises the significance of teachings in international law generally, but others such as Lauterpacht, *Development*, 25; Kammerhofer, 'Lawmaking', 324, are more sceptical.

[331]   Thirlway, *Sources*, 127.

[332]   ICJ Judge 2.

[333]   ICJ Judge 1.

[334]   ICJ Employee 2.

is that the Court is acting strategically and in line with its institutional culture, and that its strategic choices and its culture are shaped by the Court's unique role in international law.

The relatively low weight ICJ judges generally assign to teachings compared to ILC works and judicial decisions can be explained by teachings' lack of official authority, that judicial decisions must treat like cases alike, and that judicial decisions and works produced by state-empowered bodies are collective and diverse. Expertise and quality have no explanatory power.

In addition to this, judges may have a variety of conscious or unconscious influences when applying sources and deciding cases. This may include their backgrounds, personal opinions, and future ambitions.[335] Section 5.5 therefore examines how the judges' backgrounds correlate with their approaches to teachings and draws some overall conclusions.

The weight of teachings can vary over time. Teachings used to be more important in international law than they are today.[336] The results that are presented in this chapter are therefore not static, but only a snapshot of the Court's and the judges' practice as it was between 1948 and 2016.

Regardless of the low weight that ICJ judges assign to teachings when deciding specific legal questions, Section 3.4.2 argued that teachings seem to provide significant benefits to judges. They can improve the quality of their work and make it more authoritative. They can also contribute to the development of the law, and they help systematise the legal system and facilitate communication between international lawyers.[337] They were significant to the establishment of international law.[338]

Teachings can therefore be said to have a 'dual role' in international law: they are simultaneously insignificant and significant. This 'dual role' of teachings can be contrasted with the past. The weight that teachings used to have has largely been lost. Teachings also used to play an important role in the broader legal system, and this has to a large extent been retained. The function that teachings had in the solution of legal

---

[335] Erik Voeten, 'International Judicial Behavior' in Cesare P R Romano, Karen J Alter, and Chrisanthi Avgerou (eds.), *The Oxford Handbook of International Adjudication* (Oxford University Press 2013) 550, 550. Similarly Harry T Edwards and Michael A Livermore, 'Pitfalls of Empirical Studies That Attempt to Understand the Factors Affecting Appellate Decisionmaking' (2009) 58 *Duke Law Journal* 1895, 1915.

[336] Section 2.2.1.

[337] Section 6.1.

[338] Mary Ellen O'Connell, *The Power and Purpose of International Law: Insights from the Theory and Practice of Enforcement* (Oxford University Press 2008) 7, about Hugo Grotius. Similarly, for example, Boas, *Contemporary*, 114; Dixon, *Textbook*, 49.

questions has largely been replaced by treaties, judicial decisions, and works of state-empowered bodies. The functions that teachings have in the international legal system are much more difficult to replace.

Another question is what will happen in the future. One might imagine that the gradual decline of the weight of teachings, which has been underway for centuries, would continue over the next decades. That is not certain, however. It will depend on, among other things, whether the production of treaties, judicial decisions, and works of state-empowered bodies continues to grow. The 'judicialisation' of international law that took place in the 1990s has slowed considerably,[339] but existing institutions will continue to produce case law. The ILC, the leading state-empowered body in international law, is still active, and new treaties are regularly adopted. In any case, the practical usefulness of teachings is likely to increase. As the body of other instruments and sources grows, teachings actually become more important for navigating them, as argued in Section 3.7.7.

---

[339] Benedict Kingsbury, 'International Courts: Uneven Judicialisation In Global Order' in James Crawford and Martti Koskenniemi (eds.), *The Cambridge Companion to International Law* (Cambridge University Press 2012) 203, 223.

4

Variations between Works

4.1 Introduction

This chapter argues that the weight ICJ judges assign to teachings varies between different works.[1] The varying weight of teachings can to some extent be inferred from the wording of the ICJ Statute Article 38(1)(d), which speaks of 'the most highly qualified publicists'. This wording assumes that some writers are more qualified than others, and that only the 'most qualified' are to be applied by the ICJ. The wording of the Statute suggests a distinction between 'the most highly qualified' and other writers, where the ICJ can only cite the former. However, the concept of 'qualification' should instead be seen as a gradual progression from the least to the most qualified, where the more highly qualified are assigned more weight.[2] A rejected proposal in the ACJ was to establish a formal ranking of teachings.[3] While the proposal itself was unrealistic, it reveals an underlying view that the weight of teachings varies between different works.

Sections 4.2 and 4.3 show that the ICJ judges treat individual works differently in terms of frequency (how often a work is cited) and substance (how that work is described and treated when it is cited). Section 4.3 identifies 'factors' that seem to determine the weight of a specific work. Section 4.4 tries to explain why judges prefer to distinguish between teachings. Section 4.5 then reflects on how the foregoing sections show that authority in international law is established and maintained through a collective process, which is largely implicit instead of being conducted openly. Section 4.6 provides a conclusion.

---

[1] As assumed by, for example, ILC, *Report of the Sixty-eighth session,* 111; Murphy, *Dimensions,* 26; ALI, *Restatement,* 38.

[2] Section 2.2.6.

[3] ACJ, *Procès-Verbaux,* 336; Peil, 'Writings', 140.

4.2 Variations by Frequency

4.2.1 The Most-Cited Writers in ICJ Opinions

The ICJ has cited some writers more often than others. Table 4.1 lists the ten most-cited writers, and how many times they have been cited (not counting self-citations).[4] Antônio Augusto Cançado Trindade has been cited 297 times, but only by himself.

Thus, the most-cited writers are Shabtai Rosenne, Hersch Lauterpacht, Gerald Fitzmaurice, Manley O. Hudson, and Lassa Oppenheim. A list of the forty most-cited writers is included in Appendix 1. Under the assumption that citation to some extent reflects weight,[5] those most-cited writers are apparently the ones whose works have the most weight.

More generally, a small number of writers have been cited many times. The top ten most-cited writers have been cited a total of 726 times. This represents 17.9 per cent of a total 4050 citations (again excluding self-citations). While a total of 1280 writers have been cited in ICJ opinions, more than half of them (694) were cited only once. In other words, the top 0.8 per cent writers have more citations (726) than the bottom 50 per cent (640). Another significant number is that the top 10 per cent most-cited writers have 2077 citations, which is just over 50 per cent of the total. By contrast, the 10 per cent least-cited writers have 128 citations, which is 3 per cent of the total.

Table 4.1 *The ten most-cited writers*

Rank	Writer	Citations
1	Rosenne, Shabtai	233
2	Lauterpacht, Hersch	119
3	Fitzmaurice, Gerald	67
4	Hudson, Manley O.	55
5	Oppenheim, Lassa	53
6	Jennings, Robert	52
7	de Visscher, Charles	51
8	Brownlie, Ian	42
9	Watts, Arthur	32
9	Stone, Julius	32

---

[4] Self-citations are excluded for the reasons given in Section 5.2.
[5] Section 1.3.4.

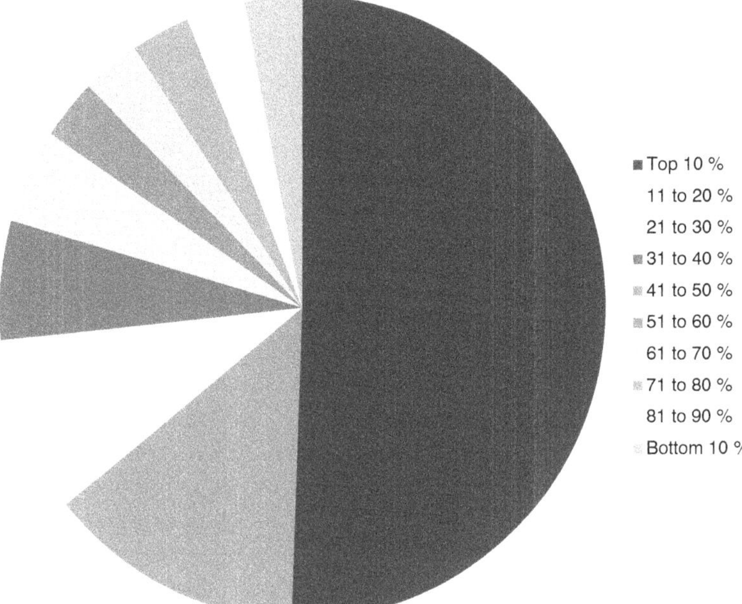

Figure 4.1   Writers' shares of all citations

The results are illustrated in Figure 4.1. The largest slice represents the top 10 per cent most-cited writers, the second largest represents the 10–20 per cent most-cited writers, and so on, until the last slice that represents the bottom 10 per cent.

In individual PCIJ opinions, the differences between how often writers are cited are much smaller. The most-cited writer is cited only three times. That writer is 'M. Planiol', who is cited on points on national law.[6]

The ICJ also seems to treat individual works differently in substance (and not just by frequency). This can be seen in the tendency to rank teachings according to various 'factors',[7] which are discussed in Section 4.3.

---

[6] *Case Concerning the Payment of Various Serbian Loans in France (France v. Kingdom of the Serbs, Croats and Slovenes), Judgment No. 14, 12 July 1929, P.C.I.J. Reports Series A No. 20*, p. 5, Dissenting opinion by M. Pessôa 73; *Brazilian Loans*, Dissenting opinion by M. Pessôa 150; *The Diversion of Water from the Meuse, Judgment 28 June 1937, P.C.I.J. Reports Series A/B No. 70*, p. 4, Individual Opinion by Mr. Hudson 77.

[7] Similarly Hall, *International Law*, 59; Nils Jansen, *The Making of Legal Authority: Non-legislative Codifications in Historical and Comparative Perspective* (Oxford University Press 2010) 95; Bordin, 'Reflections', 537.

The data that have been collected for the ICJ allow for some tentative conclusions concerning which 'publicists' the ICJ judges consider to be the 'most highly qualified', as per the ICJ Statute Article 38(1)(d). While this standard is to some extent subjective, as outlined in Section 2.2.6, this section presents rankings across three measures that are in themselves objective: the writers who have been cited the most; the writers who have been cited by the most judges; and the writers who have been subject to the highest number of the 'justifications' discussed earlier. Since the data set is relatively small and contains 'outlier' judges,[8] it is best not to look solely at how many times a writer is cited.

Scholars are sometimes compared by using the 'h index', which counts the number of scholarly works by an author to have received more than a given number of citations (in other scholarly works).[9] For example, if an author has written nine works that have been cited at least nine times, their h index would be nine. It would be possible to do a similar count for scholarly works cited by ICJ judges. However, ICJ judges generally cite very few individual works by any one writer. An 'h-count' would therefore not add much compared to a regular citation count. The regular citation count also has the advantage of being simpler (in terms of data collection and presentation) and is, therefore, the preferred method here.

Precise numbers are given in Appendix 1.

- The ten most-cited writers: Rosenne, H. Lauterpacht, G. Fitzmaurice, Hudson, Oppenheim, Jennings, de Visscher, Brownlie, Watts, and Stone.
- The ten writers who are cited by the highest number of judges: Rosenne, H. Lauterpacht, Oppenheim, Jennings, Hudson, G. Fitzmaurice, de Visscher, Brownlie, Watts, and Waldock. The data are listed in Table 4.2.
- The ten writers being subject to the highest number of 'justifications' (i.e., where judges justify a reference to teachings by emphasising the quality of a work or the expertise or official position of the writer): H. Lauterpacht, Rosenne, Jiménez de Aréchaga, G. Fitzmaurice, Hudson, Jennings, Oppenheim, Huber, and Jenks are the first nine, while the tenth place is shared between Elias, Morelli, Pufendorf, Radbruch, Scelle, and Wolff. The data are shown in Table 4.3.

This shows that while the numerical analyses identify Shabtai Rosenne as the most-cited writer among ICJ judges, the most 'justified' writer is

---

[8] Peil, 'Writings', 160.

[9] Proposed by J E Hirsch, 'An Index to Quantify an Individual's Scientific Research Output' (2005) 102 *Proceedings of the National Academy of Science of the United States of America* 16569.

Table 4.2 *Writers by number of judges citing them*

Writer	Number of judges citing
Rosenne, Shabtai	40
Lauterpacht, Hersch	39
Oppenheim, Lassa	31
Jennings, Robert	25
Hudson, Manley O.	24
Fitzmaurice, Gerald	22
de Visscher, Charles	22
Brownlie, Ian	16
Watts, Arthur	16
Waldock, Humphrey	15

Table 4.3 *Writers by number of 'justifications' of citations*

Writer	Justifications
Lauterpacht, Hersch	23
Rosenne, Shabtai	18
Aréchaga, Eduardo Jiménez de	10
Fitzmaurice, Gerald	9
Hudson, Manley O.	9
Jennings, Robert	8
Oppenheim, Lassa	8
Huber, Max	6
Jenks, C. Wilfred	6
(Multiple writers)	5

Hersch Lauterpacht. None of these statistics say anything final or decisive about who the 'most highly qualified publicists' are, but they do say something about which writers the judges think highly of and prefer to cite. It can also be mentioned that Lauterpacht is cited on, and wrote about, a wider variety of topics than Rosenne, who focused heavily on the procedural law of the ICJ itself. One ICJ judge thus emphasises that 'the work of Rosenne [...] has canonical status on procedural issues'.[10]

---

[10] ICJ Judge 1.

Another ICJ judge explains that Rosenne is the one writer who most closely studied the ICJ's procedure,[11] which makes his writings particularly useful when the Court is dealing with procedural matters. The same judge labels Lauterpacht as a 'thinker' whose works many judges find 'inspiring',[12] which surely adds to his appeal and citation count. If the discussion concerns 'the most highly qualified publicists' in international law generally, rather than in the ICJ specifically, Lauterpacht would seem to be more significant. Who are 'the most highly qualified publicists' should depend on which area of international law one is talking about.

4.2.2   *The Demographics of the Most-Cited Writers*

This section will show that the most-cited writers in individual ICJ opinions comprise a homogeneous group.[13] This is shown through an examination of the nationality and gender of the most-cited writers.[14]

Appendix 1 shows the forty most-cited writers in individual ICJ opinions, and for the top twenty it lists nationality as well as the countries where they were educated and employed. Thirteen of the writers were UK nationals. Two were US nationals, two from France, and one each from Italy and Belgium. Only one was a citizen of a non-Western country, Eduardo Jiménez de Aréchaga of Uruguay, and he has been described as 'close' to Western legal traditions.[15] The numbers for the top twenty writers' countries of education and employment are similar, with the United Kingdom being dominant and Jiménez de Aréchaga being the only non-Western writer. Thus, while the Court itself is relatively heterogeneous in terms of geography and culture,[16] the teachings cited by the judges are less so.

---

[11] ICJ Judge 2.

[12] Ibid.

[13] Jean d'Aspremont, 'Non-State Actors from the Perspective of Legal Positivism: the Communitarian Semantics for the Secondary Rules of International Law', in Jean d'Aspremont (ed.), *Participants in the International Legal System: Multiple Perspectives on Non-State Actors in International Law* (Routledge 2011) 23, 32; Michael Waibel, 'Interpretive Communities in International Law' in Andrea Bianchi, Daniel Peat, and Matthew Windsor (eds.), *Interpretation in International Law* (Oxford University Press 2015) 147, 161.

[14] As in Deborah J Merritt and Melanie Putnam, 'Judges and Scholars: Do Courts and Scholarly Journals Cite the Same Law Review Articles' (1996) 71 *Chicago-Kent Law Review* 871, 895–897.

[15] Cassese, *Five Masters,* ix (and similarly 49–50).

[16] Section 3.9.6.

Eighteen of the twenty most-cited writers are men (all except Rosalyn Higgins and Geneviève Guyomar).[17] The next women on the list of most-cited writers are Dinah Shelton (number 44), Edith Brown Weiss (number 75), and Suzanne Bastid (number 79). Gender diversity among judges is not mandated by the ICJ Statute. As of April 2020, three of the Court's fifteen permanent judges are women (20 per cent). Similar numbers are found in other courts and tribunals.[18]

4.2.3 Explaining the Skewed Demographics of the Most-Cited Judges

The ICJ may be afflicted with a structural or systemic bias.[19] This bias may extend to the judges' choice of teachings. However, the skewed representation of different groups of writers in the teachings cited by the ICJ does not have to be the result of bias among judges. A judge searching for teachings may not even be aware of the nationality or gender of the different authors, even if they cared about it at all. Bias is a possibility, but the numbers cited here do not prove it.

The different rates of citations of Western and non-Western and male and female writers may instead reflect patterns in the teachings that are published, just like, for example, an overrepresentation of male judges can be the result of more men applying for diplomatic jobs.[20] There may simply be more teachings written by male or Western writers. This possibility is raised by an ICJ employee, who 'do[es] not believe that' the relevant 'works have been produced by a diverse range of people'.[21] Different levels of university funding in different countries probably play a role.[22] This point, about where 'the money is', is also made by an ICJ employee.[23] Another important factor is the level of development of each state's legal education system.[24]

---

[17] Black and Richter, 'My Name', 392–393 find the same in the Canadian Supreme Court.

[18] Terris, Romano, and Swigart, *International Judge*, xviii and 18; Nienke Grossman, 'Achieving Sex-Representative International Court Benches' (2016) 110 *American Journal of International Law* 82, 82.

[19] Martti Koskenniemi, *From Apology to Utopia: The Structure of International Legal Argument* (2nd edn, Cambridge University Press 2006) 607; Andrea Bianchi, 'Choice and (the Awareness of) its Consequences: The ICJ's "Structural Bias" Strikes Again in the Marshall Islands Case' (2017) 111 *AJIL Unbound* 81, 84.

[20] Fernando R Tesón, 'Feminism and International Law: A Reply' (1993) 33 *Virginia Journal of International Law* 647, 653.

[21] ICJ Employee 1.

[22] D'Aspremont, 'Wording', 587.

[23] ICJ Employee 1.

[24] Susan D Franck, 'The Diversity Challenge: Exploring the "Invisible College" of International Arbitration' (2015) 53 *Columbia Journal of Transnational Law* 429, 465.

Western teachings may be seen as better because academic freedom allows scholars to take less biased positions than those from certain other states.[25] It is apparently impossible to find a Russian scholar who believes that the 2014 annexation of Crimea was contrary to international law,[26] or a Chinese scholar who believes that the 2016 *South China Sea Arbitration*[27] got anything right.[28] It is not difficult to find a UK scholar who believes that the 2003 Iraq invasion was illegal,[29] or a US scholar who respects the ICJ's *Nicaragua* decision.[30] The uniform views of Russian and Chinese scholars on these issues are apparently enforced by their governments.[31]

Western countries may have more experts on international law,[32] and a disproportionate number of them may be men. This book does not attempt to investigate whether this is true, nor why it may be so.[33] One factor found in Section 4.3.4 to influence the weight of teachings is the official position(s) of the writer. Examples of such positions include international judges (especially in the ICJ), members of the ILC, and government representatives. Official positions such as those of ICJ judge and member of the ILC are relatively well distributed geographically because of formal rules requiring this. Writers from any state can obtain official positions in their

[25] Roberts, *Is International Law International?*, 254 argues that on the *South China Sea* arbitration, '[t]he uniformity of these Chinese opinions works to undermine their credibility'.

[26] Anton Moiseienko, 'Guest Post: What do Russian Lawyers Say about Crimea?', *Opinio Juris* (24 September 2014) http://opiniojuris.org/2014/09/24/guest-post-russian-lawyers-say-crimea/. Similarly, for example, Oleksandr Zadorozhnii, 'To Justify against All Odds: The Annexation of Crimea in 2014 and the Russian Legal Scholarship' (2015) 35 *Polish Yearbook of International Law* 139, 168–169; Maria Issaeva, 'Quarter of a Century on from the Soviet Era: Reflections on Russian Doctrinal Responses to the Annexation of Crimea' (2017) 5 *Russian Law Journal* 86, 87 and 107–108.

[27] PCA, *The South China Sea Arbitration (The Republic of Philippines v. The People's Republic of China)*, Case 2013–19, Award, 12 July 2016.

[28] Julian G Ku, 'China's Legal Scholars Are Less Credible After South China Sea Ruling', *Foreign Policy* (14 July 2016) http://foreignpolicy.com/2016/07/14/south-china-sea-lawyers-unclos-beijing-legal-tribunal. Similarly Roberts, *Is International Law International?*, 240.

[29] The Iraq Inquiry, 'International Law Submissions' (undated) www.iraqinquiry.org.uk/other-material/submissions-international-law/. The report itself did not discuss the legality of the invasion: The Iraq Inquiry, 'Introduction' (6 July 2016) www.iraqinquiry.org.uk/media/247882/the-report-of-the-iraq-inquiry_introduction.pdf, 17.

[30] Ku, 'Scholars', 240.

[31] Roberts, *Is International Law International?*, 231 and 241; Lauri Mälksoo, *Russian Approaches to International Law* (Oxford University Press 2015) 31; Issaeva', 108–111.

[32] For example, Cassese, *Five Masters*, 254.

[33] Grossman, 'Achieving', 84; Nienke Grossman, 'Shattering the Glass Ceiling in International Adjudication' (2016) 56 *Virginia Journal of International Law* 339, 358–363, is sceptical towards a similar explanation for female judges in international courts.

government, although some states will presumably employ a larger share of its population in international law-related jobs, and some states' civil services are more meritocratic than others. Many official positions are generally not required to reflect gender balance, however.

Citations are probably skewed in favour of older writers, since their writings have been available longer and thus in a larger number of cases.[34] While many works will gradually become outdated as the law evolves, parts of certain works can remain relevant for several decades, or even centuries, after publication. Citations should also be skewed towards generalist writers, whose writings will presumably be relevant in a larger number of cases.[35] However, Western writers cannot be assumed to be older or more generalist than others. More citations of older writers *can*, however, explain some of the dominance of male writers, since the dominance of men in international law academia was even greater in the past than it is today. The same pattern affects the representation of women in international courts, where fewer women were judges in the past, which explains why older courts have a smaller share of women among their total number of judges.[36]

The selection of teachings may also be affected by what is available to the judges.[37] No one person can be familiar with all the teachings on international law, and some selection or filtering is inevitable.[38] Western teachings could be preferred by the Court's librarians or clerks or be easier to acquire or consult in the Hague or other cities where the judges spend time. Additionally, judges may be more familiar with certain teachings. This may depend, for example, on the teachings they were instructed to read as students.[39] In that context, it is worth noting that most judges, including the non-Western ones, have studied at Western universities.[40] As shown in Appendix 2, of the 146 judges for whom data are available, only twenty have no education from an OECD member state.

---

[34] Posner, 'Citations Analysis', 10; Duxbury, *Judges*, 16; Gregory Scott Crespi, 'The Influence of Two Decades of Contract Law Scholarship on Judicial Rulings: An Empirical Analysis' (2004) 57 *SMU Law Review* 105, 110–111.

[35] Stanton, 'Scholarship', 204.

[36] Analogously, Grossman, 'Shattering', 390.

[37] Kammerhofer, 'Lawmaking', 323.

[38] Crawford, *Chance*, 153.

[39] Duxbury, *Judges*, 20–21, citing Louis J Sirico Jr and Jeffrey B Margulies, 'The Citing of Law Reviews by the Supreme Court: An Empirical Study (1986) 34 *UCLA Law Review* 131, 133–134. Section 1.3.4 also discusses the influence of teachings on students.

[40] Similarly Prott, *Culture*, 203; Kurt Taylor Gaubatz and Matthew MacArthur, 'How International Is "International" Law?' (2001) 22 *Michigan Journal of International Law* 239, 262; Hernández, *Judicial Function*, 133–134.

The teachings cited in pleadings can also matter.[41] One ICJ judge explains that '[w]here counsel refer to individual works in the pleadings [. . .] they are much more likely to be referred to by judges'.[42] This book has examined pleadings in three ICJ cases. Among the judges' 469 citations of teachings in individual opinions in those cases, 100 (21 per cent) were also cited in pleadings. Conversely, of the teachings cited in the pleadings, 37 per cent were later cited in judges' individual opinions. Among the twenty most-cited writers in the pleadings, four were non-OECD nationals (from Sri Lanka, Argentina, and Uruguay, respectively). A list of the most-cited writers in the pleadings is included in Appendix 6. Thus, overrepresentations in ICJ judges' citations can, to some extent, be a result of similar overrepresentations in pleadings. The selection of teachings in pleadings is in turn governed by what the parties expect to be most influential with the judges.[43] Pleadings may therefore overrepresent certain writers because counsel sees that those writers are already overrepresented in judicial opinions. Similar citation patterns in pleadings and opinions can thus reinforce each other.

Judges' nationality, native language, and even gender seem to play a role in determining the teachings they prefer to cite. This is the conclusion of a closer examination of twenty writers who have been cited in ICJ opinions. It was not possible to do a nationality-based study of *all* the writers who have been cited by ICJ judges, simply because it is often impossible to find reliable information about writers' national backgrounds. Instead, the study focuses on the five most-cited writers from common law English-speaking countries,[44] the five most-cited writers from Romance-language civil law countries,[45] the five most-cited writers from non-OECD countries,[46] and the five most-cited women.[47] This seems to be the most interesting and least crude way to measure the connections between judges' and writers' nationalities that is still realistically possible to perform. Since the geographical distribution of the Court's membership has been quite stable throughout history, all writers will have had the chance

---

[41] Merryman, 'Theory', 414. Cole, 'Non-Binding', 316 argues that arbitrators should seek out teachings beyond the pleadings.

[42] ICJ Judge 1.

[43] Thirlway, *Sources*, 127; (in the context of national law) Earlsferry, 'Judges', 29–30.

[44] Rosenne; Lauterpacht; Fitzmaurice; Hudson; Jennings.

[45] de Visscher; Guyomar; Guillaume; Reuter; Anzilotti.

[46] Jiménez de Aréchaga; Elias; Singh; Bedjaoui; Jesús María Yepes.

[47] Higgins; Guyomar; Shelton; Weiss; Bastid.

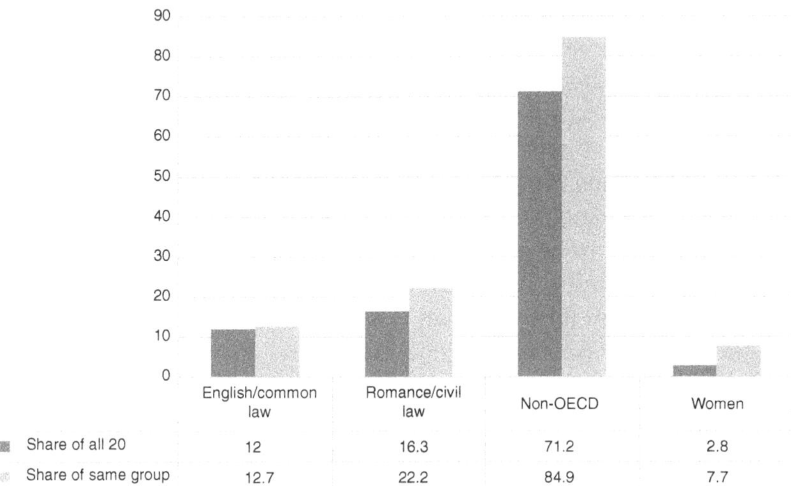

	English/common law	Romance/civil law	Non-OECD	Women
Share of all 20	12	16.3	71.2	2.8
Share of same group	12.7	22.2	84.9	7.7

Figure 4.2   Overrepresentation by groups of judges and writers

to be cited by judges from roughly the same regions, and the study thus treats writers from different eras in the same way.

The result of the study is that judges cite teachings in their own language and from their own culture somewhat more often than they cite other teachings. More specifically, judges from majority English-speaking common law countries made 12 per cent of references to all of the twenty writers, and 12.7 per cent to the five writers from majority English-speaking common law countries. A stronger link can be observed for the five Romance-speaking civil law writers. Judges from Romance-language civil law countries made 16.3 per cent of references to all the twenty writers, and 22.2 per cent of references to the five Romance-speaking civil law writers. Similar results are seen for non-OECD and female judges. Judges from non-OECD countries made 71.2 per cent of references to all twenty writers, but 84.9 per cent of references to the five non-OECD writers. Female judges made 2.8 per cent of references to all twenty writers, but 7.7 per cent of references to female writers.

The numbers are summarised in Figure 4.2, with overrepresentation presented in terms of percentages, within a clustered column chart. The differences between the black and grey bars show the overrepresentation for each group.

Thus, all four groups of writers are to some extent overrepresented in terms of how often they are cited by judges from the same group. The overrepresentation is smallest for English-speaking common law lawyers and largest for women.

Overrepresentation can signify different things. It is intuitively plausible that English-language teachings are more familiar and accessible to an English-speaking judge and vice versa with other languages. Perhaps the greater overrepresentation between Romance-language judges and writers compared with English-language judges and writers can be explained by knowledge of English being more widespread (meaning that those who can read French can also read English more than those who can read English also can read French).[48] Judges may also find perspectives and views that they more readily understand and agree with in teachings that are written by writers from their own group.[49]

Of the twenty most-cited writers, ten are originally from the United Kingdom, two from the United States, and two from France. Thus, twelve out of twenty writers (or 60 per cent) can be presumed to be native English speakers. A further three (15 per cent) are native French speakers.[50] Since English is the dominant international law language,[51] and French and English are the official languages of the Court,[52] it is fair to assume that more judges can read them than can read most other languages. This is probably one reason why the judges cite many English-speaking and some French-speaking writers.[53] This can in turn explain some of the dominance of Western writers in ICJ opinions, since English and French are Western languages. Thus, generally, the role of language in international law and in the ICJ does, to some extent, explain why the ICJ's citations of teachings are skewed in favour of Western writers.

This does not fully explain the preponderance of British writers over other English- and French-speaking writers, though. The overrepresentation of British writers may also, for example, be a result of a British tradition of writing general textbooks, which are popular with courts, and from many non-British judges having studied in Britain or lived under British rule.

---

[48] Mackenzie and others, *Selecting*, 44.

[49] Roberts, *Is International Law International?*, 46.

[50] Similarly for the ICTY: Bohlander, 'Influence', 197.

[51] Parry, *Sources*, 108; Roberts, *Is International Law International?*, 47 and 260–267.

[52] ICJ Statute Article 39(1) .

[53] Similarly for the ICTY: Michael Bohlander and Mark Findlay, 'The Use of Domestic Sources as a Basis for International Criminal Law Principles' (2002) 2 *The Global Community Yearbook of International Law and Jurisprudence* 3, 6.

Furthermore, non-native English writers can, and do, write in English. Among the top twenty most-cited writers, Hersch Lauterpacht grew up in a Yiddish-speaking home in a then-Polish-speaking city (Lviv), studied in a German-speaking city (Vienna), and subsequently moved to the United Kingdom and wrote in English. Lassa Oppenheim was born and studied in Germany but wrote in English after moving to the United Kingdom. The same story is true for Georg Schwarzenberger. Eduardo Jiménez de Aréchaga was a native Spanish speaker, but mostly wrote in English. Edvard Hambro was Norwegian but wrote his most significant international law works in English. This shows that non-native English speakers can write in English, even though they may do so less often or less successfully than native speakers. It is more difficult to write well in a non-native language, especially if that language is radically different from one's native language. One can compare, for example, English and Mandarin, which are more different than English and German. Non-native speakers may refrain from writing in English or French because of personal preferences or convictions, or because of institutional incentives. Roberts reports that French, Chinese, and Russian scholars largely publish in their own language (88, 90, and 98 per cent, respectively).[54] She explains that French scholars have strong institutional incentives to publish in French, whereas the Chinese and Russians have more mixed incentives, but many of them lack English language skills and exposure to English legal thinking.[55] Because non-native speakers can, in principle, write in English (or French), the judges' preference for English (and French) teachings may not be all that problematic. As long as all judges can read English or French, and English is the dominant international law language, non-Western writers who wish to influence the ICJ should be encouraged to write in those languages. That being said, there are problems involved in encouraging everyone to write in English. While it does ease cross-border communication, it poses risks to the intellectual diversity and global acceptability of international law.[56]

The conclusion is that the citation of teachings in ICJ judges' opinions is probably to a large extent determined by familiarity, availability, and relevance. Section 6.2.2 discusses potential benefits from diversifying its range of writers who are cited. These benefits could apply regardless of the causes of the current patterns.

---

[54] Roberts, *Is International Law International?*, 92–96.
[55] Ibid., 93–97 and 266–267.
[56] Ibid., 264–269.

4.3   Variations by Substance: Factors That Influence the Weight of Teachings

4.3.1   Introduction

This section identifies factors that influence the weight of teachings. These discussions are mainly based on apparent attempts by judges to 'justify' references to teachings, by highlighting the quality of a work, the expertise of a writer, the official authority of a writer, agreement among multiple writers, and diversity between agreeing writers.

Some judges do not justify any of their references to teachings. Those who do, however, do not justify *all* of their references. There are examples of opinions where some references are justified while others are not, and even footnotes where only some references are justified. One reason for this is that a single justification may apply to multiple references. For example, in *Bosnia Genocide,* Judge ad hoc Kreća referred to teachings by William A. Schabas multiple times, but called Schabas 'the learned author' only once.[57] However, a judge may also justify one reference because they perceive the work in question to have less weight than other works that are cited (without being justified). For example, it is interesting that Judge ad hoc Pirzada in the *Aerial Incident of 10 August 1999* case justified his reference to R. P. Anand by calling him a 'well-known Indian writer',[58] but did not justify references to Ian Brownlie or Shabtai Rosenne. The latter two are among the most-cited writers among ICJ judges, and Judge ad hoc Pirzada may have felt that it was necessary to justify including Anand in the same context. On the other hand, a judge may justify one reference to show that it has a greater significance than other references. An example could be Judge ad hoc Van den Wyngaert in the *Arrest Warrant* case, who referred to one work as 'very thorough' and the rest as 'other'.[59] In any of these cases, the implication seems to be that different teachings have different levels of weight.

It is possible to compare how often each type of justification is made. This gives an indication of the relative importance of each factor. The quality of works and expertise of writers are the most common types of justifications, with 198 mentions of quality and 190 of expertise. The official positions of writers were mentioned 107 times, while agreement between writers was mentioned 32 times. This may mean that expertise

---

[57] *Bosnia Genocide, 2007,* Separate Opinion of Judge ad hoc Kreća 542.
[58] *Aerial Incident of 10 August 1999,* Dissenting Opinion of Judge ad hoc Pirzada 95–96.
[59] *Arrest Warrant, 2002,* Dissenting Opinion of Judge ad hoc Van den Wyngaert 166.

and quality are the most important factors. However, one ICJ employee similarly says that at the ICJ, *who* proposes an idea is not typically important or dispositive, what matters is whether an idea is good.[60] The employee makes exceptions for certain writers in certain areas of international law and mentions Rosenne on the Court's procedural law as a specific example.[61] While the purely quantitative analysis done in this paragraph suggests that expertise and quality are equally important in practice, that does not finally settle the matter. It is not possible to know precisely how important each judge considers the two factors (to the extent they even have a clear view on the matter). The most plausible view is that this varies from judge to judge.

4.3.2   Expertise

This section argues that judges give more weight to writers whom they consider experts.[62] This is indicated by judges' practice of justifying references to teachings by emphasising the expertise of the writer.[63] For example, judges have used terms that reflect the general competence of writers, calling them 'expert',[64] 'learned',[65] 'distinguished',[66] and a variety of similar terms. Judges have also used terms that apparently focus on other actors' perceptions of the writers, such as 'well-known',[67]

---

[60] ICJ Employee 2. ILC, *Report of the Sixty-eighth session,* 111 and Sivakumaran, 'Influence', 12 agree.

[61] ICJ Employee 2.

[62] That expertise affects weight is generally assumed by, for example, Lauterpacht, *Development,* 24; Oppenheim, 'Science', 345; ILC, *Report of the Sixty-eighth session,* 111.

[63] Sivakumaran, 'Influence', 11.

[64] For example, *Temple Interpretation, 2013,* Separate Opinion of Judge Cançado Trindade 339–340; *TimorLeste v. Australia, 2014,* Separate Opinion of Judge Cançado Trindade 174, and many other opinions by Judge Cançado Trindade.

[65] For example, *Nauru,* Separate Opinion of Judge Shahabuddeen 289; *Application of the International Convention on the Elimination of All Forms of Racial Discrimination (Georgia v. Russian Federation), Preliminary Objections, Judgment, I.C.J. Reports 2011,* p. 70, Dissenting Opinion of Judge Cançado Trindade 288; *Croatia Genocide, 2015,* Separate Opinion of Judge Owada 169.

[66] For example, *Fisheries case,* Dissenting Opinion of Sir Arnold McNair 182; *Fisheries Jurisdiction (Spain v. Canada), Jurisdiction of the Court, Judgment, I.C.J. Reports 1998,* p. 432, Dissenting Opinion of Vice-President Weeramantry 504; *Aerial Incident of 10 August 1999,* Dissenting Opinion of Judge ad hoc Pirzada 91.

[67] For example, *North Sea,* Dissenting Opinion of Vice-President Koretsky 157; *Libyan Arab Jamahiriya/Malta, 1984,* Dissenting Opinion of Vice-president Sette-Camara 87; *Aerial Incident of 10 August 1999,* Dissenting Opinion of Judge ad hoc Pirzada 95–96.

'famous',[68] and 'influential',[69] and other similar terms. Some statements highlight the consistent quality of an author's works, such as 'characteristically thoughtful',[70] 'characteristically thorough',[71] and 'characteristic cogency'.[72] That is another way of saying that the author is an expert. Yet another writer was praised for having 'so often and so brilliantly contributed to the cause of international law and justice'.[73] Some statements draw more historical lines. Judge Trindade often discusses the 'founding fathers' of international law.[74] Among them is 'Grotius himself',[75] as referred to by Judge Weeramantry. Weeramantry has also (and similarly) referred to 'fountainheads of international law'.[76] Some judges have designated writers, works, or institutions as being or having 'authority',[77] being 'authoritative',[78] and similar terms. Further praise has focused on more specific competence. One writer was called 'a keen observer of the origins and evolution of Pan-African organizations, and an advocate of an "*uti possidetis* africain"',[79] another 'one of the forerunners of the international protection of human rights',[80] yet others the 'first writer

---

[68] *Corfu Channel*, Dissenting Opinion by Judge Krylov 72.

[69] *Bosnia Genocide, 1993*, Separate Opinion of Vice-President Weeramantry 378.

[70] *Namibia*, Separate Opinion of Judge Dillard 168.

[71] *Fisheries Jurisdiction (United Kingdom v. Iceland)*, Separate Opinion of Judge Dillard 68.

[72] *Military and Paramilitary Activities in and against Nicaragua (Nicaragua v. United States of America), Provisional Measures, Order of 10 May 1984, I.C.J. Reports 1984*, p. 169, Dissenting Opinion of Judge Schwebel 197–198.

[73] *South West Africa, Second Phase*, Dissenting Opinion of Judge Jessup 325–326 (also cited by *Nicaragua, 1986*, Dissenting Opinion of Judge Schwebel 267–268).

[74] For example, *Kosovo*, Separate Opinion of Judge Cançado Trindade 552–553; *Jurisdictional Immunities of the State (Germany v. Italy), Application for Permission to Intervene, Order of 4 July 2011, I.C.J. Reports 2011*, p. 494, Separate Opinion of Judge Cançado Trindade 515–516; *Judgment No. 2867 of the Administrative Tribunal of the International Labour Organization upon a Complaint Filed against the International Fund for Agricultural Development, Advisory Opinion, I.C.J. Reports 2012*, p. 10, Separate Opinion of Judge Cançado Trindade 71 and 73.

[75] *Land and Maritime Boundary, 1998*, Dissenting Opinion of Vice-President Weeramantry 372–373.

[76] *Jan Mayen*, Separate Opinion of Judge Weeramantry 239.

[77] For example, *Guardianship of Infants*, Separate Opinion of Judge Sir Hersch Lauterpacht 96; *Namibia*, Dissenting Opinion of Judge Gerald Fitzmaurice 303; *Nicaragua, 1986*, Dissenting Opinion of Judge Schwebel 313.

[78] *Aerial Incident of 3 July 1988*, Separate Opinion by Judge Schwebel 137; *Legality of Use of Force*, Dissenting Opinion of Vice-President Weeramantry 191–192; *Arrest Warrant, 2002*, Joint Separate Opinion of Judges Higgins, Kooijmans and Buergenthal 72.

[79] *Frontier Dispute (Burkina Faso/Niger), Judgment, I.C.J. Reports 2013*, p. 44, Separate Opinion of Judge Yusuf 136.

[80] *Georgia v. Russian Federation*, Dissenting Opinion of Judge Cançado Trindade 306.

on intervention before the PCIJ',[81] 'one of the foremost experts on the international law of procedure',[82] an 'expert on the law of civil procedure',[83] 'the leading author on genocide',[84] 'the most learned commentator on the Court's procedure',[85] 'a most authoritative commentator of the Statute',[86] 'one of the deepest researchers into judicial reasoning in our time',[87] '[a] well-known writer, devoted to problems related to the International Court of Justice',[88] someone who 'studied Article 63 intensively in a number of published papers',[89] and many similar designations.

A single reference to a writer being 'most qualified' is the only one that mirrors the wording of the ICJ Statute Article 38(1)(d).[90] However, the terms mentioned here all generally seem to express the same sentiment that was inferred from the ICJ Statute in Section 2.2.6, that some writers are more 'highly qualified' than others and that this affects the weight of their teachings.

Writers have also been singled out for being 'one of the directors of [Revista peruana de Derecho internacional]'[91] and 'Secretary of the Institute of International Law'.[92] The point seems to be that these positions imply and require a certain expertise. Along with the reference to the 'Secretary of the Institute of International Law', the Institute was said to have 'had a substantial share in the preparation of the first drafts of the Convention' that was discussed.[93] This means that the expertise was not just on a general level, but related specifically to the legal instrument that was at issue in the case.

---

[81] *Sovereignty over Pulau Ligitan und Pulau Sipadan (Indonesia/Malaysia), Application for Permission to Intervene, Judgment, I.C.J. Reports 2001*, p. 575, Separate Opinion of Judge ad hoc Weeramantry 647.

[82] *Libyan Arab Jamahiriya/Malta, 1984*, Separate Opinion of Judge Jiménez de Aréchaga 57.

[83] Ibid., 67–68.

[84] *Bosnia Genocide, 2007*, Separate Opinion of Judge Tomka 347.

[85] *Bosnia Genocide, 1997*, Separate Opinion of Judge ad hoc Lauterpacht 279.

[86] *Aerial Incident of July 27th, 1955*, Joint Dissenting Opinion by Judges Sir Hersch Lauterpacht, Wellington Koo and Sir Percy Spender 174.

[87] *Nuclear Tests (New Zealand) Examination*, Dissenting opinion by Judge Weeramantry 359–360.

[88] *Libyan Arab Jamahiriya/Malta, 1984*, Dissenting Opinion of Vice-president Sette-Camara 87.

[89] *Nicaragua, Jurisdiction and Admissibility 1984*, Dissenting Opinion of Judge Schwebel 236.

[90] *Nuclear Tests (Australia)*, Dissenting Opinion of Judge de Castro 381.

[91] *Asylum*, Dissenting Opinion by Judge Azevedo 344.

[92] *Guardianship of Infants*, Separate Opinion of Judge Sir Hersch Lauterpacht 84.

[93] Ibid.

According to one ICJ employee, one proxy of expertise is whether a writer works at a good university.[94] The judges' opinions do not reveal whether they use this proxy, but it seems plausible.

The IDI as such has also been the subject of praise.[95] It has been called 'authoritative'[96] and 'learned'[97] (alongside the ILA). Judge Weeramantry in *Nuclear Weapons* noted that an IDI resolution was supported by 'an illustrious list of the most eminent international lawyers of the time'.[98] The implication was that even though the IDI as an institution has a certain authority, the expertise of the specific individuals who are at any time involved in its work affects the weight of that work.

In the PCIJ, terms and phrases that hint at the expertise of writers include 'an eminent authority on international law',[99] 'the best known authors' and 'writers of the highest authority',[100] and 'learned writers'.[101]

4.3.3   Quality

Judges justify some citations of teachings by saying something about the quality of the specific work.[102] Various terms have been used.

Some terms relate to qualities of the text itself, such as 'clear' and 'clearly',[103] 'objective',[104] 'comprehensive',[105] and various others.

---

[94] ICJ Employee 3. D'Aspremont, 'Wording', 582 agrees.

[95] For example, *Nuclear Weapons*, Dissenting Opinion of Judge Weeramantry 500 and 518–519; *Arrest Warrant, 2002*, Dissenting Opinion of Judge ad hoc Van den Wyngaert 162–163.

[96] *Namibia*, Separate Opinion of Judge Dillard 162–163.

[97] *Jurisdictional Immunities, 2012*, Dissenting Opinion of Judge Cançado Trindade 194 and 197.

[98] *Nuclear Weapons*, Dissenting Opinion of Judge Weeramantry 508.

[99] *Lotus*, Dissenting Opinion by M. Moore 91–92.

[100] *Brazilian Loans*, Dissenting Opinion by M. de Bustamante 133.

[101] *Lighthouses Case between France and Greece, Judgment 17 March 1934, P.C.I.J. Series A/B No. 62*, p. 4, Separate Opinion by M. Séfériadès 50.

[102] The assumption that quality is affected by weight is shared by, for example, Oppenheim, 'Science', 345; Andrew Clapham, *Brierly's Law of Nations: An Introduction to the Role of International Law in International Relations* (7th edn, Oxford University Press 2012) 67; ILC, *Report of the Sixty-eighth session*, 111.

[103] *Barcelona Traction, 1970*, Separate Opinion of Judge Jessup 192; *Border and Transborder Armed Actions*, Separate Opinion of Judge Shahabuddeen 149–150.

[104] *Fisheries Jurisdiction (United Kingdom v. Iceland)*, Separate Opinion of Judge de Castro 80.

[105] *North Sea*, Dissenting Opinion of Judge Sorensen 242; *Jan Mayen*, Separate Opinion of Judge Weeramantry 233.

Other authors have been said to write 'with insight',[106] 'foresight',[107] and 'admirable clarity'.[108] Other terms focus specifically on the judges' use of the teachings, such as 'useful',[109] 'valuable',[110] 'helpful',[111] and various others. Yet other terms are about other actors' perceptions of the teachings. These include, among others, 'generally accepted',[112] 'celebrated',[113] and 'influential'.[114] The terms 'standard'[115] and 'leading'[116] may also be taken as attributes that are shaped by the perceptions of other actors: What is a standard or leading work in a field depends on the views of the actors in that field. Some terms denote inherent qualities of works. These include 'authoritative',[117]

[106] *Prosecute or Extradite*, Dissenting Opinion of Judge Cançado Trindade 196; *Certain Activities Carried Out by Nicaragua in the Border Area (Costa Rica v. Nicaragua); Construction of a Road in Costa Rica along the San Juan River (Nicaragua v. Costa Rica), Provisional Measures, Order of 22 November 2013, I.C.J. Reports 2013*, p. 354, Separate Opinion of Judge Cançado Trindade 380; *Questions relating to the Seizure and Detention of Certain Documents and Data (Timor-Leste v. Australia), Request for the Modification of the Order Indicating Provisional Measures of 3 March 2014, Order of 22 April 2015, I.C.J. Reports 2015*, p. 556, Separate Opinion of Judge Cançado Trindade 2.

[107] *Jurisdictional Immunities, 2010*, Dissenting Opinion of Judge Cançado Trindade 336–337.

[108] *Judgement No. 158*, Separate Opinion of Judge Dillard 237.

[109] *Bosnia Genocide, 1993*, Separate Opinion of Judge Shahabuddeen 368; *Territorial and Maritime Dispute (Nicaragua v. Colombia), Judgment, I.C.J. Reports 2012*, p. 624, Declaration of Judge Keith 743.

[110] *Application for Revision of the Judgment of 11 July 1996 in the Case concerning Application of the Convention on the Prevention and Punishment of the Crime of Genocide (Bosnia and Herzegovina v. Yugoslavia), Preliminary Objections (Yugoslavia v. Bosnia and Herzegovina), Judgment, I.C.J. Reports 2003*, p. 7, Separate Opinion of Judge ad hoc Mahiou 70.

[111] *Aerial Incident of 3 July 1988*, Separate Opinion by Judge Shahabuddeen 157.

[112] *Aegean Sea*, Dissenting Opinion of Judge de Castro 69.

[113] For example, *Certain expenses of the United Nations (Article 17, paragraph 2, of the Charter), Advisory Opinion of 20 July 1962, I.C.J. Reports 1962*, p. 151, Dissenting Opinion of President Winiarski 229; *Nuclear Weapons*, Dissenting Opinion of Judge Weeramantry 520–521; *Jurisdictional Immunities, 2011*, Separate Opinion of Judge Cançado Trindade 522.

[114] *Tunisia/Libyan Arab Jamahiriya*, Dissenting Opinion of Judge Oda 199; *Pedra Branca/ Pulau Batu Puteh*, Separate Opinion of Judge ad hoc Sreenivasa Rao 168.

[115] *Barcelona Traction, 1970*, Separate Opinion of Judge Sir Gerald Fitzmaurice 85; *Arbitral Award of 31 July 1989*, Dissenting Opinion of Judge Weeramantry 167; *Jan Mayen*, Separate Opinion of Judge Weeramantry 240.

[116] For example, *Case of Certain Norwegian Loans, Judgment of July 6th, 1957: I.C.J. Reports 1957*, p. 9, Separate Opinion of Judge Sir Hersch Lauterpacht 49 and 50; *Land, Island and Maritime Frontier Dispute, 1992*, Dissenting Opinion of Judge Oda 737; *Aerial Incident of 10 August 1999*, Dissenting Opinion of Judge ad hoc Pirzada 65.

[117] *Application of the Convention on the Prevention and Punishment of the Crime of Genocide, Preliminary Objections, Judgment, I.C.J. Reports 1996*, p. 595, Joint

'one of the best',[118] 'classic',[119] and many others. The adjective 'well' is also used in various contexts, as in 'well described' and the like.[120] Similar phrases are 'fittingly summarizes'[121] and 'convenient summary'.[122]

Other works have been labelled 'characteristically thoughtful'[123] and 'characteristically thorough'.[124] In other works a 'characteristic thoroughness'[125] and 'characteristic cogency'[126] has been noted. One writer was said to have drawn conclusions 'not without reasons'.[127] The IDI has been said to have been 'preside[d] [over] with such distinction'.[128] One writer's observations were 'useful to note'.[129] Another writer was part of a 'predominant legal theory',[130] while yet another's work contained some of 'the insights of modern analytical jurisprudence'.[131] One judge referred to '*De Jure Belli ac Pacis* itself',[132] apparently implying that this work has a special status. One work had 'never been surpassed'.[133] Other writings were 'without any exaggeration

> Declaration of Judge Shi and Judge Vereshchetin 631; *LaGrand (Germany v. United States of America), Provisional Measures, Order of 3 March 1999, I.C.J. Reports 1999*, p. 9, Separate Opinion of President Schwebel 21–22; *Arrest Warrant, 2002*, Joint Separate Opinion of Judges Higgins, Kooijmans and Buergenthal 72.

[118] *Croatia Genocide, 2015*, Dissenting Opinion of Judge ad hoc Vukas 447.

[119] For example, *Nicaragua, 1986*, Separate Opinion of Judge Sir Robert Jennings 546; *Land, Island and Maritime Frontier Dispute, 1992*, Dissenting Opinion of Judge Oda 747; *Armed Activities on the Territory of the Congo (Democratic Republic of the Congo v. Uganda), Order of 11 April 2016, I.C.J. Reports 2016*, p. 222, Declaration of Judge Cançado Trindade 227.

[120] For example, *Tunisia/Libyan Arab Jamahiriya*, Separate Opinion of Judge Ago 97; *Nicaragua, Jurisdiction and Admissibility 1984*, Separate Opinion of Judge Sir Robert Jennings 547–548; *Land and Maritime Boundary between Cameroon and Nigeria, Provisional Measures, Order of 15 March 1996, I.C.J. Reports 1996*, p. 13, Separate Opinion by Judge Ajibola 45.

[121] *Jan Mayen*, Separate Opinion of Judge Weeramantry 237.

[122] *Barcelona Traction, 1970*, Separate Opinion of Judge Jessup 204.

[123] *Namibia*, Separate Opinion of Judge Dillard 168.

[124] *Fisheries Jurisdiction (United Kingdom v. Iceland)*, Separate Opinion of Judge Dillard 68.

[125] *Judgement No. 158*, Separate Opinion of Judge Dillard 237.

[126] *Nicaragua, Provisional Measures 1984*, Dissenting Opinion of Judge Schwebel 197–198.

[127] *Arrest Warrant, 2002*, Dissenting Opinion of Judge ad hoc Van den Wyngaert 169.

[128] *Nuclear Weapons*, Dissenting Opinion of Judge Weeramantry 518–519.

[129] Ibid., 543.

[130] *Nuclear Weapons*, Dissenting Opinion of Vice-President Schwebel 322–323.

[131] *Arbitral Award of 31 July 1989*, Dissenting Opinion of Judge Weeramantry 163.

[132] *Land and Maritime Boundary, 1998*, Dissenting Opinion of Vice-President Weeramantry 372–373.

[133] *Nicaragua, 1986*, Dissenting Opinion of Judge Schwebel 285–286.

whatever'.[134] Yet another work 'better described' the law.[135] Other works have been called 'the most exhaustive treatise on the subject'[136] and 'respectable authority'.[137] One work was said to have 'persuasive force'.[138] In another case there was 'not better' writing on a subject than the teachings that were cited.[139] Another opinion cited 'a unique systematic work'.[140] One judge argued that 'a court of law need not look beyond the words of Charles de Visscher'.[141]

In the PCIJ, Vogt in *Eastern Greenland* cites a work where the 'subject' under discussion 'has been fully dealt with'.[142]

Some justifications straddle the line between referring to the author (as described in Section 6.3.2) and the work itself (as described in this section). For example, Judge Schwebel in the *Nicaragua* case referred to an 'authoritative' interpretation (which is about the work), but did so in connection with mentioning that the author was a former legal director of the OAS.[143] The joint separate opinion of Judges Higgins, Kooijmans and Buergenthal in the *Arrest Warrant* case referred to 'the authoritative Pictet commentary'.[144] This is a reference to the work, but its author was employed by the ICRC, which also published the text and which plays a significant role in the field of international humanitarian law. These references should be seen as belonging to both categories, illustrating that both quality and expertise are important to the weight of teachings.

That works of high quality have more weight also means that works of low quality have less. An example of a judge pointing to the low quality of specific teachings is found in the opinion by Judge Oda in *Land, Island and Maritime Frontier Dispute*. He noted that while scholars were unanimous, this had 'little [. . .] value' because their conclusions were based on a single decision of the PCA, which they, according to Oda, had read too much into.[145]

---

[134] *Anglo-Iranian Oil Co.*, Dissenting Opinion of Judge Levi Carneiro 167.

[135] *Jan Mayen*, Separate Opinion of Judge Ajibola 287.

[136] *Voting Procedure*, Separate Opinion of Judge Lauterpacht 104.

[137] *Barcelona Traction, 1970*, Separate Opinion of Judge Jessup 183.

[138] *Guardianship of Infants*, Separate Opinion of Sir Percy Spender 124–125.

[139] *Asylum*, Dissenting Opinion by M. Caicedo Castilla 364.

[140] *Croatia Genocide, 2015*, Separate Opinion of Judge ad hoc Kreća 495.

[141] *Arbitral Award of 31 July 1989*, Separate Opinion of Judge Shahabuddeen 119.

[142] *Legal Status of Eastern Greenland, Judgment 5 April 1933, P.C.I.J. Series A/B No. 53*, p. 22, Dissenting Opinion by M. Vogt 108.

[143] *Nicaragua, 1986*, Dissenting Opinion of Judge Schwebel 388.

[144] *Arrest Warrant, 2002*, Joint Separate Opinion of Judges Higgins, Kooijmans and Buergenthal 72.

[145] *Land, Island and Maritime Frontier Dispute, 1992*, Dissenting Opinion of Judge Oda 748.

The 'relevance' of teachings has been emphasised by judges.[146] However, relevance is a not an appropriate factor for determining the weight of teachings; it is instead significant when deciding whether it is useful to consult and cite them in the first place. The same goes for age.[147] Age in this sense is already covered by 'relevance', since older works will grow less relevant as the law changes.

As noted in Section 4.2.1, Rosenne is the most-cited author in the ICJ. One judge explains why Rosenne's book on *The Law and Practice of the International Court* is popular with the judges: The book 'records the Court's practice in a fairly open way, it does not insist on its point of view much'.[148] This illustrates a more general point, which is that judges may prefer works that are objective and stick to *lex lata* discussions, as opposed to straying into *lex ferenda* territory.[149]

One ICJ employee mentions how the reputation of the journal in which an article is published can be used as a proxy for the quality of the article.[150] This assumption is plausible, but the ICJ opinions do not reveal whether ICJ judges hold it.

4.3.4 *Official Positions*

According to ICJ opinions, the official position of a writer seems to affect the weight of their teachings.[151] Many of the most-cited writers in the ICJ are themselves ICJ judges or have held other official positions, for example, as government legal advisers or counsel. Among the ten most-cited writers, five were judges of the PCIJ and ICJ: Hersch Lauterpacht, Gerald Fitzmaurice, Manley O. Hudson, Robert Jennings, and Charles de Visscher. Watts was a government legal adviser, and

---

[146] For example *Armed Activities on the Territory of the Congo (New Application: 2002) (Democratic Republic of the Congo v. Rwanda), Provisional Measures, Order of 10 July 2002, I.C.J. Reports 2002*, p. 219, Declaration by Judge Elaraby 262. Oraison, 'L'Influence', 228 that this is a relevant factor in determining quality.

[147] Which is mentioned in Oraison, 'L'Influence', 228 and Hall, *International Law*, 59–60 as a relevant factor in determining quality.

[148] ICJ Judge 1.

[149] For example, ILC, *Third report*, 45; ILC, *Report of the Sixty-eighth session*, 111; US Supreme Court, *The Paquete Habana* 175 US 677 (1900), 700; English High Court of Justice, *West Rand Central Gold Mining Co. v. R* [1905] 2 KB 391, 402.

[150] ICJ employee 3. D'Aspremont, 'Wording', 582 agrees.

[151] This assumption is shared by, for example, Hall, *International Law*, 60; Clapham, *Brierly's*, 67; Wolfke, *Custom*, 156.

Rosenne was an ambassador. This is an indication that the official position of the writer affects the weight accorded to their teachings.

Judges have, moreover, justified their references to teachings by mentioning some official position held by the author. In ICJ opinions, there are many references to a writer being either a 'Judge'[152] or 'President'[153] of the ICJ itself. Having been a 'Judge'[154] or 'President'[155] of the PCIJ has also been mentioned (as has as membership of 'both courts'[156]). A 'President of the Arbitral Tribunal of Upper Silesia' has been cited,[157] and one writer was described generally as an 'international judge'.[158] Some opinions have referred to judges 'writing extra-judicially',[159] 'out of court',[160] and 'in another context'[161] (than as a judge). One possible interpretation of this is that the writer also being a judge gave the teachings added weight.

These references may have had varying motivations. The argument here is that the primary motivations are the writer's special insights, general expertise, and acceptability to states: Having an official position of the kind discussed here usually means being involved in the creation and application of international law, which gives a special insight into the rules in question.[162] Those who are appointed or elected to such positions must generally possess significant expertise in international law in order

---

[152] For example, *Temple*, Separate Opinion of Sir Gerald Fitzmaurice 64–65; *North Sea*, Dissenting Opinion of Vice-President Koretsky 160; *Libyan Arab Jamahiriya/Malta, 1984*, Dissenting Opinion of Judge Ago 115–116.

[153] For example, *East Timor*, Dissenting Opinion of Judge Skubiszewski 266; *Nuclear Weapons*, Dissenting Opinion of Judge Higgins 592; *Pulp Mills*, Joint Dissenting Opinion Judges Al-Khasawneh and Simma 114.

[154] For example, *Admission of a State to the UN*, Dissenting Opinion by M. Krylov 109; *Corfu Channel*, Dissenting Opinion by Judge Azevedo 100; *Aerial Incident of July 27th, 1955*, Joint Dissenting Opinion by Judges Sir Hersch Lauterpacht, Wellington Koo and Sir Percy Spender 174.

[155] *Corfu Channel*, Dissenting Opinion by Judge Winiarski 53; *Georgia v. Russian Federation*, Dissenting Opinion of Judge Cançado Trindade 259.

[156] *Oil Platforms (Islamic Republic of Iran v. United States of America), Counter-Claim, Order of 10 March 1998, I.C.J. Reports 1998*, p. 190, Dissenting Opinion by Judge ad hoc Rigaux 229.

[157] *South West Africa, Second Phase*, Dissenting Opinion of Judge Jessup 434–435.

[158] For example, *Marshall Islands v. United Kingdom*, Separate Opinion of Judge Tomka 10.

[159] *Jan Mayen*, Separate Opinion of Judge Weeramantry 236; *Fisheries Jurisdiction (Spain v. Canada)*, Dissenting Opinion of Vice-President Weeramantry 504.

[160] *Land, Island and Maritime Frontier Dispute, Order 1990*, Dissenting Opinion of Judge Shahabuddeen 21.

[161] *Nuclear Weapons*, Dissenting Opinion of Judge Koroma 563.

[162] Pellet, 'Article 38', 869 considers this significant, but as argued here it cannot be considered the main explanation of the extra weight given to teachings written by judges.

to be considered in the first place. Appointments and elections are often made by states. Being appointed or elected will therefore usually imply that one's views on and approach to international law is found acceptable by at least one state.

Some references included the nationality of the author and judge, in cases where that country or region was involved in the case (one reference was to Canada[163] and another to Latin America[164]). This may be because those writers are seen as having a special relevance to the case. A similar example is the reference to writings by 'a former President of the Court himself',[165] when the legal question under discussion concerned the meaning of the ICJ statute. Most of the presidents and judges are designated as 'former'. Some references instead refer to the writings of someone who only later became a judge at the Court: One writer was 'now' a judge of the International Court of Justice',[166] two others were 'later' a member and vice-president of the Court, respectively,[167] while one was 'shortly to become' an ICJ judge.[168] In those cases, special insight gained from the position at the Court could not be the motivation for the reference. Rather their later election or appointment to the Court should be seen as a proxy for their expertise and their acceptability to states.

In the cases mentioned here, there are more references to presidents (seventeen) of the ICJ as there are to regular judges (twelve). This despite there being fourteen times as many judges as presidents on the Court at any time. Regardless of the fact that all presidents have also been judges and that the average tenure as president is shorter than that of a judge, there are more former judges than former presidents of the ICJ. This discrepancy may be caused by the assumption that the position of president requires more personal competence, gives a greater insight into the work of the Court, and represents a greater degree of trust from states. Having been president thus carries more weight, amplifying the incentive to emphasise it when citing teachings. This point can be generalised, in that the added weight of an official position correlates with how difficult the position is to achieve.[169]

---

[163] *Fisheries Jurisdiction (Spain v. Canada)*, Dissenting Opinion of Judge Torres-Bernárdez, Judge ad hoc 656.

[164] *Obligation to Negotiate Access to the Pacific Ocean*, Separate Opinion of Judge Cançado Trindade 6.

[165] *Judgment No. 2867*, Separate Opinion of Judge Cançado Trindade 80.

[166] *Aerial Incident of 10 August 1999*, Dissenting Opinion of Judge ad hoc Pirzada 105.

[167] *Libyan Arab Jamahiriya/Malta, 1984*, Dissenting Opinion of Judge Schwebel 141; *Gabčikovo*, Separate Opinion of Vice-President Weeramantry 91.

[168] *Nicaragua, 1986*, Dissenting Opinion of Judge Schwebel 394.

[169] Waibel, 'Communities', 156.

Judges citing teachings have also mentioned that writers have been 'Registrars' of the ICJ.[170] This position has some of the same features as that of judge, in that it may denote insight into the work of the Court, personal competence, and proximity to states. Furthermore, judges have mentioned that writers have been members of the ILC.[171] ILC membership is based on personal competence, gives insight into the development of specific areas of international law, and constitutes an approval by states.

A different group of references to teachings has mentioned the writer's participation in the drafting of the rules that the judge was discussing. They include negotiators, delegates, and advisers in the negotiations of legal documents,[172] and (other) members of drafting or revision committees or conferences.[173] One writer had prepared a draft of a treaty provision[174] and another made a 'prominent contribution to the discussion leading to the drafting of' the ICJ's own rules.[175] A similar reference is to a writer who was 'Secretary of the Institute of International Law, which had a substantial share in the preparation of the first drafts of' a treaty (as mentioned in Section 4.3.2), to a 'former Belgian delegate and jurisconsult whose knowledge of the United Nations dates from the San Francisco Conference',[176] and to a writer 'who was present on behalf of [the] Court both in the Committee of Jurists at Washington and in the relevant Committee of the Conference of San Francisco'.[177] The motivation behind these references seems to be the special insight that participation in negotiations may provide. This in some sense is similar to citing

[170] For example, *Military and Paramilitary Activities in and against Nicaragua (Nicaragua v. United States of America), Declaration of Intervention, Order of 4 October 1984, I.C.J. Reports 1984*, p. 215, Dissenting Opinion of Judge Schwebel 236; *Land, Island and Maritime Frontier Dispute, Order 1990*, Dissenting Opinion of Judge Shahabuddeen 56; *Bosnia Genocide, 1993*, Separate Opinion of Vice-President Weeramantry 377–378.

[171] *Application of the Interim Accord*, Dissenting Opinion of Judge ad hoc Roucounas 746, *Jurisdictional Immunities, 2012*, Separate Opinion of Judge Keith 169–170.

[172] For example, *Namibia*, Dissenting Opinion of Judge Gerald Fitzmaurice 240; *Kosovo*, Declaration of Judge Tomka, Vice President 464; *Obligation to Negotiate Access to the Pacific Ocean*, Declaration of Judge Gaja 1.

[173] For example, *Aerial Incident of July 27th, 1955*, Joint Dissenting Opinion by Judges Sir Hersch Lauterpacht, Wellington Koo and Sir Percy Spender 174; *Nicaragua v. Colombia*, Declaration of Judge Keith 743; *Obligation to Negotiate Access to the Pacific Ocean*, Declaration of Judge Bennouna 1.

[174] *Jan Mayen*, Separate Opinion of Judge Weeramantry 237.

[175] *Bosnia Genocide, 1997*, Dissenting Opinion of Vice-President Weeramantry 290.

[176] *Namibia*, Dissenting Opinion of Judge Gerald Fitzmaurice 240.

[177] *Aerial Incident of July 27th, 1955*, Joint Dissenting Opinion by Judges Sir Hersch Lauterpacht, Wellington Koo and Sir Percy Spender 174.

preparatory works. In the same vein, one judge in an interview explains that 'Gidel on the law of the sea [has canonical status] because of his role in the early development of the modern law of the sea'.[178] Similarly, in the PCIJ, Kellogg in *Upper Savoy and the District of Gex* commented on the 'clear distinction between a Court of arbitration and a Court of justice' and cited teachings written by 'Director of the Division of International Law of the Carnegie Endowment and Legal Assistant to Mr. Root during the work of the Jurists Committee at The Hague in 1920'.[179] These credentials seem to have given the author special knowledge of the purposes behind the creation of the PCIJ.

However, some citations cannot have been motivated by special insights: For example, one reference is to a writer who 'later became a member of the Committee which drafted the Statute of the Permanent Court'.[180] Since this author at the time the cited text was written had yet to participate in the negotiations, the reference cannot have been motivated by any special insight that the writer could have gained. Writers having participated in negotiations also say something about their personal competence more generally, and it is a form of proximity to states.

Some references have concerned writers who have held official positions in intergovernmental organisations and the like: one 'Attorney-General of Palestine' during the mandate period,[181] one 'Secretary-General of both the Stockholm and the Rio Conferences',[182] one 'Deputy Secretary of the United Nations Sea-Bed Committee',[183] one 'Vice-Chairman of the Permanent Mandates Commission' (and 'one of the most active members'),[184] and one 'former Director of the Department of Legal Affairs of the OAS'.[185] These references too may have been about expertise, insight gained from experience, and acceptability to states. Other opinions refer to writers' positions in state governments. This includes positions as legal adviser at 'the Foreign Office'

---

[178] ICJ Judge 1.

[179] *Free Zones of Upper Savoy and the District of Gex (second phase), Order made on 6 December 1930, P.C.I.J. Series A No. 24*, p. 4, Observations by M. Kellogg 34–35.

[180] *Legality of the Use by a State of Nuclear Weapons in Armed Conflict, Advisory Opinion, I.C.J. Reports 1996*, p. 66, Dissenting Opinion of Judge Weeramantry 142.

[181] *Kosovo*, Separate Opinion of Judge Cançado Trindade 546.

[182] *Nuclear Tests (New Zealand) Examination*, Dissenting opinion by Judge ad hoc Sir Geoffrey Palmer 407–408.

[183] *Fisheries Jurisdiction (United Kingdom v. Iceland)*, Declaration by Judge Ignacio-Pinto 38.

[184] *South West Africa*, Dissenting Opinion of President Winiarski 451.

[185] *Nicaragua, 1986*, Dissenting Opinion of Judge Schwebel 384.

and 'the United Kingdom's Permanent Mission to the United Nations'.[186] Other writers have worked at 'the British Embassy at Constantinople' and 'the Ministry for Foreign Affairs'.[187] Yet others have represented their governments at 'the Special Committee on the Question of Defining Aggression' and 'the Council of the Organization of American States',[188] and one writer was 'Assistant Secretary of State for International Organization Affairs'.[189] Another writer served as 'President of the Supreme Court of Senegal'.[190] The posts of supreme court judge and legal adviser require some competence as a lawyer, and the references may in part be about the expertise of the writer. However, the position of Assistant Secretary of State is more of a political than a legal job and does not to the same extent imply competence on legal questions. It rather implies proximity to state power. The position of legal adviser to the UN was brought up in connection to a question of UN law, which shows that at least this reference could have also been about insight gained from the position.

Finally, some references do not fit any of the aforementioned paragraphs, but nonetheless seem to focus on the official authority of a writer. A general reference to a writer being 'no less an insider than' is one example.[191] Another reference was to a writer who was a 'well-known [...] statesman',[192] and yet another was to writings by the 'counsel' in the present case.[193] One judge mentioned that a writer was 'cited in the Counter-Memorial of Peru as an authority in matters of American international law'.[194] The implication seems to be that when a state approves of teachings by incorporating arguments into their memorial, this gives the teachings a veneer of official authority.[195]

---

[186] Ibid., 394; *Bosnia Genocide, 2007,* Separate Opinion of Judge Tomka 320.

[187] *Aegean Sea,* Separate Opinion of Judge Tarazi 56; *Asylum,* Dissenting Opinion by Judge Azevedo 341.

[188] *Asylum,* Dissenting Opinion by M. Caicedo Castilla 365–366.

[189] *Oil Platforms, 2003,* Separate Opinion of Judge ad hoc Rigaux 387–388.

[190] *Gabčikovo,* Separate Opinion of Vice-President Weeramantry 91.

[191] *Pulp Mills,* Joint Dissenting Opinion Judges Al-Khasawneh and Simma 114.

[192] *North Sea,* Dissenting Opinion of Vice-President Koretsky 157.

[193] *Nuclear Tests (New Zealand) Examination,* Dissenting opinion by Judge ad hoc Sir Geoffrey Palmer 386.

[194] *Asylum,* Dissenting Opinion by M. Caicedo Castilla 365.

[195] This is analogous to, for example, the WTO Appellate Body's practice of only accepting amicus curiae briefs when approved by a party to a case, as described by Helmersen, 'WTO', 340–341.

4.3.5 Agreement between Multiple Writers

Another factor that affects the weight of teachings is whether multiple works agree.[196] Various examples can be found in ICJ practice.

First of all, the ICJ's majority opinions contain seven references to specific teachings.[197] One of those references is to multiple works ('the successive editors of Oppenheim's International Law'). Another three are to collective bodies (the IDI and the ICRC twice). Thus, only a minority of the citations of specific works (three out of seven) are to individual works by individual writers. Other majority opinions have contained unspecific references to 'writers' and 'writings', which should be read as a reference to multiple agreeing works. Thus, the ICJ's majority opinions have mostly invoked multiple writers at once, as opposed to individual writers.[198]

In individual opinions, some judges have referred to works that have received 'eminent juristic support'[199] or 'wide acceptance',[200] have been 'quoted with approval by many scholars',[201] or have a 'generally approved view',[202] a 'generally accepted doctrine',[203] 'widely recognized as one the century's leading authorities',[204] or 'a recognized authority'.[205] Moreover, some works have been called 'celebrated', as mentioned in Section 4.3.3. This 'celebration' was presumably done (at least partly) by other writers who concurred with the work in question. All this should mean that a work has more weight if other writers agree with it.

Judges have also found it significant that there existed a 'vast',[206] 'considerable',[207] or 'impressive'[208] support for a view. One judge often

---

[196] This is assumed by, for example, English Court of Admiralty, *The 'Renard'* [1778] 165 All ER 51–52; Lauterpacht, *Development*, 24; Oraison, 'L'Influence', 228.

[197] Section 3.2.

[198] Wolfke, *Custom*, 156; Sivakumaran, 'Influence', 26.

[199] *Nuclear Weapons*, Dissenting Opinion of Judge Weeramantry 500.

[200] *Bosnia Genocide, 1993*, Separate Opinion of Vice-President Weeramantry 382.

[201] *Tunisia/Libyan Arab Jamahiriya*, Dissenting Opinion of Judge Oda 198.

[202] *Barcelona Traction, 1970*, Separate Opinion of Judge Tanaka 144.

[203] *Aegean Sea*, Dissenting Opinion of Judge de Castro 69.

[204] *Nicaragua, 1986*, Dissenting Opinion of Judge Schwebel 342–343.

[205] *Nicaragua, 1986*, Separate Opinion of Judge Lachs 169.

[206] *Nuclear Tests (New Zealand) Examination*, Dissenting opinion by Judge Weeramantry 360.

[207] *Nuclear Weapons*, Dissenting Opinion of Judge Weeramantry 508–509.

[208] *Jan Mayen*, Separate Opinion of Judge Weeramantry 235. See also 156–157, where he also seems to consider it significant that multiple writers agree.

sees a 'trend' in teachings.[209] Teachings have also been 'fairly unanimous'[210] and 'generally in agreement'.[211] More simply, teachings can 'agree'[212] or '[appear] satisfied'.[213] A view can receive 'growing attention',[214] 'support',[215] or even 'wide acceptance' in relevant teachings.[216] Such views may be 'echoed by other commentators'[217] and 'quoted with approval'.[218]

One judge ad hoc asked rhetorically whether 'the Court [should] not have given more consideration to the factor that war crimes and crimes against humanity have, by many, been considered to be customary international law crimes'.[219] Thus, the opinion of 'many', presumably writers, mattered. The same judge argued that 'some authorities seem to support' one view, but 'most authorities do not mention' it 'and even reject it'.[220] This too was a reference to the numerical strength of a group holding a particular view. Another judge ad hoc found it significant that a 'controversial interpretation' was 'not upheld by the greater part of scholarly opinion'.[221] Judge ad hoc Kreća in *Croatia Genocide* cited an ILC text which 'however, mentions only one article', implying that the failure to cite multiple works that agreed with each other reduced the weight of the ILC text.[222]

In the PCIJ, judges have mentioned that 'there [was] no difference of opinion [...] between legal writers'[223] and that they are citing 'the predominant view of authorities'.[224]

Works by collective institutions such as the IDI will, by definition, be backed by multiple concurring individuals. This should give them a default

---

[209] *Obligation to Negotiate Access to the Pacific Ocean*, Separate Opinion of Judge Cançado Trindade 17–18; *Kosovo*, Separate Opinion of Judge Cançado Trindade 534; *Jurisdictional Immunities, 2012*, Dissenting Opinion of Judge Cançado Trindade 264.

[210] *Guardianship of Infants*, Separate Opinion of Judge Sir Hersch Lauterpacht 96.

[211] *Bosnia Genocide, 2007*, Dissenting Opinion of Judge ad hoc Mahiou 419.

[212] *Arbitral Award of 31 July 1989*, Separate Opinion of Judge Ni 100.

[213] *Kosovo*, Separate Opinion of Judge Cançado Trindade 550–551.

[214] *Certain Activities Carried Out by Nicaragua in the Border Area (Costa Rica v. Nicaragua); Construction of a Road in Costa Rica along the San Juan River (Nicaragua v. Costa Rica), Order of 22 November 2013*, Separate Opinion of Judge Cançado Trindade 380.

[215] *Temple*, Separate Opinion of Vice-President Alfaro 41.

[216] *Bosnia Genocide, 1993*, Separate Opinion of Vice-President Weeramantry 378.

[217] *Oil Platforms, 1998*, Dissenting Opinion by Judge ad hoc Rigaux 229.

[218] *Tunisia/Libyan Arab Jamahiriya*, Dissenting Opinion of Judge Oda 198.

[219] *Arrest Warrant, 2002*, Dissenting Opinion of Judge ad hoc Van den Wyngaert 156.

[220] Ibid., 157–158.

[221] *Bosnia Genocide, 2007*, Dissenting Opinion of Judge ad hoc Mahiou 404.

[222] *Croatia Genocide, 2015*, Separate Opinion of Judge ad hoc Kreća 495.

[223] *Lighthouses*, Separate Opinion by M. Séfériadès 50.

[224] *Upper Savoy and the District of Gex*, Opinion by M. Dreyfus 44.

level of weight that is greater than that of 'regular' teachings.[225] There are examples of judges apparently considering IDI texts to be authoritative.[226] A particularly interesting example is Judge Weeramantry's opinion in *Nuclear Weapons*, where he emphasised how an IDI resolution 'was adopted by sixty votes, with one against and two abstentions'.[227] Thus, it was significant not just that the resolution came from the IDI, but that such a large number of people concurred. Judge Tomka similarly 'expressed his scepticism regarding the value of resolutions adopted by learned societies purporting to reflect customary international law when, for instance, few members of that society are present and the resolution is adopted by a thin majority'.[228] Individual ICJ opinions contain a total of 191 references to 'institutional' teachings: eighty-five to the IDI, twenty-nine to the ICRC, eighteen to the ILA, fifteen to ALI, and fourteen to Harvard Law School.

It may also be significant that a single writer has held the same view consistently. For example, Judge Jessup in *South West Africa* noted that '[a]fter a decade had passed, Lord McNair evidently found no reason to change his view'.[229] As mentioned earlier, one of the two references to specific teachings in ICJ majority opinions was to 'the successive editors of Oppenheim's International Law'. The significance of this may have been not only that multiple editors agreed but also that individual editors held on to their views throughout successive editions.

More generally, judges often cite multiple authors for the same point. One motivation for this is probably that citing multiple writers is seen as more authoritative than citing only one.

The ICJ Statute Article 38(1)(d) focuses on 'publicists of the various nations'. A logical inference is that teachings have more weight when writers from multiple geographic regions and legal cultures agree.[230] This should give collective institutions, such as the IDI, more weight.[231] It is also a reason why judicial decisions and state-empowered bodies such as

---

[225] This is also assumed by, for example, Sørensen, *sources*, 183; Stahn and De Brabandere, 'Future', 4–5; ILC, *Third report*, 45.

[226] *Case concerning the Arbitral Award made by the King of Spain on 23 December 1906, Judgment of 18 November 1960: I.C.J. Reports 1960*, p. 192, Dissenting Opinion of Judge Urrutia Holguin 224; *Barcelona Traction, 1970*, Separate Opinion of Judge Ammoun 292.

[227] *Nuclear Weapons*, Dissenting Opinion of Judge Weeramantry 508.

[228] Judge Tomka quoted in Keene (ed.), 'Outcome Paper', 260.

[229] *South West Africa*, Separate Opinion of Judge Jessup 406.

[230] Sivakumaran, 'Influence', 9.

[231] For example, ILC, *Report of the Sixty-eighth session*, 112; Virally, 'Sources', 116, 153; Wolfke, *Custom*, 156.

the ILC have more weight, as argued in Section 3.9.6. The significance of diversity is not, however, evident from the Court's and the judges' opinions. ICJ judges mostly cited Western teachings, as explained in Section 4.2.2. Adjusting this aspect of the Court's practice could be beneficial, as argued in Section 6.2.2.

There is a limit to the significance of unanimity between writers. Teachings are 'subsidiary means',[232] which means that no agreement between writers can create new law.[233]

4.4 Reasons for Distinguishing between Teachings

4.4.1 Introduction

The foregoing sections have argued that the weight of teachings varies between different works, and that factors that determine the weight of teachings include quality, expertise, the writers' official positions, and unanimity among multiple writers. This section seeks to explain why judges assign different weight to different works, and why they rely on the aforementioned factors when doing so. Three explanations are considered: a desire to increase the authority of an opinion (Section 4.4.2), the opportunity to save time (Section 4.4.3), and compliance with the ICJ Statute Article 38 (Section 4.4.4).

4.4.2 Increased Authority

Citing an authoritative work may make a judicial opinion look more authoritative. Lawyers aspire to have their work accepted by others. This holds true of academics who publish research and of lawyers pleading before judges, but also of judges themselves.[234] Therefore, one reason why judges cite teachings may be that they think it will improve how they are perceived by other actors.[235]

---

[232] Section 2.2.8.

[233] English Court for Crown Cases Reserved, *R* v. *Keyn* [1876] 2 Ex D 63, 202. The case is discussed in John P Grant, *International Law* (Dundee University Press 2010) 22.

[234] *Qatar and Bahrain, 2001*, Joint Dissenting Opinion of Judges Bedjaoui, Ranjeva and Koroma 151.

[235] For example, Cole, 'Non-Binding', 303 and 309; Duxbury, *Judges,* 9–11; Robert J Hume, 'Strategic-Instrument Theory and the Use of Non-Authoritative Sources by Federal Judges: Explaining References to Law Review Articles' (2010) 31 *Justice System Journal* 291, 295.

However, the opposite effect is also possible, in that an absence of references to teachings may make a judicial decision look more authoritative. The implication of not citing teachings could be that the judge considers their opinion to be authoritative enough on its own. This is a plausible reason why ICJ majority opinions almost never cite teaching (as noted in Section 3.5.9), while teachings are cited more frequently in individual opinions, which have a lower inherent authority.[236]

It is intuitive that higher-quality works are more authoritative. A work that is better written, more thorough, or more 'celebrated' (as per Section 4.3.3) will be more likely to espouse views that other lawyers agree with. This is significant when authority is seen as a collective process, as discussed in Section 4.5.

When judges cite works that their audiences are unfamiliar with, the judges must themselves be in a position to distinguish authoritatively between higher-quality and lower-quality teachings in order for the authority-by-association effect to apply. ICJ judges have this authority, but not all lawyers do. However, if audiences repeatedly disagree with a judge's designation of high-quality teachings, trust in the judge's assessments is undermined. Judges therefore have an incentive not to invoke quality too often and to do so only when they actually believe that the work is good.

An additional effect of emphasising the quality of a cited work is that it shows that the judge has made an effort to assess the work and a conscious choice about citing it. Judges can cite works that they have not even read,[237] but by emphasising the quality of a cited work, the judge shows that the citation is 'genuine'. This makes the opinion look more thorough and informed, which contributes to its authority.

Much of this also applies to expertise. The title of expert is generally extended to writers who have a history of espousing views that others have agreed with, and writers who possess outstanding knowledge and insight about the law, in turn making them more likely to hold views that are shared by others. More expert writers therefore have more authority. Citing them contributes more to the authority of an opinion than citing less expert writers. ICJ judges are in a position to distinguish authoritatively between more and less expert writers.

According to the analysis presented in Section 4.3.4, references to a writer's official position are used as proxies for their expertise and

---

[236] Manley, 'Citation', 1006.
[237] For example, Merritt and Putnam, 'Judges and Scholars', 873.

their acceptability to states. Citing a writer who is acceptable to states in an opinion increases the likelihood that states will have a favourable view of the opinion. This is particularly important to the ICJ, since it is states that bring the Court's cases, and compliance with the Court's decisions is dependent on states accepting them (since decisions are not enforced).

While judges rely on their own authority when they assess quality and expertise, such authority is less important when judges refer to writers' official positions. There is a rough but broad agreement about which official positions confer what authority in international law to a much greater extent than there is agreement on the precise quality and expertise of every specific writer and scholarly work.

Judges also tend to emphasise that multiple writers agree. All else being equal, when more writers agree on a point, it is more likely that they are correct. This point is nevertheless tightly bound up with expertise and quality. The opinion of one outstanding writer is worth more than the opinion of multiple poor ones. The significance of agreement between writers as an authority-enhancing factor therefore increases exponentially when it is combined with the other factors discussed here.

4.4.3 Saving Time

On a more practical level, citing authoritative writers can save time for judges. This is in part because authoritative writers are, at least presumably, more likely to be correct about the law.[238] This means that judges can trust the views of authoritative writers and spend less time on independent research or prolonged deliberation.[239]

Relying on a writer whose expertise is reputed can undoubtedly save a judge time. If the judge knows that the writer is good, they can look at their work and trust that is likely to be correct. The same is true for a writer who holds or has held an important official position, since official positions can be seen as proxies for expertise, as discussed in Section 4.3.4. In addition to this, citing a writer who holds an official position may contribute to the persuasiveness of the opinion towards the institution in question. Citing the writings of a sitting ICJ judge could increase the likelihood that the opinion will be accepted by that judge or even by the Court as a whole.

---

[238] For example, Hernández, *Judicial Function*, 171; Cole, 'Non-Binding', 301 and 303.
[239] Wolfke, *Custom*, 156; Cole, 'Non-Binding', 308–309.

By contrast, reading (and citing) multiple writers who agree necessarily takes time and is therefore not something that will save time for judges. A similar point can be made about citing high-quality works. A work must usually be read quite thoroughly in order to establish its quality, which also takes time. If a judge already knows that a work is good, they can consult it more quickly next time. If the second time around they consult a specific passage or chapter whose quality they have not yet assessed, they can build on a *presumption* of quality, which can save time. If the presumption is extended to *other works* by the same writer, it is more correct to say that what is invoked is the writer's expertise, rather than the quality of the work.

4.4.4   Compliance with the ICJ Statute Article 38

ICJ judges are bound by the ICJ Statute, including Article 38. They should therefore be interested in grounding their methodological approach in the wording of Article 38.

The first three of the factors discussed in Section 4.3 – expertise, quality, and official positions – can be linked to the phrase 'the most highly qualified publicists' in the ICJ Statute Article 38(1)(d), as noted in Section 2.2.6. The 'most highly qualified publicists' are those with the most expertise. Often, they will also write the highest-quality teachings. Holding an important official position should also be seen as an aspect of being 'most highly qualified'. This is because election or appointment requires expertise and because doing the work enhances expertise. Moreover, the official positions in question are ones that confer a certain authority merely by holding the office. With regard to the fourth factor, unanimity, this too has a connection to the ICJ Statute Article 38(1)(d), which speaks about 'teachings' and 'publicists', in plural. That writers should represent different regions is in line with the wording of the ICJ Statute Article 38(1)(d) and its focus on 'publicists of the various nations'. All of the factors that were identified in Section 4.3 can thus be traced back to the ICJ Statute Article 38(1)(d). The factors are part of the legal framework that governs the work of the ICJ and its judges.

That being said, the determination of what constitutes 'quality' and 'expertise' will to some extent be subjective. Judges can form their own opinion on what constitutes good legal writing, who is a good lawyer, and (to a lesser extent) which official positions are the most authoritative. While the community of international lawyers have developed certain shared guidelines, as discussed in Section 4.5, individual lawyers and judges are to some extent free to form their own views. Thus, while the factors are part of the Court's legal framework, they do not 'bind' or restrict the judges to any significant extent.

4.5   The Collective Nature of Authority in International Law

This section argues that the weight of teachings and of judicial decisions and works by state-empowered bodies is determined through a collective, informal, and largely tacit process. There are numerous examples from individual ICJ opinions that, when citing teachings, use terms that imply that weight is determined through a collective process.[240] As mentioned in Section 4.3, judges have referred to works and authors as being 'well-known', 'famous', 'influential', 'celebrated', 'generally accepted', having 'been quoted with approval by many scholars', and having 'eminent juristic support'.

More generally, the concepts of quality, expertise, and authority of an institution cannot be ascertained by a single individual in a vacuum. What one person finds to constitute quality, expertise, and authority depends, at least to some extent, on the judgment of others. There is thus a continuous collective process which produces a loose consensus about what constitutes 'quality' in writing about international law, who the greatest 'experts' on international law are, and which institutions are the most authoritative.[241] International lawyers have a rough notion of how a court ranks relative to other courts and how much of an expert various writers are on various topics and can give some examples of good and bad international legal writing. However, the process itself and its results are rarely explicitly discussed or written down. The process is, instead, informal and largely tacit.

An interesting aspect of the process is that it is in some sense self-reinforcing. This may be called 'The Matthew Effect', which means that 'rewards tend to be skewed towards those who are already highly reputed'.[242] When a specific work is cited in a judicial decision, this

---

240 There are also examples in teachings, for example, in J L Brierly, *The Law of Nations: An Introduction to the International Law of Peace* (Sir Humphrey Waldock ed, 6th edn, Oxford University Press 1963) 66; Lassa Oppenheim, *International Law: A Treatise*, vol. I (Longmans, Green, and Co. 1905) 24; Lauterpacht, *Development*, 24.

241 Sureda, *Uncertainty*, 138; Mark Tushnet, 'Academics as Law Makers' (2010) 29 *University of Queensland Law Journal* 19, 20.

242 Duxbury, *Judges,* 11, referring to Robert K Merton, 'The Matthew Effect in Science' (1968) 159 *Science* 56, 58.

may have been done because that work had more weight than others, but it may also give the cited work even more weight simply by the fact that it was cited in a judicial decision.[243] This is also assumed by an ICJ employee.[244] The same ICJ employee points out that the ICJ's clerks largely '[go] to the same [. . .] key academic texts', which means that the clerks may be contributing to the effect.[245] Similarly, the weight of a judicial decision may depend on 'how well [it] is accepted in academic writings'.[246] Citation and approval of teachings by other teachings and of judicial decisions by other judicial decisions should also matter.[247]

4.6 Conclusion

The earlier sections have found that ICJ judges cite some writers more than others. Shabtai Rosenne is the most-cited writer, ahead of Hersch Lauterpacht. More generally Western writers, in particular from the United Kingdom, dominate the lists. This may be because these groups write more or better teachings, or it could be a result of bias in the Court.

ICJ judges seem to consider the following factors when assessing the weight of teachings: the quality of a work; the expertise of a writer; the official positions of a writer; and whether multiple writers agree and (if so) whether those writers represent different parts of the world.

The judges' incentives for distinguishing between teachings and citing the ones with more weight probably include a desire to make their opinions authoritative and to save time. Compliance with the Court's legal framework may also play a role, but this framework leaves judges significant discretion.

Additionally, the process by which the weight of teachings is determined is collective, informal, and largely tacit and involves both states and individual international lawyers.

---

[243] For example, Sivakumaran, 'Influence', 28; Manley, 'Citation', 1004.

[244] ICJ Employee 1 ('[t]he extent to which that work is cited by others').

[245] ICJ Employee 1.

[246] Shecaira, *Scholarship*, 57, discussing comparative national law and citing Neil MacCormick and Robert S Summers (eds.), *Interpreting Precedents: A Comparative Study* (Aldershot 1997).

[247] Harlan Grant Cohen, 'Theorizing Precedent in International Law' in Andrea Bianchi, Daniel Peat, and Matthew Windsor (eds.), *Interpretation in International Law* (Oxford University Press 2015) 268, 279.

The factors that determine the weight of teachings may also apply to other 'subsidiary means' in international law.[248] This presupposes that the weight accorded to other subsidiary means is variable, which does not seem to be controversial. For example, concerning ILC works, an ICJ employee finds that 'the articles on state responsibility [with] the commentary is treated as if it is a real authority', which makes it '[stand] apart'.[249]

The weight of judicial decisions may be affected by their quality.[250] Expertise may also matter.[251] Expertise may also be relevant to other sources,[252] such as reports by fact-finding missions,[253] or texts produced by state-empowered bodies.[254] An analogy to considering the official position of a writer may be to consider the status or nature of a court or an institution, which for some writers seems relevant to the weight accorded to their works or decisions.[255] For example, a permanent institution should be more authoritative than an ad hoc arbitral tribunal,[256] and appellate institutions superior to those whose decisions can be appealed. This informal hierarchy of international courts and institutions may also be used to determine how much extra weight teachings gain from their authors having had official positions in the court or institution. Works produced by state-empowered bodies may gain added weight by increasing degrees of state involvement, such as the UNGA, 'taking note' of ILC works.

Just as unanimity affects the weight of teachings, the weight of judicial decisions and works by state-empowered bodies may be affected by the number of judges deciding a case, the number of members of an

---

[248] Hall, *International Law*, 59; Bordin, 'Reflections', 560 argues that 'authorship, representation and procedure may establish a presumption in favour of the view endorsed in the non-legislative codification'.

[249] ICJ Employee 2.

[250] For example, Akehurst, 'Hierarchy', 280; Charlesworth, 'Law-Making', 197; ILC, *Third report*, 43.

[251] For example, Wolfke, *Custom*, 74 and 146; Onuf, 'Global', 19; Cohen, 'Theorizing', 279.

[252] Schwarzenberger, 'Province', 238.

[253] Vaios Koutroulis, 'The Prohibition of the Use of Force in Arbitrations and Fact-Finding Reports' in Marc Weller (ed.), *The Oxford Handbook of the Use of Force in International Law* (Oxford University Press 2015) 605, 612.

[254] Schachter, 'Law-Making', 134; Dugard, 'Effective', 38; Bordin, 'Reflections', 552.

[255] For example, Onuf, 'Global', 19; Malcolm N Shaw, 'A Practical Look at the International Court of Justice', in Malcolm D Evans (ed.), *Remedies in International Law: The Institutional Dilemma* (Hart 1998) 11, 27; Charlesworth, 'Law-Making', 197.

[256] For example, Wolfke, *Custom*, 146.

institution who produced a work,[257] and whether anyone dissented.[258] One aspect of this is that the weight of a judicial decision should, all else being equal, increase with the number of people who produced it. For example, a decision from all fifteen to seventeen ICJ judges should have more weight than a decision by a chamber.[259] This does not seem to be the case in practice, however.[260] Another consequence is that, for example, investment arbitration awards, which are commonly made by three arbitrators, will have less weight than ICJ decisions.

The diversity of writers who agree is another factor likely to affect the weight of teachings. The equivalent for judicial decisions or state-empowered bodies is to look at whether the institution is global rather than regional, or whether concurring regional institutions represent different parts of the world.[261]

---

[257] Wolfke, *Custom*, 146; (in the context of national law) Shecaira, *Scholarship*, 57.

[258] ILC, *Third report*, 43; (in the context of national law) Shecaira, *Scholarship*, 57.

[259] Shahabuddeen, *Precedent*, 173.

[260] Section 1.3.1.

[261] For example, Schwarzenberger, *International Law*, 30–31; ALI, *Restatement*, 37; Currie, *International Law*, 108.

5

Variations between Judges

5.1 Introduction

The previous chapter compared the weight accorded to different teachings. This chapter compares the weight accorded to teachings by different judges. Section 5.2 shows that ICJ judges vary in how often and how they cite teachings. A categorisation of judges is proposed in Section 5.3, with three distinct groups: judges who never cite teachings, judges who frequently cite and engage with teachings, and a median. Section 5.4 presents factors that could explain the variations between judges, while Section 5.5 presents data that correlate with the variations between judges. Section 5.6 is a conclusion.

5.2 Variations by Frequency and Substance

Judges cite teachings with varying frequency.[1] Precise numbers for the ICJ are given in Appendix 2. The individual judges are divided into three groups in Section 5.3, largely based on how many times they have cited teachings. The counts include self-citations (by judges who are also writers). This differs from the count of the most-cited writers, which excludes self-citations. That is because a self-citation does not say much about the how the writer is viewed by the Court as a whole, while it does say something about the individual judge's attitude towards teachings. Self-citations are therefore included when comparing judges, but they are excluded when comparing writers.

There are 165 judges who have written at least one individual opinion. Eighty-four of them were permanent judges, sixty-three were ad hoc, and eighteen were both. Five permanent judges and thirty-three judges ad hoc have not written any individual opinion.

---

[1] (In the context of national law) David L Schwartz and Lee Petherbridge, 'The Use of Legal Scholarship by the Federal Courts of Appeals: An Empirical Study' (2011) 96 *Cornell Law Review* 1345, 1352.

Among the 165 who have, Judge ad hoc Wyngaert has the highest average number of teachings citations per opinion, with 41.5. Judge Cançado Trindade is just behind with 40.9. Another four judges have more than twenty references per opinion on average. Of the 165 judges, 53 have never cited teachings. That is around 33 per cent of the total. Another 51 have between 0.1 and 1.0 citations of teachings on average per opinion. Thus, only slightly more than a third of the judges have more than 1.0 teachings citations per opinion on average, ranging from 1.1 for Judge Wellington Koo to 41.5 for Judge ad hoc Wyngaert.

Judges also differ in the share of their opinions that include at least one citation of teachings. Twenty-five judges (15 per cent) have referred to teachings in all their individual opinions. A further twenty judges are above 50 per cent, and twelve have precisely 50 per cent. The remaining fifty-six, or around one-third, lie between 50 and 0.1 per cent, while fifty-three have (as mentioned) never cited teachings.

Figure 5.1 illustrates the distribution of judges by average number of citations of teachings per opinion. The judges are grouped as percentages of the total, with the respective slices showing the top 10 per cent of most-citing judges, 11–20 per cent, and so on, with the last slice showing the bottom 40 per cent.

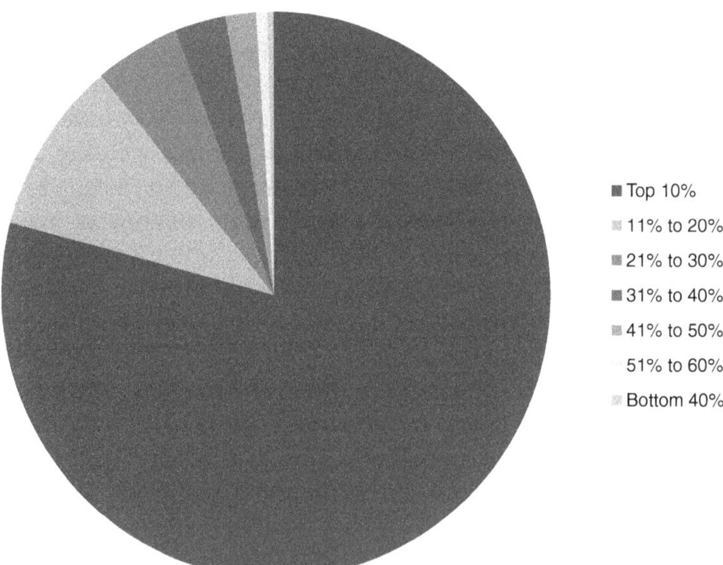

Figure 5.1   Groups of judges ranked by a total number of references to teachings

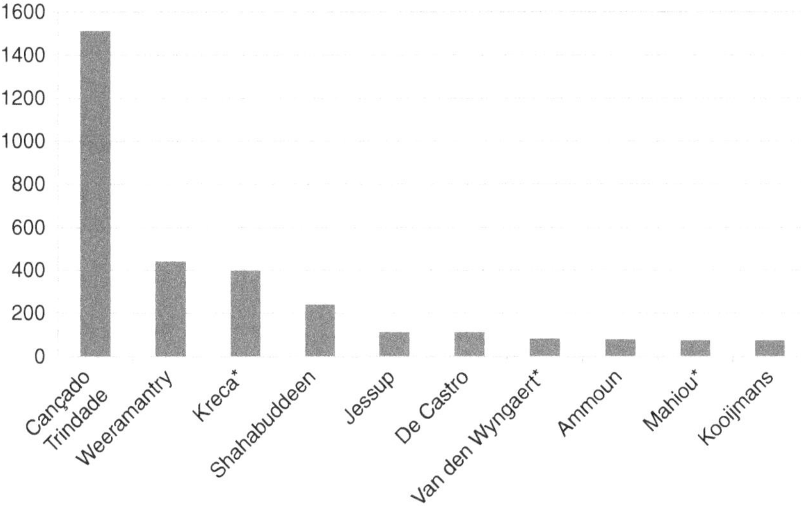

Figure 5.2   The ten most-citing judges

The same pattern exists in the PCIJ, where the top 10 per cent of judges are responsible for more than two-thirds of citations.

Figure 5.2 shows the top ten most-citing judges in ICJ opinions. The judges are listed along the horizontal x-axis, while their citation numbers are on the vertical y-axis. A star (*) means that the judge was a judge ad hoc.

The judges of the PCIJ are ranked by their number of teachings citations in Appendix 4.

If one accepts the premise that the rate of citation of teachings is an indication of the weight accorded to them (discussed in Section 1.3.2), the weight varies significantly between ICJ judges.

Judges vary not only in frequency (how often they cite teachings) but also in substance (how they apply the teachings when they cite them). Section 3.7 lists instances of judges applying teachings in ways that imply that teachings have some weight, such as applying teachings as a main argument, criticising others for not considering teachings, trying to clarify teachings, citing teachings the judge disagrees with, and citing disagreements between teachings. These instances stem mostly from the opinions of only a few judges, with most judges being completely absent. As shown in Appendix 3, only forty-eight of the 112 judges who have ever cited teachings have ever applied teachings in ways that are covered by Section 3.7. Of those forty-eight, twenty-three have done so only once. At the opposite end of the spectrum, Judge Shahabuddeen is represented twenty times and Judge Weeramantry seventeen times. Three more judges (Judge Cançado Trindade, Judge Sir Hersch Lauterpacht, and Judge Schwebel) are represented more than ten times.

In conclusion, judging from how different judges apply (and do not apply) teachings, the weight they accord to teachings varies significantly.

5.3 Categorising Judges

5.3.1 Introduction

This section proposes a classification of ICJ judges into three categories: judges who never cite teachings, judges who often cite teachings, and a 'median' in between. This classification is meant descriptively, without normative implications. None of the groups is 'wrong'; the judges in question are simply more or less removed from an observable median between them.[2]

The numbers for PCIJ judges are presented in Appendix 4.

5.3.2 Category 1: Judges Who Never Cite Teachings

One category consists of judges who do not cite teachings at all. This category includes fifty-three judges, which is almost one-third (32 per cent) of the 165 judges who have written at least one individual opinion. However, of these fifty-three judges, twenty-one have written only a single opinion. Only eight of the judges have written more than ten opinions. The fewer opinions a judge writes, the fewer opportunities they have to cite teachings. It is quite possible that some of these judges would have cited teachings if they had participated in more cases and written more opinions. No attempt has been made here to set a lower limit of how many opinions a judge must have written in order to be relevant, as that would be arbitrary, and make the presentation incomplete. Instead, a parenthesis after the name of each judge shows how many opinions they have written.

The following judges belong to this category (with the number of opinions in parenthesis):
Permanent judges:

> Parra-Aranguren (28); Petren (16); Alvarez (13); Basdevant (12); Xue (12); Klaestad (11); Morozov (11); Kojevnikov (8); Moreno Quintana (8); Tarassov (7); Bengzon (6); Herczegh (6); Elias (5); Córdova (3);

---

[2] Lachs, *Teacher*, 13–158 distinguishes between 'deniers', 'utopians', and a 'mainstream' in international law generally, but those terms have a normative connotation that is not part of the argument in this book.

El-Khani (3); Ferrari Bravo (2); de Visscher (2); Benegal Rau (1); de Lacharrière (1); Gevorgian (1)

Judges who have been both permanent and ad hoc:

Nagendra Singh (17); Muhammad Zafrulla Khan (9); Morelli (9); Spiropoulos (9); Fleischhauer (6); Sepúlveda (6)

Judges ad hoc:

Garfield Barwick (6); Vinuesa (3); Callinan (2); Chagla (2); Stassinopoulos (2); Sur (2); Thierry (2); Verhoeven (2); Abi-Saab (1); Alayza y Paz Soldán (1); Arbour (1); Bastid (1); Beb a Don (1); Berman (1); Boni (1); Broms (1); Brower (1); Carry (1); Daudet (1); Fischer (1); Goitein (1); Kateka (1); Guggenheim (1); Mensah (1); Offerhaus (1); Orrego Vicuña (2); Reddy (1)

In the PCIJ, twenty-six of the forty judges who have written at least one individual opinion have not cited teachings. These judges are (with the number of opinions in parenthesis):

Anzilotti (17); Altamira (15); Hurst (8); Nyholm (8); Negulesco (6); Rolin-Jaequemyns (5); Erich (4); Huber (4); Urrutia (4); Adatci (3); Fromageot (3); Römer'is (3, ad hoc); Visscher (3); Wang (3); Nagaoka (2); Papazoff (2, ad hoc); Yovanovitch (2); Caloyanni (1); Guerrero (1); Hammarskjold (1); Loder (1); Novacovitch (1); Oda (1); Rabel (1); Tien-Hsi (1); Tomcsanyi (1)

5.3.3   Category 2: The Median

Another category is the Court's 'median'. The 'median' category includes judges who have cited teachings on average between 0.1 and 10 times per opinion. There are also some judges who have more than ten references per opinion on average, but are not represented at all, or only represented once, among the applications of teachings that are listed in Section 3.7. That section contains instances where judges seem to have accorded some weight to teachings. A listing of these instances, organised by judge, is included as Appendix 3. Judges who rarely or never apply teachings in ways that imply that teachings have weight are included here in the 'median' rather in the final group, which contains judges who 'often cite and engage with teachings'.

The 'median' category thus encompasses 102 of the 165 judges who have written at least one individual opinion. These judges have cited teachings in between 6.7 per cent (Donoghue) and 100 per cent (several judges) of their opinions.

Of the 102 judges who are listed here, seventeen have only written a single opinion. This means that, as with the previous category, the sample size is small. Therefore, the same parentheses are included in this section (and in the next section).

The median judges, in terms of citations of teachings per opinion, are Lachs and Ruda, with 0.5 references per opinion on average. However, this is lower than the average for all opinions, which is 3.5 references per opinion. Judge Alfaro is closest to this average. All of these judges lie comfortably within the 'median' category as defined here.

The following judges belong to the 'median' category:
Permanent judges:

> Oda (70); Koroma (62); Ranjeva (40); Kooijmans (36); Higgins (33); Schwebel (30); Elaraby (23); Owada (23); Gros (21); Vereshchetin (21); Shi (20); Lachs (19); Al-Khasawneh (17); Buergenthal (16); Keith (16); Tomka (16); Abraham (15); Badawi (15); Donoghue (15); Onyeama (14); Winiarski (13); Dillard (12); Greenwood (12); Spender (12); Read (12); Ignacio-Pinto (11); Bhandari (10); Forster (10); Wellington Koo (10); Ago (9); Fitzmaurice (9); Rezek (9); Waldock (9); McNair (8); Padilla Nervo (8); Sebutinde (8); Azevedo (7); H. Lauterpacht (7); Krylov (6); Levi Carneiro (6); Robinson (6); Tanaka (6); Bustamante (6); Hackworth (6); Koretsky (5); Aguilar Mawdsley (4); Hsu Mo (4); Ni (4); Zoricic (4); Crawford (3); Tarazi (3); Alfaro (2); Guerrero (2); El-Erian (1)

Judges who have been both permanent and ad hoc:

> Guillaume (25); Gaja (20); Bennouna (19); Jiménez de Aréchaga (19); Yusuf (19); Skotnikov (15); Bedjaoui (14); Simma (12); Ruda (11); Ajibola (9); Jennings (8); Evensen (7); Mosler (7); Armand-Ugon (6); Mbaye (5); Sette-Camara (5)

Judges ad hoc:

> Dugard (8); Torres-Bernárdez (8); Mahiou (6); Valticos (4); Caicedo Castilla (2); Cot (3); E. Lauterpacht (3); Mampuya (3); Vukas (3); Ečer (2); El-Kosheri (2); Franck (2); Mavungu (2); Mbanefo (2); Skubiszewski (2); Van den Wyngaert (2); Charlesworth (1); Daxner (1); Luchaire (1); Sorensen (1); Urrutia Holguin (1); Caron (1); Dimitrijevic (1); Fernandes (1); Fortier (1); Palmer (1); de Cara (1); Paolillo (1); Pirzada (1); Riphagen (1); Roucounas (1); Sreenivasa Rao (1)

A potential problem with labelling these judges as 'median' is that their approach is somewhat different from that found in the Court's majority opinions, which almost never cite teachings. However, Section 3.5.11 argues that the approach taken in majority opinions is mainly the result of the ICJ's institutional role. Moreover, Section 1.2 pointed out that individual opinions can actually give a more accurate view of the judges' approaches to teachings, and Section 3.4 that teachings are used more often than they are cited. Therefore, it seems safe to label the approach of this category of judges as the Court's 'median'.

From the PCIJ, all judges who have cited teachings in individual opinions would be in the 'median' described here. PCIJ judges have cited teachings on average between 0.1 and 4 times per opinion. Full numbers are listed in Appendix 4. The judges in question are (with number of opinions in parenthesis):

> Eysinga (14); Rostworowski (12); Shucking (9); Bustamante (6); Hudson (6); Finlay (4); Pessoa (4); Dreyfus (3); Moore (3); Weiss (3); Kellogg (2); Seferiades (2); Otavsky (1); Vogt (1)

5.3.4   Category 3: Judges Who Often Cite and Engage with Teachings

The final category covers judges who cite and engage with teachings significantly more than do the 'median' judges. These judges have cited teachings more than ten times on average per opinion, and they have applied teachings twice or more in ways that are listed in Section 3.7. They have cited teachings in between 60 per cent (Ammoun) and 100 per cent (multiple judges) of their opinions. Their average citation rate per opinion is between 40.9 (Cançado Trindade) and 11 (Shahabuddeen). As in the previous sections, the parenthesis after each name lists the number of opinions the judge has written.

The category includes the following judges:
Permanent judges:

> De Castro (9); Jessup (6); Ammoun (5)

Judges who have been both permanent and ad hoc:

> Cançado Trindade (37); Weeramantry (27); Shahabuddeen (24)

Judges ad hoc:

> Kreća (24); Rigaux (3); Bula-Bula (2); van Wyk (2)

Among these ten judges, Cançado Trindade, Weeramantry, Shahabuddeen, and Kreća have written many more opinions than the others. The combination of a large number of citations per opinion and many opinions means that these judges significantly influence the Court's overall citation numbers. They are therefore treated as 'outliers' and are removed from certain statistical analysis throughout the book.

5.4   Factors That May Explain Variations Between Judges

5.4.1   Introduction

This section seeks to explain why different judges apply teachings differently, as was shown in Section 5.2. This section has parallels with Section 3.5, which explains why ICJ majority opinions rarely cite teachings. The section explained the differences in citation between majority opinions and individual opinions, while this section explains the differences between different judges' individual opinions.

5.4.2   Strategic Citations

As noted in Section 3.5.9, judges can be seen as political actors who respond to incentives. That section found the ICJ as a whole had incentives not to cite teachings. Some judges do not cite teachings, and they may be motivated by the same strategic considerations as the Court's majority. That respect for the institutional role of the Court motivates judges is suggested by an ICJ employee, who notes that 'the judges' who 'have a policy of not referring to academic opinion' have a style that 'reflects the style of the Court as a whole'.[3]

The need to protect the Court's institutional role should be less acute in individual opinions, since they do not represent the Court as such. Some judges may still have it in mind when composing individual opinions and therefore refrain from citing teachings. In this connection, it is interesting that former national and international judges cite few teachings compared to other groups of judges, as discussed in Section 5.5.6. These judges may be particularly attuned to the Court's institutional role, and how the Court's prestige may be enhanced or diminished by what the judges do. A related possibility is that one purpose of an individual opinion is to convince the Court's majority, which may be facilitated by writing in the style that the majority generally adopts, which is without references to teachings.

However, many individual judges cite teachings. This may be a strategic choice, since judges may think that it improves how they are

---

[3] ICJ Employee 1.

perceived by other actors.[4] Citing authoritative teachings can improve the authority of an opinion, as argued in Section 4.4.2.

It is difficult to measure how much of the variance between judges is due to differing views on the strategic functions of teachings. Regardless of the difficulty of testing this empirically, it is a plausible explanation. It can also explain some of the variance in citations of teachings over time, outlined in Section 3.7.7. This was shown to be influenced by the election and appointment of specific judges, and it could also in part be due to changes in the Court's political context.

5.4.3 Philosophical Perspectives

Judges' attitudes to teachings may in some cases reflect a broader philosophical perspective on the law.[5] For example, in the context of US courts and US politics, several writers have found that left-leaning judges include more references to teachings in their decisions.[6] The most plausible interpretation is that such political views tend to correlate with legal philosophies that affect how judges approach teachings.

Two specific ICJ judges will be discussed here (as 'case studies').

The first is Judge Cançado Trindade. He alone is responsible for 34 per cent of the total number of references to teachings.[7] Judge Cançado Trindade's opinions have often gone into philosophical discussions, especially of the concept 'jus gentium'.[8] In discussing this concept, Judge Cançado Trindade has invoked numerous teachings. Judges who do not discuss *jus gentium* in their opinions have no reason to cite those teachings, of course. Additionally, it is likely that Judge Cançado Trindade's *jus gentium* perspective on the law is connected with his propensity to cite teachings when discussing legal questions in general. This finds some support in one of Judge Cançado Trindade's own monographs (first delivered as the General Course at the Hague Academy of International Law), titled *International Law for Humankind:*

---

[4] Duxbury, *Judges,* 9; Cole, 'Non-Binding', 303 and 309. Yonatan Lupu and Erik Voeten, 'Precedent in International Courts: A Network Analysis of Case Citations by the European Court of Human Rights' (2011) 42 *British Journal of Political Science* 413, 413 make the same point about judges citing judicial decisions.

[5] Cole, 'Non-Binding', 313. Similarly Earlsferry, 'Judges', 30.

[6] For example, Hume, 'Strategic', 303 and 309; Schwartz and Petherbridge, 'Scholarship', 1367–1370; Newton, 'Scholarship', 408.

[7] Section 5.2.

[8] For example, *Jurisdictional Immunities, 2011,* Separate Opinion of Judge Cançado Trindade 509–528; *Frontier Dispute, 2013,* Separate Opinion of Judge Cançado Trindade 130–131.

Towards a New Jus Gentium. In the preface to that book, he explains that 'in the pursuance of the consideration of [*jus gentium*], I see no reason whatsoever to limit myself to positive International Law',[9] and that 'the fulfilment of the "common interests of mankind" [...] may prevail over the policies of individual states'.[10] His focus is thus on normative and philosophical ideas rather than State will. This makes it natural to rely more heavily on teachings than in narrowly positivistic discussions focused on State practice.

Additionally, Cançado Trindade was a judge at the IACtHR before being elected to the ICJ. Judge Buergenthal served on the same two courts, and contrasts them by saying that '[o]n the Inter-American Court, you were relatively free to strategize about judicial policy, focusing on the policy implications of a case'.[11] It is plausible that the freedom that Buergenthal describes had some influence on Cançado Trindade's legal philosophy and judicial approach, which in turns affects his approach to teachings.

Judge Weeramantry is the second case study. His opinions have often referred to religious philosophy.[12] He invokes in particular Buddhist philosophy. In his book *Universalising International Law*, Judge Weeramantry writes about 'major global traditions which have not yet been sufficiently used to enrich and invigorate public international law' and lists 'Buddhism', 'Confucianism', 'Hinduism', 'Islam', 'Judaism', and 'Christianity'.[13] Judge Weeramantry's practice thus is an exception from the judges' tendency to focus on Western writers, as discussed in Section 4.2.2. Similar to Judge Cançado Trindade's focus on *jus gentium*, Judge Weeramantry seeks answers beyond the confines of State practice and State will, for which it is natural to look to and cite teachings.

It is significant that the two ICJ judges with the most references to teachings espouse legal-philosophical approaches that seem to call for the application of teachings. This is a good indication that frequent reference to teachings by other judges too can be a result of their more general approach to the law and to philosophy.

This can be contrasted, for example, with Judge Sir Hersch Lauterpacht, who is classified as a 'median' user of teachings in

---

[9] Antônio Augusto Cançado Trindade, *International Law for Humankind: Towards a New Jus Gentium* (Martinus Nijhoff 2010) 2.

[10] Ibid., 3.

[11] Judge Buergenthal quoted in Terris, Romano, and Swigart, *International Judge*, 97–98.

[12] For example, *Nuclear Weapons,* Dissenting Opinion of Judge Weeramantry 478–482; *Gabčikovo,* Separate Opinion of Vice-President Weeramantry 198–199.

[13] C G Weeramantry, *Universalising International Law* (Martinus Nijhoff 2004) 17–30.

Section 5.3.3. He was a decidedly pragmatic lawyer.[14] One ICJ judge highlights Lauterpacht as a judge whose 'influence [...] was a very strong one', even though (or perhaps partly because) he 'did not refer very often to individual works'.[15] Another ICJ judge agrees with the general proposition, saying that individual judicial philosophies and views of the judicial function affect how some judges apply teachings in their opinions.[16]

A possible indication of the importance of the individual judge's attitude to teachings would be if judges consistently maintained their approach to teachings when moving from one institution to another. This book only examines the ICJ and does not enable a systematic examination of judges who have moved between institutions. One example is available, however. As mentioned in Section 3.5.11, Judge Shahabuddeen cited teachings far more than other judges in the ICTY, and he was also one of the most frequent citers of teachings in the ICJ. This suggests that the personal attitude of the individual judge is an important factor in how they apply teachings.

5.4.4 Expertise

Judges may have enough expertise to render the application of teachings unnecessary, at least in certain fields. The flip side of this is that judges will cite more teachings when dealing with areas or questions of law that they are less familiar with.

As shown in Section 3.4.2, ICJ judges cite teachings more often in individual opinions attached to judgments than in those that are attached to orders. The latter are often focused on ICJ-specific procedural law, whereas judgments generally involve substantive questions of international law that are not specific to the ICJ. ICJ judges may believe that they have more expertise on their own procedural law than certain other fields of international law and, therefore, cite more teachings when dealing with the latter.

Expertise may also explain variations between individual judges, since an ICJ judge's perception of their own expertise may explain why they find it more or less necessary to cite teachings.[17] This also applies to judges' drafting abilities, which can affect whether they see the need to borrow phrases from teachings. One ICJ employee assumes a link

---

[14] For example, Martti Koskenniemi, *The Gentle Civilizer of Nations: The Rise and Fall of International Law 1870–1960* (Cambridge University Press 2001) 399–406.

[15] ICJ Judge 1.

[16] ICJ Judge 2.

[17] Earlsferry, 'Judges', 38.

between drafting ability and approach to teachings, when talking about a specific judge.[18] Beyond such anecdotal evidence, this possibility is difficult to test empirically.

In short, expertise is a possible explanation for why ICJ judges cite more teachings in some cases than in others. There are indications of this in the ICJ's practice, even though it cannot be conclusively proven.

5.4.5   The Availability of Better Arguments

One reason why individual opinions resort to teachings more often than majority opinions is may be that the views espoused in majority opinions systematically have better support in available sources, as suggested in Section 3.5.8. Something similar could cause differences between individual judges as well, since some judges may systematically take stances that have less support in available sources, giving them a greater incentive to resort to teachings. For example, Judge ad hoc Kreća, in most of the cases he has participated in, has been a lone or almost lone dissenter from the majority opinion and has been highly critical of most aspects of that opinion. He is also among the judges with the most citations of teachings.

Section 5.5.2 discusses the possibility that judges ad hoc cite teachings more often than do permanent judges because of an absence of better arguments. However, the conclusion here is that the pattern is better explained by the style and philosophy of the individuals appointed as judges ad hoc. In short, the lack of better arguments is a reasonable explanation for the approaches of specific judges, but not for the entire group of judges ad hoc.

5.4.6   Practical Factors

Practical factors can also affect how a judge applies teachings.[19] How a judge applies teachings may, for example, be affected by the assistance the judge receives in identifying and processing relevant works. The ICJ Registry prepares bibliographies relating to each case.[20] However, this does not mean that judges or other employees always find this useful in practice, as they may be 'recycled', 'too general', and sent out too late.[21]

---

[18] ICJ Employee 1 ('[i]t is probably rare to find somebody who can express something better than [the judge] can').
[19] Sivakumaran, 'Influence', 28.
[20] Section 3.4.3.
[21] ICJ Employee 2.

Similarly, the availability and use of law clerks and assistants might also affect how teachings are applied.[22] In the ICJ, clerks produce background documents for judges, and these documents usually cite teachings.[23] The ICJ's Registry also assists judges.[24] However, judges use the support staff differently.[25] It is therefore difficult to draw firm conclusions about specific judges, since their use of clerks is not public knowledge. What can be compared are developments over time. The number of ICJ clerks has expanded over time,[26] coinciding with a general increase in the citation of teachings by the Court's judges. This increase was found in Section 3.7.7 to be largely due to the election and appointment of four judges in particular. However, the expansion of the clerk system may also have been a factor in the evolution of the judges' application of teachings.

Another practical factor that may affect how a judge approaches teachings is time pressure. This may be because judges cite more teachings when they have more time available for research (and vice versa).[27] One ICJ judge explains that 'there is not a great deal of time to produce a separate or dissenting opinion. You have [...] a period of about two to three weeks [...] to produce a separate opinion. You do not have time to go off on research'.[28] A contrary effect is also possible, in that teachings are more necessary when there is less time for independent thought. An ICJ employee thus claims that '[i]f you [...] have five minutes to put together a position on something, or an hour to write an advice, you are much more heavily dependent upon [...] whichever work you use'.[29]

For ICJ judges, it is possible to test whether citations of teachings correlate with the number of individual opinions written, creating what could be termed a measure of 'busyness'. Figure 5.3 is a graphical representation of the number of individual ICJ opinions per year.

---

[22] Earlsferry, 'Judges', 29; Forest, 'Listening', 75; Sivakumaran, 'Influence', 28.

[23] Section 3.4.3.

[24] Thirlway, 'Drafting', 19.

[25] Terris, Romano, and Swigart, *International Judge*, 56.

[26] For example, Dapo Akande, 'International Court of Justice to Appoint 6 New Clerks', *EJIL: Talk!* (16 February 2010) www.ejiltalk.org/international-court-of-justice-to-appoint-6-new-clerks.

[27] Hume, 'Strategic', 292; Louis J Sirico Jr and Beth A Drew, 'The Citing of Law Reviews by the United States Courts of Appeals: An Empirical Analysis' (1991) 45 *University of Miami Law Review* 1051, 1053.

[28] ICJ Judge 1.

[29] ICJ Employee 1.

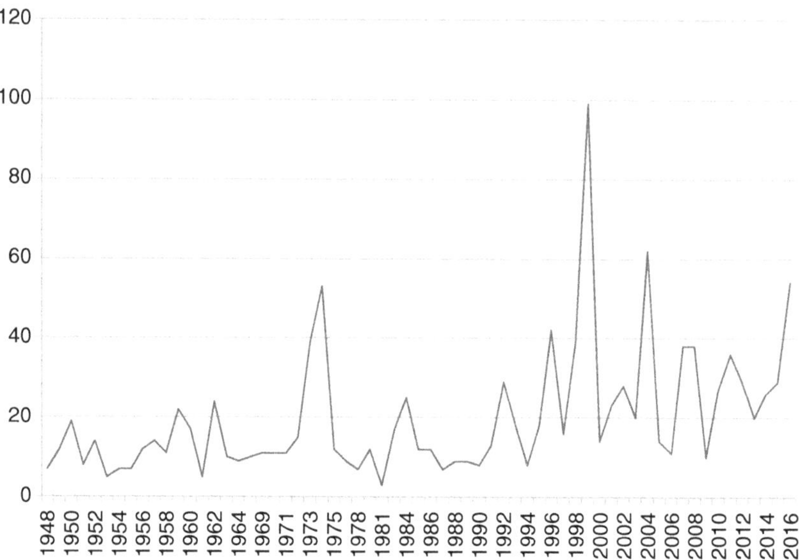

Figure 5.3   Individual opinions per year

Years are on the horizontal x-axis, while the total number of individual opinions published each year is on the vertical y-axis.

Figure 5.3 can then be combined with Figure 3.1, which showed the number of citations of teachings per year. This is done in Figure 5.4.

From this combined figure, it can be seen that each variable is often high when the other is low. In other words, they appear to be inversely correlated. This is consistent with the hypothesis that when judges write more opinions, they generally include fewer references to teachings in each opinion. This picture is muddied by the fact that some of the judges who frequently cite teachings in their opinions are also judges who frequently write individual opinions. Examples include Judge Cançado Trindade, Judge Weeramantry, and Judge Shahabuddeen.

Judges' application of teachings in a given case can also be affected by how teachings are used in the pleadings. In the three cases where pleadings have been examined in this book, judges cited teachings 469 times in individual opinions. Among these, 100 (21 per cent) involved authors who were cited in pleadings. If pleadings had cited more or fewer teachings, or cited different works, this could have affected the teachings cited by the judges. Another conclusion is that many of the teachings that

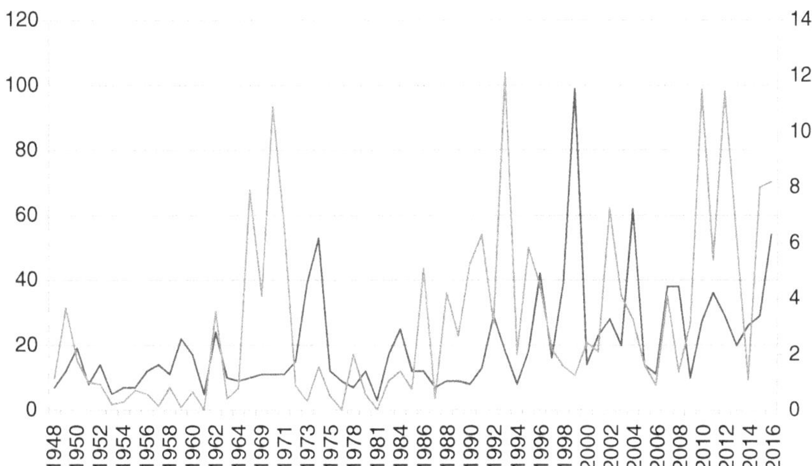

Figure 5.4   Number of opinions per year and number of citations of teachings per year

judges cite are not found in pleadings. They are the result of the judges' (or clerks') own research, which requires time, which in turn means that judges' time pressure, research assistance, and facilities matter. The exact share of judges' citations that are also found in pleadings varies from opinion to opinion, from 0 to 100 per cent. An overview is given in Appendix 5.

As a final practical factor, the variation between how often judges cite teachings may also be influenced by the availability of relevant teachings in each specific case. If judge A decides to write an individual opinion in a case where there is a wealth of relevant teachings, while judge B decides to write an individual opinion in a case with a dearth of teachings, this alone could explain why Judge A cited more teachings. Judges ad hoc are particularly susceptible to this, because they (by design) decide fewer cases than permanent judges, and their numbers are therefore more affected by the particular circumstances of specific cases. Controlling for this factor would require an examination of the field of available relevant teachings at the time each of the ICJ's cases was decided. That is not attempted in this book. However, that the availability of teachings can account for much of the variation between judges would seem unlikely, since variations are also found between different judges in the same cases. For example, in the merits phase of *Fisheries Jurisdiction (UK)*, Judge Sir Humphrey Waldock's opinion had a single reference to teachings,[30] while Judge De Castro's similarly lengthy opinion cited teachings on almost every page.[31]

5.5   Data That Correlate with Variations between Judges

5.5.1   *Introduction*

This section tests ICJ judges' approaches to teachings against various sets of data to see how they correlate. While these data cannot in themselves explain why or how judges apply teachings, they do suggest that some of the factors discussed in Section 5.4 are more plausible than others. Five data sets are examined: whether a judge is permanent or ad hoc; whether opinions are separate or dissenting; judges' nationalities; judges' educations; and judges' professional backgrounds.

5.5.2   *Permanent Judges and Judges Ad Hoc*

The application of teachings by ICJ judges varies between permanent and ad hoc judges. As shown in Appendix 2, judges ad hoc had on average 5.5 references to teachings in their opinions, while the number for permanent judges is 2.8. While 51.6 per cent of opinions by judges ad hoc contain references to teachings, only 27.6 per cent of opinions by permanent judges do so. In short, judges ad hoc cite more teachings. The numbers are similar if the four most-citing judges (Cançado Trindade, Weeramantry, Shahabuddeen, and Kreća) are excluded: an average of 3.7 citations for judges ad hoc and 1.1 for permanent judges, and citations in 43 per cent of opinions for judges ad hoc and 24 per cent for permanent judges.

As for why this may be the case, it is possible that the nature of the role as judge ad hoc motivates judges to cite more teachings. Ad hoc judges are not supposed to act as additional counsel for the state that appointed them,[32] but part of their duties is to ensure that the views and perspectives of that state is understood by the other judges.[33] In practice they tend to vote in favour of the appointing state.[34] Thus, judges ad hoc may resort to legal arguments that are less supported by relevant sources than

---

[30] *Fisheries Jurisdiction (United Kingdom* v. *Iceland)*, Separate Opinion of Judge Sir Humphrey Waldock 119.

[31] Ibid., Separate Opinion of Judge de Castro 78–87, 91, 94–97, 100.

[32] Eduardo Jiménez de Aréchaga quoted in Cassese, *Five Masters*, 90; Rosenne and Ronen, *Law and Practice*, 1081.

[33] *Bosnia Genocide, 1993*, Separate Opinion of Judge ad hoc Lauterpacht 409.

[34] Rosenne and Ronen, *Law and Practice*, 1082–1083.

are the arguments of permanent judges. This may in turn call for citing teachings, since no more authoritative sources or arguments are available (as discussed in Section 5.4.5).

Appendix 2 also looks at the opinions of the judges who have served both as permanent judges and as judges ad hoc. As judges ad hoc, these judges included an average of 1.7 citations of teachings in each opinion and cited teachings in 45.5 per cent of their opinions. In their opinions as permanent judges, the same judges cited teachings on average 3.9 times per opinion and cited teachings in 34.3 per cent of their opinions. Thus, the judges actually cited *more* teachings in their opinions as permanent judges (although as judges ad hoc they cited teachings in a slightly higher share of their opinions). If the different citation rates between permanent and ad hoc judges are caused by differences between the two roles, one would expect judges who had held both roles to have more citations as judges ad hoc. The numbers show the opposite. This suggests that the different citation rates between permanent judges and judges ad hoc are caused not by the differences between the two roles, but rather by differences between the individuals who have held the respective positions.

However, if the two most-citing, 'outlier' judges who have been both permanent judges and judges ad hoc (Weeramantry and Shahabuddeen) are removed, the remaining judges who have served in both roles cited teachings more often when they were judges ad hoc: 1.1 citations per opinion as judge ad hoc versus 0.7 as permanent judges, and citations in 41.5 per cent of opinions as judge ad hoc versus 22 per cent of opinions as permanent judges. The numbers for judges ad hoc and permanent judges are therefore somewhat inconclusive.

Even so, differences between individuals may be systematic, for example, states tend to elect individuals of one type as permanent judges and appoint another type as judges ad hoc. A relevant factor in this context is that permanent judges need the support of a large number of states in order to be elected, while judges ad hoc are appointed by a single state. States are therefore freer to appoint more creative or combative judges as judges ad hoc. Such creativity and combativeness can be classified as part of a judge's philosophical outlook or approach, which were discussed in Section 5.4.3.

5.5.3 *Separate and Dissenting Opinions*

It is possible to compare the rates of citations in separate and dissenting opinions. Intuitively, one might think that dissenting opinions would have more citations, since these will usually be further removed from the

Court's median view and have less support in other, more authoritative sources than teachings. That is to some extent confirmed by the data: Judges cite teachings on average 4.7 times per separate opinion and 5 times per dissenting opinions. Teachings are cited in 41.9 per cent of both separate and dissenting opinions. The results are similar when the four most-citing judges (Cançado Trindade, Weeramantry, Shahabuddeen, and Kreća) are excluded. In that case separate opinions have 2.0 citations on average, while dissenting have 2.3. There are thus slightly more teachings in dissenting opinions than in separate opinions, and the mostly plausible explanation is that this is because of differences in the availably of better arguments, as discussed in Section 5.4.5.

Individual ICJ opinions also include declarations, where teachings are cited only 0.1 times per opinion and in 9 per cent of opinions. This is unsurprising, as declarations are generally short and uncomplicated. Twelve opinions from the early days of the Court are officially labelled neither 'separate' nor 'dissenting' nor 'declaration', but rather 'individual'. Those twelve opinions are not included in these statistics.

5.5.4 Judges' Nationalities

Statistically, there is a correlation between judges' citation rates and whether they are nationals of an OECD member State. Appendix 2 gives precise numbers. Data on nationality were available for all judges from the Court's website.[35] OECD membership can be seen as a proxy for whether a country is 'rich' or 'poor', or 'developed' or 'developing'. This is not a perfect proxy,[36] but it has the advantage of being simple and reasonably accurate.[37] OECD membership can also be used as a proxy for distinguishing between Western and non-Western States.[38]

The appendix shows that judges from non-OECD countries cited teachings an average of 4.7 times per opinion, compared to 1.5 for judges from OECD member States. Judges from non-OECD countries cited

---

[35] ICJ, 'All Members' (2017) www.icj-cij.org/en/all-members; ICJ, 'All Judges *ad hoc*' (2017) www.icj-cij.org/en/all-judges-ad-hoc.

[36] Gaubatz and MacArthur, 'How International', 250.

[37] It is used by, for example, Susan D Franck, 'Development and Outcomes in Investment Treaty Arbitration' (2009) 50 *Harvard International Law Journal* 438, 446–447; but is supplemented by other proxies by Franck, 'Diversity', 462; Shashank P Kumar and Cecily Rose, 'A Study of Lawyers Appearing before the International Court of Justice, 1999–2012' (2014) 25 *European Journal of International Law* 893, 899.

[38] For example, Gaubatz and MacArthur, 'How International', 250.

teachings in 34.9 per cent of their opinions, compared to 26.2 per cent for judges from OECD member States.

A plausible explanation of this correlation is that certain philosophical and methodological perspectives on the law (as discussed in Section 5.4.3) are more prevalent in some countries than in others. However, if the four 'outlier' judges (Cançado Trindade, Weeramantry, Shahabuddeen, and Kreća) are excluded, the numbers for the two groups of judges are almost exactly the same: 1.5 citations per opinion per OECD judges and 1.3 per non-OECD judge. Both groups cited teachings in 26 per cent of opinions. Thus, the differences between OECD and non-OECD judges seem to be primarily caused not so much by different approaches in different parts of the world as by the individual approaches of certain specific judges.

It would be interesting to see whether individual judges' approaches correlate with the approach of their national courts. If certain philosophical and methodological perspectives on the law are more prevalent in some countries than in others, these could also affect national judges. The practices of some national courts are described in Section 6.3, but not enough to do a systematic analysis.

That judges are influenced by their national background would be in line with the ICJ Statute Article 9, according to which 'the representation of the main forms of civilization and of the principal legal systems of the world should be assured' among the Court's members. The existence of observable differences between judges is in line with the Court's institutional design.

There is also a correlation between how often judges cite teachings and whether they are nationals of countries with civil law or common law systems.[39] The eight judges from 'mixed' countries (South Africa, Israel, Guyana, Somalia, Sri Lanka, Philippines, and Cameroon) are counted under both categories. The United States, Canada, and China are not counted as mixed, even though Louisiana, Quebec, and Hong Kong use a different system than the country as a whole. The results are shown in Appendix 2. Judges from civil law countries cite teachings more often, 3.8 times per opinion, compared to 2.8 for judges from common law

---

[39] As classified by the University of Ottawa's 'Juriglobe' project: University of Ottawa, 'Alphabetical Index of the 192 United Nations Member States and Corresponding Legal Systems' (undated) www.juriglobe.ca/eng/syst-onu/index-alpha.php.

countries. This is line with conventional wisdom.[40] The differences
between judges from civil law and common law countries nonetheless
disappear when the four most-citing judges (Cançado Trindade,
Weeramantry, Shahabuddeen, and Kreća) are excluded from the statistics: without them, civil law judges cite teaching on average 1.4 times per
opinion (and 25 per cent of opinions) and common law judges 1.5 times
(and 29 per cent of opinions). There is thus no apparent systematic
difference between the two groups. Regardless, it is plausible to assume
that ICJ judges carry with them habits that have been internalised from
their educations and professional lives in their national legal systems.
These affect the judges' 'personal philosophy', which was discussed in
Section 5.4.3. Such philosophies are not wholly a matter of choice and
reflection on the part of the judge; they are also the result of subconscious
influences and conditioning.

The numbers are illustrated in Figure 5.5. The groups of judges are
distributed along the horizontal x-axis, while the average number of
citations of teachings per opinion is on the vertical y-axis.

5.5.5   Judges' Educations

The previous section distinguished between judges who are nationals of
OECD member States and those that are not.[41] It is also possible to
distinguish between judges who have and have not *studied in* an OECD
member State. This is done in Appendix 2, which contains data on 146 of
the 165 judges who have written at least one individual opinion. Data
were unavailable for two permanent judges,[42] sixteen judges ad hoc,[43]
and one who was both.[44] As the appendix shows, 126 judges have taken at
least one degree in an OECD member State, while twenty judges have
not. The latter group cites teachings more often than the former.

The non-OECD judges cite teachings on average 3.6 times per opinion
and in 37 per cent of all opinions. The corresponding numbers for

---

[40]   Expressed, for example, by Bohlander, 'Influence', 208; Forest, 'Listening', 88;
      Jan Paulsson, 'Scholarship as Law' in Mahnoush H Arsanjani and others (eds.), *Looking
      to the Future: Essays in Honor of Michael Reisman* (Martinus Nijhoff 2011) 183, 188.
[41]   Studies at the Hague Academy of International Law, professional qualifications (e.g., from
      the English Inns of Court), and honorary degrees are not counted.
[42]   Alfaro, Basdevant.
[43]   Alayza y Paz Soldán, Beb a Don, Boni, Bula-Bula, Caicedo Castilla, Carry, Daxner, Ečer,
      Fernandes, Louis Mbanefo, Mavungu, Reddy, Roucounas, Theirry, Urrutia Holguin,
      van Wyk.
[44]   Armand-Ugon.

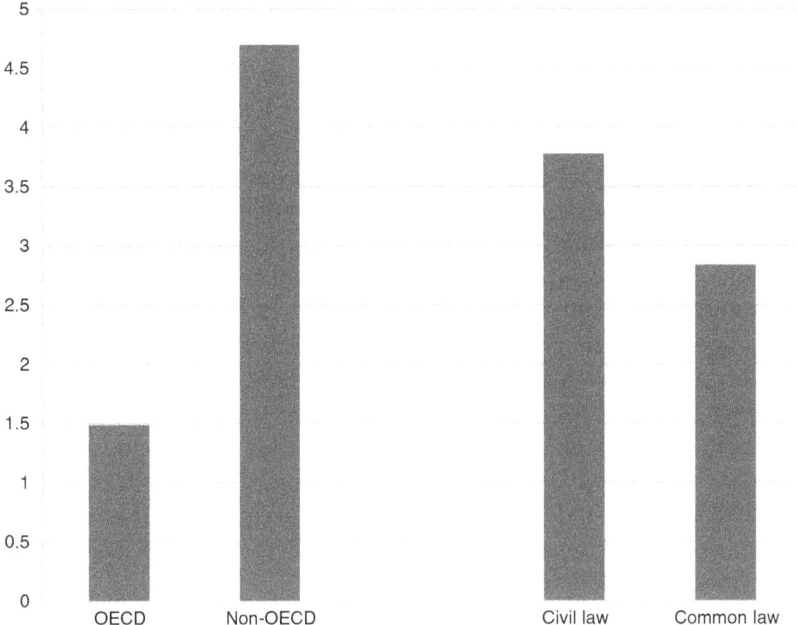

Figure 5.5 Citations of teachings by judges' nationalities

OECD-educated judges are lower, at 3.1 references per opinions and 31 per cent of all opinions. However, if the four most-citing judges (Cançado Trindade, Weeramantry, Shahabuddeen, and Kreća) are excluded, the situation is reversed, with judges with no OECD education citing teachings on average 0.9 times per opinion and in 24 per cent of opinions and judges with some OECD education citing 1.4 times per opinion and in 27 per cent of opinions. Thus, the initial difference between the groups is largely down to these four specific judges, as with the data on nationality.

The previous section suggested that 'certain philosophical and methodological perspectives on the law' are 'more prevalent in some countries than in others'. That assumption is also plausible for variations based on where judges were educated. If there are differences in 'philosophical and methodological perspectives on the law' between different countries and regions, which affect how teachings are viewed and applied, those differences should be reflected in and reproduced by educational institutions. The result will be that it matters where a judge was educated.

The previous section also compared judges who are nationals of countries with civil law systems and common law systems, respectively. It is similarly possible to compare judges who *studied in* countries with civil law systems and common law systems. This is also done in Appendix 2. While civil law country nationals cited more teachings, the results based on education say the opposite: Judges who studied only in civil law countries cite the least teachings (at 1.9 per opinion), while judges who studied only in common law countries cite considerably more (at 3.3 per opinion). The judges who studied in either a country with a mixed system or in multiple countries with different systems cite considerably more teachings than both groups, however (at six per opinion). Since the 'middle group' is an outlier, the results are inconclusive and difficult to interpret in a meaningful way. If the four most-citing judges (Cançado Trindade, Weeramantry, Shahabuddeen, and Kreća) are excluded, common law-educated judges still cite teachings more often than civil law-educated judges, with 1.6 versus 1.4 citations per opinion and citations in 33 per cent versus 25 per cent of opinions. Judges with educations from both systems cite less than both the other groups when the most-citing judges are excluded, with 0.8 citations per opinion on average and citations in 20 per cent of opinions.

These results undermine the neat conclusion from Section 5.5.4 that 'civil law judges' cite more teachings. The conclusion is instead that simple conclusions cannot be drawn, and the conventional wisdom that civil lawyers cite more teachings does not hold up in the context of the ICJ judges' application of teachings.[45]

The numbers are illustrated in Figure 5.6. The vertical axis plots the average number of citations of teachings per opinion, while the horizontal axis names the different groups of judges.

5.5.6   Judges' Professional Backgrounds

Judges' professional backgrounds are correlated with how often they cite teachings. Judges have generally had more than one job,[46] but here they

---

[45] This realisation echoes Duxbury's scepticism against drawing any sharp distinctions between the role of teachings in France, England, and the US: Duxbury, *Judges*, 115 and 117.

[46] Terris, Romano, and Swigart, *International Judge*, 102. Similarly Leigh Swigart and Daniel Terris, 'Who are International Judges' in Cesare P R Romano, Karen J Alter, and Yuval Shany (eds.), *The Oxford Handbook of International Adjudication* (Oxford University Press 2015) 619, 626; Vera Shikhelman, 'Diversity and Decision-Making in International Judicial Institutions' (2018) 36 *Berkeley Journal of International Law* 60, 78.

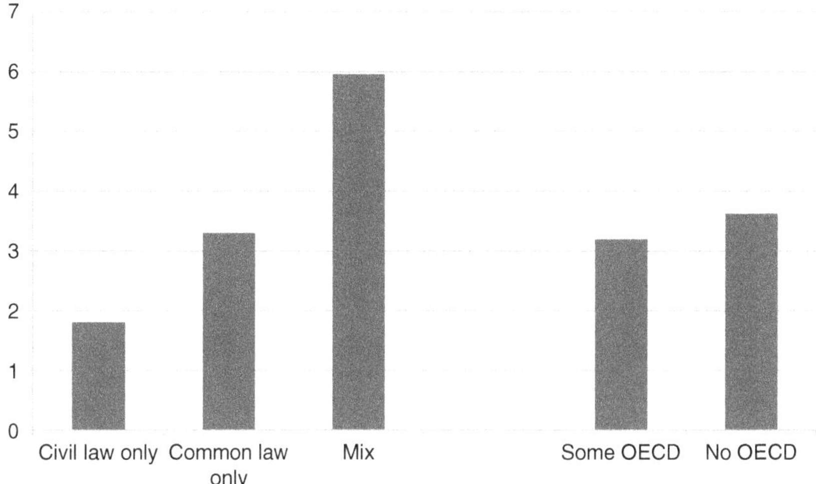

Figure 5.6 Citations of teachings by judges' educations

have been classified in only one former profession, which is the one that they have spent the most time in. An alternative approach would have been to count the most recent employment, but that would have been arbitrary for shorter stints. Another possibility would have been to count the number of years each judge spent in each position and attempt to weigh the citation numbers accordingly, but that would have been confusingly complex. Comprehensive biographical data were obtained for all but 14 of the 165 judges who had written at least one individual opinion.[47] The 14 missing judges were all ad hoc judges, and they were responsible for only 20 of the 1409 individual opinions that are counted in the study. The full data on judges' citations and backgrounds are included in Appendix 2.

Former academics cite teachings more often than other judges, with averages of 4.9 and 1.6 references per opinion, respectively. The non-academics can be broken into subgroups, with average citation numbers in parenthesis: diplomats (1.6); national civil servants (0.4); international civil servants (1.1); politicians (5.7); national judges (0.4); international judges (0.4); and practising lawyers (1.8).

---

[47] Data were unavailable for: Alayza y Paz Soldán, Beb a Don, Boni, Bula-Bula, Caicedo Castilla, Carry, Daxner, Ečer, Fernandes, Louis Mbanefo, Mavungu, Urrutia Holguin, Reddy, van Wyk.

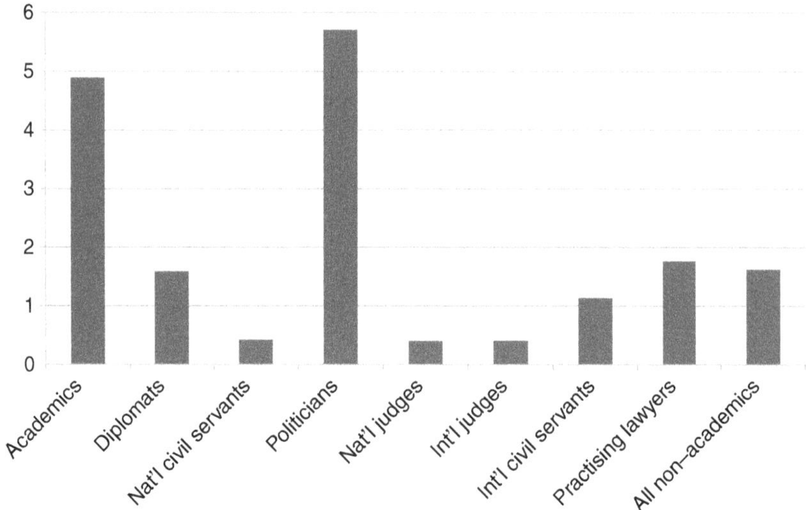

Figure 5.7   Citations of teachings by judges' professional backgrounds

Figure 5.7 illustrates the data, which show average references per opinion on the vertical y-axis and judges' professional backgrounds on the horizontal x-axis.

The main professional backgrounds of ICJ judges are as academics and diplomats, with smaller groups of national judges, international judges, national civil servants, international civil servants, practising lawyers, and politicians.[48] Of the 151 judges for whom data were available, 69 were former academics, 44 were former diplomats, while the remaining 38 belonged to other categories. This means that for all groups except academics and diplomats, the sample sizes were small (between three and eleven judges). For example, one judge (Shahabuddeen) made 249 out of 291 citations by politicians.

The differences nonetheless persist when the four most-citing judges (Cançado Trindade, Weeramantry, Shahabuddeen, and Kreća) are excluded from the statistics. Academics (1.7 citations per opinion) and politicians (1.6 citations per opinion) still cite teachings most often, while diplomats are at 1.0 citations per opinion. The other groups are not affected by the removal of the four judges.

---

[48] Similarly, Terris, Romano, and Swigart, *International Judge*, 20.

That judges who are former academics cite more teachings is assumed by an ICJ judge, who says that '[a]cademics are more liable to cite' teachings, and that '[t]here is a light majority of judges who have given legal advice to governments [...] they are less likely to cite [teachings] than academics'.[49] The findings presented here are therefore 'not at all a statistical anomaly'.[50]

The different approaches to teachings by academics and non-academics can have various explanations. The two groups may entertain different judicial philosophies, as discussed in Section 5.4.3. One ICJ judge thus explains Shahabuddeen's high citation rate by noting that, even though he was not employed as an academic, he 'was an inherently scholarly man'.[51] Academics' higher citation rate may also be a matter of habit, since academics are used to frequently citing teachings in their work. This is the opinion of another ICJ judge.[52] Academics may also be more familiar with the breadth and depth of available teachings[53] and may moreover have more respect for them, since they and their colleagues have been involved in producing them. It is also possible that judges who were academics have a more 'academic' judicial style, where it is more appropriate and relevant to cite teachings.

5.6 Conclusion

This chapter has shown that ICJ judges vary in how they use teachings and proposed that they can be classified into three groups: those who never cite teachings; those who frequently cite and engage with teachings; and the median, who occasionally cite but rarely engage with teachings. A significant majority of the Court's judges belongs to the median.

The most important factors that determine a judge's approach to teachings seem to be their individual judicial philosophy and style. Practical factors also seem to matter, especially their workload, since the judges overall cite fewer teachings when they write more individual opinions. Judges probably think strategically about when and how to apply (or not to apply) teachings, even though this is difficult to prove

---

⁴⁹ ICJ Judge 1.
⁵⁰ Ibid. For example, Forest, 'Listening', 73; Black and Richter, 'My Name', 387; Gordon Bale, 'Lederman and the Citation of Legal Periodicals by the Supreme Court of Canada' (1994) 19 *Queen's Law Journal* 36, 58 agree.
⁵¹ ICJ Judge 1.
⁵² ICJ Judge 2.
⁵³ Duxbury, *Judges*, 37.

conclusively. It is also likely that judges are to some extent motivated by their views on their own legal expertise when deciding whether and how to apply teachings.

The judges' application of teachings correlates with their professional and educational background, the wealth of their home country, whether they are ad hoc or permanent judges, and whether they are writing a separate or a dissenting opinion. The best interpretation of these data is that professional background, education, and nationality influence judges' style and judicial philosophy. The difference between permanent and ad hoc judges is best explained by systematic differences in style and philosophy among the relevant individuals, while the differences between separate and dissenting opinions are best explained by separate opinions having more support in other sources.

The significant variations between judges show that the ICJ Statute Article 38(1)(d) leaves significant discretion to judges, as also noted in Section 4.4.4. This is also the view of one ICJ judge, who explains that judges have considerable discretion, because the law at some point 'runs out'.[54] The wording of the ICJ Statute does not contradict this conclusion, since it gives few clear directions on when and how teachings are to be cited, as discussed in Section 2.2. The ICJ Statute Article 38(1)(d) may be supplemented by more informal directives. According to one ICJ judge, '[t]here are house practices' that guide the judges, but this judge 'would not call them rules'.[55] An ICJ employee similarly talks about 'social norms', primarily 'what has happened before' in the institution 'and the preferences of whomever I am working for' as the main determinants for how they apply teachings.[56]

---

[54] ICJ Judge 2.
[55] ICJ Judge 1.
[56] ICJ Employee 1.

6

Concluding Reflections

6.1 Teachings and the Development of International Law

So far, this book has focused on the role that teachings play when ICJ judges answer legal questions. The book has analysed ICJ judges' application of teachings in the context of the ICJ Statute Article 38, across three dimensions: (1) the weight assigned to teachings, which was found to be low; (2) the weight of different teachings, which was found to be variable; and (3) the weight assigned to teachings by different judges, which was also found to be variable. A separate but related question is what role teachings play in the broader development of international law. That is explored here.

Teachings can contribute to the development of international law.[1] This is in line with the preparatory works of the PCIJ Statute. An alternative draft produced by Mr. Root and Lord Phillimore included 'the opinions of writers as a means for the *application and development* of law' (emphasis added) in a formal hierarchy of sources.[2] The use of this distinction suggests an assumption that teachings were capable not only of affecting how specific legal questions were answered but also of influencing the broader development of the law. It is, however, difficult to draw a sharp distinction between 'application' and 'development'. The terms are reminiscent of 'codification' and 'progressive development', which were discussed in the context of the ILC in Section 2.3.6. The distinction between them was found not to be sharp, in the sense that the ILC can hardly do the one without doing the other.

---

[1] For example, Oscar Schachter, 'The Invisible College of International Lawyers' (1977) 72 *Northwestern University Law Review* 217, 223; William R Slomanson, *Fundamental Perspectives on International Law* (5th edn, Thomson Wadsworth 2007) 27; Ademola Abass, *International Law: Text, Cases, and Materials* (2nd edn, Oxford University Press 2014) 55, and others.

[2] ACJ, *Procès-Verbaux*, 344. It was also used by ACJ, *Procès-Verbaux*, 351, and, for example, by Daillier, Forteau, and Pellet, *Droit international*, 435.

157

One way in which teachings can influence the development of international law, is by affecting the views and practices of states.[3]

Additionally, teachings influence the ICJ. This book has shown that this statement has many nuances and reservations, but that there is some degree of influence. International courts and tribunals, in particular the ICJ, are often said to contribute to the development of international law.[4] The ICJ recognised in *Nuclear Weapons* that 'in stating and applying the law, the Court necessarily has to specify its scope and sometimes note its general trend'.[5] The Court has recognised that one of its judgments (in *North Sea*) 'made the greatest contribution to the formation of customary law' regarding the continental shelf.[6] Judge Sir Gerald Fitzmaurice wrote in *Barcelona Traction* that 'judicial pronouncements of one kind or another constitute the principal method by which the law can find some concrete measure of clarification and development'.[7] Shahabuddeen, who was an ICJ judge, argues 'that the Court has a faculty of limited creativity'.[8] The ICJ's effect on the development of international law is also recognised in the ICJ's own *Handbook*.[9] Judicial decisions can contribute to the development of international law even though they are 'subsidiary means' and, therefore, cannot themselves 'create' international law, as discussed in Section 2.2.8. Teachings' influence on judicial decisions, which can in turn influence international law, is one way in which teachings can influence the development of international law.

The ICJ's ability to influence the development of international law comes largely from the view that its decisions are accurate guides to the contents of international law.[10] This assumption is held despite the

---

[3] For example, English High Court of Justice, *West Rand Central Gold Mining Co. v. R* [1905] 2 KB 391, 402; Onuf, 'Global', 22; Dixon, *Textbook*, 49.

[4] For example, Rosalyn Higgins, *Problems and Process: International Law and How We Use It* (Oxford University Press 1995) 202; Boyle and Chinkin, *Making*, 266–269, 310–311; Robert Kolb, *The Elgar Companion to the International Court of Justice* (Edward Elgar 2014) 376, and others.

[5] *Nuclear Weapons*, 237.

[6] *Delimitation of the Maritime Boundary in the Gulf of Maine Area, Judgment, I.C.J. Reports 1984*, pp. 246, 293.

[7] *Barcelona Traction, 1970*, Separate Opinion of Judge Sir Gerald Fitzmaurice 64.

[8] Shahabuddeen, *Precedent*, 232.

[9] ICJ, 'Handbook' (last updated 31 December 2013) www.icj-cij.org/files/publications/handbook-of-the-court-en.pdf, 99–107.

[10] For example, Rosalyn Higgins, 'A Babel of Judicial Voices? Ruminations from the Bench' (2006) 55 *International and Comparative Law Quarterly* 791, 797; *Asylum*, Dissenting Opinion by Judge Azevedo 332; Boyle and Chinkin, *Making*, 293.

general view that there is no formal '*stare decisis*' or system of 'binding' precedent in international law. There are de facto systems of precedent, which means that judicial decisions can be of great significance without being formally binding (except on the parties to each case).[11]

An important caveat here is that this book is mainly examining individual opinions, which have less weight than majority opinions.[12] It cannot be presumed that any single individual opinion has much weight. However, the book aggregates results from *all* individual opinions, which is significant, because it is likely to say something of importance about how the majority opinions were written and decided, and the role teachings played in this process. As noted in Section 1.2, individual opinions may even be more accurate than majority opinions as guides to the role of teachings in the Court's decision-making process.

In conclusion, teachings probably contribute to the development of international law. Whether this is a good thing depends partly on whether one approves of the substantive outcomes of the developments. However, it can be valuable in itself that the law can be developed even when some actors are deadlocked. In this context it is relevant that international law does not have a legislature, which in national legal systems is an important agent in the development of the law.[13] Teachings may contribute by clarifying the law to discussing and agreeing on solutions to previously unresolved legal questions.[14] This contributes to legal certainty.[15] Teachings also play a role in systematising international law.[16]

Academics who read this book may take heart from seeing that teachings are not *entirely* ignored by the ICJ judges and from the assumption that citations are not exhaustive, as argued in Sections 1.3.2 and 3.4. Academics who find themselves on the list in Appendix 1 (and

---

[11] Section 3.7.7.

[12] Section 1.2.

[13] Anand, 'International Court', 228; Quincy Wright, 'The Strengthening of International Law' (1959) 98 *Recueil des Cours* 1, 284.

[14] For example, Schwarzenberger, 'Inductive', 8; Jean d'Aspremont, *Epistemic Forces in International Law* (Edward Elgar 2015) 239. Van Hoof, *Rethinking*, 177 is more sceptical.

[15] For example, Sourang, 'Jurisprudence', 283; Jennings, 'What is International Law', 46; Jutta Brunnée, 'The Sources of International Environmental Law: Interactional Law' in Samantha Besson and Jean d'Aspremont (eds.), *The Oxford Handbook on the Sources of International Law* (Oxford University Press 2017) 960, 977.

[16] For example, Van Hoof, *Rethinking*, 291; Oraison, 'L'Influence', 209; d'Aspremont, *Formalism*, 211; Wood, 'Teachings', para 3.

are thus still alive) can take this as a confirmation that they have written something that appeals to the Court's judges. They may also assume that their teachings have influenced the judges and thus the development of international law.

6.2   Potentially Beneficial Adjustments of the Court's Practice

6.2.1   Introduction

The previous chapters have described the practices of the Court and its judges in applying teachings. This section discusses whether any changes to that practice could be beneficial. This means that the arguments are normative. Three arguments are put forward: That the Court could benefit from diversifying its selection of writers, from more transparency about its application of teachings, and from more regulation of the application of teachings.

The arguments are grounded in larger normative debates about diversity, transparency, and regulation in international law. These debates have so far not been extended to the ICJ's application of teachings, and that is what this section does.

Other normative arguments about the application of teachings are possible. This includes arguments about the role that teachings should play in resolving contested legal issues,[17] and whether judges should be able to use teachings that the parties were not aware of.[18] The latter is permitted due to the principle of *jura novit curia*, according to which judges are assumed to know the law.[19] However, the ICJ Rules of Court[20] Article 72 prohibits ICJ judges from doing the same with evidence.[21] Such arguments cannot be connected with the examination that is done in this book and are therefore not discussed further.

---

[17] Cole, 'Non-Binding', 309.

[18] For example, *Barcelona Traction, 1970*, Separate Opinion of Judge Jessup 184; (in the context of national law) Bernstein, 'Secondary', 63; Beatson, 'Academics', 537.

[19] *Brazilian Loans*, 124; *Nicaragua, 1986*, 24–25; Rüdiger Wolfrum and Mirka Möldner, 'International Courts and Tribunals, Evidence', *Max Planck Encyclopedia of Public International Law* (article last updated August 2013) http://opil.ouplaw.com/view/10 .1093/law:epil/9780199231690/law-9780199231690-e26, para 15.

[20] ICJ, 'Rules of Court (1978)' (1978) www.icj-cij.org/en/rules.

[21] The same rule is found in ITLOS, 'Rules of the Tribunal' (17 March 2009) www.itlos.org /fileadmin/itlos/documents/basic_texts/Itlos_8_E_17_03_09.pdf, Article 87; Rome Statute Article 74(2) .

Normative arguments about the Court's practice could be phrased in terms of 'legitimacy'.[22] Legitimacy is often classified as either normative or sociological.[23] The first focuses on philosophical arguments about the right to rule, the second on sociological beliefs about whether a ruler has such a right.[24] Perceptions about legitimacy depend on who the perceiver is.[25] For the ICJ, such audiences may include litigants, other states, international lawyers, and other politically interested people.[26] An accurate way of discovering the views of the Court's different audiences would be to poll or interview relevant individuals, but that is beyond the scope of this book. Instead, the book makes arguments about how the Court's practice could be better aligned with recognised ideals in international law and the text of the ICJ Statute. Legitimacy is a contested and elusive term,[27] and it is not used in the following.

It is necessary to distinguish between the Court as a whole and individual judges. The argument about diversity is based mainly on citation patterns in individual opinions. The argument about transparency is largely about the Court's majority opinions. Even so, the practices of both the institution as a whole and of individual judges should be conscious of ideals such as diversity and transparency.

Changing the Court's practice as suggested later could affect its support from the international community, which in turn matters for its funding and supply of new cases, which are essential to its existence. The Court currently seems generally well respected among relevant audiences. This is reflected in, for example, the fact that the size of its docket remains relatively constant and involves states from most parts of the world. This does not mean that potential improvements need not be

---

[22] For example, Weeramantry, *Treaty Interpretation*, 137, argues that dealing with such sources and instruments in a transparent manner 'generally enhances the legitimacy of the adjudicative process'.

[23] For example, Allen Buchanan, 'The Legitimacy of International Law' in Samantha Besson and John Tasioulas (eds.), *The Philosophy of International Law* (Oxford University Press 2010) 79, 79; Geir Ulfstein, 'International Courts and Judges: Independence, Interaction, and Legitimacy' (2014) 46 *NYU Journal of International Law and Politics* 849, 862 (with further references).

[24] Harlan Grant Cohen and others, 'Legitimacy and International Courts – A Framework' in Harlan Grant Cohen and others (eds.), *Legitimacy and International Courts* (Cambridge University Press 2018) 1, 4.

[25] Ibid. Similarly Prott, *Culture,* 137.

[26] Prott, *Culture,* 152. Similarly Lupu and Voeten, 'Precedent', 417.

[27] For example, Koskenniemi, *Apology,* 591; Anne Peters, Geir Ulfstein, and Jan Klabbers, *The Constitutionalization of International Law* (Oxford University Press 2009) 42; Cohen and others, 'Legitimacy', 4.

discussed, however. The Court's practice could also affect compliance with its judicial decisions.[28] Such compliance is particularly important in international law, compared to many national legal systems, due to the lack of enforcement powers in international law.[29] The weight accorded to judicial decisions may also be affected by changes the Court's practice.[30]

6.2.2   Increased Diversity

Section 4.2.2 showed that ICJ judges cite mostly Western, and in particular British, writers. International law seeks to be global, insofar as it applies to every state in the world. Different states have different legal cultures,[31] and they have different approaches to international law.[32] International law should aim to be universal and accommodate all states.[33] The ICJ Statute Article 38(1)(d) thus talks about writers 'of the various nations', as discussed in Section 2.2.7. If ICJ judges cited a more diverse selection of writers, their practice would be more in line with the universal ideal of international law.[34] It would also be more in line with the wording of the ICJ Statute.[35]

International law is not infrequently accused of being Eurocentric.[36] The perceived bias of the investment arbitration system has led to several

---

[28] Thomas M Franck, *The Power of Legitimacy Among Nations* (Oxford University Press 1990) 49; Boyle and Chinkin, *Making*, 301.

[29] C G Weeramantry, 'Cultural and Ideological Pluralism in Public International Law' in Nisuke Ando, Edward McWhinney, and Rüdiger Wolfrum (eds.), *Liber Amicorum Judge Shigeru Oda*, vol 2 (Kluwer 2002) 1491, 1491; Weeramantry, *Universalising*, 3; Shikhelman, 'Diversity', 62 and 68–69.

[30] Boyle and Chinkin, *Making*, 301; Zarbiyev, 'Credibly', 312; Ingo Venzke, 'Semantic Authority, Legal Change and the Dynamics of International Law' (2015) 12 *No Foundations* 1, 3 (apparently).

[31] William E Butler, 'Regional and Sectional Diversities in International Law' in Bin Cheng (ed.), *International Law: Teaching and Practice* (Stevens and Sons 1982) 45, 47. Similarly, for example, Antonio Cassese, *International Law in a Divided World* (Oxford University Press 1986) 123; Schachter, *Theory*, 38.

[32] David Kennedy, 'The Disciplines of International Law and Policy' (2008) 12 *Leiden Journal of International Law* 9, 17.

[33] For example, Allott, 'Interpretation', 384 (talking about 'interpretation'). Similarly, for example, *Gabčikovo*, Separate Opinion of Vice-President Weeramantry 108; Mark W Janis, 'Introduction' in Mark W Janis and Carolyn Maree Evans (eds.), *Religion and International Law* (Martinus Nijhoff 1999) xi, xi.

[34] Bohlander and Findlay, 'Use', 22 suggests a similar argument for the ICTY.

[35] Virally, 'Sources', 153; ILC, *Report of the Sixty-eighth session*, 112.

[36] For example, Martti Koskenniemi, 'Histories of International Law: Dealing with Eurocentrism' (2011) 19 *Rechtsgeschichte* 152; Arnulf Becker Lorca, 'Eurocentrism in

developing states criticising or leaving it.[37] The ICC has been accused of being biased against African States.[38] Several African States have threatened to leave the ICC,[39] and Burundi has done so.[40] The lack of diversity in the ICJ judges' application of teachings fits into a broader pattern.

ICJ judges cite men far more often than women, as shown in Section 4.2.2. Roughly half the world's population is female, but they do not participate equally in the practice of international law.[41] However, the attitudes among the relevant diplomats and politicians towards increased female representation in international courts and tribunals seem to be 'ambivalent'.[42] This may be because some states do not practice gender equality internally. Another reason is that while the authority of international law formally rests on the consent and participation of states in all regions of the world, this argument does not apply to men and women. The gender of writers is not mentioned in the ICJ Statute Article 38(1). Gender diversity is, in any case, another area where the ICJ judges' practices are part of a broader pattern.

More consultation and citations of non-Western and female writers in ICJ opinions would not necessarily result in different substantive outcomes in specific cases.[43] Such writers may or may not have different attitudes, assumptions, preferences, and prejudices than their male and Western counterparts (which would be similar to how judges'

---

the History of International Law' in Bardo Fassbender and Anne Peters (eds.), *The Oxford Handbook of the History of International Law* (Oxford University Press 2012) 1034.

[37] For example, Emmanuel Gaillard, 'The Denunciation of the ICSID Convention', *Transnational Dispute Management* (2007).www.transnational-dispute-management.com/article.asp?key=1074.

[38] The Economist, 'Nice idea, now make it work' (4 December 2014) www.economist.com/news/international/21635470-international-criminal-court-struggling-justify-itself-amid-accusations-bias.

[39] For example, Associated Press In Addis Ababa, 'African leaders plan mass withdrawal from international criminal court', *The Guardian* (31 January 2017) www.theguardian.com/law/2017/jan/31/african-leaders-plan-mass-withdrawal-from-international-criminal-court.

[40] Agence France-Presse, 'Burundi becomes first nation to leave international criminal court', *The Guardian* (28 October 2017) www.theguardian.com/law/2017/oct/28/burundi-becomes-first-nation-to-leave-international-criminal-court.

[41] Hilary Charlesworth and Christine Chinkin, *The Boundaries of International Law: A Feminist Analysis* (Manchester University Press 2000) 50. Similarly Hilary Charlesworth, Christine Chinkin, and Shelley Wright, 'Feminist Approaches to International Law' (1991) 85 *American Journal of International Law* 613, 622.

[42] Mackenzie and others, *Selecting*, 49.

[43] Dermot Feenan, 'Editorial Introduction: Women and Judging' (2009) 17 *Feminist Legal Studies* 1, 4; Rosemary Hunter, 'More than Just a Different Face? Judicial Diversity and Decision-making' (2015) 68 *Current Legal Problems* 119, 140; Franck, 'Diversity', 498.

approaches to teachings vary by national background, as discussed in Section 5.5.4). The argument made in this section does not depend on affecting the outcome of any future case.[44] The main purpose is rather to show that this part of international law, too, aspires to be global and universal, even if this ideal is often achieved only imperfectly in practice.

The current citation patterns may have various causes, as explored in Section 4.2.3. They do not show that ICJ judges are biased. They may be a result of individual judges making a rational calculation about what citations will improve the authority of their decisions.[45] Even so, the citation patterns are not aligned with the ideal of universality. This has a parallel with rules about recusal for judges in international and national courts. These focus on perception rather than substance, in that justice must be *'seen to be done'*.[46] Actual influence or bias on the part of the recused judge is not a requirement.[47]

A more diverse citation of teachings may not only result in less authoritative judicial decisions. Teachings can save judges' time, not least because judges can trust the legal analyses in authoritative works. If judges were to consult and cite less authoritative works, this benefit too may disappear.[48] Judges must balance potential advantages and disadvantages of a more diverse citation pattern against each other.[49]

6.2.3 Increased Transparency

Section 3.4 argued that teachings are used by ICJ judges more often than they cite them in their opinions. There is, therefore, a potential for increased transparency in the judges' application of teachings.[50]

---

[44] Similarly Grossman, 'Shattering', 403.

[45] Kumar and Rose, 'Study', 912; Sergio Puig, 'Social Capital in the Arbitration Market' (2014) 25 *European Journal of International Law* 387, 423 make analogous arguments about the selection counsel in the ICJ and investment arbitration.

[46] For example, English High Court of Justice, *R* v. *Sussex Justices, Ex parte McCarthy* [1923] 1 KB 256, 259 (emphasis added).

[47] ICTY Appeal Chamber, *Prosecutor* v. *Anto Furundzia*, Judgment, 21 July 2000, Case IT-95-17/1-A, 58; ECtHR, 'Resolution on Judicial Ethics' (23 June 2008) www.echr.coe.int /Documents/Resolution_Judicial_Ethics_ENG.pdf, Section II; Sands, McLachlan, and Mackenzie, 'Principles', para 9.2, 12.1, 13.1, 14.2.

[48] Similarly, Avidan Kent and Jamie Trinidad, 'International Law Scholars as Amici Curiae: An Emerging Dialogue (of the Deaf)?' (2016) 29 *Leiden Journal of International Law* 1081, 1088.

[49] Shikhelman, 'Diversity', 104.

[50] Other meanings of the term 'transparency' as applied to the ICJ are discussed by Philippe Sands quoted in Keene (ed.), 'Outcome Paper', 249.

Transparency is an essential component of the rule of law.[51] Actors in a legal system should be made able to foresee the legality of their actions. This means that judges should show what sources they rely on to decide a given case. This gives the parties to the case a full understanding of why they won or lost, and it gives potential future litigants the ability to predict the outcomes of their cases.[52]

Judges do cite teachings in individual opinions, as emphasised by an ICJ judge.[53] This gives some degree of transparency about the role of teachings in the judges' decision-making.

Transparency is not just about *citing* teachings. Judges can also show and explain how teachings affected their decision by 'engaging' with teachings, as explained in Section 3.7. The section noted that ICJ judges engage little with teachings even when citing them. Arguments from teachings are usually not explicitly assessed on their merits, no effort is usually made to elucidate the precise views of the teachings consulted, and comparisons between different works are usually not attempted. This may be done in private, of course, but is rarely seen in the text of opinions. This means that here too there is a potential for increased transparency. For example, judges could consistently refer to and rebut perspectives that go against the legal solution favoured in a decision.[54] Because teachings lack official authority,[55] their arguments should be evaluated on their merits.[56]

More generally, the Court and its judges could also be more transparent about how they view and apply the ICJ Statute Article 38(1) in specific cases.[57]

The ICJ Statute Article 38(1)(d) says that the ICJ 'shall apply' teachings when deciding cases based on international law. This does not entail obligation to cite them.[58]

---

[51] For example, Boyle and Chinkin, *Making,* 302; Samantha Besson, 'Theorizing the Sources of International Law' in Samantha Besson and John Tasioulas (eds.), *The Philosophy of International Law* (OUP 2010) 163, 172.

[52] Philippa Webb, *International Judicial Integration and Fragmentation* (Oxford University Press 2013) 224; Michael A Becker and Cecily Rose, 'Investigating the Value of Site Visits in Inter-State Arbitration and Adjudication' (2017) 8 *Journal of International Dispute Settlement* 219, 248–249, make this point about judicial decisions and site visits and by Cole, 'Non-Binding', 316, regarding teachings in investment tribunals.

[53] ICJ judge 2.

[54] Similarly Cole, 'Non-Binding', 310 and 316; Shecaira, *Scholarship,* 80.

[55] Section 3.9.2.

[56] Cole, 'Non-Binding', 316.

[57] Yee, 'Applicable Law', 498; Sir Michael Wood, 'What Is Public International Law? The Need for Clarity about Sources' (2011) 1 *Asian Journal of International Law* 205, 205–207.

[58] Section 2.2.3.

Judges may adopt the text of scholarly work without attribution.[59] Unlike academic writers, such judges are not guilty of plagiarism in a strict legal sense.[60] Even so, they will not have been transparent about the sources that influence their decision-making.[61]

Section 3.5 presented explanations for why the ICJ's majority opinions rarely cite teachings. Some of these explanations are also valid justifications of a lack of transparency. That teachings lack official authority is one such justification. The ICJ's institutional role and authority probably renders it particularly uneasy about seeming to rely on scholars. The need to keep a decision relatively short and readable is another valid concern. As shown in Section 4.2.2, the writers that individual judges cite are largely Western nationals. That is another reason why the Court's majority may prefer not to cite teachings, since an increased reference to teachings would likely expose the lack of diversity in the relevant teachings that the judges consult. However, in that case the lack of diversity should be the main issue, not the risk that it gets exposed.

In short, reasons for not citing teachings must be counterbalanced by the potential benefits from increased transparency. As with diversity, this balancing must be done by the individual judge.[62]

Regarding the future of the 'unwritten rule' that majority decisions do not cite teachings (mentioned in Section 3.4.3), one ICJ judge reveals that 'there is no pressure for change', and 'I do not see this changing'.[63] Even so, former ICJ Registrar Thirlway describes 'an unwritten rule of drafting that the Court [. . .] never to arbitral awards', which 'appears now to have been abandoned'.[64]

6.2.4   Increased Regulation

The exercise of public authority should generally be regulated.[65] Judges exercise authority when deciding cases, and their decision-making

---

[59]   Beatson, 'Academics', 524 gives specific examples (from national law).

[60]   For example, Richard A Posner, *The Little Book of Plagiarism* (Pantheon 2007) 21; Earlsferry, 'Judges', 32; Stanton, 'Scholarship', 206.

[61]   Jennings, 'Subsidiary Means', 329; Duxbury, *Judges*, 65.

[62]   Similarly, Bernstein, 'Secondary', 80.

[63]   ICJ Judge 1.

[64]   Hugh Thirlway, *The Law and Procedure of the International Court of Justice: Fifty Years of Jurisprudence* (Oxford University Press 2013) 248.

[65]   Armin von Bogdandy, Philipp Dann, and Matthias Goldmann, 'Developing the Publicness of Public International Law: Towards a Legal Framework for Global Governance Activities' (2008) 9 *German Law Journal* 1375, 1376–1382; Pauwelyn, 'Is It

should be regulated. The application of teachings is one aspect of that decision-making. The application of teachings in the ICJ is regulated only by the ICJ Statute Article 38(1), which, as concluded in Section 2.2, at best provides limited guidance to judges.

The limited regulation of teachings can be compared to the use of legal experts in international courts and tribunals. These experts have a role that has similarities with that of teachings, but they are regulated in much more detail.[66] This discrepancy may, however, be justified by the same differences that prompted the classification of legal experts as distinct from 'teachings' in Section 2.3: Legal experts give their views in the context of a specific dispute, and do so orally, directly before the judges. Unlike teachings, they therefore have much in common with regular witnesses, whose role in the ICJ is also heavily regulated.

The ICJ Statute Article 38(1) could be supplemented with a codification of principles similar to the conclusions drawn in this book, about the general weight of teachings compared to judicial decisions and ILC works, and that their weight depends on quality, expertise, official positions, and agreement between multiple writers.

Amending the ICJ Statute itself is not realistic, as it would require agreement among all UN member States, nor desirable, since it would be inflexible. An alternative would be to add certain principles to the ICJ Rules of Court. This would be more flexible and practical as well as more realistic to accomplish. The application of teachings by judges could also be a subject of discussion in bodies such as the ILC, the IDI, the ILA, and the like, but such bodies include members who write teachings, leading to potential conflicts of interest. Ideally any regulation should be developed by judges themselves. Unofficial guidelines for international judges, such as the Burgh House Principles and the Oslo Recommendations,[67] have

International Law', 157; Joost Pauwelyn and George Pavlakos, 'Principled Monism and the Normative Conception of Coercion under International Law' in Malcolm D Evans and Panos Koutrakos (eds.), *Beyond the Established Orders: Policy Interconnections Between the EU and the Rest of the World* (Hart 2011) 317, 319.

66 ICJ, 'Rules of Court (1978)' (1978) www.icj-cij.org/en/rules, Articles 57–58, 62–65, 67–68, 70–71. Their use is also regulated in ICSID cases: ICSID Convention Article 22; ICSID, Rules of Procedure for Arbitration Proceedings (last amended 10 April 2006) http:// icsidfiles.worldbank.org/icsid/icsid/staticfiles/basicdoc/partf-chap04.htm Article 34–36.

67 Sands, McLachlan, and Mackenzie, 'Principles'; Brandeis Institute for International Judges, *Oslo Recommendations for Enhancing the Legitimacy of International Courts* (26 July 2018) www.brandeis.edu/ethics/pdfs/Oslo%20Reccs%20Legitimacy%20of% 20ICs.pdf.

included some judges in their drafting processes. This makes them more significant and interesting, but they have not covered the application of teachings.

Regulating teachings could also give more transparency and diversity in the application of teachings. Regulations could encourage judges to cite teachings more openly and select a more diverse set of writers. Even loose regulation apparently makes a difference when it comes to gender diversity among international judges.[68]

However, as pointed out in Section 6.2, there are important counter-arguments against both transparency and diversity. Any regulation on these points should allow judges to give ample weight to those counter-arguments in specific cases. There is no sense in proposing strict instructions about when or how teachings should be cited. There cannot be quotas on how many authors from each region are to be cited in each opinion, for example. It would, moreover, be unfair that certain authors are to be cited solely because of their nationality or gender. A better approach would be to encourage (rather than oblige) judges to consult a diverse range of teachings. Like judicial ethics, for which few international courts have formal rules,[69] the application of teachings is not a matter 'strictly of hard and fast rules'.[70] Teachings should constitute an open marketplace of ideas, where judges can pick and weigh ideas on their merits.[71]

6.3 The ICJ Compared to Other International Courts and Tribunals

6.3.1 Introduction

This section compares the ICJ's practice with that of other courts and tribunals. Several of them have been subjected to analyses similar to the ones made in this book. The data from different courts and tribunals are not always comparable, and some studies do not reveal their full numbers

---

[68] Grossman, 'Achieving', 82; Grossman, 'Shattering', 388.

[69] Terris, Romano, and Swigart, *International Judge*, 195.

[70] *Legal Consequences of the Construction of a Wall in the Occupied Palestinian Territory, Order of 30 January 2004, I.C.J. Reports 2004*, p. 3, Dissenting Opinion of Judge Buergenthal 9.

[71] Similarly, for example, Lachs, 'Teaching', 237; Zachary Douglas, *The International Law of Investment Claims* (Cambridge University Press 2009) xxiv; John Westlake, *The Collected Papers of John Westlake on Public International Law* (Cambridge University Press 1914, Lassa Oppenheim ed) 83.

or methodologies. For example, WTO Appellate Body reports mostly do not have individual opinions, while ICJ judges mostly cite teachings in individual opinions. Comparing how frequently ICJ judges cite teachings in their individual opinions with how often the WTO Appellate Body refers to teachings in its reports is not perfect, but it is all that the data allow.[72]

Most of the comparisons are with international courts and tribunals, but some are with national courts. That gives an added dimension to this section, but with the caveat that the institutional differences between the ICJ and national courts are even bigger than between the ICJ and other international courts and tribunals.

The following sections will show that different institutions apply teachings differently. International law is a single unified system of law,[73] and most international courts and tribunals adhere to the same general international law on sources of law.[74] Section 2.2.2 thus argued that all international lawyers are subject to the customary international law equivalent of the ICJ Statute Article 38(1). It is because this provision gives such limited guidance on the application of teachings that different institutions can have different practices and yet be subject to the same law. This book cannot determine whether judges in other institutions believe that they are applying Article 38(1) or rather some *lex specialis* on the application of teachings or the sources of international law more generally. If such *lex specialis* were to exist, it would mean that

---

[72] The same point is made in Sondre Torp Helmersen, 'The Application of Teachings by the International Tribunal for the Law of the Sea' (2020) 11 *Journal of International Dispute Settlement* 20.

[73] For example, ILC, *Fragmentation of International Law: Difficulties Arising From the Diversification and Expansion of International Law: Report of the Study Group of the International Law Commission, Finalized by Martti Koskenniemi (A/CN.4/L.682)* (UN 2006) 8; ILC, 'Conclusions of the work of the Study Group on the Fragmentation of International Law: Difficulties arising from the Diversification and Expansion of International Law' in *Yearbook of the International Law Commission 2006 Volume II Part Two (A/CN.4/SER.A/2006/Add.1 (Part 2))* (UN 2006) 177, 177–178; *Diallo, 2012*, Declaration of Judge Greenwood 394.

[74] Thirlway, *Sources*, 9; Boyle and Chinkin, *Making*, 299 (the 'ECHR and ACHR'); Fabián Raimondo, *General Principles of Law in the Decisions of International Criminal Courts and Tribunals* (Martinus Nijhoff 2008) 73 (international criminal courts and tribunals); Werner Zdouc and Peter Van den Bossche, *The Law and Policy of the World Trade Organization* (Cambridge University Press 2013) 59 (WTO tribunals). By contrast Cole, 'Non-Binding', 292, argues that 'the rules that should guide [international investment arbitration] tribunals in their use of non-binding documents and literature cannot be derived from Article 38'.

international law is fragmented on this point.[75] It is difficult, neverthe-less, to imagine a practice that could be radical enough to be wholly outside the broad and flexible principles in Article 38(1).

Fragmentation is also a more general policy concern in the application of teachings specifically and in international law more generally. It could threaten the coherence of international law, which in turn contributes to legal certainty.[76] Vastly different approaches to teachings in different fields of international law could contribute to undermining the coherence of the international legal system, but the variations described in this section are not big enough to warrant such a warning.

6.3.2   The General Role of Teachings

Section 3.2 showed that the ICJ almost never cites teachings in majority opinions. Teachings have only been cited 7 times in 155 cases, which is an average of 0.04 citations per case, and citations are found in only 3 per cent of cases. In individual opinions, the average citation rate per opinion is 3.5 per opinion, and 32 per cent of such opinions cite teachings.

These numbers differ from findings from other international courts and tribunals. The ICTY cited 'academic sources' on average 7.2 times in majority opinions and 4 in individual opinions up to 2003.[77] International criminal courts and tribunals in general have 7.4 on average.[78] The WTO Appellate Body has an average of exactly one citation per report.[79] The ITLOS has no citations in majority opinions,[80] which

---

[75] Charlesworth, 'Law-Making', 189 points out that '[s]pecialised fields of international law [. . .] also differ in the priority that they accord to different sources and the approaches they take to them'. Pauwelyn, *Conflict of Norms,* 394–395 mentions '[s]pecial customary law prevailing as *lex specialis* over general customary law'. A similar methodological question was faced by Van Damme, *Treaty Interpretation*: Does the WTO Appellate Body apply the general international law of treaty interpretation, or does it have its own rules of interpretation? In that case, however, the question is answered by the DSU Article 3(2), which says the Appellate Body shall apply 'customary rules of interpretation of public international law'.

[76] ILC, *Fragmentation of International Law: Difficulties Arising From the Diversification and Expansion of International Law: Report of the Study Group of the International Law Commission, Finalized by Martti Koskenniemi (A/CN.4/L.682)* (UN 2006) 248.

[77] Bohlander, 'Influence', 198–202.

[78] Stappert, 'Influence', 964 and 973.

[79] Helmersen, 'WTO', 317 reports an average of 1.4 citations, but as explained at 334, 30 per cent ILC of them are to ILC works, which are not considered teachings in this book.

[80] Helmersen, 'Law of the Sea', 25.

makes it strikingly different from the other courts and tribunals mentioned here, but quite similar to the ICJ. ITLOS judges nonetheless cite an average of 1.7 citations in individual opinions.[81] ICSID tribunals cited teachings in 74 per cent of all awards between 1998 and 2006. The ECtHR also cites teachings,[82] but exact numbers are not available. The same goes for various arbitral tribunals.[83]

If courts and tribunals are arranged on a spectrum based on how often they cite teachings, the ICJ's majority opinions sit firmly on one end, along with ITLOS majority opinions. International criminal courts and tribunals are on the other end of the spectrum. The ICJ's individual opinions sit somewhere in the middle, with around half the citation rate of international criminal courts and tribunals, but double that of ITLOS individual opinions, and more than three times that of the WTO Appellate Body. This book identified a 'median' approach among ICJ judges in Section 5.3.3. In the community of international courts and tribunals, the ICJ's individual opinions as a whole seem to constitute a 'median'.

International courts and tribunals can also be compared qualitatively, based on how they use teachings when they are cited. In the ICJ, foregoing discussions have shown that teachings have on the whole 'generally low weight' (Section 3.10), even though this varies greatly between teachings and between judges. In the ITLOS, teachings also seem to have 'low weight'.[84] Even when teachings are cited in individual opinions, there is often 'a lack of engagement' with them.[85] This too is similar to the ICJ. In the WTO Appellate Body, teachings are used with 'an apparent tendency to be careful'.[86] In ICSID tribunals, Fauchald finds that teachings were 'an essential interpretive argument'.[87] Despite frequent citations, Bohlander believes that the 'influence' of teachings on the ICTY is 'marginal'.[88] Stappert, by contrast, argues that in international criminal courts and tribunals, 'academic writings overall seem to play a more influential role [...] than its characterization as a subsidiary means indicates'.[89] Similarly,

---

[81] Ibid., 27.
[82] Wood, 'Teachings', para 14, contradicting Twining and others, 'Academics', 945.
[83] Kaczorowska, *International Law*, 59; Crawford (n 12) 43.
[84] Helmersen, 'Law of the Sea', 32.
[85] Ibid., 29.
[86] Helmersen, 'WTO', 332.
[87] Fauchald, 'Legal Reasoning', 352.
[88] Bohlander, 'Influence', 195.
[89] Stappert, 'Influence', 975, 976, and 979.

Jain argues that international criminal courts and tribunals used teachings as 'a *de facto* source of law' in 'the development of modes of liability'.[90] To this it should be added that teachings can have significant weight while formally being used as a subsidiary means. That judges rely significantly on teachings does not mean that they are more than a subsidiary means. This would be the case only if judges base their legal conclusions on teachings rather than treaties or customary international law. In any case, the other conclusions mentioned here offer interesting points of comparison with the ICJ.

National courts also cite teachings. This includes at least US courts generally,[91] French courts,[92] and the British House of Lords between 1990 and 2009.[93] Numbers are available for, for example, Australian state Supreme Courts (1.38 citations per case on average),[94] the Australian High Court (gradually rising from 0.7 to 4.0),[95] the Canadian Supreme Court (2.0),[96] and the New Zealand Court of Appeal (3.32).[97] In Italy, by contrast, the legislature has instructed the judiciary not to cite teachings.[98] Prohibitions of citations have existed, for example in Italian states in the 1700s and in the Prussian *Landrecht*.[99] The national courts for which data are available would also fall in the middle of the spectrum discussed earlier. This suggests that there is nothing anomalous about the citation rate in individual ICJ opinions. In this context, it is also relevant that teachings are cited in pleadings and arguments before international courts and tribunals, official communications, the works of state-empowered bodies such

---

[90] Neha Jain, 'Teachings of Publicists and the Reinvention of the Sources Doctrine in International Criminal Law', in Kevin Heller et al (eds.), *The Oxford Handbook of International Criminal Law* (Oxford University Press, 2020) 106, 124.

[91] Duxbury, *Judges*, 35.

[92] Ibid., 55 and 59.

[93] Stanton, 'Scholarship', 218.

[94] Smyth, 'Outside', 705 (with a definition at 692).

[95] Russell Smyth, 'Other Than "Accepted" Sources of Law?: A Quantitative Study of Secondary Source Citations in the High Court' (1999) 22 *UNSW Law Journal* 19, 28 (with a definition at 20).

[96] Black and Richter, 'My Name', 382. Similarly Bale, 'Lederman', 55.

[97] Russell Smyth, 'Judicial Robes or Academic Gowns? Citations to Secondary Authority and Legal Method in the New Zealand Court of Appeal', in Rick Bigwood (ed), *Legal Method in New Zealand* (Butterworths 2001) 101, 105 (with a definition at 101).

[98] John Henry Merryman and Rogelio Pérez-Perdomo, *The Civil Law Tradition: An Introduction to the Legal Systems of Europe and Latin America* (3rd edn, Stanford University Press 2007) 59. Similarly Earlsferry, 'Judges', 32.

[99] Braun, 'Burying', 29; Stefan Vogenauer, 'An Empire of Light? Learning and Lawmaking in the History of German Law' (2005) 64 *Cambridge Law Journal* 481, 492.

as the ILC, as well as in teachings themselves, as noted in Section 1.2. Citing teachings is the rule rather than the exception for texts on international law.

National courts have also made some general statements about the weight of teachings in international law. According to the dissenting opinion of Chief Justice Fuller in the *Paquete Habana* case of the US Supreme Court, teachings 'may be persuasive, but not authoritative'.[100] The *Franconia* case from the English Court for Crown Cases Reserved held that 'writers [...] cannot make the law', even if 'entire unanimity had existed'.[101]

The US Court of Appeals for the Second Circuit in *Flores* v. *Southern Peru Copper Corp* noted that teachings were more important in international law in the past,[102] as discussed in Section 2.2.1.

Section 3.5.1 noted that ICJ majority opinions not only rarely cite teachings, but they also rarely cite judicial decisions from other institutions. The same pattern is found for other international courts and tribunals,[103] including the ECtHR, the European Court of Justice, the WTO Appellate Body, and the Iran-US Claims Tribunal.[104] Not citing a source that is probably widely used in practice is not unique to the ICJ or to teachings.

That judges probably read more teachings than they cite (as argued in Section 3.4) is also not unique to the ICJ. Interviews with international criminal judges and staff 'indicates' the same.[105] A specific example of influence without citation in the ICTY is that '*Krstić* [...] seems to have been influenced [...] by William A. Schabas' 2000 treatise, *Genocide in International Law*', which was 'referred to [...] only once, on an unrelated point of law'.[106]

---

[100] US Supreme Court, *The Paquete Habana* 175 US 677 (1900), 720. Similarly William J Aceves, 'Symposium Introduction; Scholarship as Evidence of International Law' (2003) 26 *Loyola of Los Angeles International and Comparative Law Review* 1, 1.

[101] English Court for Crown Cases Reserved, *R* v. *Keyn* [1876] 2 Ex D 63, 202-203 (discussed in John P Grant, *International Law* (Dundee University Press 2010) 22).

[102] Court of Appeals for the Second Circuit, *Flores* v. *Southern Peru Copper Corp.*, 343 F 3d 140 (2nd Cir. 2003), para 28.

[103] Terris, Romano, and Swigart, *International Judge*, 120.

[104] Marcelo Dias Varella, *Internationalization of Law: Globalization, International Law and Complexity* (Springer 2014) 150.

[105] Stappert, 'Influence', 974 and 979.

[106] Diane Marie Amann, 'Group Mentality, Expressivism, and Genocide' (2002) 2 *International Criminal Law Review* (2002) 93, 112–113.

The Court's practice suggests that judicial decisions have more weight than teachings, as argued in Section 3.8.2. The same idea seems to be implicit in a decision by the Special Court for Sierra Leone Trial Chamber. In a footnote to its judgment in *Prosecutor v. Charles Ghankay Taylor*, it noted 'that the Defence [. . .] has cited only a textbook, but no jurisprudence, in support of its submission'.[107] The Trial Chamber preferred judicial decisions to teachings.[108] The same notion can be found in national courts. The *Paquete Habana* decision by the US Supreme Court held that 'resort must be had [. . .] to the works of jurists' apparently only 'where there is no [. . .] judicial decision'.[109] Lord Summer in *Kronprinsessan Margreta* found that 'prize courts must always attach chief importance to [. . .] decisions' over 'the opinions of [. . .] writers'.[110] He also thought that 'the more the field is covered by decided cases the less becomes the authority of commentators and jurists'.[111]

That ICJ majority opinions cite ILC texts but not teachings is an indication that ILC texts have more weight, as argued in Section 3.8.3. Other international courts and tribunals also cite ILC texts. This includes ITLOS majority opinions, which have never cited teachings.[112] A report by the UN Secretary General finds that the ILC's work on *Responsibility of States for Internationally Wrongful Acts* has been cited 392 times by judges between 2001 and 2016.[113] Various other international courts and tribunals also cite teachings, however, as noted earlier. Thus, they may not necessarily show such a stark contrast between the application of ILC texts and teachings. The WTO Appellate Body has cited both, but it has increasingly preferred to cite ILC works over teachings.[114] No such preference is apparent in ICSID decisions.[115]

---

[107] Special Court for Sierra Leone Trial Chamber, *Prosecutor* v. *Charles Ghankay Taylor*, Judgment, SCSL-03-01-T, 18 May 2012, 171.

[108] Borda, 'Formal Approach', 660.

[109] US Supreme Court, *The Paquete Habana* 175 US 677 (1900), 700.

[110] Lord Summer in Privy Council, *Kronprinsessan Margreta* [1921] AC 486, 495.

[111] Ibid. The point is echoed by, for example, Jennings and Watts (eds), *Oppenheim's*, 43; Parry, *Sources*, 104.

[112] Helmersen, 'Law of the Sea', 26.

[113] UNGA, *Responsibility of States for internationally wrongful acts: Compilation of decisions of international courts, tribunals and other bodies, Report of the Secretary-General, Addendum (A/71/80/Add.1)* (UN 2017) 3.

[114] Helmersen, 'WTO', 334.

[115] Fauchald, 'Legal Reasoning', 352.

6.3.3   Variations between Teachings

Section 4.2 showed that ICJ judges cite some writers more than others. Other courts and tribunals also cite some writers more than others. Lists have been produced for the ITLOS and the WTO Appellate Body.[116]

Shabtai Rosenne is the most-cited writers in individual ICJ opinions, as noted in Section 4.2.1. He is also the most-cited writer in individual ITLOS opinions. In the WTO Appellate Body, Lassa Oppenheim tops the list. Oppenheim is also in the top ten in both the ICJ and ITLOS. Ian Brownlie appears in both the ICJ and the WTO Appellate Body. Otherwise there is no overlap between the top ten in the three institutions. Such overlap will be limited by the different mandates of the three institutions. The ITLOS cites much work on the law of the sea,[117] the WTO Appellate Body some on international trade law (but actually more on general international law),[118] and the ICJ, with its broad mandate and varied case load, naturally gravitates towards generalist works.

In the ICJ, the most-cited writers were largely found to be men from Western countries, especially the United Kingdom (Section 4.2.2). These patterns are not unique to the application of teachings in the ICJ; they show up in a variety of other contexts in international law.

In the ITLOS, fourteen of the nineteen most-cited writers were UK or US nationals. All were men. The WTO Appellate Body is relatively diverse by comparison. Among the writers of its ten most-cited works, three can be classified as non-Western.[119] All were men, though. The ICC generally cites many Western teachings, including works on German criminal law.[120]

A study of lawyers who appeared before the ICJ between 1999 and 2012 found that they were mostly a small group of Western men,[121] while a similar study for 1948–1998 found that they were mostly from OECD member States.[122] The same is true for international investment arbitrators[123] and investment arbitration

---

[116] Helmersen, 'WTO', 333–334; Helmersen, 'Law of the Sea', 33.

[117] Helmersen, 'Law of the Sea', 35.

[118] Helmersen, 'WTO', 326.

[119] The three writers are Mustafa Kamil Yasseen, Eduardo Jiménez de Aréchaga, and Mojtaba Kazazi.

[120] Elies van Sliedregt, 'International Criminal Law: Over-studied and Underachieving?' (2016) 29 *Leiden Journal of International Law* 1, 7.

[121] Kumar and Rose, 'Study', 901-903 (regarding the West), 904 (regarding men), and 912 (regarding the same individuals appearing repeatedly).

[122] Gaubatz and MacArthur, 'How International', 250–260.

[123] Susan D Franck, 'Empirically Evaluating Claims about Investment Treaty Arbitration' (2007) 86 *North Carolina Law Review* 1, 78 (regarding the West) and 81 (regarding men);

counsel.[124] The geographic concentration among arbitrators is documented in the ICSID's official statistics, according to which 68 per cent of arbitrators, conciliators, and ad hoc committee members between 1972 and 2017 were from Western Europe or North America.[125]

When international law textbooks cite state practice or teachings, there seems to be a focus on 'material from Western states in general, and core English-speaking Western states in particular'.[126] Western nationals are also overrepresented among the staff in the ICC, especially on higher levels.[127] These nationals are also overrepresented in the WTO secretariat.[128] However, by contrast, more than half of the members of WTO panels are from 'developing' countries according to the WTO definition (although 36 per cent with the World Bank's definition).[129] The significant presence of developing country nationals may be explained by the general rule that WTO panellists should not be nationals of the parties or third parties to the dispute.[130]

Section 4.2.3 discussed ICJ judges' preference for Western teachings and proposed the fact that most of them studied law in Western countries as a possible explanation. The same educational pattern is found among international judges more generally.[131]

The dominance of Western actors and materials thus seems to be a general pattern in international law.[132] This means that the ICJ judges'

Puig, 'Capital', 405 regarding (regarding the West), 404–405 (regarding men), and 407 and 422 (regarding the same individuals appearing repeatedly); Malcolm Langford, Daniel Behn, and Runar Hilleren Lie, 'The Revolving Door in International Investment Arbitration' (2017) 20 *Journal of International Economic Law* 301, 309–310 (regarding the West and men) and 310 (regarding the same individuals appearing repeatedly).

[124] Langford, Behn, and Lie, 'Revolving', 316 (regarding the West and men).

[125] ICSID, 'The ICSID Caseload – Statistics (Issue 2017-2)' (2017) https://icsid .worldbank.org/en/Documents/resources/ICSID%20Web%20Stats%202017-2%20 (English)%20Final.pdf, 19.

[126] Roberts, *Is International Law International?*, 165.

[127] Ibid., 256.

[128] Ibid., 258.

[129] Joost Pauwelyn, 'The Rule of Law without Lawyers? Why Investment Arbitrators are from Mars, Trade Adjudicators from Venus' (2015) 109 *American Journal of International Law* 761, 771.

[130] Roberts, *Is International Law International?*, 259, citing the DSU Article 8.3.

[131] Mikael Rask Madsen, 'Who Rules the World? The Educational Capital of the International Judiciary', (2020) 3 *University of California Journal of International, Transnational, and Comparative Law* 97, 111.

[132] Roberts, *Is International Law International?*, 5.

practice is not unique. They seem, on average, to be little different from other international lawyers. It also means that the potential benefits of more diversity discussed in Section 6.2.2 may be relevant to other institutions as well, even though such arguments must to some extent be particular to each specific institution.[133]

A separate finding is that in the WTO Appellate Body, 'many of the authors that have been cited the most [...] have connections with governments'.[134] That is similar to the official positions held by the most-cited writers in individual ICJ opinions, and with the judges' tendency to justify teachings by mentioning such positions (Section 4.3.4), even though the WTO Appellate Body has not said that it accords greater weight to writers who held official positions.

ICJ judges seem to give more weight to teachings where multiple writers agree (Section 4.3.5). This apparent preference can also be seen in individual ITLOS opinions[135] and in national courts.[136] ITLOS judges also emphasise the quality of teachings,[137] just like ICJ judges. ICJ judges also highlight writers' expertise and official positions (Section 4.3), but that is hardly found in the ITLOS.[138]

6.3.4 Variations between Judges

Chapter 5 showed that different ICJ judges have different approaches to teachings. They can be divided into three groups: those who never cite teachings, the 'median', and those who rely heavily on teachings. Comparable numbers are available for the WTO Appellate Body and the ITLOS.

In the ICJ, 32 per cent of the judges who have written at least one individual opinion have never cited teachings. In the WTO Appellate Body, only two out of twenty-three members have not cited teachings, that is, just under 9 per cent.[139] In the ITLOS, nineteen out of forty-two have never cited teachings (45 per cent).[140]

---

[133] Shecaira, *Scholarship*, 77.
[134] Helmersen, 'WTO', 334.
[135] Helmersen, 'Law of the Sea', 37–38.
[136] Duxbury, *Judges*, 50-53; Shecaira, *Scholarship*, 56 discusses court practice in Brazil, Germany, and Canada.
[137] Helmersen, 'Law of the Sea', 36–37.
[138] Ibid., 38.
[139] Helmersen, 'WTO', 347, but note that the numbers include ILC works.
[140] Helmersen, 'Law of the Sea', 39.

Section 5.3.3 grouped ICJ judges with average citation rates per opinion between 0.1 and 10 in the 'median', along with some judges with a higher citation rate but who did not engage much with teachings. The category includes 62 per cent of the judges. In the WTO Appellate body, no member has an average of more than ten citations per opinion. The highest are 4.3 (Bautista) and 4.0 (Bossche and Ramírez-Hernández).[141] Thus, 91 per cent of WTO Appellate Body members would be in the ICJ's 'median'. In the ITLOS, all but two of the judges who have cited teachings have average citation rates above ten: Judge Laing (22) and Judge ad hoc Servulo Correia (12). This means that twenty-one ITLOS judges, 50 per cent of the total, are within the ICJ 'median'.

Ten ICJ judges, 6 per cent of the total, were placed in the final group of judges who often cite and engage with teachings. This category would contain no WTO Appellate Body members, but 5 per cent of ITLOS judges. The highest average citation rate in the ICJ is 41.5, twice as high as that of Judge Laing in the ITLOS and nearly ten times that of Bautista in the WTO Appellate Body.

When the three institutions are compared, the WTO Appellate Body seems to be the most homogenous. More than 90 per cent of its members would be in the ICJ's 'median' category. The ICJ has the greatest variation between judges.

Section 5.3.3 identified four 'outlier' judges in the ICJ: Judges Cançado Trindade, Weeramantry, Shahabuddeen, and Kreća. In the ITLOS, Judge Laing is an identifiable outlier, since he cites and engages with teachings far more often than his colleagues.[142] He shares some characteristics with the ICJ outliers. He is a former academic and a non-OECD national. All the ICJ outliers are non-OECD nationals, and all but Shahabuddeen are former academics. This may be part of a broader pattern.

Thus, in the ICJ, former academics generally cite teachings more often than non-academics (Section 5.5.6). This is also the case in ITLOS.[143] This can be contrasted with the WTO Appellate Body, where members who have been diplomats cite teachings slightly more often than members who have been academics.[144] Stappert finds that there is 'not necessarily' any connection between professional background and approach to teachings in international criminal courts and tribunals.[145] However,

---

[141] Helmersen, 'WTO', 347, but note that the numbers include ILC works.
[142] Helmersen, 'Law of the Sea', 44.
[143] Ibid., 39.
[144] Helmersen, 'WTO', 341–342.
[145] Stappert, 'Influence', 975.

Fauchald suggests the presence of academics as arbitrators as one reason why the ICSID decisions he examined gave significant weight to teachings.[146] Studies from US nationals courts are mixed. One study found more citations by former academics,[147] while another did not.[148]

Section 5.5 examined data that correlated with variations between ICJ judges. Section 5.5.4 found that 'non-Western' judges (non-OECD nationals) generally cite teachings more often than their Western counterparts, but that the difference almost disappears when the four outlier judges are removed from the equation. The same thing can be observed in the ITLOS, where an apparently higher citation rate among non-Western judges disappears without Judge Laing.[149] In the WTO Appellate Body, there is no difference in the citation rates of OECD and non-OECD nationals.[150] Franck reports no connection between investment arbitration outcomes and the 'development status' of the presiding arbitrator's state of nationality.[151] In the HRC Shikhelman finds a mixed picture, with 'certain voting patterns' being 'associated with geographical origin, domestic legal systems, professional background, and possibly gender', even though 'on many issues' background did not have a 'significant influence'.[152]

In the ICJ, it was difficult to draw clear conclusions about the application of teachings by common law and civil law judges. In the ICTY Appeals Chamber, by contrast, Bohlander finds that common law judges cite more teachings.[153] In the WTO Appellate Body, there is no noticeable difference between civil law and common law-educated judges.[154]

Permanent and ad hoc judges were compared in Section 5.5.2, which showed that ad hoc judges have a higher citation rate. In the ITLOS the permanent judges have a slightly higher citation rate, but only because of

[146] Fauchald, 'Legal Reasoning', 352.

[147] Daniels, 'Beyond', 9 (about all 'secondary sources', not limited to scholarship).

[148] Chester A Newland, 'The Supreme Court and Legal Writing: Learned Journals as Vehicles of an Anti-Antitrust Lobby?' (1959) 48 *Georgetown Law Journal* 105, 481. Duxbury, *Judges,* 37 cites unspecified 'citation analyses [indicating] that judges who were formerly law professors [...] are disproportionately high citers of academic literature'.

[149] Helmersen, 'Law of the Sea', 42.

[150] Helmersen, 'WTO', 341.

[151] Franck, 'Development', 487.

[152] Shikhelman, 'Diversity', 65.

[153] Bohlander, 'Influence', 208: 'common law majorities in the Appeals Chamber used almost three times as many academic sources than did the civil law majorities if one looks at the percentage, and more than twice as many in absolute numbers'

[154] Helmersen, 'WTO', 341.

Judge Laing. Without him, ad hoc judges cite teachings twice as often as permanent judges.[155]

6.3.5   Explaining Variations between Institutions

Section 5.4 explored possible reasons for variations between ICJ judges in the application of teachings. Similar reasons may explain variations between the ICJ as a whole and other institutions. Such similar reasons include the composition of an institution, especially the philosophies and methodologies of the judges. Composition can be influenced by procedures for the election and appointment of judges. An institution's mandate may also play a role, in that some cases may lend themselves more to citing teachings than others. Practical support, such as the assistance available to judges, differs between institutions[156] and can influence the application of teaching.

The WTO Appellate Body cites teachings more often on points of general international law than on international trade law.[157] The DSU Article 17.3 states that '[t]he Appellate Body shall comprise persons of recognized authority, with demonstrated expertise in law, international trade and the subject matter of the covered agreements generally'. In practice, the members are mostly international trade law experts.[158] Lack of expertise in general international law can be one reason why the WTO Appellate Body cites relatively few teachings when dealing with international trade law, as opposed to dealing with general international law.[159] However, an alternative explanation is that the WTO Appellate Body does not see itself as having the authority to engage with or contribute to general international law, and prefers to hide behind teachings when doing so.[160] A similar line of argument seems to fit

---

[155]   Helmersen, 'Law of the Sea', 43–44.

[156]   Terris, Romano, and Swigart, *International Judge*, 55–56.

[157]   Helmersen, 'WTO', 326–327.

[158]   Gabrielle Marceau, 'WTO Dispute Settlement and Human Rights' (2002) 13 *European Journal of International Law* 753, 765–766, but Joost Pauwelyn, 'How to Win a World Trade Organization Dispute Based on Non-World Trade Organization Law?: Questions of Jurisdiction and Merits' (2003) 37 *Journal of World Trade* 997, 1030. Similarly Peter Van den Bossche, 'From Afterthought to Centrepiece: The WTO Appellate Body and Its Rise to Prominence in the World Trading System', in Giorgio Sacerdoti, Alan Yanovich, and Jan Bohanes (eds), *The WTO at Ten: The Contribution of the Dispute Settlement System* (Cambridge University Press 2006) 289, 301 add some nuance.

[159]   Helmersen, 'WTO', 338–339.

[160]   Ibid., 339.

national courts. National judges are generally experts on national law rather than international law. Some writers report that national courts tend to cite teachings diligently when dealing with international law matters,[161] albeit without specifically comparing those courts' citation rates in cases dealing with international and national law, respectively.

For individual ICJ opinions, Section 3.4.2 showed that judgments contain more citations than orders, possibly because orders involve legal issues more familiar to the judges. The alternative explanation for the WTO Appellate Body that was mentioned earlier, that it lacks authority to deal with general international law, cannot be extended to the ICJ. The ICJ's institutional role as a global and generalist court and part of the near-universal UN system means that there is no area of international law that the ICJ is supposed to stay away from.

Teachings are cited more often when dealing with unwritten law in the WTO Appellate Body,[162] as in the ICJ (as noted in Section 3.4.2). Recourse to teachings may be more essential where there is no formal written source to use as a starting point, and whether this is the case may vary between institutions.

A decline in the rate of citations of teachings over time can be seen in the reports of the WTO Appellate body,[163] in the ICC,[164] and in US national courts.[165] This may be because teachings are gradually displaced by a growing body of precedent in those institutions. In international criminal courts, Jain holds that reliance on teachings has been gradually supplanted by reliance on judicial decisions.[166] No decline in the citation of teachings is seen in the ICJ, however, as noted in Section 3.7.7.

A court is composed of judges, each of whom has their individual approach to the law in general and to teachings in particular. The composition of an institution is therefore a significant factor when comparing the institutions' aggregate approaches to teachings.

Judges' individual philosophies were suggested as a significant factor behind variations between ICJ judges in Section 5.4.3. Such individual philosophies probably vary between individual judges in other institutions, and when aggregated they can also create variations between the

---

[161] Section 1.2.

[162] Helmersen, 'WTO', 335.

[163] Ibid., 323–325, although Pauwelyn, *Conflict of Norms*, 50 draws the opposite conclusion.

[164] Stappert, 'Influence', 973.

[165] Merritt and Putnam, 'Judges and Scholars', 877 (citing various studies of different courts).

[166] Jain, 'Reinvention', 124.

institutions as a whole. Stappert interviewed an ICC judge who 'expressed dissatisfaction with what they perceived as an overly academic drafting style'.[167] Such concerns have also been raised by at least one national judge.[168]

Another aspect of the composition of a court is the presence of former academics, whose significance was as discussed in Section 5.5.6. Yet another is that of Western or non-Western judges, and variations between them in at least some institutions was noted in the previous chapter. The presence of female judges is also relevant. Section 4.2.3 showed that they cite more female writers in their ICJ opinions. More generally, Grossman cites '[a] number of female judges' in international courts who 'have made statements implying that their experiences as women gave them a particular sensitivity in certain cases'.[169] King and Greening report that in sexual assault cases at the ICTY, sentences are harsher when the judges have the same gender as the victim.[170]

As for practical factors, Section 5.4.6 found that ICJ judges cite more teachings in years when they decide fewer cases. In some US national courts, there seems to be a connection between judges deciding more cases per time unit and fewer citations.[171] A judge at the Canadian Supreme Court confirms that judges are less able to research teachings when they have a heavy workload.[172] The authors of *The International Judge* cite a WTO Appellate Body member, who expresses dissatisfaction with the time available to produce each report.[173] The reports 'could be much better turned out, technically and intellectually' given more time.[174] The WTO Appellate Body nonetheless cited teachings in 19 per cent of its reports up to 2013, with an average of one reference per report.[175] Then again, the authors also describe international courts as 'increasingly busy',[176] which correlates with a decline over time in the WTO Appellate Body's citations of teachings.[177]

---

[167] Stappert, 'Influence', 974.

[168] Kaye, 'One Judge's', 315.

[169] Grossman, 'Shattering', 401.

[170] Kimi Lynn King and Megan Greening, 'Gender Justice or Just Gender? The Role of Gender in Sexual Assault Decisions at the International Criminal Tribunal for the Former Yugoslavia' (2007) 88 *Social Science Quarterly* 1049, 1065–1066.

[171] Schwartz and Petherbridge, 'Scholarship', 1365–1367.

[172] Forest, 'Listening', 89.

[173] Terris, Romano, and Swigart, *International Judge*, 81.

[174] Ibid.

[175] Helmersen, 'WTO', 317 (the numbers including ILC works are 1.4 and 26 per cent).

[176] Terris, Romano, and Swigart, *International Judge*, 201.

[177] Helmersen, 'WTO', 324–325.

The presence of law clerks may influence judges' application of teachings. Pauwelyn and Pelc find that in WTO panels, 'the Secretariat exerts a stronger influence over the writing of WTO rulings than the panelists themselves',[178] but the application of teachings by such panels has not yet been studied. A judge of the Canadian Supreme Court confirms the introduction of clerks has 'stimulated the use of academic material'.[179] The authors of *The International Judge* note that '[c]riminal court judges have perhaps the most assistance among the courts considered here'.[180] Webb similarly reports that '[u]nlike the ICJ, international criminal courts rely heavily on their staff members for the drafting of motions, orders, and Judgments'.[181] This fits well with the finding that international criminal courts cite teachings more often than other courts and tribunals.

6.4 Avenues for Future Research

This book has offered a chance to test some conventional wisdom about the status of teachings in international law. A central finding in the book is that teachings generally have low weight in the ICJ. That conclusion is relatively unsurprising and uncontroversial. The conventional view of the relative status of the sources of international law is not upended by the findings in this book. The conclusion does have some important nuances, however. The most important points are that weight varies between different teachings and between different judges. Future research may reveal yet further refinements.

Such future research could examine the application of teachings by other international courts and tribunals. Some such studies exist, and their results are compared with those from the ICJ in Section 6.3, but there is room for more. It would be particularly interesting to gather data on institutions where the same judges have served. This would make it possible to say more about the behaviour of judges as they move between institutions. Do they keep to the same approach in different institutions, even if the overall approaches of those institutions are different? Or do they rather conform to an 'institutional culture'? Is their approach in

---

[178] Joost Pauwelyn and Krzysz J. Pelc, 'Who Writes the Rulings of the World Trade Organization? A Critical Assessment of the Role of the Secretariat in WTO Dispute Settlement' (2019) https://papers.ssrn.com/sol3/papers.cfm?abstract_id=3458872 20.

[179] Forest, 'Listening', 75. Similarly Bale, 'Lederman', 58.

[180] Terris, Romano, and Swigart, *International Judge*, 56.

[181] Philippa Webb, *Integration*, 193.

the second institution noticeably influenced by the overall approach of the first institution? A study of multiple institutions could also incorporate practical factors and look closer at how these are connected with the application of teachings.

Studies could also extend to how national courts use teachings when dealing with international law. How different are the approaches of courts in different countries, how different are they from the approaches of international courts and tribunals, and are they different from when national courts deal with national law? One view is that the rules of international law are generally less clear than those of national law,[182] which should enhance the potential role of teachings.[183] It would also be possible to look at the application of teachings in pleadings before international courts and tribunals and by institutions, such as the ILC, as well as even by teachings themselves.

It would be interesting to compare the application of teachings with that of other subsidiary means, especially judicial decisions. These studies can be done with similar methods and on the same institutions as studies of the application of teachings. With enough such studies, it would be possible to say something general about the application of subsidiary means in international law. It is likely that at least some of the conclusions drawn in this book are relevant to all subsidiary means. Section 4.6 already suggested that this is the case for the factors that ICJ judges apparently use to distinguish between teachings with different weight.

Future research could expand on potential benefits from adjusting citation practices, presented in Section 6.2. More data from other institutions and other subsidiary means could confirm or (less likely) rebut the pattern of disproportionate influence for Western actors. Future research could draw on research on the concept of legitimacy and judge behaviour, with the aim of making more concrete and targeted recommendations. Such research would be even more useful if it involved sitting judges themselves.

---

[182] Virally, 'Sources', 153.

[183] Paulsson, 'Scholarship', 183; Kent and Trinidad, 'Scholars', 1087; Gillian Triggs, 'The Public International Lawyer and the Practice of International Law' (2005) 24 *Australian Year Book of International Law* 201, 202; Hall, *International Law*, 59.

APPENDIX 1

The Forty Most-Cited Writers

Rank	Writer	Citations	Including self	Nationality	Education	Work	Gender
	(Trindade, A. A. Cançado)	(0)	(297)				
1	Rosenne, Shabtai	233		UK/Israel	UK/Israel	UK/Israel	Male
2	Lauterpacht, Hersch	119		Austro-Hungary/UK	Austro-Hungary /Austria/UK	UK	Male
3	Fitzmaurice, Gerald	67	(72)	UK	UK	UK	Male
4	Hudson, Manley O.	55		US	US	US	Male
5	Oppenheim, Lassa	53		Germany/UK	Germany	Germany/ Switzerland/ UK	Male
6	Jennings, Robert	52		UK	UK/US	UK	Male
7	de Visscher, Charles	51		Belgium	Belgium	Belgium	Male
8	Brownlie, Ian	42		UK	UK	UK	Male
9	Watts, Arthur	32		UK	UK	UK	Male
9	Stone, Julius	32		UK?	UK/US	UK/NZ/ Australia	Male
11	Schwarzenberger, Georg	31		Germany/UK	Germany/UK	UK	Male
12	Higgins, Rosalyn	30	(31)	UK	UK	UK	Female
12	Schachter, Oscar	30		US	US	US	Male
14	Guyomar, Geneviève	28		France	France	France	Female
14	Aréchaga, Eduardo Jiménez de	28		Uruguay	Uruguay	Uruguay	Male
16	Jenks, C. Wilfred	24		UK	UK/Switzerland	Switzerland	Male

16	McNair, Arnold	24	UK	UK	UK	Male
16	Hambro, Edvard	24	Norway	Norway, Switzerland	Norway	Male
19	Brierly, James Leslie	23	UK	UK	UK	Male
20	Guillaume, Gilbert	22	France	France	France/Belgium	Male
Total **top 20**			**15 UK, 2 US, 2 France, 2 Germany**	**11 UK, 4 US, 2 France, 2 Germany, 2 Switzerland**	**11 UK, 2 US, 2 France, 2 Belgium, 2 Switzerland**	**18 male, 2 female**

21	Anzilotti, Dionisio	21	
21	McDougal, Myres S.	21	
21	Waldock, Humphrey	21	
24	Kelsen, Hans	20	
24	Schabas, William A.	20	
26	Cheng, Bin	19	
26	Thirlway, Hugh	19	
28	Kolb, Robert	18	
28	O'Connell, Daniel Patrick	18	
	(Simma, Bruno)	(8)	(18)
30	Reuter, Paul Jean-Marie	17	
31	Grotius, Hugo	16	
31	Guggenheim, Paul	16	

(*cont.*)

Rank	Writer	Citations	Including self	Nationality	Education	Work	Gender
31	Tams, Christian	16					
31	Verhoeven, Joe	16					
31	Elias, Taslim O.	16					
	(Oda, Shigeru)	(7)	(16)				
36	Jessup, Philip C.	14	18				
36	Robinson, Nehemiah	14					
36	Singh, Nagendra	14					
36	Vattel, Emer de	14					
40	Buergenthal, Thomas	13					
40	Rousseau, Charles	13					
40	Shelton, Dinah L.	13					
40	Wright, Quincy	13					
40	Bedjaoui, Mohammed	13					

Note: Self-citations do not count towards the ranking. Writers who are part of the top forty only when self-citations are counted are listed in parenthesis.

Citations Per Judge

Judge (* = ad hoc)	State	Profession	Education	Opinions	References	Per opinion
Van den Wyngaert*	Belgium	Academic	Brussels	2	83	41.5
Cançado Trindade	Brazil	Academic	Minas Gerais, Cambridge	37	1513	40.9
van Wyk*	South Africa	?	?	2	54	27.0
Palmer*	New Zealand	Politician	Wellington, Chicago	1	27	27.0
Bula-Bula*	DR Congo	?	?	2	48	24.0
Weeramantry*	Sri Lanka	Academic	London	1	22	22.0
Roucounas*	Greece	Academic	?	1	22	22.0
Jessup	US	Academic	Hamilton, Columbia, Yale	6	114	19.0
Pirzada*	Pakistan	Int'l civil servant	Bombay (and Lincoln's Inn)	1	19	19.0
Mavungu*	DR Congo	?	?	2	36	18.0
Weeramantry	Sri Lanka	Academic	London	26	440	16.9
Kreća*	Serbia	Academic	Belgrade	24	396	16.5
Ammoun	Lebanon	Diplomat	Beirut, Lyon	5	79	15.8
Rigaux*	Belgium	Academic	St Louis (Brussels), Louvain	3	42	14.0
Jean-Yves de Cara*	France	Academic	Lyon	1	14	14.0
Mahiou*	Algeria	Academic	Toulouse, Nancy, Paris	6	76	12.7
De Castro	Spain	Academic	Madrid	9	113	12.6
Shahabuddeen	Guyana	Politician	London	22	242	11.0
Fernandes*	Portugal	?	?	1	10	10.0

Paolillo*	Uruguay	Diplomat	Uruguay	1	10	10.0
Azevedo	Brazil	Academic	Rio, Paris	7	53	7.6
El-Kosheri*	Egypt	Academic	Dijon, Rennes, Paris, Cairo	2	14	7.0
Skubiszewski*	Poland	Academic	Poznan, Nancy, Harvard	2	13	6.5
Sreenivasa Rao*	India	Diplomat	Andhra, Yale	1	6	6.0
Ajibola	Nigeria	Practising lawyer	London	5	27	5.4
Tanaka	Japan	Academic	Tokyo, 'USA and Europe'	6	32	5.3
Ečer*	Czechoslovakia	?	?	2	10	5.0
Simma	Germany	Academic	Innsbruck	12	54	4.5
Jiménez de Aréchaga*	Uruguay	Academic	Montevideo	3	12	4.0
El-Erian	Egypt	Diplomat	Cairo, Harvard, Columbia	1	4	4.0
Alfaro	Panama	Politician	?	2	7	3.5
Shahabuddeen*	Guyana	Politician	London	2	7	3.5
Ajibola*	Nigeria	Practising lawyer	London	4	14	3.5
Dillard	US	Academic	Virginia	12	40	3.3
Riphagen*	Netherlands	Diplomat	Amsterdam	1	3	3.0
Mbaye*	Senegal	Nat'l judge	Paris	3	9	3.0

(*cont.*)

Judge (* = ad hoc)	State	Profession	Education	Opinions	References	Per opinion
Fortier*	Canada	Practising lawyer	Montréal, McGill, Oxford	1	3	3.0
Dimitrijevic*	Yugoslavia	Academic	Belgrade	1	3	3.0
Crawford	Australia	Academic	Adelaide, Oxford	3	9	3.0
Levi Carneiro	Brazil	Academic	Rio	6	16	2.7
Guerrero	El Salvador	Diplomat	Salvador, Guatemala	2	5	2.5
Franck*	US	Academic	British Columbia, Harvard	2	5	2.5
Schwebel	US	Diplomat	Harvard, Cambridge, Yale	30	74	2.5
Fitzmaurice, Gerald	UK	Diplomat	Cambridge	9	22	2.4
Elaraby	Egypt	Diplomat	Cairo, NYU	23	53	2.3
Bedjaoui	Algeria	Diplomat	Grenoble	11	25	2.3
Robinson	Jamaica	Nat'l civil servant	West Indies, London	6	13	2.2
Kooijmans	Netherlands	Academic	Amsterdam	36	76	2.1
Al-Khasawneh	Jordan	Diplomat	Cambridge	17	35	2.1
Caicedo Castilla*	Colombia	?	?	2	4	2.0
Lauterpacht, Hersch	UK	Academic	Lviv, Vienna	7	14	2.0
Padilla Nervo	Mexico	Diplomat	Mexico, George Washington	8	16	2.0
Tarazi	Syria	Diplomat	Beirut	3	6	2.0

Caron*	US	Academic	US Coast Guard, Wales, Berkeley, Leiden	1	2	2.0
Dugard*	South Africa	Academic	Stellenbosch, Cambridge	8	14	1.8
Mampuya*	DR Congo	Academic	Nancy	3	5	1.7
McNair	UK	Academic	Cambridge	8	12	1.5
Bhandari	India	Nat'l judge	Jodhpur, Northwestern	10	15	1.5
Krylov	USSR	Academic	Leningrad	6	9	1.5
Jennings	UK	Academic	Cambridge (fellowship Harvard)	7	10	1.4
Torres-Bernárdez*	Spain	Int'l civil servant	Bilbao, Valladolid, Saar	8	11	1.4
Hsu Mo	China	Diplomat	Peiyang, Washington, Melbourne	4	5	1.3
Koretsky	USSR	Academic	Moscow, Kharkov	5	6	1.2
Tomka	Slovakia	Diplomat	Prague	16	19	1.2
Wellington Koo	China	Diplomat	Columbia	10	11	1.1
Daxner*	Czechoslovakia	?	?	1	1	1.0
Armand-Ugon*	Uruguay	Judge	?	1	1	1.0

(*cont.*)

Judge (* = ad hoc)	State	Profession	Education	Opinions	References	Per opinion
Urrutia Holguin*	Colombia	?	?	1	1	1.0
Bustamante	Peru	Diplomat	San Agustín, Cuzco	6	6	1.0
Mbanefo*	Nigeria	?	?	2	2	1.0
Sorensen*	Denmark	Int'l judge	Copenhagen, Geneva	1	1	1.0
Evensen*	Norway	Diplomat	Oslo, Minnesota, Columbia, Harvard	1	1	1.0
Ago	Italy	Academic	Naples	9	9	1.0
Jennings*	UK	Academic	Cambridge (fellowship Harvard)	1	1	1.0
Luchaire*	France	Academic	Caen	1	1	1.0
Yusuf*	Somalia	Int'l civil servant	Geneva, Somali, Florence	1	1	1.0
Charlesworth*	Australia	Academic	Melbourne, Harvard	1	1	1.0
Buergenthal	US	Academic	Bethany, NYU, Harvard	16	15	0.9
Keith	New Zealand	Academic	NZ, Wellington	16	14	0.9
Yusuf	Somalia	Int'l civil servant	Geneva, Somali, Florence	18	17	0.9
Aguilar Mawdsley	Venezuela	Diplomat	Caracas, McGill	4	3	0.8
Higgins	UK	Academic	Cambridge, Yale	33	23	0.7

Bennouna	Morocco	Academic	Nancy, Paris-Sorbonne	18	12	0.7
Ranjeva	Madagascar	Academic	Antananarivo, Paris	40	24	0.6
Spender	Australia	Politician	Sydney	12	7	0.6
Greenwood	UK	Academic	Cambridge	12	7	0.6
Oda	Japan	Academic	Tokyo (fellowship Yale)	70	39	0.6
Zoricic	Yugoslavia	Nat'l judge	Zagreb	4	2	0.5
Lachs	Poland	Diplomat	Vienna, Nancy, LSE London	19	10	0.5
Sette-Camara	Brazil	Diplomat	McGill	4	2	0.5
Mbaye	Senegal	Nat'l judge	Paris	2	1	0.5
Guillaume	France	Diplomat	Paris, ENA	16	8	0.5
Ruda	Argentina	Diplomat	Buenos Aires, New York	11	5	0.5
Waldock	UK	Int'l judge	Oxford	9	4	0.4
Koroma	Sierra Leone	Diplomat	KC London, Kiev	62	27	0.4
Read	Canada	Diplomat	Dalhousie, Columbia, Oxford	12	5	0.4
Badawi	Egypt	Nat'l civil servant	Cairo, Grenoble	15	6	0.4
Jiménez de Aréchaga	Uruguay	Academic	Montevideo	16	6	0.4

(*cont.*)

Judge (* = ad hoc)	State	Profession	Education	Opinions	References	Per opinion
Onyeama	Nigeria	Judge	King's College Lagos, Achimota, UCL, Oxford	14	5	0.4
Bedjaoui*	Algeria	Diplomat	Grenoble	3	1	0.3
Guillaume*	France	Diplomat	Paris, ENA	9	3	0.3
Rezek	Brazil	Academic	Minas Gerais, Paris-Sorbonne, Oxford, Harvard	9	3	0.3
Lauterpacht*	UK	Academic	Cambridge	3	1	0.3
Vukas*	Croatia	Academic	Zagreb	3	1	0.3
Cot*	France	Politician	Paris	3	1	0.3
Winiarski	Poland	Academic	Warsaw, Cracow, Heidelberg, Paris	13	4	0.3
Owada	Japan	Diplomat	Tokyo, Cambridge	23	7	0.3
Gros	France	Diplomat	Lyon, Paris	21	6	0.3
Mosler	Germany	Int'l judge	Bonn	7	2	0.3
Vereshchetin	Russia	Academic	Moscow	21	6	0.3
Abraham	France	Academic	Paris, ENA	15	4	0.3
Valticos*	Greece	Int'l civil servant	Paris	4	1	0.3

Ni	China	Diplomat	Chitz, Soochow, Dongwu (all Shanghai), Stanford	4	1	0.3
Shi	China	Academic	St John's (Shanghai), Columbia	20	5	0.3
Skotnikov	Russia	Diplomat	Moscow (fellowship Harvard)	15	3	0.2
Hackworth	US	Diplomat	Valparaiso, Georgetown, George Washington, Kentucky	6	1	0.2
Sebutinde	Uganda	Nat'l civil servant	Makerere, Edinburgh, Kampala, Colombo, Singapore, Reno	8	1	0.1
Gaja*	Italy	Academic	Rome	9	1	0.1
Forster	Senegal	Nat'l judge	Paris	10	1	0.1
Ignacio-Pinto	Benin	Int'l civil servant	Dahomey, Bordeaux	11	1	0.1
Gaja	Italy	Academic	Rome	11	1	0.1
Donoghue	US	Diplomat	Berkeley, Santa Cruz	15	1	0.1

(*cont.*)

Judge (* = ad hoc)	State	Profession	Education	Opinions	References	Per opinion
Parra-Aranguren	Venezuela	Academic	Venezuela, New York, Munich	28	1	0.0
Basdevant	France	Academic	?	12	0	0.0
Alvarez	Chile	Academic	Paris	13	0	0.0
de Visscher	Belgium	Academic	Ghent	2	0	0.0
Benegal Rau	India	Nat'l civil servant	Madras, Cambridge	1	0	0.0
Alayza y Paz Soldán*	Peru	?	?	1	0	0.0
Spiropoulos*	Greece	Diplomat	Zurich, Leipzig	1	0	0.0
Spiropoulos	Greece	Diplomat	Zurich, Leipzig	8	0	0.0
Klaestad	Norway	Nat'l judge	Oslo	11	0	0.0
Guggenheim*	Switzerland	Academic	Geneva, Rome, Berlin	1	0	0.0
Kojevnikov	USSR	Academic	Moscow	8	0	0.0
Chagla*	India	Nat'l judge	Oxford	2	0	0.0
Armand-Ugon	Uruguay	Nat'l judge	?	5	0	0.0
Moreno Quintana	Argentina	Academic	Buenos Aires	8	0	0.0
Zafrulla Khan	Pakistan	Politician	Punjab, KC London	9	0	0.0
Córdova	Mexico	Diplomat	Mexico	3	0	0.0
Offerhaus*	Netherlands	Practising lawyer	Amsterdam	1	0	0.0
Carry*	Switzerland	?	?	1	0	0.0
Goitein*	Israel	Judge	London LSE	1	0	0.0

Morelli	Italy	Academic	Rome	9	0	0.0
Petren	Sweden	Nat'l judge	Lund	16	0	0.0
Bengzon	Philippines	Nat'l judge	Manila	6	0	0.0
Morozov	USSR	Diplomat	Leningrad	11	0	0.0
Barwick*	Australia	Practising lawyer	Sydney	6	0	0.0
Boni*	Cote d'Ivoire	?	?	1	0	0.0
Elias	Nigeria	Practising lawyer	Cambridge, London	5	0	0.0
Stassinopoulos*	Greece	Academic	Athens	2	0	0.0
Evensen	Norway	Diplomat	Oslo, Minnesota, Columbia, Harvard	6	0	0.0
Sette-Camara*	Brazil	Diplomat	McGill	1	0	0.0
El-Khani	Syria	Diplomat	Damascus, Beirut, American Uni Beirut	3	0	0.0
Abi-Saab*	Egypt	Academic	Cairo, Paris, Michigan, Harvard, Cambridge, Geneva	1	0	0.0
de Lacharrière	France	Diplomat	Paris	1	0	0.0
Bastid*	France	Academic	Paris	1	0	0.0
Tarassov	Russia	Diplomat	Moscow	7	0	0.0

(*cont.*)

Judge (* = ad hoc)	State	Profession	Education	Opinions	References	Per opinion
Fischer*	Denmark	Diplomat	Copenhagen	1	0	0.0
Thierry*	France	Academic	?	2	0	0.0
Broms*	Finland	Academic	Helsinki, Michigan, Cambridge	1	0	0.0
Herczegh	Hungary	Academic	Szeged	6	0	0.0
Fleischhauer	Germany	Diplomat	Heidelberg, Grenoble, Paris	5	0	0.0
Fleischhauer*	Germany	Diplomat	Heidelberg, Grenoble, Paris	1	0	0.0
Bennouna*	Morocco	Academic	Nancy, Paris-Sorbonne	1	0	0.0
Ferrari Bravo	Italy	Academic	Naples	2	0	0.0
Verhoeven*	Belgium	Academic	Brussels, Louvain	2	0	0.0
Kateka*	Tanzania	Diplomat	East Africa, Dar es Salaam, KC London	1	0	0.0
Xue	China	Diplomat	Beijing, Columbia	12	0	0.0
Reddy*	India	?	?	1	0	0.0
Berman*	UK	Diplomat	Cape Town, Oxford	1	0	0.0
Mensah*	Ghana	Int'l civil servant	Ghana, London, Yale	1	0	0.0
Sepúlveda	Mexico	Diplomat	Mexico, Cambridge	5	0	0.0

				Opinions	References	Per opinion
Sepúlveda*	Mexico	Diplomat	Mexico, Cambridge	1	0	0.0
Vinuesa*	Argentina	Academic	Buenos Aires, Cambridge, Amsterdam, Harvard, Tufts	3	0	0.0
Orrego Vicuña*	Chile	Academic	Chile, London LSE	2	0	0.0
Daudet*	France	Academic	Paris	1	0	0.0
Gevorgian	Russia	Diplomat	Moscow	1	0	0.0
Arbour*	Canada	Academic	Montreal	1	0	0.0
Brower*	US	Practising lawyer	Harvard, Bonn, Berlin, Columbia	1	0	0.0
Callinan*	Australia	Practising lawyer	Queensland	2	0	0.0
Nagendra Singh	India	Nat'l civil servant	Agra, Cambridge	16	0	0.0
Nagendra Singh*	India	Nat'l civil servant	Agra, Cambridge	1	0	0.0
Beb a Don*	Cameroon	?	?	1	0	0.0
Sur*	France	Academic	Caen	2	0	0.0

	Number of judges	Number of judges	Number of judges	Opinions	References	Per opinion
Permanent judges	84			1243	3474	2.8
Ad hoc judges	63			186	1014	5.5
Judges who have been both, as permanent judges	18			201	791	3.9

(*cont.*)

Judge (* = ad hoc)	State	Profession	Education	Opinions	References	Per opinion
Judges who have been both, as ad hoc judges	18			44	73	1.7
OECD nationals	84 (39 permanent, 38 ad hoc, 7 both)			692	1030	1.5
Non-OECD nationals	81 (45 permanent, 25 ad hoc, 11 both)			734	3449	4.7
Civil law nationals	113 (59 permanent, 42 ad hoc, 12 both)			1045	3947	3.8
Common law nationals	44 (24 permanent, 17 ad hoc, 3 both)			471	1338	2.8
Mixed systems nationals	8 (1 permanent, 4 ad hoc, 3 both)			(counted under both)		
Academics		69 (35 permanent, 29 ad hoc, 5 both)		698	3413	4.9
Diplomats		44 (31 permanent, 6 ad hoc, 7 both)		442	705	1.6
Nat'l civil servants		5 (4 permanent, 1 both)		47	20	0.4

Politicians	6 (3 permanent, 2 ad hoc, 1 both)		51	291	5.7
Nat'l judges	11 (7 permanent, 2 ad hoc, 2 both)		85	34	0.4
Int'l judges	3 (2 permanent, 1 ad hoc)		17	7	0.4
Int'l civil servants	6 (1 permanent, 4 ad hoc, 1 both)		44	50	1.1
Practising lawyers	7 (1 permanent, 5 ad hoc, 1 both)		25	44	1.8
All non-academics	82 (49 permanent, 20 ad hoc, 13 both)		711	1151	1.6
No data	14 (14 ad hoc)				
Civil law education		75 (41 permanent, 25 ad hoc, 9 both)	684	1322	1.9
Common law education		45 (26 permanent, 13 ad hoc, 6 both)	376	1242	3.3
Mixed education		26 (15 permanent, 9 ad hoc, 2 both)	287	1709	6.0
Some OECD education		126 (68 permanent, 42 ad hoc, 16 both)	1178	3762	3.2

(*cont.*)

Judge (* = ad hoc)	State	Profession	Education	Opinions	References	Per opinion
No OECD education			20 (14 permanent, 5 ad hoc, 1 both)	139	503	3.6
No data			19 (2 permanent, 16 ad hoc, 1 both)			

Judges Engaging with Teachings

Judge	Instances
Shahabuddeen	20
Weeramantry	17
Trindade	11
Lauterpacht	10
Schwebel	10
Ammoun	6
De Castro	5
Fitzmaurice	5
Vereshchetin	5
Dillard	4
Jessup	4
Oda	4
Spender	4
Wellington Koo	3
Levi Carneiro	3
Rigaux	3
van Wyk	3
Buergenthal	2
Bula-Bula	2
Higgins	2
Jennings	2
Kooijmans	2
Kreća	2
Shi	2
Winiarski	2
Abraham	1
Al-Khasawneh	1
Jiménez de Aréchaga	1
Azevedo	1

(*cont.*)

Judge	Instances
Torres-Bernárdez	1
Caron	1
Caicedo Castilla	1
Ečer	1
Fernandes	1
Guillaume	1
Lachs	1
Mahiou	1
Mampuya	1
Padilla Nervo	1
Palmer	1
Paolillo	1
Pirzada	1
Ranjeva	1
Rezek	1
Riphagen	1
Tanaka	1
Valticos	1
Wyngaert	1

APPENDIX 4

Citations Per Judge (PCIJ)

Judge	Citations	Opinions	Avg. citations per opinion
Otavsky	4	1	4.0
Pessoa	13	4	3.3
Moore	9	3	3.0
Hudson	15	6	2.5
Seferiades	3	2	1.5
Kellogg	2	2	1.0
Vogt	1	1	1.0
Finlay	2	4	0.5
Eysinga	6	14	0.4
Bustamante	2	6	0.3
Dreyfus	1	3	0.3
Weiss	1	3	0.3
Shucking	1	9	0.1
Rostworowski	1	12	0.1

Judges' Citations Compared to Pleadings

Case	Judge (*=judge ad hoc)	Citations that were also in pleadings	All citations in the opinion	Share of all citations that were also in pleadings (%)
Bosnia Genocide	Kreća*	28	62	45
	Mahiou*	22	68	32
	Skotnikov	1	1	100
	Keith	0	1	0
	Tomka	3	7	43
	Shi and Koroma	2	2	100
	Ranjeva, Shi, and Koroma	1	1	100
	Al-Khasawneh	1	4	25
Jan Mayen	Ajibola	3	3	100
	Weeramantry	20	118	17
	Shahabuddeen	8	47	17
Pulp Mills	Greenwood	1	1	100
	Cançado Trindade	10	139	7
	Al-Khasawneh and Simma	0	15	0

Most-Cited Writers in Pleadings

Writer	Times cited	Nationality
Schabas	14	Canada
Rosenne	13	Israel/UK
Boyle	10	UK
Flangini	9	Uruguay
Jennings	9	UK
Lapeyre	9	Uruguay
Watts	9	UK
Birnie	8	UK
Oppenheim	8	Germany/UK
McCaffrey	7	US
Jayewardene	6	Sri Lanka
Pellet	6	France
Barberis	5	Argentina
Brownlie	5	UK
Caflisch	5	Switzerland
Daillier	5	France
Kirgis	5	US
Lauterpacht	5	Austrian Empire/UK
Robinson	5	Lithuania/US
Weil	5	France

Abass A, *International Law: Text, Cases, and Materials* (2nd edn, Oxford University Press 2014)

Aceves WJ, 'Symposium Introduction; Scholarship as Evidence of International Law' (2003) 26 *Loyola of Los Angeles International and Comparative Law Review* 1

Agpalo RE, *Public International Law* (Rex 2006)

Akehurst M, 'The Hierarchy of the Sources of International Law' (1975) 47 *British Yearbook of International Law* 273

Allott P, 'Interpretation—An Exact Art' in Bianchi A, Peat D, and Windsor M (eds.), *Interpretation in International Law* (Oxford University Press 2015) 373

Amann DM, 'Group Mentality, Expressivism, and Genocide' (2002) 2 *International Criminal Law Review* 93

Ambro TL, 'Citing Legal Articles in Judicial Opinions: A Sympathetic Antipathy' (2006) 80 *American Bankruptcy Law Journal* 547

American Law Institute, *Restatement of the Law of Foreign Relations of the United States*, vol. I (American Law Institute Publishers 1987)

Anand RP, 'The International Court of Justice and the Development of International Law' (1965) 7 *International Studies* 228

Andenas M and Bjorge E, 'Introduction: From Fragmentation to Convergence' in International Law' in Andenas M and Bjorge E (eds.), *A Farewell to Fragmentation: Reassertion and Convergence in International Law* (Cambridge University Press 2015) 1

Aust A, *Handbook of International Law* (2nd edn, Cambridge University Press 2010)

Bale G, 'W.R. Lederman and the Citation of Legal Periodicals by the Supreme Court of Canada' (1994) 19 *Queen's Law Journal* 36

Beatson J, 'Legal Academics: Forgotten Players or Interlopers?' in Burrows A, Johnston D, and Zimmermann R (eds.), *Judge and Jurist: Essays in Memory of Lord Rodger* (Oxford University Press 2013) 523

Becker MA and Rose C, 'Investigating the Value of Site Visits in Inter-State Arbitration and Adjudication' (2017) 8 *Journal of International Dispute Settlement* 219

Bernstein NN, 'The Supreme Court and Secondary Source Material: 1965 Term' (1968) 57 *Georgetown Law Journal* 55

Besson S, 'Theorizing the Sources of International Law' in Besson S and Tasioulas J (eds.), *The Philosophy of International Law* (Oxford University Press 2010) 163

Bianchi A, 'Reflexive Butterfly Catching: Insights from a Situated Catcher' in Pauwelyn J, Wessel R, and Wouters J (eds.), *Informal International Lawmaking* (Oxford University Press 2012) 200

    'The Game of Interpretation in International Law: The Players, the Cards, and Why the Game is Worth the Candle' in Bianchi A, Peat D, and Windsor M (eds.), *Interpretation in International Law* (Oxford University Press 2015) 34

    'Choice and (the Awareness of) its Consequences: The ICJ's "Structural Bias" Strikes Again in the Marshall Islands Case' (2017) 111 *AJIL Unbound* 81

Bishop WW, 'General Course on Public International Law' (1965) 115 *Recueil des Cours* 147

Black V and Richter N, 'Did She Mention My Name?: Citation of Academic Authority by the Supreme Court of Canada, 1985–1990' (1993) 16 *Dalhousie Law Journal* 377

Boas G, *Public International Law: Contemporary Principles and Perspectives* (Edward Elgar 2012) 115

Bohlander M, 'The Influence of Academic Research on the Jurisprudence of the International Criminal Tribunal for the Former Yugoslavia – A First Overview' (2003) 3 *The Global Community Yearbook of International Law & Jurisprudence* 195

    and Findlay M, 'The Use of Domestic Sources as a Basis for International Criminal Law Principles' (2002) 2 *The Global Community Yearbook of International Law and Jurisprudence* 3

Borda AZ, 'A Formal Approach to Article 38 (1)(d) of the ICJ Statute from the Perspective of the International Criminal Courts and Tribunals' (2013) 24 *European Journal of International Law* 649

Bordin FL, 'Reflections of Customary International Law: The Authority of Codification Conventions and ILC Draft Articles in International Law (2014) 63 *International and Comparative Law Quarterly* 535

Bos M, 'The Recognised Manifestations of International Law: A New Theory of "Sources"' (1977) 20 *German Yearbook International Law* 9

Boyle A and Chinkin C, *The Making of International Law* (Oxford University Press 2007)

Braun A, 'Burying the Living? The Citation of Legal Writings in English Courts' (2010) 58 *American Journal of Comparative Law* 27

Brierly JL, *The Law of Nations: An Introduction to the International Law of Peace* (Waldock H ed., 6th edn, Oxford University Press 1963)

Brinkmann S and Kvale S, *InterViews: Learning the Art of Qualitative Research Interviewing* (3rd edn, Sage 2015)

Brunnée J, 'The Sources of International Environmental Law: Interactional Law' in Besson S and d'Aspremont J (eds.), *The Oxford Handbook on the Sources of International Law* (Oxford University Press 2017) 960

Buchanan, A, 'The Legitimacy of International Law' in Besson S and Tasioulas J (eds.), *The Philosophy of International Law* (Oxford University Press 2010) 79

Butler WE, 'Regional and Sectional Diversities in International Law' in Cheng B (ed.), *International Law: Teaching and Practice* (Stevens and Sons 1982) 45

Cameron J and Gray KR, 'Principles of International Law in the WTO Dispute Settlement Body' (2001) 50 *International and Comparative Law Quarterly* 248

Cançado Trindade, AA, *International Law for Humankind: Towards a New Jus Gentium* (Martinus Nijhoff 2010)

'Statute of the International Court of Justice', *Audiovisual Library of International Law* (2017) http://legal.un.org/avl/ha/sicj/sicj.html

Caron DD, 'The ILC Articles on State Responsibility: The Paradoxical Relationship between Form and Authority' (2002) 96 *American Journal of International Law* 857

Carty A, *The Decay of International Law? A Reappraisal of the Limits of Legal Imagination in International Affairs* (Manchester University Press 1986)

Cassese A, *International Law in a Divided World* (Oxford University Press 1986)
International Law (2nd edn, Oxford University Press 2005)
Five Masters of International Law (Hart 2011)

Charlesworth, H, 'Law-Making and Sources' in Crawford J and Koskenniemi M (eds.), *The Cambridge Companion to International Law* (Cambridge University Press 2012) 187

and Chinkin C, *The Boundaries of International Law: A Feminist Analysis* (Manchester University Press 2000)

Chinkin C and Wright S, 'Feminist Approaches to International Law' (1991) 85 *American Journal of International Law* 613

Clapham A, *Brierly's Law of Nations: An Introduction to the Role of International Law in International Relations* (7th edn, Oxford University Press 2012)

Cohen HG, 'Theorizing Precedent in International Law' in Bianchi A, Peat D, and Windsor M (eds.), *Interpretation in International Law* (Oxford University Press 2015) 268

and others, 'Legitimacy and International Courts – A Framework' in Cohen HG and others (eds.), *Legitimacy and International Courts* (Cambridge University Press 2018) 1, 4

Cole T, 'Non-Binding Documents and Literature' in Gazzini T and De Brabandere E (eds.), *International Investment Law: The Sources of Rights and Obligations* (Martinus Nijhoff 2012) 289

Corbett PE, 'The Consent of States and the Sources of the Law of Nations' (1925) 6 *British Yearbook of International Law* 20

Côté JE, 'Far-Cited' (2001) 39 *Alberta Law Review* 640

Crawford J, *International Law as an Open System: Selected Essays* (Cameron May 2002)

    Brownlie's Principles of Public International Law (8th edn, Oxford University Press 2012)

    Chance, Order, Change: The Course of International Law (Brill 2014)

Crespi GS, 'The Influence of a Decade of Statutory Interpretation Scholarship on Judicial Rulings: An Empirical Analysis' (2000) 53 *SMU Law Review* 9

    'The Influence of Two Decades of Contract Law Scholarship on Judicial Rulings: An Empirical Analysis' (2004) 57 *SMU Law Review* 105

Currie JH, *Public International Law* (2nd edn, Irwin Law 2008)

    'What Does It Mean to be an Internationalist?' (1989) 10 *Michigan Journal of International Law* 102

d'Aspremont J, *Formalism and the Sources of International Law* (Oxford University Press 2011)

    'Non-State Actors from the Perspective of Legal Positivism: The Communitarian Semantics for the Secondary Rules of International Law' in d'Aspremont J (ed.), *Participants in the International Legal System: Multiple Perspectives on Non-State Actors in International Law* (Routledge 2011) 23

    'The Idea of "Rules" in the Sources of International Law' (2014) 84 *British Yearbook of International Law* 103

    Epistemic Forces in International Law (Edward Elgar 2015)

    'Non-State Actors and the Social Practice of International Law' in Noortmann M, Reinisch A, and Ryngaert C (eds.), *Non-State Actors in International Law* (Hart 2015) 11

    'Wording in International Law' (2012) 25 *Leiden Journal of International Law* 575

Daillier P, Forteau M, and Pellet A, *Droit International Public* (8th edn, L.G.D.J. 2009)

Daniels W, '"Far Beyond the Law Reports": Secondary Source Citations in the United States Supreme Court Opinions October Terms 1900, 1940, and 1978' (1983) 76 *Law Library Journal* 1

Danilenko GM, *Law-Making in the International Community* (Martinus Nijhoff 1993)

de Aréchaga EJ, 'International Law in the Past Third of a Century' (1978) 159 *Recueil des cours* 1

De Brabandere E, 'Rationale of Amicus Curiae Interventions in International Economic and Investment Disputes' (2011) 12 *Chicago Journal of International Law* 85

Degan VD, *Sources of International Law* (Martinus Nijhoff 1997)

Dhokalia RP, *The Codification of Public International Law* (Manchester University Press 1970)

Dickinson ED, 'Changing Concepts and the Doctrine of Incorporation' (1932) 26 *American Journal of International Law* 239

Dixon M, *Textbook on International Law* (7th edn, Oxford University Press 2013)

Douglas Z, *The International Law of Investment Claims* (Cambridge University Press 2009)

Dugard J, 'How Effective is the International Law Commission in the Development of International Law? A Critique of the ILC on the Occasion of Its Fiftieth Anniversary' (1998) 23 *South African Yearbook of International Law* 34

International Law: A South African Perspective (4th ed, Juta and Co 2011)

Dupuy PM, 'The Danger of Fragmentation or Unification of the International Legal System and the International Court of Justice' (1998) 31 *NYU Journal of International Law and Politics* 791

Duxbury N, *Judges and Jurists: An Essay on Influence* (Hart 2001)

Earlsferry LRO, 'Judges and Academics in the United Kingdom' (2010) 29 *University of Queensland Law Journal* 29

Edwards HT and Livermore MA, 'Pitfalls of Empirical Studies That Attempt to Understand the Factors Affecting Appellate Decisionmaking' (2009) 58 *Duke Law Journal* 1895

Eisenberg T and Wells MT, 'Ranking and Explaining the Scholarly Impact of Law Schools' (1998) 27 *Journal of Legal Studies* 373

Elias TO, 'Modern Sources of International Law' in Friedmann W, Henkin L, and Lissitzyn O (eds.), *Transnational Law in a Changing Society: Essays In Honor of Philip C. Jessup* (Columbia University Press 1972) 34

Falk RA, 'On the Quasi-Legislative Competence of the General Assembly' (1966) 60 *American Journal of International Law* 782

Fastenrath U, 'Article 4' in Simma B and others (eds.), *The Charter of the United Nations: A Commentary* (3rd edn, Oxford University Press 2012) 341

Fauchald OK, 'The Legal Reasoning of ICSID Tribunals – An Empirical Analysis' (2008) 19 *European Journal of International Law* 301

Feenan D, 'Editorial Introduction: Women and Judging' (2009) 17 *Feminist Legal Studies* 1

Fitzmaurice G, 'The General Principles of International Law Considered from the Standpoint of the Rule of Law' (1957) 92 *Recueil des cours* 1

'The Contribution of the Institute of International Law to the Development of International Law' (1973) 138 *Recueil des cours* 203

'Some Problems Regarding the Formal Sources of International Law' in Koskenniemi M (ed.), *Sources of International Law* (Ashgate 2000) 57

Franck SD, 'Empirically Evaluating Claims about Investment Treaty Arbitration' (2007) 86 *North Carolina Law Review* 1

'Development and Outcomes in Investment Treaty Arbitration' (2009) 50 *Harvard International Law Journal* 438

'The Diversity Challenge: Exploring the "Invisible College" of International Arbitration' (2015) 53 *Columbia Journal of Transnational Law* 429

Franck TM, *The Power of Legitimacy Among Nations* (Oxford University Press 1990)

Friedman L and others, 'State Supreme Courts: A Century of Style and Citation' (1981) 33 *Stanford Law Review* 773

Gaillard E, 'The Denunciation of the ICSID Convention', *Transnational Dispute Management* (2007) www.transnational-dispute-management.com/article .asp?key=1074

Gardiner R, *Treaty Interpretation* (2nd edn, Oxford University Press 2017)

Gaubatz KT and MacArthur M, 'How International Is "International" Law?' (2001) 22 *Michigan Journal of International Law* 239

Goff L, 'The Search for Principle' (1983) 67 *Proceedings of the British Academy* 169

Goldsmith J, 'Remarks by Jack Goldsmith' (2000) 94 *ASIL Proceedings* 318

Grant JP, *International Law* (Dundee University Press 2010)

Green LC, *International Law: A Canadian Perspective* (2nd edn, The Carswell Company 1988)

Greig DW, *International Law* (2nd edn, Butterworths 1976)

'Sources of International Law' in Blay S, Piotrowicz R, and Tsamenyi M (eds.), *Public International Law: An Australian Perspective* (2nd edn, Oxford University Press 2005) 52

Grossman N, 'Achieving Sex-Representative International Court Benches' (2016) 110 *American Journal of International Law* 82

'Shattering the Glass Ceiling in International Adjudication' (2016) 56 *Virginia Journal of International Law* 339

Hall S, *International Law* (2nd edn, LexisNexis Butterworths 2006)

Harner M and Cantone JA, 'Is Legal Scholarship Out of Touch? An Empirical Analysis of the Use of Scholarship in Business Law Cases' (2011) 19 *University of Miami Business Law Review* 1

Harris DJ, *Cases and Materials on International Law* (8th edn, Sweet & Maxwell 2015)

Helmersen ST, 'The Use of Scholarship by the WTO Appellate Body' (2016) 7 *Goettingen Journal of International Law* 309

Hernández GI, *The International Court of Justice and the Judicial Function* (Oxford University Press 2014)

'Interpretative Authority and the International Judiciary' in Bianchi A, Peat D, and Windsor M (eds.), *Interpretation in International Law* (Oxford University Press 2015) 166

Higgins R, *Problems and Process: International Law and How We Use It* (Oxford University Press 1995)

'A Babel of Judicial Voices? Ruminations from the Bench' (2006) 55 *International and Comparative Law Quarterly* 791

Hillier T, *Sourcebook on Public International Law* (Cavendish 1998)

Hirsch JE, 'An Index to Quantify an Individual's Scientific Research Output' (2005) 102 *Proceedings of the National Academy of Science of the United States of America* 16569

Hudson MO, *The Permanent Court of International Justice 1920–1942: A Treatise* (Macmillan 1943)

Hume RJ, 'Strategic-Instrument Theory and the Use of Non-Authoritative Sources by Federal Judges: Explaining References to Law Review Articles' (2010) 31 *Justice System Journal* 291

Hunter R, 'More than Just a Different Face? Judicial Diversity and Decision-Making' (2015) 68 *Current Legal Problems* 119

Issaeva M, 'Quarter of a Century on from the Soviet Era: Reflections on Russian Doctrinal Responses to the Annexation of Crimea' (2017) 5 *Russian Law Journal* 86

Jain N, 'Teachings of Publicists and the Reinvention of the Sources Doctrine in International Criminal Law' in Kevin Heller, et al. (eds.), *The Oxford Handbook of International Criminal Law* (Oxford University Press 2020) 106

Janis MW, 'Introduction' in Janis MW and Evans CM (eds.), *Religion and International Law* (Martinus Nijhoff 1999) xi

Jansen N, *The Making of Legal Authority: Non-legislative Codifications in Historical and Comparative Perspective* (Oxford University Press 2010)

Jennings RY, 'The Progressive Development of International Law and Its Codification' (1947) 24 *British Yearbook of International Law* 301

'General Course on Principles of International Law' (1967) 121 *Recueil des cours* 323

'The Collegiate Responsibility and Authority of the International Court of Justice' in Dinstein Y (ed.), *International Law at a Time of Perplexity: Essays in Honour of Shabtai Rosenne* (Martinus Nijhoff 1989) 343

'International Lawyers and the Progressive Development of International Law' in Makarczyk J (ed.), *Theory of International Law at the Threshold of the 21st Century: Essays in Honour of Krzysztof Skubiszewski* (Kluwer 1996) 413

'The Judiciary, International and National, and the Development of International Law' (1996) 45 *International and Comparative Law Quarterly* 1

'What is International Law and How Do We Know It When We See It' in Koskenniemi M (ed.), *Sources of International Law* (Ashgate 2000) 27

'Reflections on the Subsidiary Means for the Determination of Rules of Law', in *Studi di diritto internazionale in onore di Gaetano Arangio-Ruiz*, vol. I (Editoriale Scientifica 2004) 319

and Watts A (eds.), *Oppenheim's International Law*, vol. I (9th edn, Longman 1992)

Kaczorowska A, *Public International Law* (4th edn, Routledge 2010)

Kammerhofer J, 'Lawmaking by Scholars' in Brölmann C and Radi Y (eds.), *Research Handbook on the Theory and Practice of International Lawmaking* (Edward Elgar 2016) 305

Kaye JS, 'One Judge's View of Academic Law Review Writing' (1989) 39 *Journal of Legal Education* 313

Keene A (ed.), 'Outcome Paper for the Seminar on the International Court of Justice at 70' (2016) 7 *Journal of International Dispute Settlement* 238

Keith K, 'Challenges to the Independence of the International Judiciary: Reflections on the International Court of Justice' (2017) 30 *Leiden Journal of International Law* 137

Kennedy D, 'The Disciplines of International Law and Policy' (2008) 12 *Leiden Journal of International Law* 9

Kenny JT, 'Manley O. Hudson and the Harvard Research in International Law 1927-1940' (1977) 11 *The International Lawyer* 319

Kent A and Trinidad J, 'International Law Scholars as Amici Curiae: An Emerging Dialogue (of the Deaf)?' (2016) 29 *Leiden Journal of International Law* 1081

King KL and Greening M, 'Gender Justice or Just Gender? The Role of Gender in Sexual Assault Decisions at the International Criminal Tribunal for the Former Yugoslavia' (2007) 88 *Social Science Quarterly* 1049

Kingsbury B, 'International Courts: Uneven Judicialisation In Global Order' in Crawford J and Koskenniemi M (eds.), *The Cambridge Companion to International Law* (Cambridge University Press 2012) 203, 223.

Klabbers J, *International Law* (Cambridge University Press 2013)

Kolb R, *The International Court of Justice* (Hart 2013)

The Elgar Companion to the International Court of Justice (Edward Elgar 2014)

Koskenniemi M, 'Introduction' in Koskenniemi M (ed.), *Sources of International Law* (Ashgate 2000) xi

The Gentle Civilizer of Nations: The Rise and Fall of International Law 1870–1960 (Cambridge University Press 2001)

From Apology to Utopia: The Structure of International Legal Argument (2nd edn, Cambridge University Press 2006)

'Histories of International Law: Dealing with Eurocentrism' (2011) 19 *Rechtsgeschichte* 152

Koutroulis V, 'The Prohibition of the Use of Force in Arbitrations and Fact-Finding Reports' in Weller M (ed.), *The Oxford Handbook of the Use of Force in International Law* (Oxford University Press 2015) 605

Ku JG, 'China's Legal Scholars Are Less Credible After South China Sea Ruling', *Foreign Policy* (14 July 2016) http://foreignpolicy.com/2016/07/14/south-china-sea-lawyers-unclos-beijing-legal-tribunal

Kumar SP and Rose C, 'A Study of Lawyers Appearing before the International Court of Justice, 1999–2012' (2014) 25 *European Journal of International Law* 893

La Forest GV, 'Who is Listening to Whom? The Discourse Between the Canadian Judiciary and Academics' in Markesinis BS (ed.), *Law Making, Law Finding and Law Shaping: The Diverse Influences* (Oxford University Press 1997) 69

Lachs M, 'Teaching and Teachings of International Law' (1976) 151 *Recueil des cours* 161

The Teacher in International Law (2nd edn, Martinus Nijhoff 1987)

Langford M, Behn D, and Lie RH, 'The Revolving Door in International Investment Arbitration' (2017) 20 *Journal of International Economic Law* 301

Lauterpacht H, *The Development of International Law by the International Court* (Stevens and Sons 1958)

Lefkowitz D, 'The Sources of International Law: Some Philosophical Reflections' in Besson S and Tasioulas J (eds.), *The Philosophy of International Law* (Oxford University Press 2010) 187

Lorca AB, 'Eurocentrism in the History of International Law' in Fassbender B and Peters A (eds.), *The Oxford Handbook of the History of International Law* (Oxford University Press 2012) 1034

Lowe V, *International Law* (Oxford University Press 2007)

Lupu Y and Voeten E, 'Precedent in International Courts: A Network Analysis of Case Citations by the European Court of Human Rights' (2011) 42 *British Journal of Political Science* 413

MacCormick N and Summers RS (eds.), *Interpreting Precedents: A Comparative Study* (Aldershot 1997)

Mackenzie R and others, *Selecting International Judges: Principle, Process, and Politics* (Oxford University Press 2010)

Madsen MR, 'Who Rules the World? The Educational Capital of the International Judiciary' (2020) 3 *University of California Journal of International, Transnational, and Comparative Law* 97

Malanczuk P, *Akehurst's Modern International Law* (7th edn, Routledge 1997)

Mälksoo L, *Russian Approaches to International Law* (Oxford University Press 2015)

Manley S, 'Citation Practices of the International Criminal Court: The Situation in Darfur, Sudan' (2017) 30 *Leiden Journal of International Law* 1003

Mann RA, 'The Use of Legal Periodicals by Courts and Journals' (1986) 26 *Jurimetrics Journal* 400

Marceaug G, 'WTO Dispute Settlement and Human Rights' (2002) 13 *European Journal of International Law* 753

McClintock MD, 'The Declining Use of Legal Scholarship by Courts: An Empirical Study' (1998) 51 *Oklahoma Law Review* 659

McLeod I, *Legal Method* (9th edn, Palgrave Macmillan 2013)

Mendelson M, 'The International Court of Justice and the Sources of International Law' in Lowe V and Fitzmaurice M (eds.), *Fifty Years of the International Court of Justice: Essays in Honour of Sir Robert Jennings* (Cambridge University Press 1996) 63

Merrills JG, *International Dispute Settlement* (5th edn, Cambridge University Press 2011)

Merritt DJ and Putnam M, 'Judges and Scholars: Do Courts and Scholarly Journals Cite the Same Law Review Articles' (1996) 71 *Chicago-Kent Law Review* 871

Merryman JH, 'The Authority of Authority: What the California Supreme Court Cited in 1950' (1954) 6 *Stanford Law Review* 613

'Toward a Theory of Citations: An Empirical Study of the Citation Practice of the California Supreme Court in 1950, 1960, and 1970' (1977) 50 *Southern California Law Review* 381

and Pérez-Perdomo R, *The Civil Law Tradition: An Introduction to the Legal Systems of Europe and Latin America* (3rd edn, Stanford University Press 2007)

Merton RK, 'The Matthew Effect in Science' (1968) 159 *Science* 56

Moiseienko A, 'Guest Post: What do Russian Lawyers Say about Crimea?', *Opinio Juris* (24 September 2014) http://opiniojuris.org/2014/09/24/guest-post-russian-lawyers-say-crimea/

Murphy JF, *The Evolving Dimensions of International Law: Hard Choices for the World Community* (Cambridge University Press 2010)

Neumann T and Simma B, 'Transparency in International Adjudication' in Peters A and Bianchi A (eds.), *Transparency in International Law* (Cambridge University Press 2013) 436

Newland CA, 'The Supreme Court and Legal Writing: Learned Journals as Vehicles of an Anti-Antitrust Lobby?' (1959) 48 *Georgetown Law Journal* 105

Newton BE, 'Law Review Scholarship in the Eyes of the Twenty-First-Century Supreme Court Justices: An Empirical Analysis' (2012) 4 *Drexel Law Review* 399

Nouwen SMH, '"*As You Set out for Ithaka*": Practical, Epistemological, Ethical, and Existential Questions about Socio-Legal Empirical Research in Conflict' (2014) 27 *Leiden Journal of International Law* 227

Nouwen S, Tams CJ, d'Aspremont J, and Klabbers J, 'EJIL Editors' Choice of Books' (2015) 26 *European Journal of International Law* 1027

O'Connell DP, *International Law*, vol. I (2nd edn, Stevens and Sons 1970)

O'Connell ME, *The Power and Purpose of International Law: Insights from the Theory and Practice of Enforcement* (Oxford University Press 2008)

Onuf NG, 'Global Law-Making and Legal Thought' in Onuf NG (ed.), *Law-Making in the Global Community* (Carolina Academic Press 1982) 1

Oppenheim L, *International Law: A Treatise*, vol. I (Longmans, Green, and Co. 1905)
'The Science of International Law: Its Task and Method' (1908) 2 *American Journal of International Law* 313

Oraison A, 'L'Influence des Forces Doctrinales Académiques sur les Prononcés de la C.P.J.I. et de la C.I.J' (1999) 32 *Revue Belge de Droit International* 205

Palchetti P, 'Article 27', in Zimmermann A and others (eds.), *The Statute of the International Court of Justice: A Commentary* (2nd edn, Oxford University Press 2012) 502

Parry C, *The Sources and Evidence of International Law* (Manchester University Press 1965)

Paulsson J, 'Scholarship as Law' in Arsanjani MH and others (eds.), *Looking to the Future: Essays in Honor of Michael Reisman* (Martinus Nijhoff 2011) 183

Pauwelyn J, *Conflict of Norms in Public International Law: How WTO Law Relates to other Rules of International Law* (Cambridge University Press 2003)
'How to Win a World Trade Organization Dispute Based on Non-World Trade Organization Law?: Questions of Jurisdiction and Merits' (2003) 37 *Journal of World Trade* 997
'Is It International Law or Not, and Does It Even Matter?' in Pauwelyn J, Wessel R, and Wouters J (eds.), *Informal International Lawmaking* (Oxford University Press 2012) 125
'The Rule of Law without Lawyers? Why Investment Arbitrators are from Mars, Trade Adjudicators from Venus' (2015) 109 *American Journal of International Law* 761
and Pavlakos G, 'Principled Monism and the Normative Conception of Coercion under International Law' in Evans MD and Koutrakos P (eds.), *Beyond the Established Orders: Policy Interconnections Between the EU and the Rest of the World* (Hart 2011) 317
and Pelc, KJ, 'Who Writes the Rulings of the World Trade Organization? A Critical Assessment of the Role of the Secretariat in WTO Dispute Settlement' (2019) https://papers.ssrn.com/sol3/papers.cfm?abstract_id=3458872

Peil M, 'Scholarly Writings as a Source of Law: A Survey of the Use of Doctrine by the International Court of Justice' (2012) 1 *Cambridge Journal of International and Comparative Law* 136

Pellet A, 'Article 38' in Zimmermann A and others (eds.), *The Statute of the International Court of Justice: A Commentary* (2nd edn, Oxford University Press 2012) 731

Peters A, Ulfstein G, and Klabbers J, *The Constitutionalization of International Law* (Oxford University Press 2009)

Petherbridge PL and Schwartz DL, 'An Empirical Assessment of the Supreme Court's Use of Legal Scholarship' (2012) 106 *Northwestern University Law Review* 995

Posner RA, 'The Theory and Practice of Citations Analysis, with Special Reference to Law and Economics', *John M. Olin Program in Law and Economics Working Paper* Number 83 (1999) http://chicagounbound.uchicago.edu/cgi/viewcontent.cgi?article=1577&context=law_and_economics

The Little Book of Plagiarism (Pantheon 2007)

Preuss L, 'Survey of International Law in Relation to the Work of Codification of The International Law Commission. Memorandum Submitted by the Secretary General. (Doc. A/ CN.4/1/Rev.l.)' (1949) 43 *American Journal of International Law* 829

Prott LV, *The Latent Power of Culture and the International Judge* (Professional Books 1979)

Puig S, 'Social Capital in the Arbitration Market' (2014) 25 *European Journal of International Law* 387

Qureshi AH, 'Editorial Control and the Development of International Law' (1990) 61 *Political Quarterly* 328

Raimondo F, *General Principles of Law in the Decisions of International Criminal Courts and Tribunals* (Martinus Nijhoff 2008)

Richardson FK, 'Law Reviews and the Courts' (1983) 5 *Whittier Law Review* 385

Ripple K, 'The Judge and the Academic Community' (1989) 50 *Ohio State Law Journal* 1237, 1239

Roberts AE, 'Traditional and Modern Approaches to Customary International Law: A Reconciliation' (2001) 95 *American Journal of International Law* 757

Is International Law International? (Oxford University Press 2017).

and Sivakumaran S, 'Lawmaking by Nonstate Actors: Engaging Armed Groups in the Creation of International Humanitarian Law' (2012) 37 *Yale Journal of International Law* 107

Rohrbacher B, 'Decline: Twenty-Five Years of Student Scholarship in Judicial Opinions' (2006) 80 *American Bankruptcy Law Journal* 553

Rona G, 'The ICRC's Status: In a Class of Its Own', *International Committee of the Red Cross* (17 February 2004) www.icrc.org/eng/resources/documents/misc/5w9fjy.htm

Rosenne S, *Practice and Methods of International Law* (Oceana Publications 1984)

The Perplexities of Modern International Law (Martinus Nijhoff 2004)

with the Assistance of Ronen Y, *The Law and Practice of the International Court 1920–2005*, Vol. III (4th edn, Martinus Nijhoff 2006)

Rosenstock R, 'The ILC and State Responsibility' (2002) 96 *American Journal of International Law* 792

Rubin E, 'Seduction, Integration and Conceptual Frameworks: The Influence of Legal Scholarship on Judges' (2010) 29 *University of Queensland Law Journal* 101

Sands P, McLachlan C, and Mackenzie R, 'The Burgh House Principles on the Independence of the International Judiciary' (2005) 4 *Law and Practice of International Courts and Tribunals* 247

Schachter O, 'The Invisible College of International Lawyers' (1977) 72 *Northwestern University Law Review* 217

International Law in Theory and Practice (Martinus Nijhoff 1991)

'Law-Making in the United Nations' in Jasentuliyana N (ed.), *Perspectives on International Law* (Kluwer 1995) 119

Schwartz DL and Petherbridge L, 'The Use of Legal Scholarship by the Federal Courts of Appeals: An Empirical Study' (2011) 96 *Cornell Law Review* 1345

Schwarzenberger G, 'The Inductive Approach to International Law' (1947) 60 *Harvard Law Review* 539

'The Province of the Doctrine of International Law' (1956) 9 *Current Legal Problems* 235

International Law, Volume 1: International Law as Applied by International Courts and Tribunals: I (3rd edn, Stevens and Sons 1957)

Schwebel SM, 'The Inter-Active Influence of the International Law Court of Justice and the International Law Commission' in Barea CAA and others (eds.), *Liber Amicorum in Memoriam of Judge José María Ruda* (Kluwer 2000) 479

Shahabuddeen M, *Precedent in the World Court* (Cambridge University Press 1996)

Shapiro FR and Pearse M, 'The Most-Cited Law Review Articles of All Time' (2012) 110 *Michigan Law Review* 1483

Shaw MN, 'A Practical Look at the International Court of Justice' in Evans MD (ed.), *Remedies in International Law: The Institutional Dilemma* (Hart 1998) 11

International Law (7th edn, Cambridge University Press 2014)

Shecaira FP, *Legal Scholarship as a Source of Law* (Springer 2013)

Shikhelman V, 'Diversity and Decision-Making in International Judicial Institutions' (2018) 36 *Berkeley Journal of International Law* 60

Simma B, 'Remarks by Bruno Simma' (2000) 94 *American Society of International Law Proceedings* 319

Simmonds N, *Law as a Moral Idea* (Oxford University Press 2008)

Sirico Jr LJ and Drew BA, 'The Citing of Law Reviews by the United States Courts of Appeals: An Empirical Analysis' (1991) 45 *University of Miami Law Review* 1051

Sirico Jr LJ and Margulies JB, 'The Citing of Law Reviews by the Supreme Court: An Empirical Study (1986) 34 *UCLA Law Review* 131

Sivakumaran S, 'Beyond States and Non-State Actors: The Role of State-Empowered Entities in the Making and Shaping of International Law' (2017) 55 *Columbia Journal of Transnational Law* 343

'The Influence of Teachings of Publicists on the Development of International Law' (2017) 66 *International and Comparative Law Quarterly* 1

Sloan B, 'What Are We Writing For? Student Works As Authority and Their Citation by the Federal Bench, 1986–1990' (1992) 62 *George Washington Law Review* 221

Slomanson WR, *Fundamental Perspectives on International Law* (5th edn, Thomson Wadsworth 2007)

Smyth R, 'Citing Outside the Law Reports: Citations of Secondary Authorities on the Australian State Supreme Courts Over the Twentieth Century' (2009) 18 *Griffith Law Review* 692

'Other Than "Accepted" Sources of Law?: A Quantitative Study of Secondary Source Citations in the High Court' (1999) 22 *UNSW Law Journal* 19

'Judicial Robes or Academic Gowns? Citations to Secondary Authority and Legal Method in the New Zealand Court of Appeal' in Bigwood R (ed.), *Legal Method in New Zealand* (Butterworths 2001) 101

Sornarajah M, *Resistance and Change in the International Law on Foreign Investment* (Cambridge University Press 2015)

Sourang M, 'Jurisprudence and Teachings' in Bedjaoui M (ed.), *International Law: Achievements and Prospects* (Martinus Nijhoff/UNESCO 1991) 283

Stahn C and De Brabandere E, 'The Future of International Legal Scholarship: Some Thoughts on "Practice", "Growth" and "Dissemination"' (2014) 27 *Leiden Journal of International Law* 1

Stanton K, 'Use of Scholarship by the House of Lords in Tort Cases' in Lee J (ed.), *From House of Lords to Supreme Court: Judges, Jurists and the Process of Judging* (Hart 2011) 201

Stappert N, 'A New Influence of Legal Scholars? The Use of Academic Writings at International Criminal Courts and Tribunals' (2018) 31 *Leiden Journal of International Law* 963

Sureda SAR, *Investment Treaty Arbitration: Judging under Uncertainty* (Cambridge University Press 2012)

Swigart L and Terris D, 'Who are International Judges' in Romano CPR, Alter KJ, and Shany Y (eds.), *The Oxford Handbook of International Adjudication* (Oxford University Press 2015) 619

Sørensen M, *Les sources du droit international: étude sur la jurisprudence de la cour permanente de justice internationale* (E. Munksgaard 1946)

Talmon S, 'Determining Customary International Law: The ICJ's Methodology Between Induction, Deduction and Assertion' (2015) 26 *European Journal of International Law* 417

Terris D, Romano CPR, and Swigart L, *The International Judge: An Introduction to the Men and Women Who Decide the World's Cases* (Oxford University Press 2007)

Tesón FR, 'Feminism and International Law: A Reply' (1993) 33 *Virginia Journal of International Law* 647

Thirlway H, 'The Drafting of ICJ Decisions: Some Personal Recollections and Observations' (2006) 5 *Chinese Journal of International Law* 15

The Law and Procedure of the International Court of Justice: Fifty Years of Jurisprudence (Oxford University Press 2013)

The Sources of International Law (Oxford University Press 2014)

Triggs G, 'The Public International Lawyer and the Practice of International Law' (2005) 24 *Australian Year Book of International Law* 201

Tunkin GI, *Theory of International Law* (George Allen and Unwin 1974)

Tushnet M, 'Academics as Law Makers' (2010) 29 *University of Queensland Law Journal* 19

Twining W and others, 'The Role of Academics in the Legal System' in Tushnet M and Cane P (eds.), *The Oxford Handbook of Legal Studies* (Oxford University Press 2005) 920

Tzanakopoulos A, 'Judicial Dialogue as a Means of Interpretation' in Aust HP and Nolte G (eds.), *The Interpretation of International Law by Domestic Courts* (Oxford University Press 2016) 72

Ulfstein G, 'International Courts and Judges: Independence, Interaction, and Legitimacy' (2014) 46 *NYU Journal of International Law and Politics* 849

Van Damme I, *Treaty Interpretation by the WTO Appellate Body* (Oxford University Press 2009)

Van den Bossche P, 'From Afterthought to Centrepiece: The WTO Appellate Body and Its Rise to Prominence in the World Trading System' in Sacerdoti G, Yanovich A, and Bohanes J (eds.), *The WTO at Ten: The Contribution of the Dispute Settlement System* (Cambridge University Press 2006) 289

Van Hoof GJH, *Rethinking the Sources of International Law* (Kluwer 1993)

van Sliedregt E, 'International Criminal Law: Over-Studied and Underachieving?' (2016) 29 *Leiden Journal of International Law* 1

Varella MD, *Internationalization of Law: Globalization, International Law and Complexity* (Springer 2014)

Venzke I, 'Semantic Authority, Legal Change and the Dynamics of International Law' (2015) 12 *No Foundations* 1

Villiger ME, *Customary International Law and Treaties* (Martinus Nijhoff 1985)

Virally M, 'The Sources of International Law' in Sørensen M (ed.), *Manual of Public International Law* (St. Martin's Press 1968) 116

Voeten E, 'International Judicial Behavior' in Romano CPR, Alter KJ, and Avgerou C (eds.), *The Oxford Handbook of International Adjudication* (Oxford University Press 2013) 550

Vogenauer S, 'An Empire of Light? Learning and Lawmaking in the History of German Law' (2005) 64 *Cambridge Law Journal* 481

von Bernstorff J, 'The Relationship Between Theory and Practice in International Law' in d'Aspremont J and others (eds.), *International Law as a Profession* (Cambridge University Press 2017) 222

von Bogdandy A, Dann P, and Goldmann M, 'Developing the Publicness of Public International Law: Towards a Legal Framework for Global Governance Activities' (2008) 9 *German Law Journal* 1375

von Bogdandy A and Venzke I, *In Whose Name? An Investigation of International Courts' Public Authority and Its Democratic Justification* (Oxford University Press 2014)

Waibel M, 'Interpretive Communities in International Law' in Bianchi A, Peat D, and Windsor M (eds.), *Interpretation in International Law* (Oxford University Press 2015) 147

Waldock CHM, 'General Course on Public International Law' (1962) 106 *Recueil des cours* 1

Wallace RMM and Martin-Ortega O, *International Law* (7th edn, Sweet & Maxwell 2013)

Watson JS, 'Legal Theory, Efficacy and Validity in the Development of Human Rights Norms in International Law' (1979) 3 *University of Illinois Law Forum* 609

Watts A, *The International Law Commission 1949–1998*, vol. I (Oxford University Press 1999)

Webb P, *International Judicial Integration and Fragmentation* (Oxford University Press 2013)

Weeramantry CG, 'Cultural and Ideological Pluralism in Public International Law' in Ando N, McWhinney E, and Wolfrum R (eds.), *Liber Amicorum Judge Shigeru Oda*, vol. II (Kluwer 2002) 1491
Universalising International Law (Martinus Nijhoff 2004)

Weeramantry JR, *Treaty Interpretation in Investment Arbitration* (Oxford University Press 2012)

Westlake J, *The Collected Papers of John Westlake on Public International Law* (Cambridge University Press 1914, Lassa Oppenheim ed.) 83

Wolfke K, *Custom in Present International Law* (2nd edn, Martinus Nijhoff 1993)

Wolfrum R and Möldner M, 'International Courts and Tribunals, Evidence', *Max Planck Encyclopedia of Public International Law* (article last updated August 2013) http://opil.ouplaw.com/view/10.1093/law:epil/9780199231690/law-9780199231690-e26

Wood M, 'Teachings of the Most Highly Qualified Publicists (Art. 38 (1) ICJ Statute)', *Max Planck Encyclopedia of Public International Law* (article last updated October 2010) http://opil.ouplaw.com/view/10.1093/law:epil/9780199231690/law-9780199231690-e1480

'What Is Public International Law? The Need for Clarity about Sources' (2011) 1 *Asian Journal of International Law* 205

Wright Q, 'The Strengthening of International Law' (1959) 98 *Recueil des Cours* 1

Yee S, 'Article 38 of the ICJ Statute and Applicable Law: Selected Issues in Recent Cases' (2016) 7 *Journal of International Dispute Settlement* 472

Zadorozhnii O, 'To Justify Against All Odds: The Annexation of Crimea in 2014 and the Russian Legal Scholarship' (2015) 35 *Polish Yearbook of International Law* 139

Zarbiyev F, 'Saying Credibly What the Law Is: On Marks of Authority in International Law' (2018) 9 *Journal of International Dispute Settlement* 291

Zdouc W and Van den Bossche P, *The Law and Policy of the World Trade Organization* (Cambridge University Press 2013)

Zidar A, 'Interpretation and the International Legal Profession: Between Duty and Aspiration' in Bianchi A, Peat D, and Windsor M (eds.), *Interpretation in International Law* (Oxford University Press 2015) 133

INDEX

Abraham, Ronny, 73
Academic, 1, 13, 33, 86, 123, 153, 154, 155, 159, 178, 179, 182
ACJ, 19, 25, 27, 28, 29, 93
   Procès-Verbaux, 13, 19, 21, 25, 27, 28, 29, 32, 37, 81, 93, 157
Ajibola, Bola, 62
Alfaro, Ricardo J., 9, 136
ALI, 122
Ambiguity, 28, 71
Amici curiae, 37,
Ammoun, Fouad, 6, 66, 68, 76, 89, 137
Arbitral Tribunal for Upper Silesia, 115
Arbitration, 129, 166, 171, 176, 179
   Investment, 35, 130, 162, 175, 179
Azevedo, José Philadelpho de Barros e, 76

Bautista, Lilia R., 178
Bedjaoui, Mohammed, 59
Belgium, 98, 117
Bias, 15, 26, 55, 56, 57, 75, 99, 128, 162, 163, 164
Blog post, 30
Brownlie, Ian, 96, 106, 175
Buddhist, 140
Buergenthal, Thomas, 57, 60, 113, 140
Burgh House Principles on the Independence of the International Judiciary, the, 56, 167
Bustamante y Sirven, Antonio Sánchez de, 55, 73

Canada, 116, 149
Cançado Trindade, Antônio Augusto, 6, 10, 45, 51, 62, 64, 67, 71, 78, 81, 94, 108, 132, 134, 137, 139, 140, 144, 146, 148, 149, 150, 151, 152, 154, 178
Carneiro, Levi Fernandes, 34, 71
Caron, David, 73
Case law, 79, 92
Caveat, 6, 159, 169
Charter of the United Nations (UN Charter), 20, 71
China, 100, 149
Citations
   Exhaustive, 13, 159
   Indirect, 8
   Self-, 94, 131
   Strategic, 58, 59, 80, 91, 139, 155
Civil law and common law, 3, 102, 103, 150, 152, 179
Communication, 91, 105
Conflict of interest, 56, 167
Convention on the Settlement of Investment Disputes between States and Nationals of Other States (ICSID Convention), 22
   Article 42, 21
   Article 48, 21
Covenant of the League of Nations
   Article 14, 19
Crimea, annexation of, 100

de Castro, Federico, 50, 69, 71, 76, 146
de Visscher, Charles, 96, 113, 114
Descamps, Edouard, 21, 25, 29
Dictionary, 34, 44
Dillard, Hardy Cross, 50, 69
Diplomat, 13, 99, 153, 154, 163, 178
Discretion, 72, 128, 156
Dispute Settlement Understanding (DSU)
   Article 17, 86, 89, 180

DSU (cont.)
 Article 3, 170
 Article 8, 176
DSU. See Dispute Settlement
 Understanding

ECHR. See European Convention on
 Human Rights
ECtHR, 171, 173
ECtHR Rules of Court
 Article 4, 56
 Article 74, 21
El-Erian, Abdullah, 62
Encyclopaedia, 33
European Convention on Human
 Rights (ECHR)
 Article 20, 89
 Article 21, 56
European Court of Justice, 173
Evidence, 35, 36, 160

Fact-finding mission, 129
Facts, 8, 33, 34, 62
Female. See Women
Finlay, Robert, 64
Fitzmaurice, Gerald, 68, 69, 81, 94, 96,
 114, 158
France, 98, 104

General principles of law, 22, 27, 29,
 61, 67
Genocide, 44, 109
Gidel, Gilbert, 44, 118
Greenwood, Christopher, 64
Grotius, Hugo, 73, 108
Guillaume, Gilbert, 76

Hague Codification Conference, 39, 41
Hambro, Edvard, 105
Harvard Law School, 38, 122
Higgins, Rosalyn, 99, 113
Human rights, 108
Hurst, Cecil, 44

IACtHR, 60, 140
ICC, 163, 175, 176, 181, 182
ICJ
 Advisory opinions, 7

Appointment of judges ad hoc, 78,
 116, 139, 142, 143, 146, 147,
Authority, 1, 6, 28, 124
Chambers, 7, 130
Clerks, 49, 51, 101, 128, 143, 145
Composition, 7
Counsel, 56, 102, 119
Declarations, 5, 148
Docket, 45, 161
Drafting Committee, 11, 54, 61
Election of permanent judges, 78,
 116, 139, 140, 143, 147
Experts, 35, 36
Handbook, 22, 35, 36, 158
Jurisdiction, 4, 61
Library, 49, 101
Orders, 7, 48, 141, 181, 183
Pleadings, 8, 46, 52, 70, 102, 145
President, 11, 115, 116
Registry, 49, 117, 142, 143
Vice-President, 11, 116
ICJ Rules of Court
 Amendment, 167
 Article 19, 11
 Article 57, 35, 167
 Article 58, 35, 167
 Article 62, 167
 Article 63, 167
 Article 64, 167
 Article 65, 35, 167
 Article 67, 167
 Article 68, 35, 167
 Article 70, 167
 Article 71, 35, 167
 Article 72, 160
 Article 95, 21
ICJ Statute. See Statute of the
 International Court of Justice
ICRC, 41, 42, 44, 84, 85, 113, 120, 122
ICSID, 171, 174, 176, 179
ICSID Convention. See Convention on
 the Settlement of Investment
 Disputes between States and
 Nationals of Other States
ICSID Rules of Procedure for
 Arbitration Proceedings
 Article 32, 167
 Article 34, 167

Article 35, 167
Article 36, 167
ICTY, 61, 141, 170, 171, 173, 179, 182
Ideas, marketplace of, 168
IDI, 4, 32, 37, 38, 89, 110, 112, 120, 121, 167
ILA, 4, 37, 38, 89, 110, 122, 167
ILC
  1956 Yearbook, 38
  1966 Yearbook, 52
  1974 Yearbook, 82
  2001 Yearbook, 82
  2006 Yearbook, 169
  Election of members, 38, 87
  First report on formation and evidence of customary international law, 4, 37
  Fourth report on identification of customary international law, 40
  Fragmentation of International Law, 169, 170
  Identification of customary international law, Statement of the Chair of the Drafting Committee, 32
  Identification of Customary International Law, Text of the draft conclusions, 32
  Identification of Customary International Law, Text of the draft conclusions as adopted by the Drafting Committee on second reading, 32
  Report of the Sixty-eighth session, 29, 32, 33, 40, 55, 93, 107, 110, 114, 122, 162
  Report of the Sixty-fifth session, 41
  Responsibility of States of Internationally Wrongful Acts, 38, 82, 174
  Special Rapporteur, 39
  State comments, 39
  Survey of International Law in Relation to the Work of Codification of the International Law Commission, 23, 39, 40,
  Third report on identification of customary international law, 21,
    32, 37, 40, 47, 88, 114, 122, 129, 130
ILC Statute
  Article 1, 38, 83
  Article 8, 89
  Article 15, 40
Impartiality, 56
Incentive, 58, 59, 87, 105, 116, 124, 128, 138, 142
Inference, 9, 12, 26, 50, 80, 81, 93, 109, 122
Information, 29, 46, 47
Inter-Allied Committee on the Future of the Permanent Court of International Justice, 20
International community, the, 42, 60, 80, 161
International courts and tribunals
  Advisory opinions, 36
  Appeal, 129
  Clerks, 143, 183
  Composition, 58, 180, 181, 182
  Counsel, 2, 8, 35, 51, 55, 81, 114, 176
  Election and appointment of judges, 86, 87, 116, 126, 180
  Experts, 35, 36, 37, 167
  General comments, 36
  Generalist and specialist, 4, 57, 60, 61, 87, 181
  Global and regional, 57, 181
  Hierarchy, 5, 129
  Pleadings, 4, 35, 144, 172, 184
International humanitarian law, 113
International law
  Codification and progressive development of, 38, 39, 41, 83, 157, 167
  Customary, 1, 11, 18, 23, 24, 27, 29, 32, 33, 47, 52, 57, 61, 67, 69, 71, 75, 82, 83, 121, 122, 158, 169, 172
  Fragmentation of, 170
  General and special, 169, 175, 180, 181
  Judicialisation of, 92
  Sources of, 23, 28, 169, 172, 183
  Systemisation of, 41, 91, 159
  Written and unwritten, 2, 22, 47, 49, 166, 181

International trade law, 175, 180,
Iran-US Claims Tribunal, 173
Iraq War, 100
Italy, 98, 172
ITLOS, 170, 171, 174, 175, 177, 178, 179
ITLOS Rules of the Tribunal
    Article 87, 160
    Article 125, 21
ITLOS Statute. See Statute of the
    International Tribunal for the Law
    of the Sea

Jennings, Robert Yewdall, 13, 24, 51, 71,
    96, 114
Jessup, Philip C., 51, 57, 68, 122
Jiménez de Aréchaga, Eduardo, 72, 96,
    98, 105
Judges
    Behaviour, 183, 184
    Plagiarism, 166
    Recusal, 164
    Style, 10, 66, 138, 142, 155, 156, 182
Judicial decisions
    Authority of, 4, 59, 87, 124, 128, 129
    Compliance with, 125, 162
    Enforcement of, 125, 162
    Interpretation of, 47, 71, 81
Jura novit curia, 160
Jus gentium, 139, 140

Keith, Kenneth, 64
Kellogg, Frank B., 118
Kooijmans, Pieter, 113
Koroma, Abdul, 59
Kreća, Milenko, 6, 45, 70, 78, 106, 121,
    137, 142, 146, 148, 149, 150, 151,
    152, 154, 178
Krylov, Sergei Borisovitch, 9, 68

Laing, Edward Arthur, 178, 179,
    180
Language, 7, 53, 102, 103, 104, 105,
Latin America, 77, 116
Lauterpacht, Hersch, 9, 24, 40, 71, 73,
    81, 94, 96, 97, 98, 105, 114, 128,
    134, 140
Law of the sea, 118, 175
League of Nations

Assembly, 20, 39
Council, 19
Mandates, 69
Permanent Mandates
    Commission, 118
Lecture, 29
Legal certainty, 16, 159, 170
Legal culture, 122, 162
Legal positivism, 140
Legitimacy, 59, 161, 184
Lemkin, Raphael, 44
Letter, 29, 57
Lex lata and lex ferenda, 114
Lex specialis, 169

Mahiou, Ahmed, 75, 82
Mampuya Kanunk'a Tshiabo,
    Auguste, 77
Matthew Effect, the, 127
McNair, Arnold, 35, 36, 122
Moore, John Bassett, 68
Motivation, 115, 116, 117, 118, 122,
    138, 146, 156

National courts, 5, 53, 57, 149, 164, 169,
    172, 174, 177, 181, 184
    Australian state Supreme Courts,
        172
    Canadian Supreme Court, 172,
        182, 183
    French courts, 172
    House of Lords, 172
    New Zealand Court of Appeal,
        172
    Supreme Court of Senegal, 119
    US Court of Appeals for the Second
        Circuit, 173
    US courts, 139, 172, 179, 181,
        182
    US Supreme Court, 173, 174
National judges. See National courts
NGO, 38
Non liquet, 29
Norway, 105

OAS, 113, 118, 119
Obiter dicta, 70
Oda, Shigeru, 9, 70, 75, 113

OECD, 13, 101, 102, 103, 148, 148, 150, 151, 175, 178, 179
Opinio juris, 39, 47
Oppenheim, Lassa, 10, 44, 50, 64, 94, 96, 105, 120, 122, 175
Oslo Recommendations for Enhancing the Legitimacy of International Courts, 167
Outlier, 6, 61, 77, 78, 96, 138, 147, 149, 152, 178, 179

Padilla Nervo, Luis, 69
Palmer, Geoffrey, 51
Paolillo, Felipe H., 51
PCA, 75, 113
PCIJ, 5, 7, 11, 44, 45, 55, 64, 65, 68, 69, 72, 73, 79, 95, 109, 110, 113, 114, 115, 118, 121, 133, 134, 135, 137
PCIJ Statute. See Statute of the Permanent Court of International Justice
Pirzada, Sharifuddin, 106
Politics, 56, 57, 59, 119, 138, 139, 153, 154, 161, 163
Precedent, 41, 77, 80, 85, 159, 181
Proposals for the Establishment of a General International Organization, 20
Proxy, 14, 26, 110, 114, 116, 148,
Prussia, 172

Ramírez-Hernández, Ricardo, 178
Ranjeva, Raymond, 59, 80, 81
Relevance, 105, 114, 116
Reputation, 114
Riphagen, Willem, 66, 68,
Rome Statute of the International Criminal Court (Rome Statute), 22
    Article 21, 20
    Article 36, 86, 89
    Article 41, 56
    Article 74, 21, 160
Rosenne, Shabtai, 94, 96, 97, 98, 106, 107, 114, 128, 175
Russia, 100, 105

Schücking, Walther, 65
Schwarzenberger, Georg, 69, 105

Schwebel, Stephen M., 64, 82, 113, 134
Servulo Correia, José Manuel, 178
Shahabuddeen, Mohamed, 6, 11, 27, 45, 57, 61, 65, 71, 72, 73, 76, 78, 81, 82, 133, 137, 141, 144, 146, 147, 148, 149, 150, 151, 152, 154, 155, 158, 178
Sivakumaran, Sandesh, 14
Smuts, Jan, 44
Special Court for Sierra Leone, 174
Speech, 29, 82
Spender, Percy, 47, 68, 71
Stare decisis. See Precedent
State practice, 21, 33, 41, 47, 52, 140, 176
State-empowered bodies
    Definition, 38
    Election and appointment to, 86
    Election of members, 116, 126
    Global and regional, 130
Statute of the International Court of Justice (ICJ Statute)
    Amendment of, 167
    Article 2, 86
    Article 3, 89
    Article 9, 89, 149
    Article 17, 56
    Article 26, 7
    Article 39, 104
    Article 59, 77
    Draft version, 20
    Preparatory works to, 19, 20
Statute of the International Tribunal for the Law of the Sea (ITLOS Statute)
    Article 3, 89
    Article 7, 56
    Article 8, 56
Statute of the Permanent Court of International Justice (PCIJ Statute)
    Article 38, 19, 23
    Creation of, 19, 22
    Draft version, 20, 21
    Drafting of, 39
    Inclusion of teachings, 21, 22
    Preparatory works to, 19, 32, 37, 81, 157

Terminology, 28, 30, 32
Textbook, 9, 28, 41, 104, 174, 176
Thirlway, Hugh, 11, 16, 49, 82, 90, 166
Tomka, Peter, 49, 53, 122
Torres Bernárdez, Santiago, 70
Treaties
    Collections of, 33
    Conclusion of, 38, 40
    Draft, 30, 117
    Interpretation of, 18, 19, 26, 27, 47,
        61, 68, 70
    Preparatory works to, 40
    Wording of, 11, 27, 64, 72
Truman Declaration, 33

UK, 98, 100, 104, 105, 128,
    175
UN
    Charter. See Charter of the United
        Nations
    Committee of Jurists, 20
    Conference on International
        Organization, 20, 23
    HRC, 16, 179
    Sea-Bed Committee, 118
    Secretary General, 174
    UNCITRAL, 36
    UNGA, 38, 39, 53, 82, 129
UNCLOS. See United Nations
    Convention on the Law of the Sea
United Nations Convention on the Law
    of the Sea (UNCLOS), 22
    Article 73, 24
    Article 83, 24

Article 293, 20
Uruguay, 98
US, 98, 100, 104, 139, 149, 172, 175, 179,
    181, 182

Van den Bossche, Peter, 178
Van den Wyngaert, Christine, 10,
    106, 132
van Eysinga, Jonkheer, 72
van Wyk, J. T., 35, 69
VCLT. See Vienna Convention on the
    Law of Treaties
Vienna Convention on the Law of
    Treaties (VCLT)
    Article 32, 18, 19
Vogt, Zahle, 113

Waldock, Humphrey, 49, 82, 96, 145
Weeramantry, Christopher, 6, 45, 50,
    51, 64, 65, 72, 73, 75, 78, 108,
    110, 122, 133, 137, 140, 144, 146,
    147, 148, 149, 150, 151, 152,
    154, 178
Wellington Koo, Vi Kyuin, 132
Women, 99, 99, 101, 102, 103, 104, 163,
    182,
WTO
    Appellate Body, 54, 169, 170, 171,
        173, 174, 175, 177, 178, 179, 180,
        181, 182,
    Definition of 'developing
        countries', 176
    Panels, 176, 183
    Secretariat, 176, 183

Ingram Content Group UK Ltd.
Milton Keynes UK
UKHW020617190723
425395UK00033B/585